BEST PRACTICES IN LITERACY INSTRUCTION

BEST PRACTICES IN LITERACY INSTRUCTION

Second Edition

Lesley Mandel Morrow
Linda B. Gambrell
Michael Pressley
Editors

Foreword by Dorothy S. Strickland

THE GUILFORD PRESS
New York London

© 2003 The Guilford Press
A Division of Guilford Publications, Inc.
72 Spring Street, New York, NY 10012
www.guilford.com

Printed in the United States of America

This book is printed on acid-free paper.

Last digit is print number: 9 8 7 6 5 4 3 2 1

Library of Congress Cataloging-in-Publication Data

Best practices in literacy instruction / editors, Lesley Mandel Morrow,
    Linda B. Gambrell, Michael Pressley ; foreword by Dorothy S.
    Strickland.— 2nd ed.
        p. cm.
    Includes bibliographical references and index.
    ISBN 1-57230-876-1 (hardcover : alk. paper) — ISBN 1-57230-875-3
(pbk. : alk. paper)
    1. Language arts—United States.   2. Reading comprehension—United
States.   3. Literacy—United States.   I. Morrow, Lesley Mandel.
II. Gambrell, Linda B.   III. Pressley, Michael.
LB1576.B486   2003
428.4'07—dc21   2003001091

ABOUT THE EDITORS

Lesley Mandel Morrow is Professor at Rutgers University's Graduate School of Education. She is also coordinator of the Literacy Cluster, as well as a member of the Early Childhood/Elementary Cluster. She began her career as a classroom teacher and later became a reading specialist. Her area of research deals with early literacy development, with an emphasis on organizing and managing the language arts block. In addition, Dr. Morrow has more than 200 publications. Her articles have appeared in journals such as *Reading Research Quarterly, Journal of Educational Psychology*, and *The Reading Teacher*. Her most recent books are *Literacy Development in the Early Years: Helping Children Read and Write* and *Organizing and Managing the Language Arts Block*. She received the Rutgers University awards for research and teaching, the International Reading Association's Outstanding Teacher Educator of Reading Award, and Fordham University's Alumni Award for Outstanding Achievement. She is also President of the International Reading Association for 2003–2004.

Linda B. Gambrell is Professor and Director of the School of Education at Clemson University. Prior to coming to Clemson University, she was Associate Dean for Research at the University of Maryland, where she taught graduate and undergraduate reading and language arts courses. She began her career as an elementary classroom teacher and reading specialist in Prince George's County, Maryland, has written books on reading instruction, and has had articles published in such journals as *Reading Research Quarterly, The Reading Teacher, Educational Psychologist*, and *Jour-*

nal of Educational Research. From 1992 to 1997, Dr. Gambrell was principal investigator at the National Reading Research Center, where she directed the Literacy Motivation Project, and has served as an elected member of the Board of Directors of the International Reading Association, National Reading Conference, and College Reading Association. She has also served as President of the National Reading Conference and the College Reading Association. From 1993 to 1996, she was coeditor of the *Journal of Reading Behavior,* a publication of the National Reading Conference. She has received professional awards including the 1998 International Reading Association Outstanding Teacher Educator in Reading Award, the 2001 National Reading Conference Albert J. Kingston Award, and the 2002 College Reading Associate Laureate Award. Her current interests are in the areas of reading comprehension strategy instruction, literacy motivation, and the role of discussion in teaching and learning.

Michael Pressley is a member of the faculty of the College of Education (Teacher Education and Educational Psychology) at Michigan State University and is past editor of the *Journal of Educational Psychology.* He has also been a visiting faculty member at both the University of Wisconsin–Madison and the Max Planck Institute. He earned a PhD in child psychology, specializing in children's learning, and has published over 250 articles, chapters, and books, with his writing reflecting a wide range of interests and expertise, from work on children's memory, to research on the development of cognitive monitoring skills, to his studies of effective reading instruction. Dr. Pressley's book *Reading Instruction That Works: The Case for Balanced Teaching,* now in its second edition, has received considerable critical acclaim and is a leading seller in the area of literacy research. His most recent coauthored books include *Learning to Read: Lessons from Exemplary First-Grade Classrooms* and *Comprehension Instruction: Research-Based Best Practices,* and he is a leading expert in primary-level literacy education. His recent recognitions include the Oscar Causey Award from the National Reading Conference for career contributions to reading research, and induction into the Reading Hall of Fame from the International Reading Association.

CONTRIBUTORS

Richard L. Allington is the Irving and Rose Fien Professor of Education at the University of Florida. He has served as President of the National Reading Conference and was named to the International Reading Association Reading Hall of Fame. He has written extensively on the topics of struggling readers and exemplary classroom reading instruction. His books include *Classrooms That Work* and *Schools That Work,* both coauthored with Patricia M. Cunningham; *What Really Matters for Struggling Readers;* and most recently *Big Brother and the National Reading Curriculum: How Ideology Trumped Evidence.*

Harriette Arrington is currently Associate Professor of Curriculum and Instruction in the College of Education at the University of Kentucky, Lexington, Kentucky. In addition to teaching undergraduate- and graduate-level elementary and middle school courses, she coordinates student teaching and practicum programs. Prior to this position, she supervised Reading/Language Arts in Newport News, Virginia. Her publications include two children's picture books, *The Heart of a Friendship* (1997) and *Friends Again?* (2001). Dr. Arrington is an active member of several professional organizations, including the National Middle School Association (NMSA), International Reading Association (IRA), Kentucky Reading Association (KRA), and National Council of Teachers of English (NCTE). She is the 2002–2003 President of KRA and serves on the storytelling committee for NCTE. In addition to serving as an educational consultant with the Southern Region Education Board, Dr. Arrington works with numerous schools and organizations by providing language and literacy workshops, lectures, and demonstration lessons. She frequently makes national, state, and local presentations in the areas of storytelling, African American literacy, oral language, and best practices in literacy instruction and assessment issues.

Elizabeth Asbury is Assistant Professor in the Reading Department at Rowan University, where she teaches courses in early literacy and teaching reading to children with special needs. She has a broad range of teaching experience from preschool through university and taught music in kindergarten through eighth grade prior to becoming a classroom teacher. She currently supervises preservice teachers working at both clinical and PDS sites, and her research studies focus on guided reading and teacher professional development. As a director with the Institute for Teacher Development, she works with teachers and children to improve the quality of reading instruction. She was the 1999 recipient of the Edward Frye Endowed Fellowship and the recipient of the New Jersey Reading Association's Research Award in 2000. She is also a contributing author to *Learning to Read: Lessons from Exemplary First-Grade Classrooms* and coauthor of *Literacy Activities for the Early Childhood Classroom.*

Kim Baker is Assistant Professor in Reading and Special Education and Chair of the Education Department at The Sage Colleges in Troy, New York. In addition to teaching undergraduate- and graduate-level language arts courses, she also works closely with an after-school enrichment and literacy program in the inner city and has been an elementary school teacher in Missouri and New York. An active member of many professional organizations, she is chair of the Teacher as Researcher Committee for the International Reading Association, encouraging teachers to be active participants as they reflect on and research their classroom practice.

Thomas W. Bean is Professor of Reading/Literacy, as well as coordinator of doctoral studies and a member of the Language, Literacy, and Culture faculty in the Department of Curriculum and Instruction at the University of Nevada, Las Vegas. His research encompasses critical literacy and young adult literature, as well as work in teachers' reflective practices. His articles have appeared in *Reading Research Quarterly,* the *Journal of Educational Research, Journal of Adolescent and Adult Literacy,* and *Reflective Practice.* His most recent coauthored book is *Content Area Literacy: An Integrated Approach.* He recently received the University of Nevada College of Education Distinguished Researcher Award and served as a Visiting Scholar to the University of Queensland, Brisbane, Australia, assisting in a country-wide study of middle school literacy.

Camille L. Z. Blachowicz is a nationally known author and staff developer, as well as Professor of Education at National College of Education of National-Louis University, where she is director of the Reading Center and Reading Program. Dr. Blachowicz has been a classroom teacher, team leader, and reading specialist, as well as a university educator. Her research has been supported by grants from the Spencer Foundation, the Fulbright Council, and the International Reading Association. Dr. Blachowicz's many articles have been published in a number of journals, including *The Reading Teacher* and *Reading Research Quarterly*. She is also the coauthor of *Reading Diagnosis: An Instructional Approach; Teaching Vocabulary in All Classrooms;* and *Reading Comprehension: Strategies for Independent Learners,* and has written numerous book chapters, articles, and instructional materials for school-age learners. As a staff developer, she is a frequent speaker at national, local, and international conferences in the area of vocabulary, comprehension, and assessment. Currently, Dr. Blachowicz is codirecting a project to develop the Illinois Snapshot of Early Literacy and other projects focused on improving urban literacy instruction.

Cathy Collins Block is currently on the Graduate Faculty at Texas Christian University. She is also on the Board of Directors of the International Reading Association, America Tomorrow, and Nobel Learning Communities, Inc., and serves on the editorial review boards of *Reading Research Quarterly, Journal of Educational Psychology,* and *The Reading Teacher.* She has directed several nationally funded research projects and has published extensively in the field of comprehension, classroom instructional interventions, and professional development of teachers. Her most recent books include *Comprehension Instruction: Rethinking Theory, Research and Practice* (2003); *Comprehension Instruction: Research Best Practices* (2002); and *Scholastic Early Childhood Program* (2002).

Karen Bromley is a Professor of Literacy in the School of Education and Human Development at Binghamton University, State University of New York (SUNY), where she teaches graduate courses in literacy, language arts, and children's literature. She was a third-grade teacher and reading specialist in New York and Maryland schools and has written a number of books for teachers, including *Stretching Students' Vocabulary* (2002); *50 Graphic Organizers for Reading, Writing and More* (1998); *Graphic Organizers* (1995); *Journaling: Engagements in Reading, Writing and Thinking* (1993); *Language Arts: Exploring Connections, Third Edition* (1996); and *Webbing With Literature, Second Edition* (1996). She has also written many articles in professional journals such as *The Reading Teacher.* She received the SUNY Chancellor's Award for Excellence in Teaching at Binghamton

University in 2000 and the Reading Educator Award from the New York State Reading Association in 1992.

Norma J. Carr is a doctoral student in Language and Literacy at the University of Texas at Austin. She is a reading specialist and currently works as an instructional interventionist in San Antonio. Her professional interests include working with struggling readers, early intervention, and the history of reading instruction in the United States.

Kimberly H. Creamer is a doctoral student in Literacy Education at the University of North Carolina–Chapel Hill and works as a research assistant on the North Carolina Reading Excellence Act Evaluation Grant. She earned a master's degree in Literacy Education from the College of William and Mary and has conducted workshops for primary teachers in how to teach writing as well as the Four Blocks. She taught first grade for 7 years and second grade for 1 year in the public schools of Virginia and North Carolina.

James W. Cunningham is Professor of Literacy Education at the University of North Carolina–Chapel Hill. He is also coauthor of five books, two of which are in their fourth editions. He has numerous other publications in professional books and journals and has presented research and theoretical papers at many national conferences. In addition, he is on the editorial advisory board of several reading research journals, has been elected Fellow by the National Conference on Research in Language and Literacy, and is currently a leader in the international movement toward improving elementary classroom reading and writing instruction by implementing the Four Blocks, a balanced literacy instructional framework. He has also taught at the elementary and secondary levels in the public schools of Tennessee, Georgia, and North Carolina.

Patricia M. Cunningham is Professor at Wake Forest University. Her research interests include finding alternative ways to teach children for whom learning to read is difficult. She is the author of *Reading and Writing in Elementary Classrooms*, currently in its fourth edition, and *Phonics They Use: Words for Reading and Writing*, now in its third edition. She is also coauthor, with Richard L. Allington, of *Classrooms That Work* and *Schools That Work*. Along with Dorothy Hall, she developed the Four Blocks literacy framework, which is currently used as the balanced literacy framework in thousand of classrooms throughout the country. She and Dorothy Hall are also codirectors of the Four Blocks Literacy Center, which is housed at Wake Forest University.

Douglas Fisher is Associate Professor in the School of Teacher Education at San Diego State University (SDSU). He is also the Director of Professional Development for the City Heights Educational Pilot, an innovative collaboration between SDSU, Rosa Parks Elementary School, Monroe Clark Middle School, and Hoover High School. His research explores children's literature, struggling adolescent readers and writers, and literacy for diverse learners. In addition, Dr. Fisher has more than 100 publications, including articles that have appeared in *The Reading Teacher*, the *National Reading Conference Yearbook, Journal of Adolescent and Adult Literacy*, and *Reading Horizons*. His most recent books are *Developing Arts-Loving Readers: Top 10 Questions Teachers Are Asking about Integrated Arts Education* (with Nan McDonald) and *Teaching Reading to Every Child* (with Diane Lapp, James Flood, and Cindy Brock).

Peter J. Fisher is Professor of Education at National College of Education of National-Louis University, where he directs the Reading and Language doctoral program. He taught in elementary and high schools in England prior to coming to the United States to pursue doctoral studies at the State University of New York at Buffalo. His research interests include vocabulary development, the history of literacy, and the development of reflective practice in literacy teaching, and his work has been supported by several grant agencies, including the Spencer Foundation and the Illinois State Board of Higher Education. In 1997 he was inducted into the Illinois Reading Hall of Fame. A coauthor of *Teaching Vocabulary in All Classrooms* (2002) and the author of numerous articles and book chapters, he was coeditor of the *Illinois Reading Council Journal* from 1992 to 1996. He has also been a featured speaker at state and local conferences.

James Flood, Professor of Reading and Language Development at San Diego State University (SDSU), has taught in preschool, elementary, and secondary schools and has been a language arts supervisor and vice-principal. Currently, Dr. Flood teaches preservice and graduate courses at SDSU. He has coauthored and edited many articles, columns, texts, handbooks, and children's materials on reading and language arts issues, including the *Handbook of Research on Teaching the English Language Arts* (with Diane Lapp) and the *Handbook of Research on Teaching Literacy through the Communicative and Visual Arts*. He received the Outstanding Teacher Educator in the Department of Teacher Education award at SDSU and the Distinguished Research Lecturer from SDSU's Graduate Division of Research, and was elected to the California Reading Hall of Fame. Dr. Flood was a Fulbright scholar at the University of Lisbon in Portugal, and is also a member of the Board of Directors of the International Reading Association as well as President of the National Reading Conference.

Leila Flores-Dueñas is Assistant Professor in the Department of Language, Literacy and Sociocultural Studies at the University of New Mexico, where she teaches courses in reading methodology for preservice teachers; the reading and writing process; language, literacy, and culture; and family literacy. She has been a regular, bilingual, and English as a Second Language classroom teacher in inner-city schools and has also taught ESL to many recently arrived immigrant adults. She is most interested in the following areas of research: multiethnic literature and text comprehension; bilingualism and text interpretation; home and school discourse and literacy learning; and culturally relevant pedagogy and teacher education. In 1998, she won an award from the National Association of Bilingual Education for her 1997 dissertation entitled, *Second Language Literacy: Mexican American Student Voices on Reading Mexican American Literature.*

Linda B. Gambrell (*see* About the Editors).

James V. Hoffman is Professor of Language and Literacy Studies at the University of Texas at Austin, where he directs a reading specialization program at the undergraduate level and teaches graduate courses in reading and research. He is a former elementary classroom teacher and reading specialist and has served as President of the National Reading Conference, as well as editor of *Reading Research Quarterly.* He is currently editor of the *Yearbook of the National Reading Conference.* His major research interests are in the areas of teacher preparation, beginning reading instruction, and the texts used in reading instruction.

Melanie R. Kuhn is Professor of Literacy Education at Rutgers University. She began teaching in Boston public schools, taught adult literacy for a year, and spent 3 years teaching struggling readers at an American school in London. Her research interests include fluency development, literacy–technology connections, and work with struggling readers. She is the principal investigator on a 5-year Interagency Education Research Initiative grant that will explore the development and remediation of fluent reading among second graders. In addition, she has worked with the National Reading Research Center at the University of Georgia and has published an overview of fluency development, with Steven Stahl, through the Center for the Improvement of Early Reading Achievement.

Linda D. Labbo is Professor in the Department of Reading Education at the University of Georgia. Her early career included teaching kindergarten through fifth grade and providing in-service staff development as an educational specialist in a regional education service center. She conducts research on early literacy development, with a focus on computer-related literacy instruction and preservice teacher preparation, and has published articles in such journals as *Reading Research Quarterly, Language Arts, Jour-*

nal of Literacy Research, and *The Reading Teacher.* She is coeditor, with David Reinking, Michael C. McKenna, and Ronald D. Kieffer, of *Handbook of Literacy and Technology: Transformations in a Post-Typographic World,* which won an American Library Association Award as an Outstanding Academic Book of the Year in 1998 and the Edward B. Fry Book Award from the National Reading Conference in 1999. She also received a Keizai Koho Center Fellowship to conduct research and write curriculum materials about educational technology in Japan. In addition, she received the Computers in Reading Research Award from the International Reading Association Technology in Literacy Education Special Interest Group and a Phi Delta Kappa Faculty Research Award in 2000. She currently serves as a coprimary investigator on a $5.6 million grant funded by the National Science Foundation and Interagency Education Research Initiative to develop and examine the effectiveness of interactive, multimedia anchor cases on preservice teachers' professional development.

Diane Lapp is Professor of Reading and Language in the Department of Teacher Education at San Diego State University (SDSU) and has taught in elementary and middle schools. She codirects and teaches field-based preservice and graduate courses, and spent a recent sabbatical team teaching in a public school first-grade classroom. Although her sabbatical has been completed, she continues to team teach in public school classrooms. Dr. Lapp has coauthored and edited many articles, columns, texts, handbooks, and children's materials on reading and language arts issues. These include the following two books, which were codeveloped with James Flood: *Teaching Reading to Every Child,* a reading methods textbook now in its fourth edition, and the *Handbook of Research on Teaching the English Language Arts, Second Edition,* soon to be released. She has also chaired and cochaired several International Reading Association (IRA) and National Reading Conference (NRC) committees. Her many educational awards include being named as the Outstanding Teacher Educator and Faculty Member in the Department of Teacher Education at SDSU, the Distinguished Research Lecturer from SDSU's Graduate Division of Research, a member of the California Reading Hall of Fame, and the IRA's 1996 Outstanding Teacher Educator of the Year. Dr. Lapp is the coeditor of California's major literacy journal, *The California Reader.*

Susan Anders Mazzoni is a literacy coach for public school systems and a doctoral student in the Department of Curriculum and Instruction at the University of Maryland, College Park (UMCP), where she is studying reading education. She has taught reading methods at UMCP and has worked as a research assistant at the National Reading Research Center. Her work has been published in *The Reading Teacher, Reading Psychology,* and *Educa-*

tional Psychology Review, as well as in a number of edited books. Ms. Mazzoni has teaching experience in Baltimore County and Baltimore City public schools and also has extensive experience teaching adult literacy. Her research interests are in the area of metacognition, comprehension, and motivation.

Michael C. McKenna is Professor of Reading at Georgia Southern University in Savannah, where he teaches graduate courses and conducts research. He has authored or coauthored nine books and more than 70 articles, chapters, and technical reports on a range of literacy topics. His research has been sponsored by the National Reading Research Center and the Center for the Improvement of Early Reading Achievement. He recently coedited the *Handbook of Literacy and Technology: Transformations in a Post-Typographic World* (with David Reinking, Linda D. Labbo, and Ronald D. Kieffer), which won an American Library Association Award as an Outstanding Academic Book of the Year in 1998 and the Edward B. Fry Book Award from the National Reading Conference in 1999. He has twice served as a featured speaker at national meetings of the International Reading Association and has delivered two invited addresses at international forums. Dr. McKenna serves on the editorial boards of *Reading Research Quarterly,* the *Journal of Literacy Research,* and *Scientific Studies in Reading,* and his articles have appeared in each of these journals, as well as in the *Journal of Educational Psychology, Educational Researcher,* and *The Reading Teacher,* among others. He has also coedited themed issues of the *Peabody Journal of Education* and *Reading and Writing Quarterly.* His research interests include comprehension in content settings, reading attitudes, technology applications, and beginning reading.

Lesley Mandel Morrow (*see* About the Editors).

P. David Pearson is Dean of the Graduate School of Education and a faculty member in the Language and Literacy program at the University of California, Berkeley. His current research, as a principal investigator for the Center for the Improvement of Early Reading Achievement (CIERA), focuses on issues of reading instruction and reading assessment policies and practices at local, state, and national levels. Prior to coming to the University of California in 2001, he served as the John A. Hannah Distinguished Professor of Education in the College of Education at Michigan State University and as codirector of CIERA, with faculty appointments in Teacher Education and Educational Psychology. He has been active in professional organizations, serving the International Reading Association and the National Council of Teachers of English in many capacities, both as President of the National Reading Conference and the National Conference of Research in English, and as a member of the Board of the American Association of Colleges of Teacher Education. In 1989, Dr. Pearson received the Oscar Causey Award from the National Reading Conference for outstanding contributions to reading research. In 1990, he was awarded the William S. Gray Citation of Merit from the International Reading Association for his contributions to theory, research, and practice. He has written and coedited several books about research and practice, most notable being the *Handbook of Reading Research*, now in its third volume, and most recently, a coedited volume, *Effective Schools and Accomplished Teachers* (with Barbara Taylor). He has served on the boards of numerous educational research journals, and has served as Editor of *Reading Research Quarterly*, the *Yearbook of the National Reading Conference*, and *Review of Research in Education*.

Michael Pressley (*see* About the Editors).

Taffy E. Raphael is Professor of Literacy Education in the Department of Curriculum and Instruction at the University of Illinois–Chicago. Dr. Raphael's work in teacher education earned her the Outstanding Teacher Educator in Reading award from the International Reading Association. Her research has focused on question–answer relationships, strategy instruction in writing, and Book Club, a literature-based research program. She has published articles in such journals as *Reading Research Quarterly, The Reading Teacher*, the *National Reading Conference Yearbook*, and *Language Arts*, and has coauthored and edited several books on literacy instruction, including *Book Club: A-Literature-Based Curriculum, Second Edition*. She is past-president of the National Reading Conference and was associate director of the Center for the Improvement of Early Reading Achievement. She is also a member of the Reading Hall of Fame of the International Reading Association.

David Reinking is Professor of Education and Head of the Department of Reading Education at the University of Georgia. He is currently the editor of *Reading Research Quarterly*. Dr. Reinking is widely recognized in the field for his work investigating how computer-based forms of reading and writing affect literacy. His publications have appeared in the leading outlets in the field, and he is lead editor (with coeditors, Linda D. Labbo, Michael C. McKenna, and Ronald D. Kieffer), of the *Handbook of Literacy and Technology: Transformations in a Post-Typographic World*, which won an American Library Association Award as an Outstanding Academic Book of the Year in 1998 and the Edward B. Fry Book Award from the National Reading Conference in 1999.

D. Ray Reutzel is the Emma Eccles Jones Endowed Professor of Early Childhood Education at Utah State University, as well as director of the Emma Eccles Jones Center for Early Childhood Education and a member of the Department of Elementary Education. He began his career as a kindergarten classroom teacher and later taught first, third, and sixth grades. His area of research deals with early literacy in comprehension, fluency, and book selection strategies. In addition, Dr. Reutzel has more than 135 publications. His articles have appeared in journals such as *Reading Research Quarterly, Journal of Educational Research, Journal of Literacy Research,* and *The Reading Teacher,* and his most recent books are *Your Classroom Library: New Ways to Give It More Teaching Power* and *Strategies for Reading Assessment and Instruction: Helping Every Child Succeed.* He received Brigham Young University's Karl G. Maeser Research Award in 1992, the College Reading Association's A. B. Herr Award for Published Contributions to Reading Education, and Utah State University's Alumni Award for Outstanding Professional Achievement. He is also Editor-Elect of *The Reading Teacher.*

Nancy L. Roser is Professor of Language and Literacy Studies, the Flawn Professor of Early Childhood, and Distinguished Teaching Professor at the University of Texas at Austin. A former elementary teacher, she now teaches undergraduate elementary reading and language arts, as well as graduate courses in teaching the English language arts and children's literature. Her research interests include close inspection of children's book conversations in classrooms. She is coeditor of *Book Talk and Beyond* (with Miriam Martinez) and *Adventuring with Books* (with Julie Jensen), as well as over 100 chapters and articles related to teaching reading and the language arts.

Lisa Patel Stevens is a Lecturer in the Middle Years of Schooling Program at the University of Queensland in Australia and has worked as a reading teacher, literacy specialist, and policy maker. Her research interests include literacy pedagogy for adolescents, critical literacy, and discourse analysis in educational settings. She has published articles in the *Journal of Adolescent and Adult Literacy, The Reading Teacher,* and *Reflective Practice,* and has coauthored chapters on multiliteracies, critical discourse analysis, and the marginalization of young people. Dr. Stevens is currently working on a comparative study of adolescent literacy research, practice, and policy in the United States and Australia.

Peter Winograd serves as Director of the Center for Teacher Education and Educational Policy in the College of Education at the University of New Mexico. His current responsibilities include working with state and national organizations in the area of educational reform, particularly those dealing with teacher quality. In addition, Dr. Winograd helps organize and facilitate teacher education programs across the college. Dr. Winograd's previous experience includes serving as chair of the Department of Curriculum and Instruction at the University of Kentucky in Lexington. He also served as the director of the University of Kentucky Institute for Educational Research and codirector of the University of Kentucky and University of Louisville Joint Center for the Study of Educational Policy. Dr. Winograd's research focuses on education policy and reform, assessment in literacy, helping children become strategic readers, and the cognitive and motivational factors involved in the reading difficulties of children at risk. He served on the Board of Directors of the National Reading Conference and the National Advisory Board of the National Reading Research Center, and currently serves as a consultant to a number of school districts and state departments of education across the nation. He has published over 60 book chapters, policy briefs, and journal articles.

FOREWORD

Learning to read and write is arguably the most complex task humans face. Becoming literate requires experiences that help make the meaning and importance of print transparent. It requires active involvement and engagement to ensure that the joys of being literate, and the value of what literacy can do in a very practical sense, are appreciated. Although it is undoubtedly true that becoming literate still involves the development of some basic skills and strategies, today low-level basic skills that merely involve surface-level decoding and the recall of information are hardly enough. Critical thinking and the ability to personalize meanings to individual experience and apply what is read or written in the real world, under many different circumstances and with many different types of texts, may now be termed the "new basics."

Not only has what we are required to do with texts changed—the texts themselves have changed. Today, texts are presented to us and generated by us in endless variety: books, magazines, and pamphlets of every conceivable design; letters and memoranda arriving via fax, e-mail, and snail mail; television screens, computer screens, and numerous other electronic screens and displays in our kitchens as well as our offices; and the indecipherable array of documentation for everything we buy that must be assembled, cared for, or operated. The list goes on and on. It serves as a constant reminder that the definition of what it means to be literate has evolved with the increasing demands of all aspects of our lives—personal, social, and economic. It is also a reminder of the critical role schooling plays in making literacy accessible to every child.

Best Practices in Literacy Instruction could not have been conceived at a better time. Its content takes on special meaning in a time when national, state, and local school reform efforts in the United States have raised expectations for what readers and writers should know and be able to do. The public awareness of the critical need for proficient readers and writers has never been greater—nor, I might add, has its criticism of the job the schools are doing. An unprecedented amount of open dissension and debate about the content of literacy instruction has led to state directives and legislative mandates that dictate specific curriculum content.

Fortunately, the knowledge base for improving literacy has never been richer. The scholars contributing to *Best Practices in Literacy Instruction* are representative of those whose work has contributed to that knowledge. In addition to being highly respected researchers in the field of literacy, the contributors to this volume represent a wide range of perspectives and specialization within literacy education. *Best Practices in Literacy Instruction* offers both practical suggestions and a research base for educators, policy makers, and others as they consider how they might help children meet today's higher literacy standards. The first edition has become a major resource for practitioners and policy makers.

Becoming literate in the modern world is indeed an increasingly complex task. Reading and writing abilities don't just happen. They are acquired, nurtured, and refined through the acts of those who provide appropriate instructional contexts and support. The best of these practices is what this book is about. All who read *Best Practices in Literacy Instruction* will be indebted to the editors for their superb efforts in bringing clarity to where so much confusion and dissent often exists.

DOROTHY S. STRICKLAND
Samuel DeWitt Proctor Professor of Education
Rutgers—The State University of New Jersey

ACKNOWLEDGMENTS

We would like to thank the authors for their outstanding contributions to this second edition of *Best Practices in Literacy Instruction*. They represent some of the most well-known reading researchers in the country. Thank you to Chris Jennison, Senior Editor at The Guilford Press, for having the confidence in this volume to consider it for a second edition. Thank you as well to Jacquelyn Coggin for her excellent editing and to Anna Nelson for keeping the publication date on time. And thanks also to Lara Heyer and Allison Poro for their help in providing information to the authors, collecting the bios, and dealing with the many other details involved when working on such a publication. Finally, thank you to Catharine Brasch, Tammi-Lyn Eisen, and Amy Sass for taking the chapter-opening photographs of their students engaged in literacy activities.

CONTENTS

PART III: SPECIAL ISSUES

BEST PRACTICES IN LITERACY INSTRUCTION

INTRODUCTION

Lesley Mandel Morrow
Linda B. Gambrell
Michael Pressley

The second edition of *Best Practices in Literacy Instruction* is a volume containing recent insights from research that have direct implications for classroom practice. We designed this book to help beginning and experienced classroom teachers become more effective literacy teachers. We hope that it will provide teachers at all levels with fresh ideas and insights about literacy instruction. With that in mind, and to reflect the current concerns on a national level, in this volume, we focus on research-based best practices in literacy instruction and provide practical suggestions for enhancing the literacy development of all students. The book has been designed for preservice and in-service teachers, and for use in reading and language arts courses and staff development workshops that focus on literacy development. It should also be of value in graduate courses and to reading specialists and administrators of school literacy programs.

In recent years, literacy research has begun to address specific questions about the efficacy of instructional techniques and procedures. Researchers now take into account various influences such as classroom context, motivation, teaching methods, social interaction, and teacher–student interactions. In this volume, we want to emphasize that the *what* and the *how* of literacy research are important. *What* research reveals about literacy instruction should inform *how* we go about the very important job of providing literacy experiences and instruction for our students. The contributors to this volume have been active in conducting classroom-based research and program innovations that focus on literacy development. They believe that teachers must be informed decision makers and provide thorough and consistent information that integrates new, research-based information with valid, traditional ideas about literacy instruction. Thus, the chapters in this book provide practical, classroom-based strategies and techniques, as well as principles to assist in instructional decision making.

This book is organized into three parts: Perspectives on Exemplary Practices in Literacy, Strategies for Learning and Teaching, and Special Issues. In Part I, the authors explore core beliefs and philosophies of classroom literacy instruction and acknowledge the collaborative and change-oriented nature of the field of literacy. We believe that multiple perspectives increase awareness of the theoretical bases for best practices in literacy instruction. Readers of this volume should consider the merits of the different positions described as they interpret and translate these ideas into practice. Part II presents current, research-based information about classroom literacy practices. Topics include current practices in early literacy development, phonics instruction, vocabulary development, comprehension strategies, building fluency, developing writing, the use of literature in literacy programs, adolescent literacy, and best practices in assessment. Part III provides an overview of many of the current issues in the field of literacy instruction, including a discussion concerning the best use of basal reading materials, organizing effective literacy instruction, teaching children with special needs, the use of technology in literacy programs, and achieving best practices in literacy instruction.

PART I: PERSPECTIVES ON EXEMPLARY PRACTICES IN LITERACY

In Chapter 1, Susan Anders Mazzoni and Linda B. Gambrell contend that it is time for literacy researchers and educators to move beyond terms, labels, and factions, and move toward "common ground." In order to accomplish this goal, they describe a number of research-based best practices, as well as principles of best practices. However, Mazzoni and Gambrell warn that although best practices can be *de*scribed, they cannot be *pre*scribed. They assert that best practices can only be achieved when knowledgeable, dedicated, and reflective teachers adapt instruction to fit the strengths and needs of children in their classrooms.

In Chapter 2, P. David Pearson and Taffy E. Raphael describe how narrow, oversimplified views of literacy and instruction mask critical areas that educators must balance to promote lifelong learning. They begin this chapter with a summary of historical and current debates in literacy education and describe how "narrow" views of balanced instruction are detrimental to best practices. They then offer a broader, restructured view of balanced instruction using the metaphor of multiple balance beams—each possessing its own set of dimensions. The authors specifically describe content and contextual aspects of literacy instruction that need balance, such as curricular-/student-centered instruction, reader response/text-driven understandings, and narrative/expository texts, and argue that it is crucial that teachers be afforded the opportunity to balance literacy instruction along each continuum.

PART II: STRATEGIES FOR LEARNING AND TEACHING

In order to create a model of effective early literacy instruction, Lesley Mandel Morrow and Elizabeth Asbury visited the classrooms of six first-grade teachers identified as exemplary by their administrators. In Chapter 3, the authors present a case study of one exemplary, first-grade teacher who possessed all of the characteristics associated with best practices in literacy instruction. They then present overarching characteristics of exemplary early literacy instruction, including knowledge of effective instructional strategies and efficient, effective classroom management practices. Readers will glean general guiding principles, as well as specific ideas and activities, for implementing best practices for a balanced early literacy program.

After summarizing "what we know" about phonics, reading, and writing, Patricia M. Cunningham, in Chapter 4, describes a balanced approach for primary reading and writing instruction, called "The Four Blocks." She provides a detailed, vivid description of "The Words Block," which enables students to learn high-frequency words and strategies for decoding and spelling. Cunningham offers clear explanations of activities that practitioners can use in their classrooms and illustrates points with many practical examples. She also provides a rationale for employing an analogic approach to teaching phonics in the literacy program.

In Chapter 5, Camille L. Z. Blachowicz and Peter J. Fisher present five research-based guidelines for vocabulary instruction. They share the research that underpins each and give examples of instruction reflecting targeted guidelines. The authors describe a classroom that utilizes this type of instruction. They wrap up their chapter by sharing some valuable resources for vocabulary instruction.

In Chapter 6, Cathy Collins Block and Michael Pressley begin by exploring the theory, research, and current issues concerning comprehension instruction. They examine how comprehension is affected by word-level processes, vocabulary instruction, and above-word-level contexts. Recent developments in comprehension processes instruction are also presented. Block and Pressley discuss recently developed comprehension instructional practices, including teacher reader groups, comprehension process motion signals, following an author's train of thought, and use of bookmarked texts. They also suggest directions for future comprehension research and practice.

In Chapter 7, Melanie Kuhn discusses the role that fluency plays in the overall reading process. She describes how fluency development has often been overlooked as an instructional component of reading in literacy curricula and teacher development courses. Kuhn identifies several effective ways to integrate fluency instruction into the classroom literacy curriculum using strategies such as paired repeated readings, reader's theater, the fluency development lesson, and a fluency-oriented literacy program. She concludes by providing a simple measure for teachers to assess the fluency of the students in their classroom.

In Chapter 8, Karen Bromley asserts that sound writing instruction must balance process and product approaches, and she describes many effective methods for addressing both in kindergarten through eighth-grade (K–8) classrooms. She provides numerous concrete ideas that teachers can use for writing instruction. Her chapter includes a discussion of topics that range from standards and assessment, direct instruction, the value of literature and peer interaction in children's writing development, graphic organizers, and writing across the curriculum, to how to integrate electronic literacy in the language arts curriculum. Bromley embeds many examples of effective writing instruction within descriptions of real-life classrooms.

Douglas Fisher, James Flood, and Diane Lapp shed insight into the value of a literature-based literacy curriculum in Chapter 9. Readers visit a third-grade teacher's multicultural classroom in which literature is used as the cornerstone for instruction. The authors also describe research to support the contribution of literature to children's literacy growth. Practical, instructional strategies that can be incorporated into a literature-based classroom are also provided, as well as suggestions for literature selection, grouping, and assessment.

In Chapter 10, Lisa Patel Stevens and Thomas W. Bean discuss adolescent literacy and secondary literacy instruction. They explore the dichotomies between secondary school–sanctioned literacies and literacies used by adolescents outside of school. Stevens and Bean briefly review the literature on content area and adolescent literacy, then provide a model of how one teacher has been able to move beyond a text-centered approach to create an environment in which adolescent literacy instruction meets the demands of the ever-changing landscape of the 21st century. Stevens and Bean encourage readers to explore the implications of this model on their practices and future instruction.

In Chapter 11 Peter Winograd, Leila Flores-Dueñas, and Harriette Arrington contend that best practices in literacy assessment need to include a variety of indicators that address the needs of multiple audiences, improve teaching and learning, and help to ensure that schools are thriving. However, they contend that in order to improve the lives of students in our nation's schools, we must understand both broad and particular issues related to education, such as national statistics, the need for an adequate supply of well-prepared teachers and teacher-supportive schools, the tension that exists between assessment for accountability and instruction, ethical and constructive use of assessments, the limited role of assessment in improving the lives of children, and the influence of sociopolitical and economic contexts on education. Although the authors hesitate to identify which literacy practices are "best" (because effectiveness depends primarily on how wisely assessments are used), they explicitly describe authentic assessment strategies that can be beneficial for students, teachers, and parents; performance tasks and rubrics; portfolios; observation/anecdotal records/developmental checklists; and student–teacher conferences. They conclude with a presentation of questions that provide insight into the trends that will affect the assessment of literacy in the future.

PART III: SPECIAL ISSUES

As D. Ray Reutzel points out in Chapter 12, teachers often group students in order to meet individual needs. However, he cites extensive research suggesting that persistent, static ability grouping is detrimental in many ways. So what is the alternative? Reutzel recommends that educators incorporate a variety of grouping patterns in their classrooms, including flexible groups, basal reader selection groups, literature circles, cooperative learning groups, needs grouping, and guided reading groups. He provides descriptions of each type of grouping pattern and illustrates his points with examples, then presents an instructional framework that incorporates a variety of grouping patterns in K–2 classrooms, called the Primary Grades Literacy Workshop. This framework consists of five parts: (1) reading and writing together, (2) working with words and strategies, (3) guided reading, (4) fluency development, and (5) independent center study and individual assessment.

Nancy L. Roser, James V. Hoffman, and Norma J. Carr offer an in-depth look at basal readers in Chapter 13. The authors begin by tracing the history of basals, "born" approximately 150 years ago. They discuss the development of basals and point out criticisms that have been levied against them, then examine changes that have occurred in basals and teachers' guides over the past decade and describe the struggles that today's publishers face in developing texts for a diverse community. The teaching philosophy and language arts instruction of three teachers are also presented—each teacher eliciting instruction in different ways, yet all resisting the practice of strictly adhering to teachers' guides and the sole use of basal readers. The authors conclude with a discussion of their concern about how the notion of balanced instruction will materialize in new basal series.

In Chapter 14, Richard L. Allington and Kim Baker contend that, first and foremost, struggling readers and writers must have access to high-quality literacy instruction if they are to succeed. They point out that exemplary classroom teachers have a positive impact on the literacy achievement of their lowest achieving children, whereas there is some evidence to suggest that paraprofessionals—who are often poorly trained—do not. Allington and Baker assert that some children do need extra support, and that specialists must both foster and enhance classroom instruction. They provide two case studies that illustrate high-quality instruction. The first is a description of a day in the life of an exemplary first-grade teacher; the second describes the practices of an exemplary reading resource teacher. The authors conclude by summarizing practices that characterize exemplary early intervention efforts.

According to Michael C. McKenna, Linda D. Labbo, and David Reinking in Chapter 15, best practices can (and must) successfully embrace technology. The authors present scenarios from two classrooms that illustrate how two teachers have successfully used technology in their literacy instruction. The authors also show how the integration of technology into the social environment of the classroom encourages increased collaboration among students and provides additional support for students with special needs, including struggling readers and writers, nonfluent, reluctant, and English as a Second Language (ESOL) readers. Many practical activities, as well as principles for integrating technology into literacy teaching, are provided.

Finally, in Chapter 16, James W. Cunningham and Kimberly H. Creamer raise a number of current, critical issues regarding conditions that prohibit best practices in classrooms. More specifically, they argue that faddism and holding teachers accountable for students' literacy are particularly prohibitive conditions. The authors also explain why they believe that these conditions are unlikely to change in the near future. Cunningham and Creamer then offer suggestions for promoting effective instruction. They recommend professional consensus, a school-by-school/team approach to reform, school-based assessments, and balanced literacy programs as keys to promoting best practices in America's schools.

Part I

PERSPECTIVES ON EXEMPLARY PRACTICES IN LITERACY

Chapter 1

PRINCIPLES OF BEST PRACTICE: FINDING THE COMMON GROUND

Susan Anders Mazzoni
Linda B. Gambrell

This chapter will:

- Describe the characteristics of proficient readers.
- Discuss the importance of the teacher as decision maker in working toward a best practice approach to literacy instruction.
- Present 10 research-based best practices for literacy instruction.
- List and explain eight principles of best practice.

Research-based principles of best practice in reading can provide the foundation for instruction that can help all students become more proficient readers. Converging evidence from a number of national reports indicates that proficient readers share certain characteristics. Three of these reports, the *Reading Framework for the National Assessment of Educational Progress: 1992–1998* (National Assessment Governing Board, 1997), the National Reading Panel Report (Snow, Burns, & Griffin, 1998), and the RAND Reading Study Group Report (2002), have been the focus of much discussion about effective reading instruction. Taken together, the National Assessment of Educational Progress (NAEP), the National Reading Panel (NRP), and the RAND Reading Study Group Report identify several important characteristics that distinguish proficient readers from less proficient readers. According to the NAEP report, proficient readers:

- Have positive habits and attitudes about reading.
- Are fluent enough to focus on understanding what they read.
- Use their world knowledge to understand what they read.
- Develop an understanding of what they read by extending, elaborating, and evaluating the meaning of the text.
- Use a variety of effective strategies to enhance and monitor their understanding of text.
- Can read a variety of texts for a variety of purposes.

The foundation for all instructional practice, regardless of one's theoretical or pragmatic orientation to reading, is the goal of improving reading achievement for all students (Rasinski, 2001). In an investigation designed to explore contexts and practices for teaching reading on which experts could agree, Flippo (1998, 2001) surveyed representative experts of a contiuum of beliefs and philosophies. A major finding of Flippo's study was that, as professionals, we are not nearly as divided as some individuals would like the public to believe. The study revealed that, indeed, there are many points of agreement in the reading profession, even among individuals with the most diverse philosophies. Flippo found that experts agree on contexts and practices that both facilitate learning to read and make learning to read difficult. According to Rasinski (2001), the major finding from Flippo's study of experts is that "the perceived gulf that exists between orientations to research and practices in literacy education by literacy researchers and scholars is not as large as it may seem" (p. 159).

The importance of the teacher as decision maker was an underlying theme of the findings in Flippo's (1998, 2001) study of experts. As Pearson (1996) noted, teachers must be able to understand literacy learning well enough to adapt the learning environment, materials, and methods to particular situations and students. In other words, teachers must be adept at identifying and implementing best practices that will foster reading development. In the final analysis, effective teaching and learning rests on the shoulders of the teacher who makes informed decisions about the instructional approaches and practices that are most appropriate for a particular student.

Although we have learned a great deal about literacy and instruction over the past decades, there remains significant controversy over what constitutes "best practices" in literacy education. Interestingly, our increased understanding of the literacy process appears to have contributed to the current debate. We have become increasingly aware of the complexity of reading and instruction; consequently, many researchers have adopted broadened perspectives regarding the nature of literacy and how learning occurs. For example, since the 1970s, researchers have moved from performing laboratory controlled experiments, in which one aspect of learning was studied independent of context, to naturalistic classrooms settings, in which contextual variables such as affective environment, authenticity of tasks, social interaction, parental involvement, or types of materials could be evaluated. Research has shown that, indeed, many contextual variables make a difference in literacy learning. Furthermore, as our need for higher levels of literacy grew as a result of changes in workplace demands, we have redefined what is basic to becoming literate. Simply being able to decode and answer low-level, literal questions about a piece of text is no longer sufficient. Becoming fully literate means, among many things, being able to use strategies independently to construct meaning from text, draw upon texts to build conceptual understanding, effectively communicate ideas orally and in writing, and possess an intrinsic desire to read and write. Literacy and instruction have become complex, multifaceted tasks.

Although many literacy researchers have adopted multiple perspectives to help interpret and account for this complexity, tacitly or explicitly adopting a single lens has caused rifts and divides among members of the education community. With "pendulum-like persistence"

(Allington, 1994), we have swung from teacher-directed to child-centered teaching and learning and back; from phonics to comprehension and back; and from decoding to whole language and back; the list goes on. While the reading debates roar on in the media, many researchers call for mutual respect, conversation, and courtesy among members of the reading community (Allington, 1997; Flippo, 2001; Kamil, 1995; Stanovich, 1997). It is becoming increasingly clear that in order to achieve fully the goal of literacy for all, we must move beyond the terms and labels that are driving us apart. We must move away from dealing with trivial matters and move toward what Vail (1991) has called the "common ground." But the questions remain: Is there a common ground for best practice? If so, what best practices can we agree upon?

We believe that there is a common ground. In this chapter, we present a number of generally accepted, research-based best practices. We also present principles of best practice derived from constructivist theory that traverse the chapters in this book. However, before doing so, we must interject one important caveat: We believe there is no simple, narrow solution to the "best practices" debate. Although simple solutions are appealing by their very nature, applying simple solutions to complex enterprises, such as teaching children to become literate in the fullest sense, cannot result in best practice. For example, employing a method that research has shown to be effective for improving a particular aspect of literacy learning will not be a "best practice" if, for example, instruction is not adapted to fit the strengths and needs of a particular group of learners, or classroom management is an issue, or a "risk-taking" environment has not been fostered, or other aspects of literacy instruction are not included in the total program. Also, it is important to remember that teachers work with children who come to school with unique personalities and understandings; therefore, individual children will often respond differently to the same instruction. What does this mean? It means that best practices involve a "custom fit"—not a simple "one size fits all"—approach, and that effective teachers not only bring research into practice but they also understand their students' strengths and needs, as well as their cultural community, and adapt instruction to promote optimal learning in the fullest sense of what it means to become literate. Effective teachers constantly self-question, reflect, teach, and reevaluate in order to inform instruction.

We are reminded of an elementary school teacher who read about the practice of using Author's Chair (Graves, 1994) and PQP (Praising–Questioning–Polishing), in which student writers share their works with other children, who then comment on the author's work by Praising (positive comments only), Questioning (ask the authors questions about their work), and Polishing (constructive comments). Although Author's

Chair may be considered a "best practice" by many educators, this teacher noticed that the children in her class tended to make the same, low-level comments to the student authors, such as "That was really good," or "I liked your story." Consequently, she determined that her students would benefit from instruction on how to critique an author's work. Thus, the generally accepted practice of Author's Chair was improved as a result of her ongoing reflection and deliberation. We believe that this vignette illustrates a very important point: No matter how well a particular practice is shown to be effective by research, *optimal assessment and instruction can only be achieved when skillful, knowledgeable, and dedicated teachers are given the freedom and latitude to use their professional judgment to make instructional decisions that enable children to achieve their literacy potential.* Teachers are ultimately the instructional designers who develop practice in relevant, meaningful ways for their particular community of learners. In other words, best practices can be *de*scribed— but not *pre*scribed.

TEN RESEARCH-BASED BEST PRACTICES

With the notion of the teacher as ultimate instructional designer in mind, we present ten research-based best practices that are generally accepted by experts in the field and are worthy of consideration (see Table 1.1). Notice that these practices are based on a rich model of the reading process, one that incorporates the full range of experiences that children need in order to reach their literacy potential. We believe that best practices are characterized by meaningful literacy activities that provide children with both the *skill* and the *will* they need to become proficient and motivated literacy learners. The authors in this book have addressed and expanded on these best practices.

EIGHT PRINCIPLES OF BEST PRACTICE

In this section, we highlight eight *principles* of best practice that we believe represent "common ground." Because a teacher is ultimately in the best position to bring principles into practice in a meaningful way for his or her particular community of learners, the notion of principled instruction is particularly supportive of teacher empowerment and professionalization. The following eight principles are grounded in constructivist learning theory, which suggests that the goal of schools is to help students learn new meanings in response to new experiences rather than simply to learn the meanings that others have created (Poplin, 1988). This view

TABLE 1.1. Research-Based Best Practices

1. Teach reading for authentic, meaning-making literacy experiences: for pleasure, to be informed, and to perform a task.
2. Use high-quality literature.
3. Integrate a comprehensive word study/phonics program into reading/writing instruction.   *Integrated Curriculum*
4. Use multiple texts that link and expand concepts.
5. Balance teacher- and student-led discussions.
6. Build a whole-class community that emphasizes important concepts and builds background knowledge.
7. Work with students in small groups while other students read and write about what they have read.
8. Give students plenty of time to read in class.
9. Give students direct instruction in decoding and comprehension strategies that promote independent reading. Balance direct instruction, guided instruction, and independent learning.
10. Use a variety of assessment techniques to inform instruction.

of learning emphasizes the personal, intellectual, and social nature of literacy learning.

As we read each of the chapters presented in this book, we noticed that although the authors addressed a wide variety of topics, there were a number of similarities among themes. The following principles also reflect "common ground" themes related to best practices presented in this book.

1. Learning Is Meaning Making

Learning is the "natural, continuous construction and reconstruction of new, richer, and more complex and connected meanings by the learner" (Poplin, 1988, p. 404). Proficient readers and writers actively search for and construct new meanings. When students are involved in literacy tasks and activities that are purposeful and authentic, they are more motivated to learn and come to view reading and writing as relevant, dynamic, interactive processes that involve decision making and problem solving. Basic to this principle is the notion that learning most often proceeds from whole (meaning/context) to part (skills/strategy instruction) to whole (meaning). It is *wholeness* and *context* that give meaning to our experiences and to our learning. Children learn new words more easily in a personally meaningful context. Workbooks that "teach" isolated skills are seen by most children as having little relevance to what really interests them and what they want to know about. Instruction in skills and strategies (such as decoding and comprehension strategies, spelling, punctuation, and grammar) is most effectively addressed in the context of each student's own personal need for meaning making. Moreover, a whole–part–whole approach provides an opportunity for children to apply the skills and strategies they have learned to authentic, meaningful tasks.

2. Prior Knowledge Guides Learning

The best predictor of what students will learn is what they already know. Prior knowledge is the foundation upon which new meaning (or learning) is built. Effective teachers assess students' conceptual understanding, beliefs, and values, and *link* new ideas, skills, and competencies to prior understandings. They also provide experiences that equip each child with sufficient background knowledge to succeed with literacy tasks. This principle is also consistent with Vygotsky's (1978) notion of "zone of proximal development," which suggests that optimal learning occurs when teachers determine children's current level of understanding and teach new ideas, skills, and strategies that are at an appropriate level of challenge.

3. The Gradual Release of Responsibility Model and Scaffolded Instruction Facilitates Learning

Children often need concentrated instructional support when they need to learn important skills and strategies that they would have difficulty discovering on their own. The gradual release of responsibility model offers such support. In general, the model describes a process in which students gradually assume a greater degree of responsibility for a particular aspect of learning. During the first stage, the teacher assumes most of the responsibility by modeling and describing a particular skill or strategy. In the second stage, the teacher and students assume joint responsibility; children practice applying a particular skill or strategy, and the teacher offers assistance and feedback as needed. Once students are ready, instruction moves into the third stage, in which students assume all, or almost all, of the responsibility by working in situations where they independently apply newly learned skills and strategies. This gradual withdrawal of instructional support is also known as scaffolded instruction because "supports" or "scaffolds" are gradually removed as students demonstrate greater degrees of proficiency.

We view the gradual release of responsibility and scaffolded instruction as consistent with constructivist principles when they are used within meaningful, authentic contexts (Graham & Harris, 1996; Harris & Graham, 1994). Indeed, many authors in this book provide examples of how to integrate these models within meaningful reading and writing programs that include use of literature, technology, authentic writing experiences, choice, and collaborative learning.

4. Social Collaboration Enhances Learning

From a social-constructivist perspective, literacy is a social act. Readers and writers develop meanings as a result of co-constructed understandings within particular sociocultural contexts. This means, among many things, that text interpretation and level of participation are influenced by the size and social makeup of a group, the cultural conventions of literacy (e.g., "What are reading and writing *for*? What are the literacy *goals* of the community?), as well as the different perspectives others convey about text.

Specifically, collaborative learning refers to individuals who actively and substantively engage in an exchange of ideas that result in co-constructed understanding. Collaborative learning and the social perspective have brought to the fore the importance of peer talk as well as small-group learning. Interest in the positive benefits of these contexts has resulted in new classroom participation structures, such as book talk discussion groups, literacy clubs, and small-group investigations of specific topics related to a content area and communication of findings to others.

We know, however, that collaborative learning does not just "happen." Children need assistance in developing interpersonal skills. They also need a degree of teacher assistance and influence in order to stimulate new learning. However, research has shown that the rewards are great. Collaborative learning contexts have been found to result in greater student achievement and more positive social, motivational, and attitudinal outcomes for all age levels, genders, ethnicities, and social classes than individualized or competitive learning structures (Johnson & Johnson, 1983; Johnson, Johnson, & Maruyama, 1983; Johnson, Maruyama, Johnson, Nelson, & Skon, 1981; Sharan, 1980; Slavin, 1983, 1990).

5. Learners Learn Best When They Are Interested and Involved

Motivation exerts a tremendous force on what is learned, and how and when it will be learned. Motivation often makes the difference between superficial and shallow learning, and learning that is deep and internalized. Clearly, students need both the skill and the will to become competent and motivated readers (Paris, Lipson, & Wixson, 1983). Best practices include ways that teachers support students in their reading development by creating classroom cultures that foster reading motivation. Several key factors include a book-rich classroom environment, opportunities for choice, opportunities to interact socially with others, and a teacher who values reading and is enthusiastic about sharing a love of reading with students. The goal of a successful instruction program should be the development of readers who can read and who *choose* to read.

6. The Goal of Best Practice Is to Develop High-Level, Strategic Readers and Writers

The authors in this text have moved well beyond traditional, low-level conceptions of literacy. Clearly, each author describes best practices as those that promote high-level thinking and strategic, versatile reading and writing. For example, ideas are presented for how to help children to (1) become independent users of comprehension strategies to help them gain meaning from text relative to their goal; (2) comprehend texts at multiple levels; (3) acquire word-recognition skills and strategies, so that they will have "thinking power" left for meaning; (4) use literature to examine the multicultural world, as well as genres, styles, and perspectives; (5) write in different genres and for a variety of purposes and audiences; and (6) use computers in high-level literacy activities such as searching for information and making intertextual links.

We are clearly in the process of redefining what it means to be "literate" in today's world. Print, in various forms, is playing an increasingly important role in our society, and jobs are requiring a level of literacy that is unsurpassed in history. Best practices, then, must include instruction that will help meet these demands.

7. Best Practices Are Grounded in the Principle of Balanced Instruction

Although there has been considerable controversy over which practices are best for teaching children to read and write, there is evidence that effective instruction provides a balanced program in which a skillful, committed teacher adapts and integrates a multitude of components to enable each student to achieve his or her literacy potential (Slavin & Madden, 1989). Notice that many of the authors in this text have also argued for balanced instruction. For example, the authors have recommend that teachers need to balance (1) curricular- and student-centered instruction, reader response and text-driven understandings, and use of narrative and expository texts; (2) use of multiple assessment measures in a variety of meaningful contexts; (3) phonics and comprehension instruction; (4) meaning making at multiple levels; (5) use of basal texts with meaningful instruction; and (6) process and product approaches to writing. It is clear that best practice encompasses both the elegance and complexity of the reading and language arts processes. Such a model recognizes and acknowledges the importance of both form (i.e., phonics, mechanics, etc.) and function (i.e., comprehension, purpose, meaning) of the literacy processes, as well as the notion that learning occurs most often and most effectively in a whole–part–whole context.

8. Best Practices Are a Result of Informed Decision Making

One of the most striking similarities among the ideas presented in this text is the view that the teacher *is* the necessary foundation, the architectural support, for building a successful literacy program. None of the authors in this book advocate a prescriptive, programmed approach to literacy instruction. Instead, they address the issue of best practices by focusing specifically on *principles* of instruction and their relationship to effective teaching.

Effective teachers guard against the tendency to teach reading and language arts processes as solely a series of subskills or components to be taught in a prescribed, linear fashion. They recognize the important contribution that each component plays in the literacy development of their students. For example, a performer may juggle several objects of different sizes and shapes, a task that seems incredibly difficult. But by knowing how to handle each individual object, while keeping several objects in constant motion, the juggler achieves the rhythm and flow necessary for a successful performance. Exemplary teachers must also perform a challenging juggling act. A teacher must include or juggle many literacy components of varying importance and give just the right amount of emphasis to keep his or her particular community of learners moving toward the desired instructional goal. To complicate this task further, adjustments must continually be made to adapt to the changing needs of each individual child. As the juggler, the teacher remains the key to a successful reading program by guiding students, modeling strategic literacy behaviors and processes, providing support when the going gets rough, and most importantly, introducing children to books, stories, and informational text that are worth reading (Winograd & Greenlee, 1986).

FINDING THE COMMON GROUND

As literacy educators, it is critical that we avoid labels and acknowledge our "common ground." One common challenge is that as we increase our understanding of literacy and instruction, our conception of best practices broadens and deepens, and we are less able to offer simple, narrow solutions. As suggested by Strickland (1994/1995), our students need and deserve instruction that is well informed and based on a *rich* model of the reading process. Her vision of best practices embraces the richness and complexity of literacy and instruction:

> A literacy curriculum that emphasizes what is basic values and builds on the knowledge that students bring to school, emphasizes the construction of meaning through activities that require higher order thinking, and offers extensive opportunities for learners to apply literacy strategies and their underlying skills in the context of meaningful tasks. (pp. 296–297)

There is no question that this is no easy task. It requires commitment, time, and knowledge. It must begin with an enlightened teacher who looks at the strengths and needs of each individual child and plans instruction that is based on those strengths and needs. The rewards, however, are great as we help children become lifelong, engaged readers.

DISCUSSION AND ACTIVITIES

1. Reflect on the characteristics of proficient readers described in this chapter. Do you agree with these characteristics? Are there some characteristics you believe are more important than others? Are there characteristics that you would add to this list?
2. Take a look at the 10 research-based, best practices in Table 1.1. For each of the 10 practices, identify specific activities in your classroom that support research-based practices.
3. Now, take a look at the eight principles of best practice. Do the activities you have identified (in item 2) reflect principles of best practice? Do you think that your knowledge of best practice guides your instruction? Consider how these principles of best practice affect the literacy instruction you provide for your students.

REFERENCES

Allington, R. (1994). The schools we have: The schools we need. *The Reading Teacher, 48,* 14–29.

Allington, R. (1997). Why does literacy research so often ignore what really matters? In C. K. Kinzer, K. A. Hinchman, & D. J. Leu (Eds.), *Inquiries in literacy theory and practice: Forty-sixth yearbook of the National Reading Conference* (pp. 1–12). Chicago: National Reading Conference.

Flippo, R. F. (1998). Points of agreement: A display of professional unity in our field. *The Reading Teacher, 52,* 30–40.

Flippo, R. F. (Ed.). (2001). *Reading researchers in search of common ground.* Newark, DE: International Reading Association.

Graham, S., & Harris, K. R. (1996). *Making the writing process work: Strategies for composition and self-regulation.* Cambridge, MA: Brookline Books.

Graves, D. (1994). *A fresh look at writing.* Portsmouth, NH: Heinemann.

Harris, K. R., & Graham, S. (1994). Constructivism: Principles, paradigms, and integration. *Journal of Special Education, 28*(3), 233–247.

Johnson, D. W., & Johnson, R. T. (1983). The socialization and achievement crisis: Are cooperative learning experiences the solution? In L. Bickman (Ed.), *Applied social psychology* (Annual 4). Beverly Hills, CA: Sage.

Johnson, D., Johnson, R., & Maruyama, G. (1983). Interdependence and interpersonal attraction among heterogeneous and homogeneous individuals: A theoretical formulation and a meta-analysis of the research. *Review of Educational Research, 533,* 5–54.

Johnson, D., Maruyama, G., Johnson, R., Nelson, D., & Skon, L. (1981). Effects of cooperative, competitive, and individualistic goal structures on achievement: A meta-analysis. *Psychological Bulletin, 89,* 47–62.

Kamil, M. L. (1995). Critical issues: Some alternatives to paradigm wars in literacy research. *Journal of Reading Behavior, 27,* 243–261.

National Assessment Governing Board. (1997). *Reading framework for the national assessment of educational progress: 1992–1998.* Washington, DC: National Center for Educational Statistics.

Paris, S., Lipson, M., & Wixson, K. (1983). Becoming a strategic reader. *Contemporary Educational Psychology, 8,* 293–316.

Pearson, P. D. (1996). Six ideas in search of a champion: What policymakers should know about the teaching and learning of literacy in our schools. *Journal of Literacy Research, 28*(2), 302–309.

Poplin, M. (1988). Holistic/constructivist principles of the teaching/learning process: Implications for the field of learning disabilities. *Journal of Learning Disabilities, 21,* 401–416.

RAND Reading Study Group. (2002). *Reading for understanding: Toward an R&D program in reading comprehension.* Technical report for the Office of Educational Research and Improvement. Washington, DC: Office of Educational Research and Improvement.

Rasinski, T. V. (2001). A focus on communication with parents and families. In R. Flippo (Ed.), *Reading researchers in search of a common ground* (pp. 159–166). Newark, DE: International Reading Association.

Sharan, S. (1980). Cooperative learning in small groups: Recent methods and effects on achievement, attitudes, and ethnic relations. *Review of Educational Research, 50,* 241–271.

Slavin, R. E. (1983). *Cooperative learning.* New York: Longman.

Slavin, R. E. (1990). *Cooperative learning: Theory, research, and practice.* Englewood Cliffs, NJ: Prentice Hall.

Slavin, R. E., & Madden, N. (1989). *Effective programs for students at risk.* Boston: Allyn & Bacon.

Snow, C. E., Burns, M. S., & Griffin, P. (Eds.). (1998). *Preventing reading difficulties in young children.* Washington, DC: National Academy Press.

Stanovich, K. E. (1997). *Twenty-five years of research on the reading process: The grand synthesis and what it means for our field.* Oscar S. Causey Research Award address, National Reading Conference, Scottsdale, AZ.

Strickland, D. (1994/1995). Reinventing our literacy programs: Books, basic, balance. *The Reading Teacher, 48,* 294–302.

Vail, P. (1991). *Common ground: Whole language and phonics working together.* Rosemont, NJ: Modern Learning Press.

Vygotsky, L. S. (1978). *Mind in society.* Cambridge, MA: Harvard University Press.

Winograd, P., & Greenlee, M. (1986). Students need a balanced reading program. *Educational Leadership, 43,* 16–21.

Chapter 2

TOWARD A MORE COMPLEX VIEW OF BALANCE IN THE LITERACY CURRICULUM

P. David Pearson
Taffy E. Raphael

This chapter will:

- Critique the construct of balance.
- Explore the focus of current debates about balance.
- Consider the problems that arise when balance is not achieved.
- Discuss what professionals can do to ensure balance in literacy education.

There is a perennial question in literacy education: What is a "balanced" literacy program? Balance, a key term of the late 1990s, has advocates from both sides of the aisle—those who wish to infuse balance into whole-language programs (e.g., McIntyre & Pressley, 1996), and others who argue that an early code emphasis is the cornerstone of a balanced framework (e.g., Lyon, 1997). Each side claims that it is the balanced party in this debate. At stake is the experience we provide students as they enter school and—for many—begin the process of learning to read, write, and talk about all kinds of texts. The contributors to this volume want this experience to be balanced—to focus on a range of texts, to build strategies for working with today's texts and other media, and to prepare students for a future that includes sources of information we may not even envision today.

Our focus in this chapter is to try to take this term "balance" from the semantic turf of both extreme positions: (1) those who publicly assert balance, while they champion direct instruction and systematic, synthetic phonics; and (2) those who insinuate balance, while they push for a curriculum shrouded in the developmental discourse—the authentic, genuine, natural reading and writing activities of everyday (i.e., not school) communication contexts. We share our professional vision of the concept of balance, guided by three overarching questions: (1) What is this debate all about?, (2) What are the dangers in "balance gone astray"?, and (3) What is to be done?

WHAT IS THE DEBATE ALL ABOUT?

We can think of this question as a single debate or as a family of narrower debates about issues such as curricular content, nature of texts, forms and focus of teacher preparation and professional development, and control over decisions related to all of these areas. Either way, these are not new issues. Debate(s) about the issues have been going on for decades, perhaps centuries. A century ago, the debates were about ABCs (synthetic phonics) versus the analytic phonics (words first, then the letters) (Mathews, 1966). Right after World War II, the debate focused on look–say (as exemplified by the classic Dick and Jane readers) versus phonics (see Chall, 1967; Mathews, 1966). In one form or another, the debate has always been about the *emphasis* during earliest stages of formal reading instruction—*breaking the code* or *understanding what we read* (see Chall, 1967, 1997, for a historical treatment of the debate), or what Chall described as *code-emphasis* versus *meaning-emphasis*.

The code-emphasis side takes a simple view of reading (Gough & Hillinger, 1980): Reading comprehension = decoding + listening comprehension. Those who advocate the simple view argue that because the code (the cipher that maps letters onto sounds) is what students do not know, the sooner they learn it, the better. Get phonics and decoding out of the way early, so that students can begin to engage in regular reading—by translating letters into the sounds of oral language and then using the same cognitive processes that enable listening comprehension to understand what they read.

The meaning-emphasis side argues that because making meaning is the ultimate goal of reading, it is best to start students off with that very expectation. If teachers offer lots of "scaffolding" to help students determine textual meaning(s), students will, as a natural by-product, acquire the cipher for mapping sounds onto letters. Moreover, in emphasizing meaning, it is crucial that teachers begin on many fronts at once: oral reading activities; shared reading, where teachers and students together read and study a book; writing through pictures; temporary spellings and other symbols; and so forth. One side says teach them what they do not directly know; the other, bootstrap what they do not know by relying on what they do know (see Pearson, 1976, for a full treatment of these issues).

In addition to debating early emphases, the debate has also been about *instructional focus*—whether the growth of each individual *child* or the sanctity of the *curriculum* dominates the decision-making processes of the teacher. One side wants to make sure that each child experiences the optimal curriculum for his or her development. For example, Harste, Woodward, and Burke (1984) talk about approaches that ensure that the child is the primary curriculum informant. At its extreme, this position can require as many curricula as there are children in a classroom. However, more realistically, this position suggests that there are multiple activities and literacy events within a classroom, and that children will experience them differently depending on where they are in their own literacy development. The other side, while certainly acknowledging the individuality of each reader, emphasizes the importance of making sure that each and every child goes through particular stages and acquires certain requisite bodies of knowledge in acquiring reading skills. Put differently, one side argues that there are many paths to reading acquisition, while the other argues that there are many variations in the way the single path is traversed.

There are also certain "overlays" that complicate the debate by introducing peripheral issues (see Bergeron, 1990). Whole-language rhetoric is often shrouded in romanticism, sometimes incorporating aspects of radical individualism, usually couched as a right to academic freedom (Bialostock, 1997; Goodman, 1992), and occasionally hinting at a fundamental distrust of institutions of power and authority, such as governmental agencies and commercial enterprises (Bialostock, 1997; Goodman, Shannon, Freeman, & Murphy, 1988). The rhetoric of those who want to return to more skills and phonics has its own set of "shrouds," many of which are moralistic in character. The argument for a "return" to systematic phonics is sometimes characterized as a return to our national roots (Sweet, 1997), or as a struggle to return the power of literacy to individual children and their families (Honig, 1996). The complexity comes through in the very language used within these different positions (e.g., the argument for individualism and academic freedom is parallel to the argument offered by Honig for the return of literacy to families).

WHAT ARE THE DANGERS IN BALANCE GONE ASTRAY?

As parties on each side of the aisle have attempted to appropriate the term "balance," our field has seen a conflation of all sorts of issues and constructs that are not necessarily the property of one side or the other. Thus, on one side of the balance beam, along with phonics, we pile up other constructs that are sometimes related—such as direct instruction, skills emphasis, ability grouping, formal treatment of genre, and curriculum-centered instructional focus. These constructs are pitted against everything that gets piled up on the other side of the balance beam—literary response, genre study, student-centered curricula, and whole-language philosophies (see Figure 2.1). Oversimplification actually masks crucial areas that literacy educators must balance to teach literacy effectively as a lifelong process.

We believe that this oversimplification is not only inaccurate, but it can also actually contribute to a dangerous situation for the field of literacy education given our current professional context. Specifically, legislative mandates appear to be replacing the marketplace of ideas as the

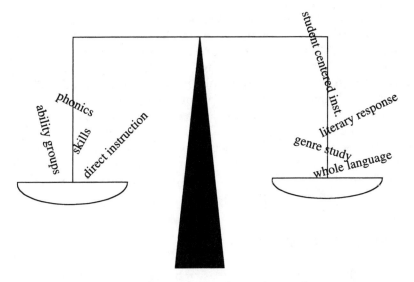

FIGURE 2.1. "Balance" out of control.

norm in our approach to curriculum change. Enacted (e.g., California Assembly 1086) and proposed (e.g., HR 2614) bills provide strong evidence for this trend. Recently, our field has experienced mandated phonics courses for all teachers (e.g., Ohio, California, Arizona), required phonics for teacher educators (California), and prior approval of the content of inservice programs (California).

This is not to say the education profession has been immune to legislative mandates in the past. In fact, colleges and universities have long lobbied for particular patterns of course work as requisite elements of teacher education programs, and they have done so in the name of quality and rigor. What is different now is the specificity of the mandate. It is one thing to have a legislative mandate or an executive order for 6 or 9 hours of course work in language arts methods; it is quite another to mandate the particular philosophical content of the course. Although teachers have a long history of responding in various ways to mandates from every level of policy making, they have not always run the risk of violating a highly specific law if they did not adopt particular practices.

If highly specific legislative mandates become the rule, then most (perhaps all) of our values regarding the professionalism of teachers and schooling will be eroded or irretrievably lost. Concepts such as empowerment, professional prerogative, inquiry and reflective practice, agency and intellectual freedom, and local curricular control make sense only under the assumption that what is available to teachers and school communities is a marketplace of research-based ideas from which to make judicious choices about the particular nature of curriculum in our corner of the world. The classic Enlightenment ideal of disseminating knowledge so that enlightened (i.e., informed by our best knowledge and practice) citizens can exercise freedom of choice is a mockery if there are no choices left to make. Notice that in the bargain, we also compromise the values and practices we have extolled in the recent reform movements (local decision making, community involvement in schools, ownership). These are high prices to pay for one particular model of research-based practice.

WHAT IS TO BE DONE?

We think that by unpacking and reassembling this phenomenon we call balance, we can build a case for the rich knowledge bases teachers need to implement a truly balanced curriculum. In so doing, we "recomplexify" balance, arguing that many independent elements must be simultaneously balanced. As we unpack this construct, we find it useful to think of a series of continua that reflect the *context* and the *content* of literacy instruction.

Contextual Continua

There are at least four contextual aspects that literacy educators attempt to balance in their daily teaching activities (see Figure 2.2). First, the notion of *authenticity* has been identified as crucial to students' literacy learning. The argument underlying the promotion of authenticity is that too many school tasks are unauthentic, unrealistic, and, by implication, not useful for engaging in real-world literacy activities; that is, instead of teaching kids how to "do school," we should be teaching them how to "do life." Writing, reading, and talking about text must be grounded in authentic tasks and goals, including writing for a real audience and purpose (Bruce & Rubin, 1993) or reading to engage in book club or literacy circle discussions with teachers and peers (e.g., McMahon, Raphael, Goatley, & Pardo, 1997), rather than writing to demonstrate knowledge of conventions or reading to answer successfully a set of comprehension questions. It may be difficult to find controversy in an emphasis on authenticity. However, if pursued too literally, some useful skills may never be acquired. There may be no occasion, if all instruction is subject to the

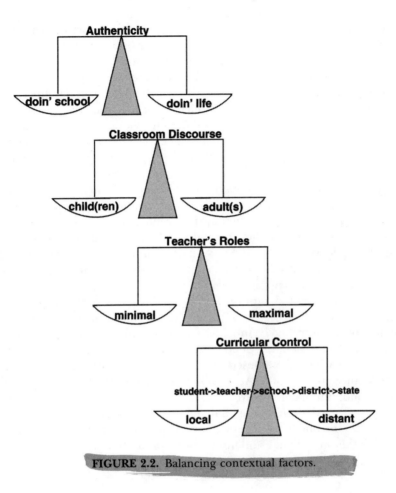

FIGURE 2.2. Balancing contextual factors.

authenticity criterion, for dealing with formal features of language, such as phonics, grammar, and punctuation, as objects of study. For example, children arguably need to understand the "code"—how sounds are captured in written language, and conventions for conveying stress and intonation—for engaging in lifelong literacy, yet the practice activities associated with becoming fluent in such areas may be limited to school practice tasks or reading practice readers. Clearly, balance is important across "doing school" and "doing life."

A second contextual aspect is the type of *classroom discourse* that students experience. Sociolinguists such as Cazden (1988) and Philips (1972) note the importance of control, specifically over topics and turn taking.

Teachers may control topics and turns, topics but not turns, turns but not topics, or neither topics nor turns. Students can exert similar control. Depending on the goal of the literacy event, activity, or lesson, different patterns of classroom talk are appropriate.

The *teachers' role(s)* within a classroom are closely related to the type of classroom discourse. Au and Raphael (1998) characterize variations in teachers' roles in terms of the amount of teacher control and student activity. They define five teacher roles: (1) explicit instructing, (2) modeling, (3) scaffolding, (4) facilitating, and (5) participating. These roles reflect decreasing control by the teacher and increased activity on the part of the student (see Figure 2.3). Thus, students are most passive when teachers are engaged in direct instruction, and most active when the teacher simply participates with them in the talk of the classroom. Au and Raphael's description implies that it is just as much a mistake to assume that literacy learning is limited to situations in which the teacher is engaged in explicit instruction as it is to assume that learning is meaningful only when the teacher is out of the picture.

A fourth aspect is that of *curricular control.* At one extreme, control is most distant from the classroom (e.g., at the national or state levels) where curriculum is controlled by those least familiar with the specific students who study the curriculum. Such control may be exerted through mandating the textbooks to be used, specifying standards or benchmarks of performance, and so forth. At the other extreme, control is in the hands of those most intimately involved with the students, specifically, classroom teachers or grade-level teams. Balancing across these two extremes is crucial. On the one hand, all educators must make clear those standards to which they would hold students accountable as they move through the

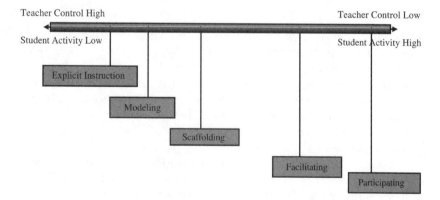

FIGURE 2.3. Teachers' roles.

curriculum. Fourth-grade teachers have the right to assume that certain curriculum content was covered and mastered prior to students' entering grade 4. Similarly, the fourth-grade teacher has a right to know the information for which these students will be held accountable when they matriculate to the next grade level. However, perhaps only the parents of these fourth graders know them better than their classroom teachers. Thus, to dictate specific instructional methods and even specific curriculum materials for reaching benchmarks and standards is to deny students the right to have those decisions made by the individuals who know them best—their teachers.

Content Continua

Balancing the contextual aspects of literacy instruction sets the stage for balance within the content of what is taught. We highlight three aspects of the curricular content that have been central to debates about literacy instruction: (1) skills contextualization, (2) text genres, and (3) response to literature (see Figure 2.4).

Skills contextualization reflects the degree to which skills related to our language system, comprehension strategies, composition strategies, and literary analysis are taught within the context of specific texts, either in response to these texts or as invited by them. At one extreme, teachers may rely on a predetermined curriculum of skills instruction, often tied to a curricular scope and sequence that operates within and across grade levels. At the other extreme, the texts and tasks are the determining force behind what is taught; the curriculum is unveiled as teachable moments occur, with the text and tasks functioning as springboards to skills or strategy instruction.

We suggest the need for teachers to operate flexibly between these two extremes. It makes a great deal of sense, for example, to teach about point of view as students read historical fiction related to the American Civil War, even if point of view happens to be scheduled at some other point in the academic year's guide to curriculum. Conversely, it makes little sense, in the context of reading Bunting's (1994) *Smoky Night* to a group of second graders, to highlight the /fl/ blend in flames, simply because it appeared in the text at the same time that the /fl/ blend popped up in an instructional scope and sequence plan. However, strict reliance on emerging questions, issues, or teachable moments as the standard by which teachers determine the content of the literacy curriculum creates problems or uncertainties because, at some point, aspects of the literacy curriculum really do have to be covered.

A second area of content balance is *genre* (see Hicks, 1998; Pappas & Pettegrew, 1998), which refers to the types of texts that form the basis of

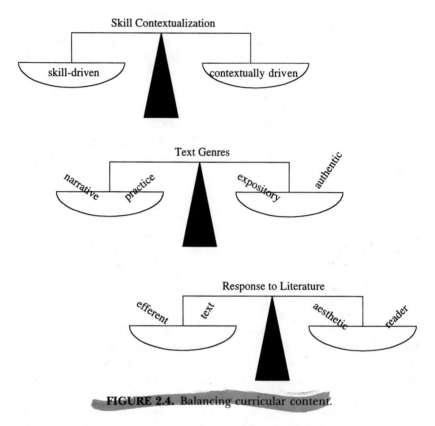

FIGURE 2.4. Balancing curricular content.

the literacy curriculum—stories, personal narratives, poems, essays, descriptions, and a whole range of specific expository structures. Results of state tests, such as the Michigan Educational Assessment Program and the National Assessment of Educational Progress, demonstrate the difficulties students have reading and understanding expository text, especially when contrasted with narrative. Although there are different explanations for the source of these disparate scores, there is agreement that young children find informational texts challenging both to read and write (Englert, Hiebert, & Stewart, 1988). In our efforts to balance the curriculum, we must ensure that students have the opportunity and the instructional support necessary to make meaning across the range of genres that exist.

The genre debate also involves authentic versus instructional texts. Some literacy educators argue that young readers learn best when reading and responding to authentic literature, which reflects purposeful use of language, complex natural language, and compelling story lines. Others have argued that such literary criteria make little sense for selecting books that young readers need to become fluent readers (e.g., Hiebert, 1998). Teachers need the flexibility to travel the full range of positions on this axis as well. Even our youngest students must be able to handle, read (even to "pretend read"), and respond to high-quality literary texts— texts written by authors to inform, persuade, entertain, and inspire. However, when it comes to acquiring the skills that enable authentic reading, relying on literature to promote skills development may serve well neither the literature nor the skills. Factors, from word placement on a page to relationships between words and pictures, may actually make wonderful literary texts poor materials for practicing and fine-tuning skills. Also, the sheer amount of practice reading in which early readers need to engage calls for a host of easy-to-read books students can read at their independent level. As engaging as these books may be to young and enthusiastic readers, many, perhaps most, may never qualify as quality literature. Neither high-quality trade books nor practice books can serve as the sole diet of books for young readers to become proficient in literacy activities.

The third dimension of content balance is *response to literature*. Here, the debate stems from complex issues related to readers' individual interpretations of text and the tensions concerning social and cultural values that almost inevitably arise in literature discussions. This debate has traveled along two axes—reader-driven versus text-driven understandings, and conventional (i.e., culturally sanctioned) versus personal interpretations. As our field has moved toward authentic literature as the basis for reading programs, teachers find themselves face-to-face with students' response to the content of literature: the enduring themes of the human experience (love, hate, prejudice, friendship, religious values, human rights, etc.). Fourth and fifth graders reading Taylor's (1990) *Mississippi Bridge* will undoubtedly initiate conversations about how the African Americans were treated by Southern whites in the 1930s, which can lead to conversations about racial relations today. Third graders reading and responding to McLerran's (1991) *Roxaboxen* unpack their own family stories and memories, and consider the relationships they have with family members across generations.

Debates about response are deeply rooted in beliefs about the functions of schooling, the separation of church and state, and the roles of parents and teachers. Furthermore, they are rooted in beliefs about the development of students' interpretive dispositions—whether we privilege the readers' interpretation of the story's meaning or author's message, or whether there is a "correct" (official or conventional) meaning that teachers are obligated to help students learn for later demonstration that they have acquired that conventional meaning. Balancing response to literature actually involves balancing the tension between the two goals of schooling—connecting to the past and preparing to meet an uncertain future. On the one hand, schools are obligated to teach students the cultural lore of our society, our history, our cultural and linguistic tools, our norms for interaction, and so forth. On the other hand, schools must build our future citizenry, helping students become adults who can live in a world that will undoubtedly differ significantly from the world we live in today. This tension, between convention and invention must be addressed through a curriculum that balances the individual with the culture.

CONCLUDING COMMENTS: RETHINKING BALANCE

We borrow from environmental science the concept of "ecological balance," which suggests a system that works to support each individual component—a curriculum that does not pit one aspect against another. In doing so, we hope to suggest that we must shift the debates about balance *away* from single-dimension discussions of what to teach and what not to teach, and *toward* the notion that achieving a balanced literacy curriculum is a logical goal of all literacy educators. The ecologically balanced curriculum that follows is based on research studying a literature-based program, Book Club, for upper-elementary-level reading instruction (Raphael, Pardo, & Highfield, 2002) and a K–5 literacy curriculum designed for the Kamehameha Early Education Program (Au, Carroll, & Scheu, 1997). Both programs are grounded in the belief that ownership of literacy is central to students' lifelong success (see Au & Raphael, 1998). The literacy instructional content that forms the ecological system consists of four areas: (1) comprehension, (2) composition, (3) literary aspects, and (4) language conventions (see Figure 2.5). Each of these four areas is supported by extensive bodies of research using a range of rigorous research methods (see Raphael & Brock, 1997). We must be conscious not to weigh in too heavily against any particular curriculum aspect, such as downplaying the role of phonics, as depicted in Figure 2.6. Nor should we be overly optimistic about teaching only a small part of the curriculum and hoping the rest will follow, as depicted in Figure 2.7.

Rather, we must recognize that the issue of balance is better described in terms of multiple dimensions of both content and context. Unpacking the cluster of dimensions in our balance beam metaphor, focusing

Comprehension	Composition	Literary Aspects	Language Conventions
Background Knowledge: prediction **Text Processing:** summarizing sequencing identifying importance **Monitoring:** clarifying planning	**Process:** planning drafting revising Writing as a Tool Writing from Sources On-Demand Writing	**Literary Elements:** theme plot character setting **Response to Literature:** personal creative critical	Sound/Symbol Grammar Syntax Interaction

FIGURE 2.5. An ecologically balanced curriculum.

Comprehension	Composition	Literary Aspects	Language Conventions
Background Knowledge: prediction **Text Processing:** summarizing sequencing identifying importance **Monitoring:** clarifying planning	**Process:** planning drafting revising Writing as a Tool Writing from Sources On-Demand Writing	**Literary Elements:** theme plot character setting **Response to Literature:** personal creative critical	Sound/Symbol Grammar Syntax Interaction

FIGURE 2.6. Lack of balance when curriculum is ignored.

on the specifics of content and contextual facets that comprise reading instruction, demonstrates some of the complexities in that debate. If we allow teachers the prerogative, for particular situations and students, of positioning themselves on each of these scales independently of the others, then we go a long way toward avoiding the oversimplifications that can so easily overwhelm us in this debate.

Teachers are not simply whole-language or skills teachers. Sometimes, for some children, they look like one; other times, for other children, they look like the other. This is because they make conscious, intentional decisions about individual students based on each of these important dimensions. We believe there is merit in the metaphor of multiple balance beams, each with at least one, and sometimes two, axes that must be traversed thoughtfully and independently. It makes balance not only a more elusive construct but also a more powerful one—one that we hope we can all strive to achieve in our teaching.

DISCUSSION AND ACTIVITIES

1. Obtain your school, district, or state's standards related to literacy education, whether those educated are pre- or inservice teachers, primary or intermediate grade students, or students in middle and high school. Examine the standards for evidence of balance across the curriculum,

Comprehension	Composition	Literary Aspects	Language Conventions
Background Knowledge: prediction Text Processing: summarizing sequencing identifying importance Monitoring: clarifying planning	Process: planning drafting revising Writing as a Tool Writing from Sources On-Demand Writing	Literary Elements: theme plot character setting Response to Literature: personal creative critical	Sound/Symbol Grammar Syntax Interaction

FIGURE 2.7. Lack of balance when curriculum is overemphasized.

the texts (i.e., genres), the nature of tasks (e.g., teacher–student control, authenticity of activities), and potential for emphasizing a variety of forms of classroom discourse. Discuss the degree to which these standards reflect balance in each area and/or obscure important aspects of literacy education. Consider the question "What can I do?" based on your findings.

2. The argument for balance in this chapter places much of the responsibility in the hands of the classroom teacher, who must make professional decisions about how to teach particular students with specific needs, use a specific curriculum to achieve particular goals, and so forth. How can the profession best support those teachers who lack the professional experiences that may be important to making wise decisions and creating balance?

3. Given your professional experiences, where do you think the challenges to providing or creating a balanced curriculum emerge? What can you do as an individual, as well as a member of a particular professional community, to infuse balance throughout the literacy curriculum and general classrooms for which you share responsibilities?

ACKNOWLEDGMENTS

This chapter was supported, in part, under the Educational Research and Development Centers Program, PR/Award Number R305R70004 to the Center for the Improvement of Early Reading Achievement (CIERA), as administered by the Office of Educational Research and Improvement, U.S. Department of Education.

REFERENCES

Au, K. H., Carroll, J. H., & Scheu, J. R. (1997). *Balanced literacy instruction: A teacher's resource book.* Norwood, MA: Christopher-Gordon.

Au, K. H., & Raphael, T. E. (1998). Curriculum and teaching in literature-based programs. In T. E. Raphael & K. H. Au (Eds.), *Literature-based instruction: Reshaping the curriculum* (pp. 123–148). Norwood, MA: Christopher-Gordon.

Bergeron, B. S. (1990). What does the term *whole language* mean?: Constructing a definition from the literature. *Journal of Reading Behavior, 22*(4), 301–329.

Bialostock, S. (1997). Offering the olive branch: The rhetoric of insincerity. *Language Arts, 74*(8), 618–629.

Bruce, B. C., & Rubin, A. D. (1993). *Electronic quills: A situated evaluation of using computers for writing in classrooms.* Hillsdale, NJ: Erlbaum.

Bunting, E. (1994). *Smoky night.* San Diego: Harcourt.

Cazden, C. (1988). *Classroom discourse: The language of teaching and learning.* Portsmouth, NH: Heinemann.

Chall, J. S. (1967). *Learning to read: The great debate.* New York: McGraw-Hill.

Chall, J. S. (1997). *Learning to read: The great debate* (3rd ed.). New York: McGraw-Hill.

Englert, C. S., Hiebert, E. H., & Stewart, S. (1988). Detection and correction of inconsistencies in the monitoring of expository prose. *Journal of Educational Research, 81,* 221–227.

Goodman, K. (1992). Whole language research: Foundations and development. In S. J. Samuels & A. E. Farstrup (Eds.), *What research has to say about reading instruction* (2nd ed., pp. 46–69). Newark, DE: International Reading Association.

Goodman, K. S., Shannon, P., Freeman, Y., & Murphy, S. (1988). *Report card on basal readers.* Katonah, NY: Owen.

Gough, P. B., & Hillinger, M. L. (1980). Learning to read: An unnatural act. *Bulletin of the Orton Society, 30,* 171–176.

Harste, J. C., Woodward, V. A., & Burke, C. L. (1984). *Language stories and literacy lessons.* Portsmouth, NH: Heinemann.

Hicks, D. (1998). Narrative discourses as inner and outer word. *Language Arts, 75*(1), 28–34.

Hiebert, E. H. (1998). Selecting texts for beginning reading instruction. In T. E. Raphael & K. H. Au (Eds.), *Literature-based instruction: Reshaping the curriculum* (pp. 195–218). Norwood, MA: Christopher-Gordon.

Honig, B. (1996). The role of skills in a comprehensive reading program. *California English, 1*(3), 16–20.

Lyon, G. R. (July 10, 1997). *Statement before the Committee on Education and the Workforce.* Washington, DC: U.S. House of Representatives.

Mathews, M. M. (1966). *Teaching to read: Historically considered.* Chicago: University of Chicago Press.

McIntyre, E., & Pressley, M. (1996). *Balanced instruction: Strategies and skills in whole language.* Boston, MA: Christopher-Gordon.

McLerran, A. (1991). *Roxaboxen.* New York: Lothrop Lee & Shepard.

McMahon, S. I., Raphael, T. E., with Goatley, V. J., & Pardo, L. S. (Eds.). (1997). *The Book Club connection: Literacy learning and classroom talk.* New York: Teachers College Press.

Pappas, C., & Pettegrew, B. S. (1998). The role of genre in the psycholinguistic guessing game of reading. *Language Arts, 75*(1), 36–44.

Pearson, P. D. (1976). A psycholinguistic model of reading. *Language Arts, 53,* 309–314.

Philips, S. U. (1972). Participant structures and communicative competence: Warm Springs children in community and classroom. In C. Cazden, V. P. John, & D. Hymes (Eds.), *Functions of language in the classroom.* New York: Teachers College Press.

Raphael, T. E., & Brock, C. H. (1997). Instructional research on literacy: Changing paradigms [Research Review Plenary Address]. In C. Kinzer, D. Leu, &

K. Hinchman (Eds.), *Inquiries in literacy theory and practice* (pp. 13–36). Chicago, IL: National Reading Conference.

Raphael, T. E., Pardo, L. S., & Highfield, K. (2002). Book Club: A literature-based curriculum (2nd ed.). Lawrence, MA: Small Planet Communications.

Sweet, R. W. (1997, May/June). Don't read, don't tell. *Policy Review*, pp. 38–42.

Taylor, M. D. (1990). *Mississippi bridge*. New York: Puffin.

Part II

STRATEGIES FOR LEARNING AND TEACHING

Chapter 3

CURRENT PRACTICES IN EARLY LITERACY DEVELOPMENT

Lesley Mandel Morrow
Elizabeth Asbury

This chapter will:

- Discuss theory, philosophy, and research that has had an impact on early childhood education and early literacy instruction.
- Discuss federal initiatives that have influenced early literacy development.
- Describe early literacy instruction through a case study demonstrating exemplary practice.
- Discuss an agenda for future research and practice in early literacy.

THEORY AND RESEARCH BASE

Historical Influences on Early Literacy Instruction

Early literacy instruction has been influenced by philosophers and theorists that dealt with child development, early childhood education, and literacy development. Philosophers such as Pestalozzi (Rusk & Scotland 1979) and Froebel (1974) talked about natural environments in which children would unfold through sensory experiences involving learning through touch, smell, taste, size and shape. Play was crucial, as was the social, emotional, and physical development of the child. Intellectual development was important; however, it was no more of a priority than social, emotional, and physical development. John Dewey's (1966) progressive education philosophy had a strong influence on preschool and kindergarten practices from the 1920s throughout the rest of the 20th century. Dewey led us to themed units of study that connect learning to meaning and purpose. He influenced the environments in preschool and kindergarten, with classrooms set up with different content area activity centers. The block corner, music and art centers, dramatic play area, science and social studies displays, and the library corner were the result of Dewey's ideas. A typical day included the following:

1. Circle time to talk about the weather, the calendar, and focus discussion on a science or social studies theme. If the theme were "good health," for example, the class would listen to a story and sing a song in keeping with this theme.
2. Free play took up a long period after circle time, when children painted at the easels, built block structures, engaged in dramatic play with dress-up clothing in the pretend kitchen set up in the classroom. Children explored and experimented with the ma-

terials in social settings, with little direction other than safety precautions.

3. Snack and rest followed free play, because good health and nutrition were emphasized.
4. If weather permitted, the children had outdoor play for large motor development. The day ended with a storybook reading.

There was no attempt at formal lessons; in fact, they were frowned on as inappropriate for the developmental stage of the child; however, teachable moments were used to advantage. There was no place in this program for formal reading instruction.

Montessori (1965) had a strong effect on early childhood and literacy instruction, believing that materials for children needed to serve a purpose for learning. She created manipulative activities to develop skills that focused on getting the right answer. Very few group lessons occur in this program, except to introduce new materials into the classroom. Children work independently at their own pace and level. According to Montessori, young children needed to use their senses to learn; therefore, she created many materials that involved the senses, such as tactile letters and wooden letters with different colors for long and short vowels.

Learning theorists Piaget (Piaget & Inhelder, 1969) and Vygotsky (1981) also had a strong impact on early childhood and literacy instruction. Both suggested social settings for learning. Those who interpret Piaget's theory of cognitive development for instruction describe a curriculum that encourages exploration of natural environments and learning rather than direct or explicit teaching. Vygotsky described learning in a similar manner to that of Piaget; however, he proposed that adults should scaffold and model behaviors they wanted children to learn.

These theories and philosophies that influenced early childhood education were concerned with the folowing:

- Prepared and natural environments for learning.
- Equal emphasis on social, emotional, physical, and intellectual development.
- Supportive adults who encourage social interaction for learning to occur.
- A focus on learning rather than teaching.
- Awareness that children must be actively involved to learn.

Reading Readiness and Early Literacy

Morphett and Washburne (1931) believed in postponing formal reading instruction until the child was developmentally "old enough." Their research concluded that children with a mental age of 6 years 6 months made better progress on a test of reading achievement than younger children. Although many educators believed that natural maturation was the precursor to literacy, others grew uncomfortable with simply waiting for children to become ready to read. They did not advocate formal reading instruction in early childhood but did begin to provide experiences that they believed would help children become ready for reading. Instead of waiting for a child's natural maturation to unfold, educators focused on nurturing that maturation by teaching children what they believed to be a set of prerequisite skills for reading, focusing on *auditory discrimination* of familiar sounds, similar sounds, rhyming words, and sounds of letters; *visual discrimination,* including color recognition, shape, and letter identification; left-to-right eye progression; *visual motor* skills, such as cutting on a line with a scissor, and coloring within the lines; and *large motor* abilities, such as skipping, hopping, and walking a straight line.

Literacy Research for the Past 35 Years

Research from the 1960s through the 1990s brought to life new information about oral language development, early writing development, emergent reading behaviors, and family literacy. With this new information and the whole language movement, we moved away from the abstract reading readiness activities thought to be the precursors to reading, toward more natural ways of developing reading once again. Although there still was a strong hands-off attitude to teaching early literacy, emergent literacy behavior was better understood and encouraged. Reading good literature to children was recognized as a very important activity, with interaction between the adult and child. Allowing and encouraging scribble writing and invented spelling was a way for children to experience the holistic form of writing. Including the family in literacy development was encouraged. Toward the end of the 1990s, the whole language philosophy was being questioned, with its lack of accountability and emphasis on specific skills development. We have entered a new phase of early literacy instruction in which acquisition of skills has become important, as has accountability for the development of these skills.

Numerous studies have found a positive relationship between reading achievement in early childhood and continued academic success (Adams, 1990; Foorman, Francis, Fletcher, Schatschneider, & Mehta, 1998). In a longitudinal study, Juel (1988) found that a child who is having difficulty reading at the end of first grade has a .88 probability of still having the difficulty in the fourth grade. It is apparent, based on this research and other, similar investigations, that it is crucial to have a good beginning when learning to read, because it can and probably will affect the rest of one's life (Snow, Burns, & Griffin, 1998).

Current Influences on Early Literacy

Publications from the federal government and professional associations, such as *Preventing Reading Difficulties in Young Children* (Snow et al., 1998), *Learning to Read and Write: Developmentally Appropriate Practices* (International Reading Association and the National Association for the Education of Young Children, 1998), and the National Reading Panel Report (NRP; 2000), all deal with concerns about early literacy instruction and how to improve it. In the spring of 2002, the Elementary and Secondary Education Act that includes the No Child Left Behind bill was passed. Although early literacy development has been a focus throughout the years, it is presently in the spotlight more than ever because of these documents.

The NRP (2000) suggests that instruction in early literacy needs to be organized and systematic. It also identifies areas on which to concentrate during instruction. The elements identified are (1) phonemic awareness, (2) phonics, (3) comprehension, (4) vocabulary, and (5) fluency. It is important to know that the Panel selected only some areas related to reading instruction to review. Members of the NRP did not study writing and its connections to reading success, nor did they study motivation. According to the NRP, some areas were omitted because there was not enough available quality research to determine their importance. In addition, they could not study everything related to reading instruction; instead, they reviewed only studies considered to be scientifically based reading research with a quantitative experimental design.

The NRP also highlights the importance of qualified teachers in developing successful readers. In the book, *Preventing Reading Difficulties in Young Children*, Snow et al. (1998) state that the best defense against failure to learn to read fluently is excellent instruction from an exemplary teacher. Investigations into exemplary and effective practice in early literacy instruction attempt to capture as many dimensions of expert performance as possible to describe teaching excellence. Effective and exemplary teachers share the following similar characteristics, which apply to effective practices not specific to literacy:

- Use of varied teaching strategies.
- Have high expectations for student achievement.
- Provide instruction designed to meet individual needs.
- Provide extensive positive feedback to students.
- Treat children with respect.

- Use of varied structures to meet individual needs when teaching, such as whole-group, small-group, and one-on-one instruction.
- Provide opportunities for children to work independently and also in collaboration with peers.
- Have excellent organization and management skills.
- Use of many assessment tools to guide instruction.
- Seek professional development on their own.
- Include parents in their program.
- Collaborate with peers (Morrow, Tracey, Woo, & Pressley, 1999; Pressley, Rankin, & Yokoi, 1996; Ruddell & Ruddell, 1995; Taylor & Pearson, 2002).

The following list of characteristics applies specifically to literacy instruction used by exemplary teachers.

- Provide a literacy rich environment with accessible materials.
- Try to carry out meaning-based literacy instruction to motivate interest.
- Provide an organized and comprehensive program of skills development in phonemic awareness, phonics, vocabulary, comprehension, and fluency.
- Use quality children's literature, along with many different materials for teaching reading and writing.
- Attend to individual literacy needs by forming small groups for some guided instruction of skills.
- Literacy instruction takes place during a long, uninterrupted time period and is integrated throughout the school day (Gambrell & Mazzoni, 1999; Morrow et al., 1999; Pressley, Allington, Wharton-McDonalds, Block, & Morrow, 2001; Pressley et al., 1996).

A comprehensive approach to early literacy is grounded in a rich model of literacy learning that encompasses both the elegance and the complexity of reading and language arts processes. Such as model acknowledges the importance of both form (phonemic awareness, phonics mechanics, etc.) and function (comprehension, purpose, meaning) of the literacy processes, and recognizes that learning occurs most effectively in a whole–part–whole context. This type of instruction is characterized by meaningful literacy activities that provide children with both the skills and the desire to achieve proficient and lifelong literacy learning (Gambrell & Mazzoni, 1999). Teaching literacy skills and providing opportunities for learning literacy skills are appropriate for young children as long as the teaching methods are appropriate for the child being taught. In such a program, teachers provide numerous literacy experiences that include the integration of reading, writing, listening, speaking, and viewing. There are multiple experience with word study activities; guided, shared, silent, collaborative, independent, and content-connected reading and writing; and oral reading to build fluency. The reading and writing take place in whole-class, small-group, one-on-one, teacher-directed, and social center settings in which children can practice what they have learned. Materials used include instructional texts, manipulatives, and meaningful children's literature. The instruction is spontaneous, authentic, and not only involves students in problem solving, but it is also direct, explicit, and systematic.

Every child is entitled to high-quality early literacy instruction. With that in mind, we describe an exemplary early childhood language arts classroom. We observed several teachers for a year as part of a study on exemplary literacy instruction. This investigation took place in five states in which supervisors nominated exemplary teachers. Teacher selection was based on supervisory observations, achievement of the students over a 5-year period, and the teachers' reputations with colleagues, parents, and children. We present a composite of the teachers' methods, highlighting the physical environment of the classroom, and the content and management of the Language Arts Block. As you read the case study, refer back to the list of exemplary characteristics to determine the degree to which the teacher fits the description.

RESEARCH-BASED PRACTICE

Danielle's Early Literacy Program

Danielle has been teaching in a suburban, middle-class community that has experienced rapid growth. During the 6 years she has taught in this school, Danielle has attained a master's degree in reading certification and is currently working toward a second master's degree. Her K–1 grade-level class consists of 24 children from the following ethnic backgrounds: 9 Caucasians, 5 Asians, 4 African Americans, 2 Native Americans, and 4 Hispanics. There are 10 girls and 14 boys. In her school, a collaborative atmosphere is apparent among teachers, administrators, and parents. Danielle shares ideas with colleagues whenever possible. At various times during her day, parent volunteers assist with classroom routines.

Teaching Philosophy

When asked to talk about her philosophy of literacy instruction, Danielle responded as follows:

> "From the first day of school, I try to create a supportive and accepting environment in my classroom. I do this with the help of parents, other teachers, administrators, and the children. The resulting class-

room community allows all of the children to feel secure as they develop socially, emotionally, physically, and intellectually. As the children grow, I attend to their individual needs and interests by using thematic instruction that integrates content areas and skills in a meaningful context. I also teach in an explicit manner when necessary. It is through small-group and individual lessons that I am able to address skills needs in a differentiated manner. Along with skills development, I hope to foster a positive attitude toward reading and writing and to make children aware of the important role that literacy will play in their lives. I want my students to be responsible about their work and to become collaborative problem solvers. As a teacher, I believe that is important for me to grow as a professional, just as my students grow as independent learners. Therefore, I always look for research-based practices that will aid me in helping my students to attain their greatest potential. In addition, I go to conferences and take courses I feel I need to stay current."

The Physical Environment in the Classroom

On entering Danielle's classroom, one is greeted with the sounds of children's voices and classical music. As the children engage in their varied activities, the value placed on literacy is very apparent. The literacy-rich environment is adorned with children's work and a host of environmental prints. An interactive Word Wall serves as a student reference for approximately 70 high-frequency words. In addition to these, which are all written on yellow cards near the top of the chart, there are new vocabulary words found in books the children have shared, and new words from themes they have studied. These words are written on light-blue cards placed under the high-frequency word cards. The children's names comprise the third group of words on pink cards, under all the rest.

In the Literacy Center are pillows, stuffed animals, a large wicker chair, a child's rocking chair, and a child-size table and chairs. The wicker chair serves as the "special chair," where Danielle or a parent reads stories to the class, and where children share their writing and read stories. One wall of the Literacy Center contains a large bulletin board, with materials for various components of the morning meeting, such as a calendar, weather/seasons and days-of-school charts, a daily schedule, daily news, and a monthly countdown. A smaller bulletin board displays materials that each child uses when teaching classmates a chosen lesson during his or her turn as "Tomorrow's Teacher." The Literacy Center includes a Reader's Corner, taped stories with headsets for listening, computers, word study manipulatives, writing materials, and storytelling materials, such as a felt board with story characters, puppets, and a roll movie box.

There are shelves containing baskets of books separated into themes, such as "Animals," "Weather," "My Family and Me," "Friends," "School," "Famous People," "Farm," "ABC's," and "123's." Some of the books are also grouped by authors' names, such as Eric Carle and Ezra Jack Keats, and there is a basket of books labeled "Old Favorite Books," and a large tote bag labeled "Books by Us." The tote contains books written and illustrated by the children, either independently or with a small group of peers. In addition, there are books sorted by level of difficulty. An area of the Literacy Center designated the Author's Spot contains various kinds of paper (lined and unlined), premade miniature blank books, various kinds of writing implements, envelopes, sight-word lists, and stickers. There is an area set aside for minilessons.

Five sets of desks in the center of the classroom are labeled with the children's names. These tables are also named with the vowels A, E, I, O, and U. Danielle uses this to help the children with letter–sound recognition. When Danielle calls groups together, the children are called by the letter name and sound on their desks. The letters change, until all 26 letters of the alphabet have been used during the year. A U-shaped table used for guided literacy instruction is located on one side of the room; its position allows Danielle to see all areas of the classroom. By this table is a cart that contains materials for guided literacy instruction. The cart's drawers contain white slates, magnetic boards, magnetic letters, and sentence strips. There are materials for writing, such as different types of paper, Magic Markers, colored pencils, pens, scissors, highlighting tape, index cards, and leveled books for the guided reading lesson.

Danielle's Literacy Center is clearly visible and child-accessible. She also has centers for art, math, science, and social studies. Charts, posters, poems, book displays, and children's work around the room clearly convey the current theme of study, animals.

Classroom Management

Good classroom organization is the foundation of effective instruction. An organized, well-managed classroom will have established clear expectations and consequences. Danielle says, "If you want them to do it, you must teach them to do it," and explains that she uses the first month of school to focus on themes such as "Manners," "School Routines," and "Cooperation." A bulletin board called "A Bunch of Magnificent Manners" highlights positive statements about manners that occur in the room. Throughout the year, Danielle continually reinforces the positive behaviors she wants the children to use. By the second week of school, she finds that the children begin to become familiar with these expectations and are able to express them in their words and actions. Transitions are a major component of the instructional day. When done efficiently, transitions can take only a few moments and help to set the stage for the next activity. Danielle uses a variety of strategies to get the children's attention, all of which are effective. In one strategy, she claps out a pattern and has the children clap it back, saying, "1, 2, 3, eyes on me"; in another strategy, she sings a series of directions to a familiar tune, such as "Twinkle, Twinkle, Little Star."

Danielle has prepared the environment to support her instruction. All materials that students need are accessible. Furthermore, all materials are assigned "a home." Various containers with labels are used to organize materials the children use. In addition, Danielle arranges her room in a way that enables her to see all areas clearly, no matter where she is.

Danielle's careful planning of lessons and materials contributes to the success of this classroom. There is a place in Danielle's plan book to jot down notes concerning what works and what needs to be changed. A small shelf by Danielle's desk contains all materials that will be needed for the week's lessons.

To actively engage children who finish activities earlier than their peers, Danielle uses a system called "Pick a Pocket." Twelve pockets, each labeled with a specific literacy activity, are taped to the front of Danielle's desk. When children finish work before others, they can take an activity card, put it in one of the pockets, then do what the activity card suggests.

Types of Reading Experiences and Skills Development

Danielle uses multiple strategies to teach reading. She used shared reading experience on the day she was being observed. The big book *Mrs. Wishy-Washy* (Cowley, 1999) was being used and reflected the theme of the week—"Farm Animals." It was obvious from the start of the reading that the children had enjoyed this story in the past. The reading was filled with the excitement of the children's voices, actions to match some of the words, and Danielle tracked the print from left to right with a pointer as the children read. After reading, Danielle carried out a lesson about onsets and rhymes in the story. She used text from the story to highlight these initial consonants and phonogram endings. During that week, other shared reading experiences focused on vocabulary development, comprehension through retelling of the story using a felt board, identification of story elements (including setting, theme, episodes, and resolution), and choral reading of some parts of the story, thus emphasizing fluency.

During the course of each day, Danielle allows her students independent reading time. She states, "This independent reading time is so valuable for the children and myself. It is a time for the children to practice their developing reading strategies. More importantly, it is a time for them to foster their own love of reading."

Another form of reading in which the class engages is a read-aloud. Before reading the book *Piggy Pie*, Danielle allowed the class a few moments to look at the cover. She asked the children to turn to a buddy and share what they thought the story would be about. After 1 minute of talk, Danielle asked a few children to share with the class their buddies' predictions.

STUDENT 1: My buddy thinks it's going to be about piggies who want to go out for pizza. But the witch is going to try to eat their pizza.

STUDENT 2: My buddy thinks it's going to be about a witch who wants to make a pie, but none of the piggies will help. Like in *The Little Red Hen*.

STUDENT 3: Me and my buddy think it's going to be about a witch who wants to eat all the pies the piggies make.

The children were visibly more excited about hearing the story, now that they had shared their predictions. Danielle read the story and used a number of character voices. She stopped at various points for predictions. Following the story, the children were asked to share their story reviews with the class. The lesson ended with Danielle asking the children to make connections between this story and other stories they had heard in the past.

Explicit skills development happens during guided literacy instruction. This instruction occurs in small groups, while other children are engaged in activities at the literacy or other learning centers. As she does with all other reading experiences, Danielle evokes a sense of excitement in the children as she makes the guided instruction highly interactive. The following excerpt is from the discussion that occurred before the book was read, to create enthusiasm and to build background meaning:

STUDENT 1: Lightning and thunder make me feel scared.

OTHER STUDENTS: Me too!

DANIELLE: What do you do when there's thunder and lightning?

STUDENT 1: I go to my mommy or daddy.

DANIELLE: What do you and your mommy or daddy do while it's storming out?

STUDENT 1: We read stories and play games.

STUDENT 2: Me and my mommy sing songs.

DANIELLE: What kinds of things do you do after a rainstorm?

STUDENT 3: Go out and play!

STUDENT 4: I make mud pies!

STUDENT 5: I jump in puddles!

STUDENT 6: I look for a rainbow!

DANIELLE: Wow! You do keep busy during and after rainstorms, and believe it or not, the lion in this story does some of the same things you do during and after a rainstorm. Let's take a picture walk through this book called *Johnny Lion's Rubber Boots.*

After the picture walk through *Johnny Lion's Rubber Boots* (Hurd, 2001), which was guided by picture cues, the group read the story together. Danielle followed up with a skills-based sound sort, in which the children discriminated between two initial consonant sounds heard in the story.

Types of Writing Experiences and Skills Development

The writing experiences in Danielle's classroom are as varied as the reading. The children begin each day with independent journal writing in their "Important to Me" Journals. Children at all stages of writing development write about things, people, or events that are important to them. Danielle uses this time to help the children individually; for example, she may reinforce the concept of leaving spaces between words in sentences or discuss how to create multiple sentences using periods rather than linking all thoughts with the word "and."

Danielle uses interactive writing many times throughout the day. As part of the morning meeting, she has the class create a daily news report. Children report news they think is important; for example, one morning a child reported, "I got a new baseball bat yesterday." The children record the news they share.

Danielle also has a Writing Workshop, in which she teaches a mini-lesson in a writing procedure. After the lesson, children are given time to write, using what they have been taught. Once the children are settled into their activity, Danielle calls a small group of students together for a guided writing session. Guided writing, another part of the Writing Workshop, provides direct, explicit instruction.

During this guided writing session, Danielle works with four children who are using only the initial and/or the final letter of a word when doing free, independent writing. Using the word "turkey," because the theme being discussed has to do with farm animals, Danielle takes a rubber band and stretched it out slowly, as she says the word "turkey," thus providing both physical and verbal segmentation of the word. She then hands out rubber bands to the four children and asks them to stretch out the rubber band and say the word "turkey" as she has just done. As the children say the word in a stretched out fashion, Danielle records it on chart paper. She follows up by asking them to stretch the word out three more times, until all of the sounds are represented on the chart paper. The group repeats the exercise with the word "chicken."

As usual, Danielle closes her Writing Workshop with the Author's Chair activity. Four children are given the opportunity to share some of their free writing.

Cross-Curricular Connections

All curriculum areas are tied together through thematic instruction in Danielle's classroom. She began a thematic unit about the "Farm Animals," with a book called *Mrs. Wishy-Washy* (Cowley, 1999). In the book, different animals get a bath. With 23 different picture storybooks about the farm and farm animals, Danielle created a reading and math activity. After looking through a book, children were asked to record the types of animals and the number of times each appeared. Danielle created a recording sheet that lists animals in the books with labels. On a line provided, the children were to write the names of the animals appearing in the book and the number times each appeared. The activity could be repeated by switching books and doing it again.

Social studies was brought into the theme with the use of a nonfiction book entitled *The Milk Makers* (Gibbons, 1987). After the read-aloud, the class engaged in interactive writing and generated a large flowchart that highlighted the farm-to-table milk-producing process. The book also engaged the class in discussions focusing on other items that come from the farm.

Teachable Moments

During one daily newswriting session, a student in Danielle's class stated, "Look! The little word *ball* is in the big word *baseball*." This simple statement made another child realize that the little word *base* was also in the word baseball. Danielle took advantage of this teachable moment as follows:

> DANIELLE: Great observation! Look at this. Ryan, come up and highlight the word *base* for us. (*The child used highlighting tape on the word.*) Now, Sophie, you highlight the word *ball*. (*This child used a different-colored highlighting tape.*) We know *baseball* is one word, because there

is no space in between the two little words. A word that has two little words in it is called a "compound word." Let me use my hands to show you how this works. I'm going to say the word *base* to one hand, and then I'm going to say the word *ball* to the other. When I move my hands together, placing one on top of the other, I get one word—a compound word—*baseball.* Can you think of other compound words?

STUDENT 1: *Football. Foot* is one word and *ball* is the other. Watch. (*The child uses his hands, just as Danielle did.*)

DANIELLE: You've got it! Anyone else?

STUDENT 2: *Butterfly!*

For the remainder of the day, students pointed out compound words both in writing and in Danielle's speech. For Danielle, this teachable moment helped to reinforce how powerful the reading strategy of finding little words inside of bigger words can be, and it also opened the door to a brand new concept of compound words.

One of Danielle's favorite teachable moments is as follows:

During a thematic unit on "Sea Creatures," the class enjoyed a read-aloud about a blue whale. In the book, the author stated that a blue whale could average 100 feet long. Michael wanted to know how long 100 feet would be. Some students thought it would be the size of the classroom; others thought it would be as tall as the school. Danielle recalls:

"It was the perfect cross-curricular, teachable moment. We gathered up all of our rulers and yardsticks, and we went outside to the black-top. We reviewed how a ruler is 1 foot long and that it would take 100 rulers to show us 100 feet. Then, we discovered that a yardstick is equivalent to three rulers. One ruler and yardstick at a time, we laid them out on the blacktop. When we ran out of measuring tools, we decided that we could mark the beginning of the line with chalk and begin placing the rulers at the other end. When we finally reached 100 feet, the children began to cheer. They asked if they could use sidewalk chalk to draw around the rulers and make it look like a real blue whale. The teachable moment turned into a price-less cross-curricular lesson."

The Daily Schedule and a Typical Day in Kindergarten

When Danielle plans her day she is always concerned that the content, materials, and time spent for activities are all age-appropriate. The following is a schedule of her day:

- *8:45–9:05. Children arrive at school.* Children enter school and engage in independent work until the day formally begins. These activities include checking in at the attendance and lunch station, folder check-in and note basket, helper chart activities, journal writing, and buddy and independent reading.
- *9:05–9:40. Morning meeting.* The whole-group morning meeting includes the following: morning message, daily schedule, daily news, Word Wall, shared read-aloud, calendar, weather report, shared reading of literature, and a skills-based lesson.
- *9:40–9:50. Introduction of learning centers activities.* The teacher describes independent and cooperative activities at centers and provides time for children to get organized, so that they are working productively. This is in preparation for meeting with individuals and small groups.
- *9:50–11:40. Guided reading.* The teacher meets with the four or more groups of children she has organized, based on similar needs for literacy instruction. Each group meets for about 20 minutes.
- *After lunch.* Writing workshop can occur during the Language Arts Block. It can begin in the morning as part of the block and continue after lunch. The entire workshop could also occur after lunch. Writing workshop includes a whole-group skills lesson, a writing assignment, and conferencing with peers and or the teacher to revise and edit.

A Description of Danielle's Language Arts Block

The children arrive at school over a 15-minute span in the morning. As they enter, children check themselves in at the attendance/lunch station, proceed to their cubbies, and unpack. They place their folders in a designated "Folder Holder," and their notes are placed in a basket labeled "Note Basket" on Danielle's desk. Following these routines, the children then complete any "Class Helper" jobs that they have been assigned.

As arrival routines are completed, the children get their "Important to Me Journals" and record an entry for the day. The date is recorded on the chalkboard and serves as a reference for the children, so they can record the date on their entry. Children can select to write about anything important to them that day or the day before. For children who may have trouble selecting a topic, a page entitled "Journal Ideas" is stapled into the cover of each child's journal. Four times a year, the children bring home a blank copy of this page and work with their families to brainstorm five things to write about in their journals. The resulting pages are stapled in the cover of the journal, so children have a variety of personally relevant topics from which to choose.

As the children are writing in their journals, Danielle greets individuals, answers notes that have been placed in her "Note Basket," and facilitates journal writing. As the children finish their journal entries, they share them with Danielle, who provides every child with specific, positive feedback. For example, when looking at Jill's work, she said, "I like how you tried to hear the beginning, middle, and ending sounds in your words."

Once all of children arrive, attendance and lunch count are recorded. Two "Class Helpers" then deliver the slips to the office, and two others lead the flag salute.

The children gather on the rug in the Literacy Center for the morning meeting. During this time, the morning message, the daily schedule, the daily news, a word study skills lesson with the Word Wall, the calendar, a read-aloud, and the weather report are all carried out.

After the other activities were completed, Danielle read a story to the class. She held up the book—*The Mitten* (Brett, 1989)—so the children could see and read the title, the author's name, and the illustrator's name. Danielle had selected the book to match their winter thematic unit. She asked the children to share their predictions about what might occur in the story related to the mitten, based on the book's cover picture and title. Before beginning to read, Danielle said, "As I read, see if what you think is going to happen in this story is what actually does happen."

As she read the story, Danielle stopped occasionally for some discussion. As she neared the end of the book, Danielle said, "I'm wondering what you think will happen at the end of the story?" When they did get to the end, the children compared predictions. After that, Danielle invited the children to share the part of the story they liked best. The students began a discussion that focused on their own stories involving mittens. Danielle made this reading an interactive discussion during which she modeled for the children some comprehension strategies.

At the end of the morning meeting, the class participated in an activity in which the children say a letter of the alphabet as they stretch to the sky, make the letter's sound as they touched their hips, and say a word that begins with that letter as they touch the ground.

Activities in the various centers were reviewed. Those available to the students were as follows:

• *Partner reading.* Children pair off and read the same book together. They may also read separate books and then tell each other about the stories they read. Because they are studying winter, they are to select books from the open-faced bookshelves that include stories and expository texts about this season. Discussion about what is read is encouraged. Each child must fill out an index card with the name of the book read and one sentence about the story.

• *Writing activity.* Children are to rewrite the story read to them earlier in the day. In their rewritings, the children can write just one word to depict a sentence, if that is what they are capable of doing, or entire sentences. They may consult the book, if necessary. Each day there is a writing activity related to the story read earlier; however, the writing assignments vary.

- *Working with words.* The words *chilly* and *slush* have been discussed as new vocabulary words with a focus on the winter theme. For this activity, children find words around the room that have the *sh* or *ch* digraph in them. In addition, they look for words that begin or end in the digraphs. After they find them, words with *sh* are written in one column and the words with *ch* in another. Children may look through books to find the digraphs.
- *Listening center.* The children listen to taped stories. For each story, there is a sheet of paper with a question to answer about the story. Two titles on tape for the unit about winter were *The Snowy Day* (Keats, 1962) and *The Wild Toboggan Ride* (Reid & Fernandes, 1992).

Once all children were in their centers and actively engaged, Danielle called her first guided literacy instruction group. When the group assembled, Danielle put on a colorful beaded necklace with 24 beads—one bead to represent each person in the class, including the teacher. Danielle refers to this as her "Cooperation Necklace." When she is wearing it, the children are not to disturb her or the group/individual she is working with, unless it is an emergency. The necklace is a constant reminder to the children that they need to work together to solve problems and to respect the learning time of others.

The four children in the first guided reading group were working with a book entitled *The Birthday Cake* (van der Meer, 1992). Danielle began the lesson by having the children sing the song "Happy Birthday to You." After singing, the group members discussed what the song made them think of. Danielle handed out a copy of the book to each child and asked the group members to predict what they thought the story might be about.

Danielle led the children through a picture walk of the book and then gave each child a rubber fingertip with a long rubber fingernail. The children slipped these on their pointer fingers and then proceeded to read chorally and point to the words in the title. They continued in this fashion as they read the book. After the choral reading, Danielle invited each child to do an independent reading of the story. She made a note that her objective for this group was to aid them in developing a one-to-one correspondence between words read and words on the page.

Once all the children finished, Danielle provided each child with a plastic bag containing index cards that had all the words from the story written on them. After modeling how to build a sentence using their word cards, Danielle asked the children to try and sequence the cards to create the story. At the end of the lesson, the children placed their book, finger pointer, and word cards for the book in their plastic bag. They put their bags in their cubbies, so that they could share their book and materials with their families.

Danielle met with two other groups. The materials and activities used varied for each group. To signal that center time was over, Danielle sang a cleanup song. The children returned to their tables after cleaning up. As part of their routine, Danielle and the children then proceeded to share compliments with one another, focusing on behaviors observed during center time. Student compliments included "I like how Ivory helped me retell the story *Lunch*" [Fleming, 1993]. Jennifer said, "Whitney, Josh, and me did a good job with finding the *sh* and *ch* words." Brandon said, "I like how I worked with somebody new in the Writing Center." These brief exchanges brought about a positive closure to this important instructional time.

Writing Workshop followed lunch. Children worked on books about winter, and the teacher led a minilesson about capital letters at the beginning of a sentence and periods at the end. Children in the final editing stages with their stories have conferences with the teacher.

At the end of the day, before going home, Danielle provides a shared reading experience of the story *The Old Woman Who Swallowed a Fly* (Westcott, 1980). Danielle guided the exercise by first reading the title of the book and author's name. She turned to the title page, where she reviewed the name of the publisher and noted the copyright date. Following the reading, the class used highlighting tape to mark the pairs of rhyming words found in the text. Next was an interactive writing experience, in which the class generated a T chart of rhyming words. Students made observations concerning the similarities in the spelling of some rhyming words and the differences in the spelling of others. Danielle encouraged and praised these student observations. After generating the list, the class chose one pair of rhyming words with which to work and made a sentence with each pair.

When it was time to go home, the children gathered their work and lined up to leave school. Once all children were in line, Danielle handed a pointer to the line leader and clapped out a pattern to get the class's attention. The line leader then pointed to the words of the poem "Ready for Going Home" as he led the class in a choral reading.

SUMMARY AND IMPLICATIONS FOR FUTURE RESEARCH

The children in this early-childhood classroom experience literacy in many different forms. The children are involved in an environment that incorporates literacy as a part of the entire day. The literacy experiences are planned to be appropriate, because there is concern for individual needs and learning styles. Danielle is enthusiastic about her teaching and excitement is contagious. As a result, her students assume a positive attitude toward literacy learning, one another, and themselves.

The children have extensive exposure to children's literature through the use of shared read-alouds, independent reading, buddy reading with a peer, and guided reading for skills development. Writing experiences included journal writing, Writing Workshop, and language experience activities. Both reading and writing include systematic skills development and, in addition, skills development is also done with an authentic purpose.

Danielle's room was rich with materials for children to experience choice, challenging activities, social interaction, and success. The school day was structured to include varied experiences that were developmentally appropriate, yet still retained an emphasis on the acquisition of skills. Children were taught rules, routines, and procedures for using the classroom materials when in self-directed roles. Danielle was consistent in her management techniques. Therefore, the children knew what was expected of them and, consequently, carried out the work that needed to be done. Consistent routine allowed the day to flow smoothly from one activity to another.

The affective quality in the room was indeed exemplary. Danielle speaks to the children with respect and in an adult manner. She does not raise her voice, nor does she use punitive remarks, facial expressions, or intonations. In this atmosphere, children learn to understand appropriate classroom behavior.

Danielle allowed time for children to unfold at their natural pace, with concern for social, emotional, and intellectual development. She also was aware of the need to foster development with appropriate materials for exploration and specific skills instruction for individual needs. She integrated the language arts curriculum and content area teaching by building one on the other to develop listening, speaking, reading, writing, and viewing. In addition, she utilized information from content areas to help to teach literacy skills.

Although we know a great deal about early literacy instruction, we need to continue to research literacy development in the early years. We need to place a great deal of emphasis on preschool literacy instruction. Most of the research has been done with children in first grade, and little has been done with preschool children. We do know a lot about early literacy; however, organizing and managing what we know within the language arts block is an untouched area. We do not know enough about the delivery of instruction, that is, comparing explicit approaches to more open, embedded approaches. We need to study exemplary teachers more to determine how they became exemplary.

DISCUSSION AND ACTIVITIES

1. Observe the Language Arts Block in an early childhood class. Using the list in this chapter that describes general and literacy exemplary practice, check an item when you observe it and record what the teacher was doing.
2. Observe the language arts block in another early childhood classroom at a different grade level. Determine the theory, philosophy, or research discussed in this chapter that influenced specific teacher behavior and instruction. Record the teacher behavior.
3. Select a social studies or science theme and create a language arts block for an early childhood classroom. Be sure to include all elements that describe a comprehensive literacy program. Be sure to integrate the theme into the literacy instruction.

REFERENCES

Professional Literature

Adams, M. J. (1990). *Beginning to read: Thinking and learning about print.* Urbana: University of Illinois Center for the Study of Reading.

Dewey, J. (1966). *Democracy and education.* New York: Free Press. (Original published 1916)

Foorman, B. R., Francis, D. J., Fletcher, J. M., Schatschneider, C. S., & Mehta, P. (1998). The role of instruction in learning to read: Preventing reading failure in at-risk children. *Journal of Educational Psychology, 90*(1), 37–57.

Froebel, F. (1974). *The education of man.* Clifton, NJ: Augustus M. Kelly.

Gambrell, L. B., & Mazzoni, S. A. (1999). Principles of best practice: Finding the common ground. In L. B. Gambrell, L. M. Morrow, S. B. Neuman, & M. Pressley (Eds.), *Best practices in literacy instruction.* New York: Guilford Press.

International Reading Association and National Association for the Education of Young Children. (1998). *Learning to read and write: Developmentally appropriate practices.* Newark, DE: International Reading Association.

Juel, C. (1988). Learning to read and write: A longitudinal study of fifty-four children from first through fourth grade. *Journal of Educational Psychology, 80*, 437–447.

Montessori, M. (1965). *Spontaneous activity in education.* New York: Schocken.

Morphett, M. V., & Washburne, C. (1931). When should children begin to read? *Elementary School Journal, 31*, 496–508.

Morrow, L. M., Tracey, D. H., Woo, D. G., & Pressley, M. (1999). Characteristics of exemplary first grade literacy instruction. *Reading Teacher, 52*, 462–476.

National Reading Panel Report. (2000). *Teaching children to read.* Washington, DC: National Institute of Child Health and Human Development.

Piaget, J., & Inhelder, B. (1969). *The psychology of the child.* New York: Basic Books.

Pressley, M., Allington, R. L., Wharton-McDonald, R., Block, C. C., & Morrow, L. M. (2001). *Learning to read: Lessons from exemplary first-grade classrooms.* New York: Guilford Press.

Pressley, M., Rankin, J. L., & Yokoi, L. (1996). A survey of instructional practices of primary teachers nominated as effective in promoting literacy. *Elementary School Journal, 96,* 363–384.

Ruddell, R. B., & Ruddell, M. R. (1995). *Teaching children to read and write: Becoming an influential teacher.* Boston: Allyn & Bacon.

Rusk, R., & Scotland, J. (1979). *Doctrines of the great educators.* New York: St. Martin's Press.

Snow, C. E., Burns, M. S., & Griffin, P. (1998). *Preventing reading difficulties in young children.* Washington, DC: National Academy Press.

Taylor B., & Pearson, P. D. (2002). *Teaching reading: Effective schools, accomplished teachers.* Mahwah, NJ: Erbaum.

Vygotsky, L. S. (1981). The genesis of higher mental functions. In J. J. Wertsh (Ed.), *The concept of activity.* White Plains, NY: Sharpe.

Children's Literature

Brett, J. (1989). *The mitten: A Ukranian folk tale.* New York: Putnam.

Cowley, J. (1999). *Mrs. Wishy-Washy.* New York: Putnam.

Fleming, D. (1993). *Lunch.* New York: Henry Holt.

Galdone, P. (1991). *The little red hen.* Boston: Houghton Mifflin.

Gibbons, G. (1987). *The milk makers.* New York: Macmillan.

Hurd, E. T. (2001). *Johnny lion's rubber boots.* New York: HarperCollins.

Keats, E. J. (1962). *The snowy day.* New York: Viking.

Palatini, M. (1997). *Piggy pie.* Boston: Houghton Mifflin.

Reid, S., & Fernandes, E. (1992). *The wild toboggan ride.* New York: Scholastic.

van der Meer, R. (1993). *The birthday cake.* New York: Random House.

Westcott, N. (1980). *I know an old lady who swallowed a fly.* Boston: Little Brown.

Chapter 4

WHAT RESEARCH SAYS
ABOUT TEACHING PHONICS

Patricia M. Cunningham

This chapter will:

- Summarize the research as it relates directly to phonics instruction.
- Describe some instructional activities consistent with that research.
- Suggest some phonics-related issues about which we need more research.

Phonics is and has been the most controversial issue in reading. Since 1955, when Rudolph Flesch's book *Why Johnny Can't Read* became a national best-seller, educators and parents have debated the role of phonics in beginning reading instruction. A variety of published phonics programs have been touted as the "cure-all" for everyone's reading problems. Enthusiasm for these programs has lasted just long enough for everyone to relearn the fact that thoughtful reading requires much more than just the ability to quickly decode words. As the chapters of this book demonstrate, the most effective literacy frameworks include a variety of instruction and activities that provide children with a balanced literacy diet. This chapter focuses on phonics and what research tells us about effective phonics instruction. When the knowledge from this chapter is combined with that from all the other chapters, good, balanced research-based literacy instruction results.

THEORY AND RESEARCH BASE

There are many things we do not know about phonics instruction, but there are also things we do know. This section summarizes six major research-based findings on which we can base sound instructional practice.

Phonemic Awareness Is One Important Component of Reading Success

Part of the understanding that many children gain from early reading and writing encounters is the realization that spoken words are made up of sounds. These sounds (phonemes) are not separate and distinct. In fact, their existence is quite abstract. Phonemic awareness has many levels and includes the concept of rhyme, the ability to blend and segment words, and to manipulate phonemes to form different words. Phonemic awareness seems to be developed gradually for most children, through lots of exposure to songs, nursery rhymes and books with rhymes, and alliteration that promote word play.

Phonemic awareness is one of the best predictors of success in learning to read (Ehri & Nunes, 2002; National Reading Panel, 2000). On learning that phonemic awareness is such an important concept, some people have concluded that it is all we need to worry about in preparing children to read. Phonemic awareness training programs have been developed and mandated for every child, every day for 30–40 minutes, when only 18 hours of phonemic awareness has been found to be necessary over a school year. This would be 10 minutes a day. In addition to phonemic awareness, children who are going to learn to read successfully must develop print-tracking skills and begin to learn some letter names and sounds, and develop a sight vocabulary. They need to develop cognitive clarity about the purpose of reading and writing, which can only be learned by spending some time each day in the presence of reading and writing.

Another problem with the overreaction to the phonemic awareness findings is that some children enter school with sufficient phonemic awareness to begin to learn to read, and others develop it from engaging in emergent literacy activities, such as shared reading of books that play with sounds and writing with invented spelling. Yopp and Yopp (2000) argue for phonemic awareness instruction as only one part of a beginning literacy program. They conclude that

> teachers must recognize that while sensitivity to the sound basis of language supports literacy development, it is also an outcome of literacy experiences. . . . To overemphasize this component of literacy instruction in the initial years of schooling is to limit children's opportunities for more comprehensive literacy development. (p. 132)

> Our concern is that in some classrooms phonemic awareness instruction will replace other crucial areas of instruction. Phonemic awareness supports reading development only if it is part of a broader program that includes— among other things—development of students' vocabulary, syntax, comprehension, strategic reading abilities, decoding strategies, and writing across all content areas. (p. 142)

Children Need to Learn Sequential Decoding but Not Necessarily through Synthetic Phonics Instruction

Sequential decoding is the ability to look at all the letters in an unknown word and associate sounds with some of these letters. Sequential decoding is not necessarily accomplished by saying a sound for each letter and then blending those individual sounds together. Beginning readers often use what is called the "consonant plane" (Berent & Perfetti, 1995) to decode words sequentially in context. Imagine a young reader who knows as sight words, *he*, *went*, *to*, *and*, and who is looking at a picture of a boy fast asleep in bed with this sentence underneath: "He went to bed and fell fast asleep." By looking at all the letters in the unknown words *bed*, *fell*, *fast*, and *asleep*, a beginning reader who knows the consonant sounds, is using the context and picture clues, and knows that reading has to make sense and sound like language, could use the consonant plane to decode the unknown words in that sentence.

Synthetic phonics approaches begin by teaching children individual sounds for letters, then having them blend those letters together to sound out words. In synthetic phonics programs, the first text children read is constructed to have them practice their decoding and is restricted to sounds they can blend to make words, plus a few essential sight words. Here are the first two pages of an early story in a synthetic phonics text (Cassidy, Roettger & Wixson, 1987, pp. 15–16)

> Dad ran. Ann ran. Dad and Ann ran.
> Dad ran. Nan ran. Dad and Nan ran.

To become fluent readers, children must learn the common sounds for vowel patterns. But in the beginning, readers can learn to do sequential decoding with the use of meaning and the consonant plane. As children decode more words in this way, they learn more about words and, particularly, patterns in words. Children must learn to decode words sequentially, but that does not mean they need to be taught with a synthetic phonics approach.

Children Need to Apply Phonics but Do Not Need to Be Restricted to Highly Decodable Text

The two sentences in the previous section about Dad, Ann, and Nan are an example of highly decodable text. Based on the finding that children need to have opportunities to apply their phonics to decode words (Juel & Roper-Schneider, 1985), some researchers have advocated the exclusive use of highly decodable texts for beginning reading. Although there is general agreement that children need text in which they have to apply their decoding skills to some words, there does not seem to be any support in the research for recommending highly decodable text as the exclusive beginning reading material for all children (Allington & Woodside-Jiron, 1998).

Hiebert (1999) makes the case for children reading text that provides practice with high-frequency words, along with opportunities to apply decoding skills and use meaning-based cues. Because she does not see these "multiple criteria" texts presently available, she suggests that teachers may want to provide different kinds of texts—some more sight word oriented, some more decoding oriented, and some more meaning-cue oriented—to children on a regular basis, so that they learn to use all the word identification cues fluent readers actually use.

As Children Learn More Words, They Use Patterns and Analogy to Decode

Imagine that you are reading and encounter the words *spew* and *spate* for the first time. You would probably quickly pronounce them in your mind and then try to make sense of them in their sentence context:

> A spate of people gathered when the oil began to spew out of the ground.

Good readers encounter new words in their reading all the time. If you have never seen a word before, you have to decode it—get it pronounced—in some way, whether overtly or covertly. Some researchers (Adams, 1990; Goswami, 2000; Goswami & Bryant, 1990; Moustafa, 1997) believe that the way we decode many, if not most, words is to use patterns learned from other words. *Spew* has two patterns—*sp* and *ew*, often called the onset and the rime. *Spate* has the same onset, *sp*, but a different rime—*ate*.

Because you are such a fluent reader when you first encounter *spew* and *spate*, you probably "automatically" decoded these words using the patterns—*sp, ew, ate*—so familiar to you from words such as *spill, spy, new, few, chew, ate, gate, date, hate*. If you had encountered these words earlier in your reading development, when you did not have the *sp, ew, ate* patterns so firmly established from so many other words, you might have had to go through a slightly longer process in which you thought of some *sp, ew,* and *ate* words you knew, used these words to find the patterns, and applied these patterns to the new words. Your brain may have thought something like: "S-p is how words like *spill* and *spy* begin. E-w is in *new* and *chew*. A-t-e is in *ate* and *date*." You use analogy to decode when your brain accesses other words you know and combines these patterns to decode new words.

Decoding by pattern and analogy uses the same units—the onset and the rime. It is difficult—if not impossible—to know which one a reader is using. In general, the more words you have read with a particular pattern, the more apt you are to have that pattern stored in your brain and not have to go through an analogy process. When you are just beginning to learn to read, you do not have enough words to use analogy or to abstract patterns. Most researchers believe that by the time children have a fluent first-grade reading level, they are using patterns and analogy as their major decoding strategy.

Gaining knowledge of rime patterns may be particularly important for learning to decode the "vowel plane" of words because of the difficulty of vowels and how vowel sounds are affected by other letters in the word, particularly the consonants that follow them (Berent & Perfetti, 1995; Goswami, 2000).

Children Decode Multisyllabic Words Using Patterns That Are Often Morphemes

What do you do when you come to big words you have never encountered before in your reading? Imagine the first time you meet the printed words *technostress* and *desertification*. Just as with smaller words, you decode or pronounce them. You probably pronounce *technostress* quite quickly and even figure out a meaning: "I know how that feels!"

Desertification probably takes a little longer and may require a sentence context to solidify the meaning:

> The desertification in Africa caused by the removal of trees and brush should be of concern to the entire world community.

Using what you know about the root word *desert* and other words that end in *ification*, such as *modification* and *unification*, along with the sentence context, you confirm your pronunciation and construct meaning for *desertification*.

Decoding big words is also accomplished by patterns and analogy. Rather than onsets and rimes, however, the patterns are often morphemes—root words, suffixes, and prefixes. English is the most morphologically connected language. Estimates are that for every word you know, you can quickly learn six or seven other words that share some of the same morphemes (Nagy & Anderson, 1984). Because morphemes provide meaning clues, as well as decoding and spelling patterns, learning how to use the morphemes in big words helps you build your meaning vocabulary. Wide reading is the most significant predictor of vocabulary size, and the best guess of experts is that you use context and morphological clues together to infer meanings for new words you encounter in your reading.

There Is No "Best Way" to Teach Phonics

In spite of the apparent importance of the question of how best to teach phonics, there have been few instructional studies comparing different types of phonics instruction, and those that have been done have often compared systematic phonics instruction with "hit-or-miss" phonics instruction. From these studies, we can conclude that any kind of well-organized and efficient phonics instruction is generally better than little or no phonics instruction that leaves learning phonics to chance! Stahl, Duffy-Hester, and Stahl (1998) reviewed the research on phonics instruction and concluded that there are several types of good phonics instruction, and that no research base supports the superiority of any one particular type. The National Reading Panel (2000) reviewed the experimental research on teaching phonics and determined that explicit and systematic phonics is superior to nonsystematic or no phonics, but that there is no significant difference in effectiveness among the kinds of systematic phonics instruction. They also found no significant difference in effectiveness among tutoring, small-group, or whole-class phonics instruction.

RESEARCH-BASED PRACTICES

Given what we know about phonics—and what we do not know, what kind of activities are supported by the research? This chapter has only reviewed the research on phonics instruction, but the research summarized in other chapters would lead us to the big conclusion that children need to spend most of their reading/language arts time actually reading and writing. Without many opportunities to apply what they are learning about phonics, children will not become fluent readers or writers. Comprehension instruction and the development of prior knowledge, meaning vocabulary, and oral language are necessary components of a balanced reading program that will produce thoughtful readers. Although most people agree on the need for balance, there is no research to indicate how time should be allocated between real reading and writing, comprehension strategy instruction, prior-knowledge/meaning vocabulary/oral language development and phonics instruction. In the Four Blocks framework, we allocate approximately one-fourth of our instructional time to phonics activities and three-fourths of our time to the other components (Cunningham & Allington, 2003; Cunningham, Hall, & Sigmon, 1999).

Although research does not tell us what kind of phonics instruction is most effective, we can use some research-based findings to evaluate phonics activities. Phonics activities for young children should include some opportunities to develop phonemic awareness. They should help children learn to look across all the letters to develop sequential decoding ability. Every activity should include opportunities for children to apply what they are learning to reading and/or writing new words. Because readers eventually use larger-than-letter units to decode, some emphasis should be placed on helping children focus on the onset–rime units in words. As children encounter more and more big words in their reading, they should learn to use morphemes to unlock the pronunciation, spelling, and meaning of polysyllabic words. The remainder of this section describes two phonemic awareness activities and four phonics activities, and explains how they are supported by research.

Sing Rhymes and Read Lots of Rhyming Books

Many children who come to school with well-developed phonemic awareness abilities have usually come from homes in which rhyming chants, jingles, and songs are part of their daily experience. These same chants, jingles, and songs should be a part of every young child's day in the classroom.

There are so many wonderful rhyming books, but because of their potential to develop phonemic awareness, two deserve special mention. Along with other great rhyming books, Dr. Seuss wrote *There's a Wocket in My Pocket* (1974). In this book, all kinds of Seussian creatures are found in various places. In addition to the wocket in the pocket, there is a vug under the rug, a nureau in the bureau, and a yottle in the bottle! After several readings, children delight in chiming in to provide the nonsensical word and scary creature that lurks in harmless-looking places. After reading the book a few times, it is fun to decide what creatures might be lurking in your classroom. Let children make up the creatures and accept whatever they say as long as it rhymes with their object:

"There's a pock on our clock!"
"There's a zindow looking in our window!"
"There's a zencil on my pencil!"

Another wonderful rhyming book for phonemic awareness is *The Hungry Thing* by Jan Slepian and Ann Seidler. In this book, a large, friendly dinosaur-looking creature (You have to see him to love him!) comes to town, wearing a sign that says, "Feed Me."

When asked what he would like to eat, he responds, "Shmancakes." After much deliberation, a clever little boy offers him some pancakes. The Hungry Thing eats them all up and demands, "Tickles." Again, after much deliberation, the boy figures out he wants pickles. As the story continues, it becomes obvious that The Hungry Thing wants specific foods and asks for them by making them rhyme with what he wants. He asks for *feetloaf* and gobbles down the meatloaf. For dessert, he wants *hookies* and *gollipops*!

The Hungry Thing is a delightful book; in many classrooms, teachers have made a poster-size Hungry Thing, complete with his sign that reads

"Feed Me" on one side and "Thank You!" on the other. Armed with real foods or pictures of foods, the children try to feed The Hungry Thing. Of course, he will not eat the food unless the children make it rhyme. If they offer him spaghetti, they have to say, "What some bagetti? [or zagetti, or ragetti—any silly word that rhymes with spaghetti!]" To feed him Cheerios, they have to offer him seerios, theerios, or leerios!

Blending and Segmenting Games

In addition to hearing and producing rhyme, the ability to put sounds together to make a word—blending, and to separate out the sounds in a word—segmenting, is a critical component of phonemic awareness. Blending and segmenting are not easy for many children. In general, it is easier for them to segment off the beginning letters—the onset— from the rest of the word—the rime—than to separate all the sounds. In other words, children can usually separate *bat* into *b-at* before they can produce the three sounds *b-a-t*. The same is true for blending. Most children can blend *S-am* to produce the name *Sam* before they can blend *S-a-m*. Most teachers begin by having children blend and segment the onset from the rime, and then move to blending and segmenting individual letters.

Lots of games children enjoy can help them learn to blend and segment. The most versatile is a simple riddle guessing game. The teacher begins the game by naming the category and giving the clue:

"I'm thinking of an animal that lives in the water and is a *f-ish* [or *f-i-sh*, depending on what level of blending you are working on]."

The child who correctly guesses "fish" gives the next riddle:

"I'm thinking of an animal that goes quack and is a *d-uck* [or *d-u-ck*]."

This sounds simplistic but children love it, and you can use different categories to go along with units you are studying.

A wonderful variation on this guessing game is to put objects in a bag and let children reach in the bag and stretch out the name of an object they choose, and then call on someone to guess "What is it?" Choose small, common objects you find in the room—a cap, a ball, chalk, a book— and let the children watch you load the bag and help you stretch out the words for practice as you put them in.

Children also enjoy talking like "ghosts." One child chooses an object in the room to say, as a ghost would, stretching the word out very slowly—"dddooooorrr." The child who correctly guesses "door" gets to ghost name another object—"bbbooookkk." Both the ghost-talk game and the guessing game provide practice in both segmenting and blending as children segment words by stretching them out, and other children blend the words together to guess them.

How Our Emphasis on Rhyme, Segmenting,
and Blending Reflects What We Know

Rhyme awareness—the ability to make and recognize rhymes—is one of the earliest developed phonemic awareness abilities. Many children come to kindergarten with developed rhyme awareness. Most of these savvy children were not given any direct instruction in rhyme, but they were immersed in an environment of songs, jingles, and books in which rhyme played a large role. Including rhyming songs, jingles, and books as part of every early childhood day allows all children to begin developing their phonemic awareness.

Segmenting and blending words is one of the more difficult phonemic awareness abilities. Children need lots of practice with oral activities in which they put sounds together to create words and pull words apart into their component sounds. Children who are able to blend and segment words orally can then combine these skills with their phonics knowledge to decode words as they read and spell words as they write.

Making Words

"Making Words" (Cunningham & Cunningham, 1992; Cunningham & Hall, 1994) is a manipulative activity in which children learn how to look for patterns in words and see how changing just one letter, or where a letter is put, changes the whole word. Each Making Words lesson has three parts. First, children manipulate letters to make 10–15 words—including a "secret" word made from all the letters. Next, they sort the words into patterns. Finally, they learn how to transfer their phonics knowledge by using rhyming words they have made to decode and spell some other rhyming words.

To plan a Making Words lesson, we begin with the "secret" word. Here is an example for a Making Words lesson in which the secret word is *unbeaten*. Using the letters in *unbeaten*, we choose 10–15 words that will give us some easy and harder words, some morphemically related words and several sets of rhymes. We then decide on the order in which words will be made, beginning with short words and building to larger words. We write these words on index cards to use in the sorting and transferring parts of the lesson.

As the children make each word, we choose one child who has made the word correctly to come and make it in the pocket chart. As the lesson begins, the letters *a e e u b n n t* are in the pocket chart. The children each have the same letters and a holder. The teacher leads them to make words by saying:

1. "Take two letters and spell *at*. 'We are all meeting *at* the mall.'"
2. "Add one letter and spell *bat*. 'A *bat* is a mammal with wings.'"
3. "Change one letter and spell *but*. 'I have never seen a bat *but* I would like to.'"
4. "Change one letter and spell *nut*. 'The squirrel was eating a *nut*.'"
5. "Use three letters to spell *eat*. 'Bats *eat* insects.'"
6. "Add one letter and spell *neat*. 'I like to keep my room clean and *neat*.'"
7. "Change one letter and spell *beat*. 'My favorite team *beat* the other team.'"
8. "Use five letters to spell *eaten*. Stretch out *eaten* and listen for the sounds you hear. 'We have *eaten* all the cookies.'"
9. "Add one letter and spell *beaten*. 'Our team has *beaten* them in the last five games.'"
10. "Add your letters to *beaten* and you will have the secret word. I will come around to see if anyone has the secret word. [The teacher circulates and finds a child who has figured out the secret word. That child makes the word in the pocket chart and the word is put in a sentence.] 'Our team was the only team that didn't lose a single game and ended the season *unbeaten*.'"

After making words, the teacher displays the words one at a time and places them in the pocket chart as the children pronounce each word and put the words in an oral sentence. Next, the teacher asks the children if they see any related words—words that have the same root and share some meaning. Children come to the pocket chart, sort out these words, and discuss how they are related in meaning, and how we use them differently in speaking.

beat	eat
beaten	eaten
unbeaten	

Next, children sort the words that rhyme:

eat	nut	at	eaten
neat	but	bat	beaten
beat			

The final step in every Making Words lesson is the transfer step. Children are shown two new words on index cards; they place them under the words with which they rhyme and use the rhyming words to pronounce the new words. Finally, the teacher pronounces two words that children spell by deciding which words rhyme with them. When the lesson ends, the transfer words are lined up under their corresponding rhyming words:

eat	nut	at	eaten
neat	but	bat	beaten
beat	shut	flat	
wheat			
treat			

How Making Words Reflects What We Know

In addition to providing lots of rhyming, blending, and segmenting activities, many of our phonics activities include opportunities for children to develop phonemic awareness. While making words, we encourage children to stretch out words and model this segmenting activity. Children hear how words change when they have different sounds added at the beginning, middle, or end. When children sort for rhymes and spell rhyming transfer words, they listen for the words that rhyme. To pronounce the transfer words, they blend the beginning letters of the new word with the rhyming parts of the words they have made.

Children learn sequential decoding as they decide which letters to put in what order. Once they have made a word, they often say the word, pointing to each letter to make sure they have them in the right order. They learn to pay attention to all the letters, because changing just one letter results in a new word. They also learn that it matters where they put the letters.

In every Making Words lesson, children apply what they have learned to reading and writing new words. In fact, as we show the two new words, we ask children to pretend they are reading and come upon this new word. As they place the new word in the pocket chart under the rhyming words they have made, we remind them that thinking of other words with the same pattern will help them decode lots of words as they are reading. Before asking them to spell two new rhyming words, we also set up a "pretend" situation.

> "Let's pretend it is writing time, and Joey is writing about his trip to see his grandma and how they had a flat tire. Let's all say *flat* and decide which of the words we made rhyme with *flat* and see how these words will help Joey spell *flat*."

Young children love to pretend, and when they are reading, they delight in finding a word in a book they can decode because they know the rhyming pattern, or in figuring out how to spell a word they need when writing.

We do not have related words in every Making Words lesson, but we always sort them out when we have them, and talk about how they are related. This activity helps children begin to learn about morphemes in words, and how morphemes help to decode, spell, and build meaning for larger words.

We always sort for rhyming words. Children soon learn to look for and use rhyming patterns to decode and spell words. This helps children move toward using onsets/rimes and analogies for decoding and spelling words.

Rounding Up the Rhymes

"Rounding Up the Rhymes" (Cunningham, 2000) is an activity to follow up the reading of a book, story, or poem that contains lots of rhyming words. Here is an example using that timeless book *I Wish That I Had Duck Feet* (Seuss, 1972), in which a boy wishes he had duck feet, so that he could splash and would not have to wear shoes, until he realizes his mother would not want him in the house like that. The boy goes on to wish for deer horns, a whale spout, a long tail, and a long nose, until he thinks of the complications each would cause and finally decides to "be just me." As with so many other Dr. Seuss books, this one has enormous appeal for children.

After reading and enjoying the book, we point out to the children that, in addition to silly stories and great illustrations, Dr. Seuss books are fun to read because of all the rhyming words. We then reread several pages of *I Wish That I Had Duck Feet*, and the children help us "round up the rhymes." On the first page, the children decide that the rhyming words are *why* and *dry*. We write these words on two index cards and place them one under the other in a pocket chart. On the next page, we round up the rhyming words *me* and *see*. We continue reading the pages and rounding up the rhymes, until we have six or seven sets of rhyming words.

why	me	brown	play	floor	don't	instead
dry	see	town	way	door	won't	head

Next, we reread these pages once more. As we get to the rhyming words, we point to them in the pocket chart and have the children say them.

Once six or seven sets of rhyming words are rounded up and displayed on index cards in the pocket chart, we have the children underline the spelling pattern in each word. We notice that most of the rhyming words have the same spelling pattern. *Me* and *see*, however, rhyme but have a different spelling pattern. We explain to the children that we only want to keep rhymes with the same spelling pattern and toss *me* and *see* in the trash can! There are now six pairs of rhyming words with the same spelling pattern in the pocket chart:

why	brown	play	floor	don't	instead
dry	town	way	door	won't	head

The final part of this activity is the transfer step—how we use rhyming words to read and spell other words. This step is exactly the same as the transfer step in a Making Words lesson. We write two words that rhyme and have the same spelling pattern as the words in the pocket chart. Children put each word in the pocket chart under the other words with the same spelling pattern and use the rhyme to decode the words.

Finally, say two words that rhyme. The children decide what words they rhyme with and use the spelling pattern to spell them. Here are the *I Wish That I Had Duck Feet* words, along with the new words read and spelled, based on their rhymes and spelling patterns:

why	brown	play	floor	don't	instead
dry	town	way	door	won't	head
sky	clown	tray			bread

How Rounding Up the Rhymes Reflects What We Know

Although very different from Making Words, Rounding Up the Rhymes helps children develop the same understandings about words. As children identify rhyming words, they are developing phonemic awareness. Underlining the spelling pattern helps them learn to process words in a sequential manner. Students apply what they have learned to new words that they decode and spell based on the rhyming words. As they decode and spell new words, their attention is drawn to the onsets and rimes, and they begin to use an onset–rime/analogy decoding strategy.

Reading/Writing Rhymes

"Reading/Writing Rhymes" (Cunningham, 2000) is an activity that gives students practice using patterns to decode and spell hundreds of words. Once all the rhyming words are generated on a chart, students write rhymes using these words and then read each other's rhymes. Because writing and reading are connected to every lesson, students learn how to use these patterns as they actually read and write. Here is an example of how one Reading/Writing Rhymes lesson might be carried out.

The teacher distributes the whole set of beginning letter cards to the children. This beginning letter deck contains 50 index letter cards, including

Single consonants: *b c d f g h j k l m n p r s t v w y z*
Digraphs (two letters, one sound): *sh ch wh th*
Other two-letter, one-sound combinations: *wr kn qu*
Blends (beginning letters blended together, sometimes called clusters): *bl br cl cr dr fl fr gl gr pl pr sc scr sk sl sm sn sp spr st str sw tr tw*

Once all the onset cards are distributed, the teacher writes a spelling pattern 10 times on a piece of chart paper. Next, the teacher invites children who have cards they think make a word to come up and place their card next to one of the written spelling patterns and pronounce the resulting word. If the word is indeed a real word, the teacher uses the word in a sentence and writes that word on the chart. If the word is not a real word, the teacher explains why she cannot write it on the chart. (If a word is a real word and does rhyme but has a different spelling pattern, the teacher explains that it rhymes but has a different pattern and includes the correct spelling on the bottom of the chart with an asterisk next to it.) The teacher writes names with capital letters, and if a word can be both a name and not a name, such as bill and Bill, she writes it both ways. When all the children who think they can spell words with their beginning letters and the spelling pattern have come up, the teacher calls children up to make the words not yet there by saying something like,

"I think the person with the *qu* card could come up here and add *qu* to *ill* to make a word we know."

The teacher tries to include all the words that any of the children would have in their listening vocabulary but avoids obscure words. If the 10 patterns the teacher wrote to begin the chart get made into complete words, she adds as many more as needed. Figure 4.1 illustrates what the completed _ill chart might look like.

Once the chart of rhyming words is written, teacher and students work together in a shared writing format to write a silly sentence using lots of the rhyming words. Then, the children write some silly sentences

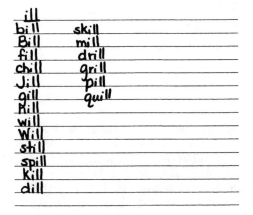

FIGURE 4.1. Completed _ill chart.

of their own. Many teachers put the children in small groups or with partners to write these sentences, and then let different children read their sentences to the class.

To make Reading/Writing Rhymes charts for the patterns with two common spellings, the teacher writes both patterns on the same chart. Students come up and tell the word their beginning letters will make, and the teacher writes it with the correct pattern. In many cases, there are two homophones, words that are spelled differently and have different meanings but the same pronunciation. The teacher writes both of these and talks about what each one means. Figure 4.2 is a chart for the *ain/ane* spelling pattern.

Children enjoy writing the silly sentences. Figure 4.3 is an example based on the *ain/ane* chart.

ain	ane	
rain	cane	
brain	crane	
train	sane	
pain	pane	
plain	plane	# reign
drain	Jane	Maine
vain	Vane	
chain	Shane	
gain	mane	
grain	Zane	
stain		
strain		
Spain		
sprain		

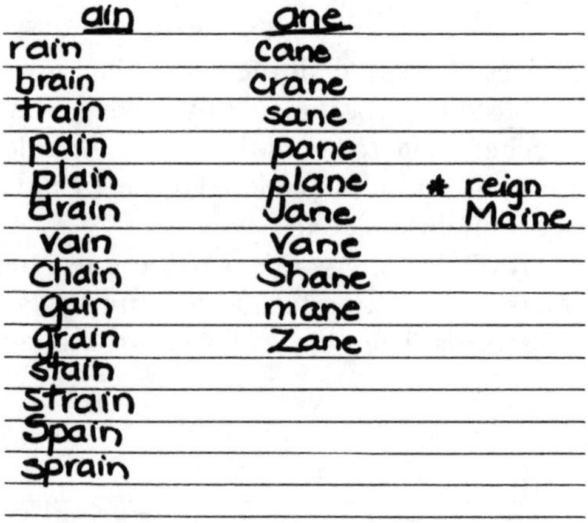

FIGURE 4.2. *Ain/ane* spelling pattern chart.

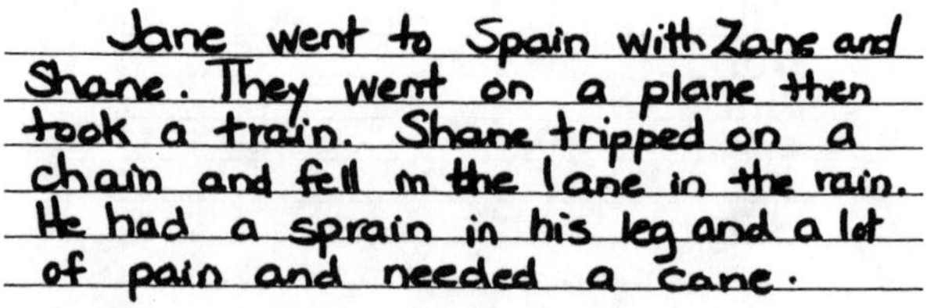

Jane went to Spain with Zane and Shane. They went on a plane then took a train. Shane tripped on a chain and fell in the lane in the rain. He had a sprain in his leg and a lot of pain and needed a cane.

FIGURE 4.3. Example based on the *ain/ane* chart.

How Reading/Writing Rhymes Reflects What We Know

Phonemic awareness is developed as children blend the vowel pattern with the beginning letters on the cards and as they read all the rhyming words before writing their silly sentences. Children apply what they have learned by writing some of the rhymes in silly sentences and then reading these to their classmates. As they engage in lots of Reading/Writing Rhymes lessons with different patterns, they get in the habit of looking at words as combinations of onsets and rimes, and this promotes the development of the onset/rime/analogy decoding strategy.

Word Detectives

"Word Detectives" is an activity we do with children when introducing big words to them. We teach the children to ask themselves two questions to "solve the mystery of big words."

1. "Do I know any other words that look and sound like this word?"
2. "Are any of these look-alike/sound-alike words related to each other?"

The answer to the first question helps children with pronouncing and spelling the word. The answer to the second question helps children discover what, if any, meaning relationships exist between this new word and others in their meaning vocabulary stores. To be most effective, children need to be word detectives throughout the school day in every subject area. Imagine that during math, students encounter the new word, *equation*. The teacher demonstrates and gives examples of equations, and helps build meaning for the concept. Finally, the teacher asks the students to pronounce *equation* and see if they know any other words that look and sound like *equation*. Students think of words that end like *equation*, such as *addition, multiplication, nation,* and *vacation*. For the beginning chuck they think of *equal* and *equator*.

The teacher lists the words, underlining the parts that are the same, and has students pronounce the words, emphasizing the part that is pronounced the same. The teacher then points out to the students that thinking of a word that looks and sounds the same as a new word will help them quickly remember how to pronounce and also spell the new word.

Next the teacher explains that words, like people, sometimes look and sound alike but are not related. If this is the first time this "words are like people" analogy is used, the teacher will want to spend some time talking with the students about people with red hair, green eyes, and so on, who have some parts that look alike but are not related, and others who are.

"Not all people who look alike are related, but some are. This is how words work, too. Words are related if there is something about their meaning that is the same. After we find look-alike/sound-alike words that will help us spell and pronounce new words, we try to think of any ways these words might be in the same meaning family."

With help from the teacher, the children discover that *equal, equator,* and *equation* are related because the meaning of *equal* is in all three. An *equation* has to have *equal* quantities on both sides of the *equal* signs. The *equator* is an imaginary line that divided the earth into two *equal* halves.

Later, during science time, the students do some experiments using thermometers and barometers. At the close of the lesson, the teacher points to these words and asks the students once again to be word detectives. The children notice that the *meters* chunk is pronounced and spelled the same. The teacher then asks the students if they think these words are just look-alikes or are related to one another. The students conclude that both are used to measure things, and the *meters* chunk must be related to measuring, as in *kilometers.* Students also noticed that *thermometer* begins like *thermostat,* and they decide that *thermometer* and *thermostat* are related, because they both involve heat or temperature.

Throughout their school day, children encounter many new big words. Because English is such a morphologically related language, most new words can be connected to other words by their spelling and pronunciation, and many new words have meaning-related words already known to the students. Children who use clues from other big words to figure out the decoding, spelling, and meaning of new big words are being word detectives.

How Word Detectives Reflects What We Know

Word Detectives is an activity specifically designed to help children become sensitive to morphology—prefixes, suffixes, and roots that provide links to the spelling, pronunciation, and meanings of big words. Because the words chosen always come from the context of what is being studied, children learn to use morphology and context together as clues to solve the mysteries of big words.

IMPLICATIONS FOR FUTURE RESEARCH

This chapter has summarized what we know from research about how to teach phonics. The major conclusions of this research are that children do need systematic phonics instruction, but there is no single best way to teach phonics. This conclusions is disturbing to some people, who would like there to be a best way, so that everyone could be mandated to do it that way. In many schools, one approach to phonics has been mandated in spite of the lack of research to prove that approach is any better than other approaches teachers might take.

In order to improve reading instruction for all children, we need to look to the research on effective literacy instruction (Allington & Johnston, 2002; Pressley, Allington, Wharton-McDonald, Block, & Morrow, 2002). These nationwide studies identified effective first- and fourth-grade classrooms, and analyzed the literacy instruction that occurred in those classrooms. They not only found many differences in these classrooms but also many commonalities. The classrooms with the most effective teachers were characterized by high academic engagement, excellent and positive classroom management, explicit teaching of skills, large amounts of reading and writing, and integration across the curriculum. Within these commonalities, there were huge differences in the way the components were orchestrated. How we teach phonics has not been demonstrated to have a huge effect on achievement, but how we orchestrate classrooms has shown that effect. To improve beginning literacy achievement, we need to continue to research how to create, maintain, and support excellent classroom teachers.

DISCUSSION AND ACTIVITIES

1. Consider other phonics activities you have done or read about. How well do they reflect what we know about how children learn phonics? Is phonemic awareness developed as an integral part of that activity? Do children learn to do sequential decoding, considering every letter in the right order? Does the activity include a transfer step when the children use what they have learned to decode and spell new words? Does the activity help move children toward onset–rime/analogy decoding used by sophisticated readers?
2. Examine the materials and activities you have available for teaching phonics and determine how much attention they pay to helping children discover morphemic links. Almost all the key words encountered in science and social studies are polysyllabic words. These big words are stumbling blocks for many children, who do not know how to use prefixes, suffixes, and roots as keys to spelling, decoding, and meaning.
3. Consider how reading is usually assessed in the schools in your area. Because assessment always plays a major role in how we teach, consider the extent to which there is a match between the reading assessments used, the phonics instruction provided, and the development of thoughtful readers.

4. Identify a school and look at the phonics instruction in the context of the total literacy program. Are children spending large amounts of time actually reading and writing? Are comprehension strategies being taught for both story and informational text? Are children being taught how to read the informational text common to science and social studies? Is the development of prior knowledge, meaning, vocabulary, and oral language a prominent feature across the school day? A balanced literacy curriculum puts phonics in a prominent but not predominant position.

REFERENCES

Professional Literature

Adams, M. (1990). *Beginning to read.* Cambridge: MA: MIT Press.

Allington, R. L., & Woodside-Jiron, H. (1998). *Adequacy of a program of research and of a "research synthesis" in shaping educational policy* (No. 1.15). Albany, NY: National Research Center on English Learning and Achievement, State University of New York at Albany.

Allington, R. L., & Johnston, P. H. (2002). *Reading to learn: Lessons from exemplary fourth-grade classrooms.* New York: Guilford Press.

Berent, I., & Perfetti, C. A. (1995). A rose is a REEZ: The two-cycles model of phonology assembly in reading English. *Psychological Review, 102,* 146–184.

Cassidy, J., Roettiger, D., & Wixson, K. K. (1987). *Join the circle.* New York: Scribner.

Cunningham, P. M. (2000). *Phonics they use: Words for reading and writing* (3rd ed.). New York: Addison-Wesley/Longman.

Cunningham, P. M., & Allington, R. L. (2003). *Classrooms that work: They can all read and write.* Boston: Allyn & Bacon.

Cunningham, P. M., & Cunningham, J. W. (1992). Making words: Enhancing the invented spelling–decoding connection. *The Reading Teacher, 46,* 106–110.

Cunningham, J. W., Cunningham, P. M., Hoffman, J., & Yopp, H. (1998). *Phonemic awareness and the teaching of reading.* Newark, DE: International Reading Association.

Cunningham, P. M., & Hall, D. P. (1994). *Making words.* Parsippany, NJ: Good Apple.

Cunningham, P. M., Hall, D. P., & Sigmon, C. (1999). *The teacher's guide to the Four Blocks.* Greensboro, NC: Carson Dellosa.

Ehri, L. C., & Nunes, S. R. (2002). The role of phonemic awareness in learning to read. In A. E. Farstrup & S. J. Samuels (Eds.), *What research has to say about reading instruction* (pp. 110–139). Newark, DE: International Reading Association.

Flesch, R. (1955). *Why Johnny can't read.* New York: Harper and Row.

Goswami, U. (2000). Phonological and lexical processes. In M. L. Kamil, P. B. Mosenthal, P. D. Pearson, & R. Barr (Eds.), *Handbook of reading research* (Vol. 3, pp. 251–267). Mahwah, NJ: Erlbaum.

Goswami, U., & Bryant, P. (1990). *Phonological skills and learning to read.* East Sussex, UK: Erlbaum.

Hiebert, E. H. (1999). Text matters in learning to read. *The Reading Teacher, 52,* 552–566.

Juel, C., & Roper-Schneider, D. (1985). The influence of basal readers on first grade reading. *Reading Research Quarterly, 20,* 134–152.

Moustafa, M. (1997). *Beyond traditional phonics.* Portsmouth: NH: Heinemann.

Nagy, W., & Anderson, R. C. (1984). How many words are there in printed school English? *Reading Research Quarterly, 19,* 304–330.

National Reading Panel. (2000). *Teaching children to read: An evidence-based assessment of the scientific research literature on reading and its implications for reading instruction* (National Institute of Health Publication No. 00-4769). Washington, DC: National Institute of Child Health and Human Development.

Pressley, M., Allington, R. L. Wharton-McDonald, R., Block, C. C., & Morrow, L. M. (2001). *Learning to read: Lessons from exemplary first-grade classrooms.* New York: Guilford Press.

Stahl, S. A., Duffy-Hester, A. M., & Stahl, K. A. (1998). Everything you wanted to know about phonics (but were afraid to ask). *Reading Research Quarterly, 33,* 338–355.

Yopp, H. K., & Yopp, R. H. (2000). Supporting phonemic awareness development in the classroom. *The Reading Teacher, 54,* 130–143.

Children's Literature

Seuss, Dr. (1972). *I wish that I had duck feet.* New York: Random House.

Seuss, Dr. (1974). *There's a wocket in my pocket.* New York: Random House.

Slepian, J., & Seidler, A. (1967). *The hungry thing.* New York: Scholastic.

Chapter 5

BEST PRACTICES IN VOCABULARY INSTRUCTION: WHAT EFFECTIVE TEACHERS DO

Camille L. Z. Blachowicz
Peter J. Fisher

This chapter will:

- Present five research-based guidelines for vocabulary instruction.
- Share the research that underpins each and give examples of instruction reflecting the targeted guideline.
- Describe a classroom that utilizes this type of instruction.
- Share resources for vocabulary instruction.

EFFECTIVE TEACHING OF VOCABULARY: FIVE EVIDENCE-BASED GUIDELINES

The term "vocabulary instruction" can encompass a number of activities that occur in a classroom. We often ask teachers to make a list of word study activities that occur during one day in their classroom. A typical list from a fourth-grade teacher included the following:

- Teach the suggested words prior to the reading selection from the basal.
- Brainstorm synonyms for the word *said* as part of a minilesson in writing.
- List word families as part of spelling instruction.
- Teach the meaning of *quadrant* for word problems in math.
- Have the Mexican American and Arab American students teach the rest of the students the Spanish and Arabic words for *plains, rivers, clouds, mountains,* and *rain* as part of social studies on the Great Plains.
- Develop a semantic web for the Great Plains, including words learned so far in the unit.
- Talk about *honesty* in relation to one student having "borrowed" a marker from another without permission.
- Clarify the meanings of some difficult words in the teacher read-aloud at the end of the day.

Clearly, for each of these teaching events, the nature of the learning task was somewhat different. In some cases, students were learning unfamiliar words (the Spanish and Arabic words) for familiar concepts (*plains, rivers,* etc.), whereas in others, they were learning new concepts (*quadrant*). In addition, we might expect that students would remember some words and use them almost immediately (synonyms for *said*), whereas students might recognize other words in a story but not choose to use them in their own writing (the basal words). Vocabulary instruction occurs in our classrooms every day at a variety of levels and for a variety of purposes. After all, words are the currency of education. However, teachers are increasingly faced with a diverse group of learners in terms of current word knowledge, linguistic background, learning styles, and literacy abilities. It is up to us as teachers to make word learning enjoyable, meaningful, and effective.

How, then, does a teacher meet all these needs in a classroom of diverse learners? Like much in education, there is no simple answer. However, research has suggested several guidelines that apply across most situations (Blachowicz & Fisher, 2000; National Reading Panel, 2000):

- *Guideline 1.* The effective vocabulary teacher builds a word-rich environment in which students are immersed in words for both incidental and intentional learning, and the development of "word awareness."
- *Guideline 2.* The effective vocabulary teacher helps students develop as independent word learners.
- *Guideline 3.* The effective vocabulary teacher uses instructional strategies that not only teach vocabulary but also model good word-learning behaviors.
- *Guideline 4.* The effective vocabulary teacher provides explicit instruction for important content and concept vocabulary, drawing on multiple sources of meaning.
- *Guideline 5.* The effective vocabulary teacher uses assessment that matches the goal of instruction.

In the next section, we look at each guideline in turn, presenting an evidence base and then some examples of instruction consistent with this guideline.

VOCABULARY INSTRUCTION: THE EVIDENCE BASE

In today's world, it is important to exemplify good practice in our classrooms and be able to articulate an evidence base for our instruction drawn from research and best practices. The research base on good practice in vocabulary instruction strongly supports the guidelines we have presented, and we examine each in more depth.

Guideline 1. The effective vocabulary teacher builds a word-rich environment in which students are immersed in words for both incidental and intentional learning, and the development of "word awareness."

Rich Oral Language

This guideline is supported by research in several areas: the importance of rich oral language in the classroom; the need for wide reading; the importance of vocabulary learning as a metalinguistic process. Just as teachers use the term "flood of books" to talk about situations in which students have many and varied opportunities to read, so "flood of words" is an important concept for general vocabulary development (Scott, Asselin, Henry, & Butler, 1997); both rich oral and rich book language provide important input for students' vocabulary growth.

Children enter school with differing levels of vocabulary knowledge (Hart & Risley, 1995), and book vocabulary, both that read to children and read by them, can stimulate considerable learning. The level of vocabulary in primary-level books is well beyond the vocabulary that even college-educated parents use in daily conversation with their children (Cunningham & Stanovich, 1998). Reading to children has been shown to have an effect on not only their recognition knowledge of new words but also their ability to use these words in their own retellings (Elley, 1988; Snow, Burns, & Griffin, 1998). In reading to students, it is important to have them actively listen and to give explanation when needed. Then, have them use the new vocabulary in talking about what they have heard, describing the pictures they have drawn about a story, or using new vocabulary in drama or through other means. This discussion and oral language component of storybook listening is essential (Dickinson & Smith, 1994; Stahl, Richek, & Vandevier, 1991).

Wide Reading

Wide reading is another hallmark of word learning, with many studies suggesting that word learning occurs normally and incidentally during normal reading (Herman, Anderson, Pearson, & Nagy, 1987; Nagy, Herman, & Anderson, 1985). Furthermore, discussion in the classroom (Stahl & Vancil, 1986) and around the dinner table (Snow, 1991) is another correlate of incidental word learning. Although this type of learning through exposure cannot guarantee the learning of specific vocabulary words, it does develop a wide, flexible, and usable general vocabulary.

Models

Teachers should also be models of word learning. We all remember the year we learned many new words in school. We had a teacher who was an avid punster, crossword puzzle aficionado, or otherwise involved in word play. Teachers can be sure that they and their classrooms are models of best practices by being good models of enthusiastic and pleasurable word learning. Using word games such as Hinky Pinkies, puns, puzzles, contests, and other playful activity develops this awareness in a playful and motivating way (Blachowicz & Fisher, in press). In a detailed study of word learning in the middle elementary grades, Beck, Perfetti, and McKeown (1982) found one classroom in which the students outperformed others in word learning. Looking around the classroom, they saw a 79¢ piece of posterboard on the wall, with words entered on it by different students. When the researchers asked about this, they were told by the teacher, "Oh, that's just a little something we do each day. If the kids encounter a new and interesting word, they can tell the rest of the class about it, put it on the chart, and earn points for their team." The students became attuned to listening for new and interesting words, and this interest was validated in the classroom on a regular basis. Techniques such as "word of the day" and "mystery word" are easy, low-maintenance, inexpensive, and time-effective ways of making sure that kids are intentionally exposed to words each day and motivated to do their own word learning.

When the goal is to have students gain control of vocabulary to use for their own expression, students need many experiences that allow them to use words in meaningful ways. Use in writing and conversation, where feedback is available, is essential to durable and deep learning. Creating personal word books and dictionaries is a good first step to word ownership; use in many situations is a second step. Using new words in discussion, writing, independent projects, and word play develops real ownership and moves new words into students' personal vocabularies.

Word Play

Word play is also an important part of the word-rich classroom. The ability to reflect on, manipulate, combine, and recombine the components of words is an important part of vocabulary learning and develops metalinguistic reflection on words as objects to be manipulated intelligently and for humor (Nagy & Scott, 2001; Tunmer, Herriman, & Nesdale, 1988). Phonemic awareness (being able to segment phonemes, such as the *am* in ambulance), morphological awareness (of word part meanings), and syntactic awareness (how a word functions in language) all play important parts in word learning (Carlisle, 1995; Willows & Ryan, 1986). There is also evidence that this type of learning is developmental over the school years (Johnson & Anglin, 1995; Roth, Speece, Cooper, & De la Paz, 1996).

Part of creating a "positive environment for word learning" involves having activities, games, materials and other resources that allow students to play with words. Who would not enjoy spending a few minutes each day figuring out a *wuzzle* or word puzzle? Wuzzles and other word games and puzzles call on students to think flexibly and metacognitively about words. Much of the fun stems from the fact that words can be used in multiple ways with humorous results (see Figure 5.1).

So our students need "word-rich" and "word-aware" classrooms, where new vocabulary is presented in rich listening and personal reading experiences, time is taken to stop and discuss new words, language is a part of all activities, and words, dictionaries, puzzles and word games, word calendars, books on riddles, and rhymes round out the environment for enthusiastic word learning.

> *Guideline 2. The effective vocabulary teacher helps students develop as independent word learners.*

Control of Learning

Good learners take control of their own learning. They can select words to study and use context, word structure, and word references to get information about important vocabulary they need to know. Studies that focus on self-selection of vocabulary suggest that when students choose words that they need to learn, they learn the word meanings more successfully and retain the meanings longer than when a teacher chooses the words. Haggard (1982) interviewed adults and secondary school learners about their memories of learning new words and found that these learners most easily retained words that were usable in their peer groups— popular among peers, occurring frequently in their readings, buzzwords

---

jobsinjobs

Q. Can you tell what phrase this Wuzzle (Word Puzzle) represents?

A. In between jobs

FIGURE 5.1. Wuzzle example.

in the media. Her subsequent teaching studies involving self-selection of words to be learned (Haggard, 1982, 1985; Rapp-Ruddell & Shearer, 2002), suggested that the control offered by self-selection is an important factor in building a generalized vocabulary. Moreover, for students for whom English is a second language, some self-selection is critical to getting a true picture of words that confound learning (Jiminez, 1997).

With the popularity of wide reading approaches and cooperative group models of classroom instruction, Fisher, Blachowicz, & Smith (1991) examined the effects of self-selection in cooperative reading groups on word learning. The fourth-grade groups analyzed in this study were highly successful in learning a majority of the words chosen for study. In a later study with fifth- and seventh-grade readers (Blachowicz, Fisher, Costa, & Pozzi, 1993) the results were repeated and new information was added. The teachers who were coresearchers in the study were not only interested in whether the words were learned but they were also interested in whether the students chose challenging words for study. In all groups studied, the students consistently chose words at or above grade level for study. These and other studies indicate that self-selection and self-study processes can work effectively in the classroom. Collaborative word choice, with the students selecting some words to be learned and the teacher also contributing words for study, may be called for in content-area learning and with difficult, new conceptual topics (Beyersdorfer, 1991). Combined with teacher selection and support, helping students learn to select words for self-study is a powerful tool for independent learning.

Context

Researchers suggest that learning words from context is an important part of vocabulary development but point out that it is unreasonable to expect single, new contextual exposures to do the job (Baldwin & Schatz, 1985). Students need to understand context and how to use it.

Although several studies have provided intensive instruction in contextual analysis with mixed results, recent instructional studies suggest that successful context-use instruction involves explicit instruction, good planning, practice and feedback, scaffolding that leads to more student responsibility, and a metacognitive focus (Blachowicz & Fisher, 2002; Buikema & Graves, 1993; Kuhn & Stahl, 1998). For example, a teacher might choose particular words from students' reading to teach how to predict meaning and look for clues. Similarly, instruction focusing on structural analysis or morphology (the learning of word parts, such as the Greek roots *tele-* and *graph*) can be helpful in learning new words while reading, as long as a teacher emphasizes problem solving.

Dictionary

Students also need supportive instruction in learning how to use the dictionary—an important word-learning tool. Every teacher who has watched a student struggle to look up a word knows that using a dictionary can be a complex and difficult task. Stories of dictionary use often take on a "kids say the darndest things" aura: The student whose only meaning of *sharp* has to do with good looks feels vindicated by finding *acute* as one meaning for sharp in the dictionary ("That sure is acute boy in my class"). Another, noting that *erode* is defined as *eats out*, produces the sentence, "Since my mom went back to work my family erodes a lot" (Miller & Gildea, 1987). Aside from providing humorous anecdotes for the teacher's room, dictionaries and dictionary use are coming under closer scrutiny by those involved in instruction. Students do not automatically understand how dictionaries work or how they can most effectively take information from them.

The use of morphology, word parts such as prefixes, sufiixes, roots, and the other elements needed to break a word's meaning apart, is also an important strategy. Breaking words apart not only helps students learn and remember those specific words but also supplies them with the building blocks to understand new words they encounter (Carlisle, 2000). For morphology instruction, contextual analysis, and work with dictionaries, it is wise to remember to work from the known to the unknown. As students engage in learning any one of these processes, it is important for them to understand the underlying rationale. This is best achieved through exploration of the "how-to" with familiar words and phrases. Once they have mastered easy words, they can practice with more and more difficult words, until the process becomes automatic.

Guideline 3. The effective vocabulary teacher uses instructional strategies that not only teach vocabulary but also model good word-learning behaviors.

The effective vocabulary teacher presents new vocabulary in ways that model good learning. This involves developing learners who are active, who personalize their learning and look for multiple sources of information to build meaning, and who are playful with words.

Good learners are active. As in all learning situations, a hallmark of good instruction is having the learners actively attempt to construct their own meanings. Learning new words as we have new experiences is one of the most durable and long-lasting ways to develop a rich vocabulary. For example, the words *thread, needle, selvage, pattern,* and *dart* may be learned naturally in the context of learning to sew, just as *hit, run, base,* and *fly* take on special meanings for a baseball player. This is particularly important with students whose primary language is not English. They may need the additional contextual help of physical objects and movement to internalize English vocabulary. Another way for students to become actively involved in discovering meaning is by answering questions that ask them to evaluate different features of word meaning (Beck & McKeown, 1983). For example, answering and explaining one's answer to the question "Would a recluse enjoy parties?" helps students focus on the important features of the word *recluse*, a person who chooses to be alone rather than with others. As noted earlier, discussion is another way to involve learners in examining facets of word meaning.

Graphic Organizers

Making word meanings and relationships visible is another way to involve students actively in constructing word meaning. Semantic webs, maps, organizers, or other relational charts, such as the one in Figure 5.2, not

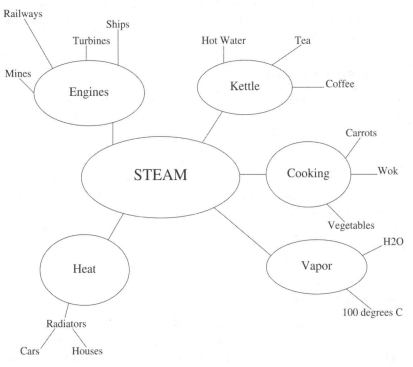

FIGURE 5.2. Web/map.

only graphically display attributes of meanings but also provide a memory organizer for later word use. Many studies have shown the efficacy of putting word meaning into a graphic form such as a map or web (Heimlich & Pittelman, 1986) or a semantic feature chart (Pittelman, Heimlich, Berglund, & French, 1991), advanced organizer, or other graphic form. It is critical to note, however, that mere construction of such maps, without discussion, is not effective (Stahl & Vancil, 1986).

Clustering Techniques

Other approaches that stress actively relating words to one another are clustering strategies that call for students to group words into related sets, brainstorming, grouping and labeling (Marzano & Marzano, 1988), designing concept hierarchies (Wixson, 1986), or constructing definition maps related to conceptual hierarchies (Bannon, Fisher, Pozzi, & Wessell, 1990/1991; Schwartz & Raphael, 1985) mapping words according to their relation to story structure categories (Blachowicz, 1986). All these approaches involve student construction of maps, graphs, charts, webs, or clusters that represent the semantic relatedness of words under study to other words and concepts. Again, discussion, sharing, and use of the words are necessary components of active involvement, as are feedback and scaffolding on the part of the teacher.

Personalizing Learning

Effective learners make learning personal. We have already commented that one of the most durable ways to learn words is in the context of learning some important skill. When we do so, word meanings are personalized by our experiences. Words not learned in firsthand experiences can also be personalized; relating new words to one's own past experiences has been a component of many successful studies. Eeds and Cockrum (1985) had students provide prior knowledge cues for new words, a method related to that used by Carr and Mazur-Stewart (1988), who asked students to construct personal cues to meaning, along with graphic and other methods. Acting out word meaning (Duffelmeyer, 1980) has also led to increased word learning.

Mnemonic Strategies

Creating one's own mnemonic or image is another way to personalize meaning. While active, semantically rich instruction and learning seem best for learning new concepts, tagging a new label onto a well-established concept can be done through the creation of associations. For example, we all know that feeling of being happy, when everything is right with the world, so we have a concept for the word *euphoria.* Mnemonic strategies, those strategies aimed at helping us remember, such as ROY G. BIV for the colors of the spectrum (red, orange, yellow, green, blue, indigo, violet), are time-honored ways to assist memory. Keyword methods are the best known of these word-learning strategies. They involve the creation of a verbal connection, an image, or a picture to help cement the meaning in memory. For example, to remember *phototropism,* the bending of plants toward light, a student created the picture in Figure 5.3 as a visual mnemonic. The verbal labels, *photographer* and *tropical plant,* aided memory for the word; the bending to the light supplied a visual image to support it. Another student created a keyword sentence, "A photo was taken of the plant bending toward light." When trying to remember, one student would call up the picture in her mind; the other would think of the sentence, with "photo" providing an acoustic cue and "bending toward light" a meaning clue.

A significant amount of research has examined the use of the keyword method as a remembering technique (Levin, 1993) for special education

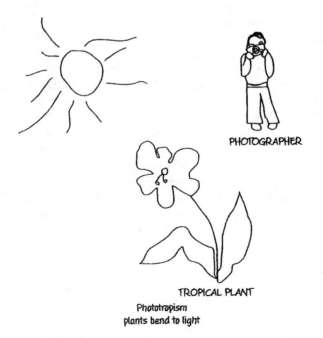

PHOTOGRAPHER

TROPICAL PLANT

Phototropism
plants bend to light

FIGURE 5.3. Keyword for phototropism. From Blachowicz and Fisher (2002). Copyright 2002 by Camille Blachowicz. Reprinted by permission.

students (Scruggs, Mastropieri, & Levin, 1985), for second-language learners, and for adult learners (McCarville, 1993). Although reviews of the research suggest that the keyword may be limited in its application, it remains a useful approach for remembering specific word labels, especially combined with imagery, drawing, and other tools for personalization.

> *Guideline 4. The effective vocabulary teacher provides explicit instruction for important content and concept vocabulary, drawing on multiple sources of meaning.*

Although contextualized word learning in wide reading, discussion, listening, and engaging in firsthand learning provides a great deal of word learning, explicit instruction can also contribute to vocabulary development (Biemiller, 2001). This is most appropriate in the content areas where students need a shared set of vocabulary to progress in their learning. It is hard to have a discussion about phototropism if the words *plant, sun, bend,* and *light* have not already been established in the learner's vocabulary. Shared content vocabulary is required for group learning.

Numerous studies comparing definitional instruction with incidental learning from context, or with no-instruction control conditions support the notion that teaching definitions results in learning. However, instructions that combined definitional information with other active processing, such as adding contextual information, writing contextual discovery, or rich manipulation of words all exceeded performance of students who received only definitional instruction (see Blachowicz & Fisher, 2000, for a review of this research). A meta-analysis of studies that compared different types of instruction (Stahl & Fairbanks, 1986) concluded that methods with multiple sources of information for students provide superior word learning. In effective classrooms, students encounter words in context and work to create or understand appropriate definitions, synonyms, and other word relations.

Therefore, teachers can model mature word-learning strategies by helping students gather information across texts and sources. Students should keep looking for different types of information that will flesh out the meaning they need to understand. Students benefit from the following:

- Definitional information
- Contextual information
- Usage examples

They also profit from manipulating words in many contexts.

Definitional information can be provide in many ways. Giving synonyms and antonyms provide information on what a word is or is not. Creating definitions using frames (see Figure 5.4, below) or other models helps students understand what a dictionary can provide. Example sentences clue students into nuance, as well as usage. Semantic maps, as exemplified earlier, webs, feature analysis, and comparing and contrasting words all help students gain definitional information.

Care must be taken that the students see the words in context and have chances to use the word with feedback. Teachers often present usage sentences for choice and discussion. For example, for the word *feedback*, the teacher might present the following and ask students to choose the correct usage.

We gave him feedback on his choices.
We were feedbacked by the teacher.

As in all vocabulary activities, discussion is the key. After choice and discussion, the teacher could ask each student to do two things: (1) Locate a sentence or paragraph in the text where the word is used and explain the meaning, and/or (2) write and illustrate an original sentence.

Guideline 5. The effective vocabulary teacher uses assessment that matches the goal of instruction.

The final guideline relates to the complexity of the vocabulary instruction suggested in our introduction. We teach words for so many different purposes, and require varying levels and types of understanding according to the task, the word, and the subject area. In general, it is helpful to think of two main dimensions for vocabulary knowledge—depth and breadth.

Depth refers to how much is known about a particular word: Can you recognize the meaning in text or conversation, can you use it appropriately, or can you define it? We all have the experience of being asked, "What does *energetic* mean?" and replying "Well, Lassie is energetic when she runs all over the house and barks at everything." We tend to supply examples to illustrate meaning rather than to give a definition. This is probably appropriate in many situations and relies on the questioner's ability to use the context we provide to elaborate on the basic meaning of the word. We often do this even when we could give a definition, but on many occasions, we do it because we know how to use a word, perhaps *calligraphy*, but are unsure of the precise meaning. Other times we can understand some of the meaning of a word when we hear or see someone use it, without feeling comfortable about using it ourselves. We learn more about words each time we see or hear them; that is, we increase our depth of understanding. In relation to classrooms, it is helpful to consider what level of understanding is needed for successful completion of the task. Perhaps, when reading a particular selection, it is enough to know that a *pallet* is a form of bed, or maybe it is necessary to know what distinguishes it from other beds (it is made of straw), because it is part of a social studies unit that connects living styles to the environment.

Breadth of knowledge of a word is related to depth insofar as it can add layers of understanding, but is concerned primarily with how a word is connected to other words in a domain of learning. For example, do students understand the relations among the words *plains, rivers, mountains, foothills,* and *erosion*? Students in fourth grade may need to see how each relates to the other when studying a unit on the Great Plains. However, their depth of understanding of *erosion* may be limited compared to that of a high-school geography student or a geomorphologist.

Baker, Simmons, and Kameenui (1995) have argued that an important principle of vocabulary instruction is that it should be aligned with the depth of word knowledge required in any setting. We understand this to mean that teachers should decide how much students need to know about a word's meaning before teaching it. For example, is it enough that students learn that an *echidna* is a small Australian mammal, or do they need to know more about its appearance and habitat? We would add that the assessment should match the instruction in relation to both depth and breadth of word knowledge. This may sound complicated, but it is not. Many instructional techniques can also be used as assessment techniques, so that a teacher can evaluate a student's understanding in authentic learning situations.

Assessing Vocabulary Breadth

One way to know what students have learned about a broad range of words is to use and analyze pre- and postinstruction graphic organizers that ask students to work with sets of related words. Knowledge ratings, semantic mapping and webbing, Vocab-O-Grams, semantic feature analysis, structured overviews, and other graphic organizers can reveal to a teacher what students have learned about groups of terms. Mapping activities can be done individually or in groups and allow a teacher to keep tabs on word learning without testing. Alternatively, a teacher can test what individuals have learned by presenting graphic organizers that are partially completed.

Assessing Vocabulary Depth

Sometimes, rather than assessing breadth of knowledge, we want to analyze how deeply students understand central terms. If we expect students to have a deep knowledge, such as a definition, an alternative to writing a definition is to have them complete a concept of definition map (Schwartz & Raphael, 1985; see Figure 5.4). Using this alternative allows a teacher to see where students' knowledge is incomplete: Do they know a category, distinguishing characteristics, and examples, or only some of these parts of a definition?

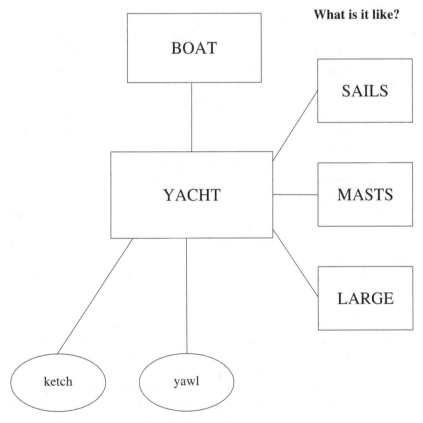

FIGURE 5.4. Concept of definition map.

The ability to use a term is often regarded as less difficult than defining it. When you want to know about students' ability to use a new term correctly, rather than a contrived method, such as "See how many of this week's new words you can use in one story"—a technique sure to produce distorted and contrived usage, you can ask students to use vocabulary in meaningful ways in the context of some larger activities. The most direct way to do this is to ask students to incorporate particular words in their responses to questions, and their summaries and retellings. Observing students' use of words in discussion, in lessons, and in writing is a means of evaluating their vocabulary usage in the most authentic way. Many teachers compose their own "rubrics," or structured ways of looking at vocabulary and rating usage. If you keep a notebook with a page for each student, you can pull out sheets for a few students each day to make observations or enter information on the sheet when you notice something in your daily anecdotal records. In addition to observing students in action in discussion and writing, you might ask students to keep lists of words that interest them, and that they encounter in reading. You can designate specific words as journal additions, and review can serve as assessment.

Another alternative for evaluating word usage is to use word monitors for discussion. A student in a discussion group can be designated as a "word monitor" to chart the number of times particular teacher-selected words are used. The monitor for that word can also be charged to survey each student in the group about the word's meaning and ask each to supply a usage for a designated word or words. Records turned into the teacher can be used as assessment.

Some teachers use Word Walls or vocabulary charts as part of assessment. Students can be assigned to construct a collection of new words in a word bank, list, or dictionary, or on a Word Wall or bulletin board. A teacher can have periodic 3-minute meetings in which she selects 10 words from the collections and asks students to use them in a meaningful way.

Along with the use of teacher assessment methods, it may be important to ask students to evaluate themselves in terms of their word learning. Using knowledge ratings and other techniques, you can encourage students to become self-reflective about the words they need to learn and the ways they need to go about learning them.

Finally, for assessing students' ability to recognize a meaning for a word, teacher-constructed tests may be appropriate. These tests can take many forms and usually test recognition (the ability to select an appropriate answer) rather than the more difficult recall (the ability to provide a word from memory). Typical teacher-made tests are types of recall assessment that involve defining a word by

1. Giving/choosing a synonym (a *diadem* is a *crown*).
2. Giving/choosing a classification (a *shrimp* is a *crustacean*).
3. Giving/choosing examples (*flowers* are things, such as daisy, rose, mum).
4. Giving/choosing an explanation of how something is used (a *shovel* is a *tool* used to dig holes).
5. Giving/choosing an opposite.
6. Giving/choosing a definition.
7. Giving/choosing a picture.
8. Giving/choosing a word to complete a context.

Tests that you make for the classroom should be easy and efficient to use. You will also want to ask the following questions:

1. Do the items and the process call on students to do the same things you typically ask them to do in class? If your normal question in class asks that students supply a synonym, then asking for an antonym on a test does not make much sense.
2. Will answering the item provide useful repetition of vocabulary or make students think more deeply about it? If the test item is an exact repetition of something you did earlier, then it may be testing rote memory rather than more creative or extensive thinking.
3. Will the knowledge you draw on be useful and relevant to the course in which the assessment is taking place? If you are testing aspects of word knowledge not relevant to the topic, your efforts may be counterproductive.
4. Does your test format match your instructional format? If you have stressed usage in instruction, test for usage. If you have emphasized word recognition, test for recognition.

An important part of all assessment is keeping records to show growth and change. Both students and teachers can keep records in the classroom to record change and growth. Students may use word files and notebooks to record their developing knowledge. These may become part of a portfolio. In addition to test records, you may also want to keep anecdotal records, using the type of techniques already suggested. The records that you keep will help you become a more effective vocabulary teacher by aligning your assessment with instruction and vice versa.

WHAT DOES THIS LOOK LIKE IN THE CLASSROOM?

You can tell that Angela, a fourth-grade teacher, loves words and word play from the moment you walk into her classroom. A poster headed "New

Words We Like" is displayed prominently on the front wall. It is filled with entries from students, with some words spilling over onto the wall on index cards. For each word, there is an entry, a description of where the student encountered the word, such as the one for "vile" which the student illustrated with a drawing and verbal description of her sister's shoes (see Figure 5.5). Each student who used the word during the week could add his or her initials to the picture with another example.

In the library area, a shelf of riddle, joke, and pun books holds many well-thumbed volumes, and a "joke of the day" is posted on the wall. The bookcase also has a multitude of dictionaries—sports dictionaries, animal dictionaries, dictionaries of tools, and others. On the bottom shelf, a number of word games are stored, including Boggle, Scrabble, Pictionary and their junior versions. There is also a basket of crossword books nearby and blank forms for making crossword puzzles. The nearby computer has a crossword puzzle program that is well used. There is also a box of discs called "Personal Dictionaries" on which students keep their own word lists. For some, a simple list in table form is used. These can be easily alphabetized and realphabetized with each addition. Other students like to use HyperCard stacks to keep their word file, so that they can resort them in different ways.

Rather than having a set of dictionaries stored on her bookshelf, Angela has dictionaries in convenient locations around the room. These range from hardbound collegiate dictionaries to more accessible softbacks at a range of levels. She also has several "learner's dictionaries (American Heritage Dictionary, 2000), which are intended for students who are learning

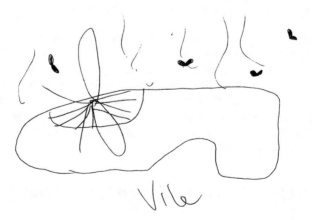

FIGURE 5.5. Personal word record: vile. "My brother says my sister's shoes smell vile. *Vile* = really bad, nasty."

English. These define words functionally instead of classically, and Angela finds that many students like to use them, not just her ESL students.

Angela's day starts with a word of the week, in which she poses a puzzle such as "Would a *ruthless* person be a good social worker?" If some students have a view, they answer and explain their reasoning. If no one has anything to offer, Angela presents the word in a few context sentences and then provides a definition. No more than 5 minutes are spent on this activity, and she varies the format. Sometimes she presents a word as a puzzle, sometimes as a guessing game, and so forth.

Today the class is starting a new unit on whales, so Angela begins with a Vocab-O-Gram (Blachowicz, 1986) brainstorming. She puts up a piece of chart paper (see Figure 5.6) and begins by having students brainstorm the words they already know about whales and entering these words on the chart. As the unit progresses, more and more words will be added and new categories will be drawn out of the "Other interesting words" category.

In math class, students are busy working on their graphic dictionary of math terms, showing types of angles labeled with their names. In literature time, students are engaged in self-selection words for study from *Castle in the Attic* (Winthrop, 1986), their core book for the unit. As they read their self-selected books on medieval life, they add to their personal lists.

FINAL THOUGHTS

All of us are vocabulary teachers when we work with students in classrooms. We teach them new ways of looking at the world and, in doing so, develop new concepts and understandings. Every day, we teach words in a variety of ways. Our obligation to the students is not just to be vocabulary teachers but the best vocabulary teachers that we can be. Following the five evidence-based guidelines will make our classrooms homes for motivated word learners whose interest and skill in learning new words will grow along with their vocabularies.

Habitat/home	Description/types	Food
Predators/prey	Life/cycle	Other interesting words

FIGURE 5.6. Vocab-O-Gram.

DISCUSSION AND ACTIVITIES

1. Choose a vocabulary word from a text selection you will use with students. Construct a vocabulary frame for that word (see Figure 5.3 for an example). Then, develop three contextual sentences, each of which gives a clue to the meaning. Last, develop two usage-choice sentences. Try them out with a classmate or with students in class. Write a reflection on what worked and what did not. How would you modify what you did?
2. Choose a vocabulary website below to use with your students. Describe the directions you would give them to use it. (See the Reading Center website *www2.nl.edu/reading_center* for some other sites to start with or search in your browser).
3. Develop a Vocab-O-Gram for a selection. Use it to select the words you would teach. Try it out with a classmate or with students in class. Write a reflection on what worked and what did not. How would you modify what you did?

RESOURCES FOR FURTHER LEARNING

Books for Further Reading

Allen, J. (1999). *Words, words, words: Teaching vocabulary in grades 4–12.* York, ME: Stenhouse.

Beck, I. L., McKeown, M. G., & Kucan, L. (2002). *Bringing words to life.* New York: Guilford Press.

Blachowicz, C., & Fisher, P. (2002). *Teaching vocabulary in all classrooms* (2nd. ed.). Columbus, OH: Prentice-Hall.

Ganske, K. (2000). *Word journeys.* New York: Guilford Press.

Johnson, D. D. (2000). *Vocabulary in the elementary and middle school.* Boston: Allyn & Bacon.

Stahl, S. S. (1999). *Vocabulary development.* Cambridge, MA: Brookline Books.

Websites

General

Vocabulary websites on the National College of Education Reading Center website.

www2.nl.edu/reading_center

Research

National Center to Improve the Tools of Educators (NCITE) Reading Research Synthesis NCITE Research Synthesis: Reading and Diverse Learners NCITE staff reviewed reading research on the design of instructional materials for diverse learners in six general areas: vocabulary acquisition, word recognition, text organization, emergent literacy, fluency, and comprehension.

idea.uoregon.edu/~ncite/documents/techre. . . .

Vocabulary Acquisition Research Group
Centre for Applied Language Studies
University of Wales
Swansea Vocabulary Research Group

www.swan.ac.uk/cals/calsres.html

Vocabulary Improvement Project (VIP)
The VIP is a national research program funded by the U.S. Department of Education. The Project's main goal is to develop intervention strategies aimed at helping children who are learning English.

mind.ucsc.edu/vip

Games

Vocabulary.com
Vocabulary puzzles and games

www.vocabulary.com

The Word Detective
Ezine with column about words and their meanings

www.word-detective.com

Adventures of Vocabulary Van
Learn new things and meet new friends in this adventure of words and creative fun. Meet Vocabulary Van and join her in her adventures.

kidslangarts.about.com/kids/kidslangarts . . .

ESL

Interactive Audio–Picture English Lessons
Offers interactive ESL with pronunciation and pictures.

www.web-books.com/Language

EnglishCLUB.net
Features grammar and vocabulary activities, word games, pen pal listings, and question-and-answer service. Includes free classroom handouts for ESL teachers.

www.englishclub.net

Learn English—Have Fun
Offers online English crosswords, ESL word games, jokes, tests, and word-search puzzles. New games and crosswords added regularly.

www.englishday.com

Interesting Things for ESL Students
Free Web-based textbook and fun study site. Daily Page for English, proverbs, slang, anagrams, quizzes, and more.

www.aitech.ac.jp/~itesls

REFERENCES

American heritage dictionary for learners of English. (2000). Boston: Houghton Mifflin.

Baker, S. K., Simmons, D. C., & Kameenui, E. J. (1995). *Vocabulary acquisition: Curricular and instructional implications for diverse learners* (Technical Report No. 14). Eugene, OR: National Center to Improve the Tools of Educators, University of Oregon.

Baldwin, R. S., & Schatz, E. I. (1985). Context clues are ineffective with low frequency words in naturally occurring prose. In J. A. Niles & R. V. Lalik (Eds.), *Issues in literacy: A research perspective* (34th Yearbook of the National Reading Conference, pp. 132–135). Rochester, NY: National Reading Conference.

Bannon, E., Fisher, P. J. L., Pozzi, L., & Wessel, D. (1990/1991). Effective definitions for word learning. *Journal of Reading, 34,* 301–303.

Beck, I. L., & McKeown, M. G. (1983). Learning words well—a program to enhance vocabulary and comprehension. *The Reading Teacher, 36,* 622–625.

Beck, I., Perfetti, C., & McKeown, M. (1982). The effects of long-term vocabulary instruction on lexical access and reading comprehension. *Journal of Educational Psychology, 74,* 506–521.

Beyersdorfer, J. M. (1991). *Middle school students' strategies for selection of vocabulary in science texts.* Unpublished doctoral dissertation, National-Louis University, Evanston, IL.

Biemiller, A. (2001). Teaching vocabulary: Early, direct, and sequential. *American Educator, 25*(1), 24–28, 47.

Blachowicz, C. L. Z. (1986). Making connections: Alternatives to vocabulary notebook. *Journal of Reading, 29,* 643–649.

Blachowicz, C. L. Z., & Fisher, P. J. L. (2000). Vocabulary instruction. In R. Barr, M. L. Kamil, P. B. Mosenthal, & P. D. Pearson (Eds.), *Handbook of reading research* (Vol. III, pp. 503–523). New York: Longman.

Blachowicz, C., & Fisher, P. (2002). *Teaching vocabulary in all classrooms* (2nd ed.). Columbus, OH: Prentice-Hall.

Blachowicz, C., & Fisher, P. (in press). Putting the "fun" back in fundamental: Word play in the classroom. In J. F. Baumann & E. J. Kameenui (Eds.), *Vocabulary instruction.* New York: Guilford Press.

Blachowicz, C. L. Z., Fisher, P. J. L., Costa, M., & Pozzi, M. (1993). *Researching vocabulary learning in middle school cooperative reading groups: A teacher–researcher collaboration.* Paper presented at the 10th Great Lakes Regional Reading Conference, Chicago, IL.

Buikema, J. L., & Graves, M. F. (1993). Teaching students to use context clues to infer word meanings. *Journal of Reading, 36,* 450–457.

Carlisle, J. (1995). Morphological awareness and early reading achievement. In L. Feldman (Ed.), *Morphological aspects of language processing* (pp. 189–209). Hillsdale, NJ: Erlbaum.

Carlisle, J. F. (2000). Awareness of the structure and meaning of morphologically complex words: Impact on reading. *Reading and Writing: An Interdisciplinary Journal, 12,* 169–190.

Carr, E. M., & Mazur-Stewart, M. (1988). The effects of the vocabulary overview guide on vocabulary comprehension and retention. *Journal of Reading Behavior, 20,* 43–62.

Cunningham, A. E., & Stanovich, K. E. (1998, Spring/Summer). What reading does for the mind. *American Educator,* pp. 8–17.

Dickinson, D. K., & Smith, M. W. (1994). Long-term effects of preschool teachers' book readings on low-income children's vocabulary and story comprehension. *Reading Research Quarterly. 29*(2), 104–122.

Duffelmeyer, F. A. (1980). The influence of experience-based vocabulary instruction on learning word meanings. *Journal of Reading, 24,* 35–40.

Eeds, M., & Cockrum, W. A. (1985). Teaching word meanings by expanding schemata vs. dictionary work vs. reading in context. *Journal of Reading, 28,* 492–497.

Elley, W. B. (1988). Vocabulary acquisition from listening to stories. *Reading Research Quarterly, 24,* 174–187.

Fisher, P. J. L., Blachowicz, C. L. Z., & Smith, J. C. (1991). Vocabulary learning in literature discussion groups. In J. Zutell & S. McCormick (Eds.), *Learner factors/teacher factors: Issues in literacy research and instruction* (40th Yearbook of the National Reading Conference, pp. 201–209). Chicago, IL: National Reading Conference.

Haggard, M. R. (1982). The vocabulary self-selection strategy: An active approach to word learning. *Journal of Reading, 26,* 634–642.

Haggard, M. R. (1985). An interactive strategies approach to content reading. *Journal of Reading, 29,* 204–210.

Hart, B., & Risley, T. R. (1995). *Meaningful differences in the everyday experience of young American children.* Baltimore: Brookes.

Heimlich, J. E., & Pittleman, S. D. (1986). *Semantic mapping: Classroom applications.* Newark, DE: International Reading Association.

Herman, P. A., Anderson, R. C., Pearson, P. D., & Nagy, W. E. (1987). Incidental acquisition of word meaning from expositions with varied text features. *Reading Research Quarterly, 22,* 263–284.

Jiminez, R. J. (1997). The strategic reading abilities and potential of five low-literacy Latina/o readers in middle school. *Reading Research Quarterly, 32,* 224–243.

Johnson, C. J., & Anglin, J. M. (1995). Qualitative developments in the content and form of children's definitions. *Journal of Speech and Hearing Research, 38,* 612–629.

Kuhn, M., & Stahl, S. (1998). Teaching children to learn word meanings from context: A synthesis and some questions. *Journal of Literacy Research, 30,* 119–138.

Levin, J. R. (1993). Mnemonic strategies and classroom learning: A twenty year report card. *Elementary School Journal, 94,* 235–244.

Marzano, R. J., & Marzano, J. S. (1988). *A cluster approach to elementary vocabulary instruction.* Newark, DE: International Reading Association.

McCarville, K. B. (1993). Keyword mnemonic and vocabulary acquisition for developmental college students. *Journal of Developmental Education, 16*(3), 2–4, 6.

Miller, G. A., & Gildea, P. M. (1987). How children learn words. *Scientific American, 257,* 94–99.

Nagy, W. E., Herman, P. A., & Anderson, R. C. (1985). Learning words from context. *Reading Research Quarterly, 20*, 233–253.

Nagy, W., & Scott, J (2001). Vocabulary processes. In M. L. Kamil, P. B. Mosenthal, P. D. Pearson, & R. Barr (Eds.), *Handbook of reading research* (Vol. III, pp. 269–283). New York: Longman.

National Reading Panel. (2000). *Report of the National Reading Panel: Teaching children to read.* Washington, DC: National Academy Press.

Pittelman, S. D., Heimlich, J. E., Berglund, R. L., & French, M. P. (1991). *Semantic feature analysis: Classroom applications.* Newark, DE: International Reading Association.

Roth, F., Speece, D., Cooper, D., & De La Paz, S. (1996). Unresolved mysteries: How do metalinguistic and narrative skills connect with early reading? *Journal of Special Education, 30*, 257–277.

Ruddell, M. R., & Shearer, B. A. (2002). "Extraordinary," "tremendous," "exhilarating," "magnificent": Middle school at-risk students become avid word learners with the vocabulary self-collection strategy (VSS). *Journal of Adolescent and Adult Literacy, 45*, 352–363.

Schwartz, R. M., & Raphael, T. E. (1985). Concept of definition: A key to improving students' vocabulary. *Reading Teacher, 39*, 198–205.

Scott, J., Asselin, M., Henry, S., & Butler, C. (1997, June). *Making rich language visible: Reports from a multi-dimensional study on word learning.* Paper presented at the annual meeting of the Canadian Society for the Study of Education, St. John's, Newfoundland.

Scruggs, T. E., Mastropieri, M. A., & Levin, J. R. (1985). Vocabulary acquisition of retarded students under direct mnemonic instruction. *American Journal of Mental Deficiency, 89*, 5451–5456.

Snow, C. (1991). The theoretical basis of the home–school study of language and literacy development. *Journal of Research in Childhood Education, 6*, 5–10.

Snow, C. E., Burns, M. S., & Griffin, P. (1998). *Preventing reading difficulties in young children.* Washington, DC: National Academy Press.

Stahl, S. A., & Fairbanks, M. M. (1986). The effects of vocabulary instruction: A model-based meta-analysis. *Review of Educational Research, 56*, 72–110.

Stahl, S. A., Richek, M. A., & Vandevier, R. J. (1991). Learning meaning vocabulary through listening: A sixth-grade replication. In J. Zutell & S. McCormick (Eds.), *Learner factors/teacher factors: Issues in literacy research and instruction* (40th Yearbook of the National Reading Conference, pp. 185–192). Chicago, IL: National Reading Conference.

Stahl, S., & Vancil, S. (1986). Discussion is what makes semantic maps work in vocabulary instruction. *Reading Teacher, 40*, 62–69.

Tummer, W. E., Herriman, M. L., & Nesdale, A. R. (1988). Metalinguistic abilities and beginning reading. *Reading Research Quarterly, 23*, 134–158.

Willows, D. M., & Ryan, E. B. (1986). The development of grammatical sensitivity and its relationship to early reading achievement. *Reading Research Quarterly, 21*, 253–266.

Winthrop, E. (1986). *The castle in the attic.* New York: Yearlong Books.

Wixson, K. K. (1986). Vocabulary instruction and children's comprehension of basal stories. *Reading Research Quarterly, 21*, 317–329.

Chapter 6

BEST PRACTICES
IN COMPREHENSION INSTRUCTION

Cathy Collins Block
Michael Pressley

This chapter will:

- Explore the theory, research, and current issues concerning comprehension instruction.
- Examine how comprehension is affected by word-level processes, vocabulary instruction, and above-word-level contexts.
- Describe recent developments in the teaching of comprehension processes.
- Present recently developed comprehension instructional practices, including teacher reader groups, comprehension process motion signals, following author's train of thought, and use of bookmarked texts.
- Suggest directions for future comprehension research and practice.

Past concerns in comprehension instruction were the need to develop more self-regulated readers (Pressley, 1999) and to include more research-based lessons in elementary school classrooms (Block, 1999). Even today, comprehension instruction does not occur as frequently as researchers recommend (Block, 2002a, 2002b, 2002c). In particular, processes used by skilled comprehenders are not being taught to elementary school, middle school, or high school students (Pressley, Wharton-McDonald, Mistretta, & Echevarria, 1998). As recently as 1998, many teachers believed that students could learn how to comprehend simply by doing massive reading. They did not understand how to deliver effective instruction (Block, 1999; Pressley, 1999).

More positively, much has happened in the last decade. Although we are most excited about the dramatic new hypotheses being researched that pertain to higher order comprehension processes, there have been some recent advances in understanding lower order cognition and some incremental understanding about how to teach the comprehension processes that have emerged. We begin the chapter with a review of some of these processes.

THEORY AND RESEARCH UPDATE

Since 1998, the attention to word-level processes has intensified. Such processes cannot be ignored when discussing comprehension. Comprehension of text is logically impossible when a reader cannot read the words.

Young readers must learn how to decode well, if they are to understand what they read. What has been said in previous chapters about decoding instruction is therefore directly relevant to comprehension development.

Word-Level Processes

In 1999, a panel of educational researchers and practitioners was convened to analyze research to date concerning reading instruction and to make recommendations for future research. One of the most prominent conclusions of the National Reading Panel (2000) was that young readers benefit from systematic phonics instruction when they are first learning to read words. There is a great deal of accumulated evidence that learning to sound out words is a good start on reading. That said, sounding out of words is just a start on word recognition, a way station that needs to be moved through with as much certainty as possible. When young readers are sounding out words, they have to devote a lot of mental effort to the activity. There is little mental capacity left over for comprehending either the individual word that is being sounded out or other words in the text (LaBerge & Samuels, 1974). Fortunately, what begins as sounding out and blending often becomes more automatic recognition of word chunks (e.g., *log* is at first sounded out as three sounds and then, as decoding ability increases, as two, the *l* sound and the sound of the chunk *–og*, which has been encountered previously through decoding of *dog*, *log*, and *hog* (Goswami, 2000). Recognition of chunks is easier than blending one sound at a time.

The ultimate goal of word recognition instruction, however, is fluent (i.e., instant) recognition of sight words. The correlation between fluent reading and comprehension is well established (e.g., National Reading Panel, 2000). Even more important, when fluency is developed through instruction and practice, comprehension improves (e.g., Tan & Nicholson, 1997; see also Breznitz, 1997a, 1997b). Therefore, instruction that develops fluent word recognition should be part of every reading program, for without fluent word recognition, comprehension will be compromised.

Vocabulary Instruction

The correlation between good reading and extensive vocabulary has been repeatedly verified through research and practice. Even more impressive is that teaching students vocabulary increases their comprehension skills, as was recently determined by the National Reading Panel and a second research panel convened to analyze research in the field of comprehension development, sponsored by the RAND Corporation (National Reading Panel, 2000; RAND Reading Study Group, 2002). An effective comprehension instructional program includes vocabulary instruction, for if readers cannot understand the individual words in text, they will not be able to understand the complex relationships specified by words in sentences, paragraphs, and passages.

Comprehension above the Word Level

As important as word-level processes are to skilled comprehension, making meaning from text involves much more than just the processing of individual words. Every little bit of new data about skilled comprehension that we encounter has confirmed a view that emerged in the mid-1990s: When good readers tackle text (Pressley & Afflerbach, 1995), they do all of the following:

- They generally read from the beginning to the end of a text, although they sometimes jump around, looking ahead in anticipation of information, or looking back to clarify an idea not understood on the first pass.
- They encounter information especially relevant to their goal in reading the text (e.g., to find out the President's perspective on educational vouchers).
- They anticipate what might be in the text based on their prior knowledge about the topic of the text.
- They monitor as they read; that is, while reading, they are very aware of which parts of a text are important, and which ideas are vague or confusing. Such self-monitoring guides decision making during reading (e.g., deciding to slow up, read faster, or skip sections of text).
- They reflect on what they read, for example, thinking about how they might use the ideas in the text. Such reflections can be interpretive, often affected by prior knowledge and present opinions.

In short, good readers are very active and strategic as they read. The research-based understanding that good reading is active reading, of course, motivates instructors to encourage young readers to be actively and intentionally strategic as they read. One approach to such comprehension processes instruction has more support than others.

Comprehension Processes Instruction

Comprehension processes instruction begins with teacher modeling and explanation of a single comprehension process. Comprehension processes can be defined as a set of meaning-making skills, strategies, and thought processes that readers initiate at specific points in a text to understand, apply, and appreciate authors' writings. Although the teacher's goal is to develop readers who are active, who use a repertoire of comprehension processes (e.g., prediction, questioning, imagery, relating to prior knowledge, monitoring and seeking clarification, summarization), she typically begins with instructing one process at a time.

Quite often, the first process taught is prediction, based on prior knowledge. In doing so, many teachers explain to students that good readers often make guesses about what will occur in a text. The teacher then models how she applies her background knowledge to the first few pages read, initiating predictive thinking processes based on the title of the story and then on the pictures. Once reading of the story begins, the teacher pauses to perform a think-aloud to demonstrate what textual feature prompted her to make a predictive inference about what might be coming up in the text. A few lines or paragraphs later, the teacher might then model awareness of whether the prediction, in fact, occurred in the story. Over the course of a few weeks, the teacher frequently describes the mental processes involved in prediction, encouraging students to make predictions, and continues to do so until the students are making predictions on their own.

Then, it is time to introduce a second process, perhaps imagery. Again, the teacher explains, thinks aloud, and models this mental process, perhaps during read-alouds. The teacher progressively demands more of the students, including that they use both predictions and imagery while processing text. Once the teacher senses that students are comfortable using the two processes together, it is time to introduce a third process, and then a fourth, until the entire repertoire of processes is introduced.

It can take a while for a teacher to introduce a full repertoire of comprehension processes, perhaps most of a year. Even then, it is far from certain that all students will be using the processes fluently (Pressley et al., 1992), although a semester to a year of comprehension processes instruction produced clear comprehension benefits, as assessed in a variety of ways, including standardized reading tests (Anderson, 1992; Block & Mangieri, 1995, 1996a, 1996b; Brown, Pressley, van Meter, & Schuder, 1996; Collins, 1991).

Much of comprehension processes instruction takes place in small reading groups that resemble guided reading groups. As students take turns reading, they are encouraged to report which mental processes they are using as they experience a text. Usually, there is a poster in the small reading group corner of the room that summarizes the repertoire, a simple list, of the processes. Comprehension processes most often taught are as follows:

- Prediction is defined as the ability to apply appropriate background experiences to authors' trains of thought, so that students imagine upcoming events prior to their appearance in text. To be successful, students must infer, combine details, and follow main ideas. Teachers often use books that have predictable story plots or repetitive phrases to develop these abilities.

- Questioning is the ability to monitor one's reading. Teachers must help students develop the ability to recognize when they misunderstand a word, sentence, or idea. Then, students must learn how to reread, determine where the confusion occurred, and ask what mental processes might be called on to make meaning. Teachers introduce specific types of questions that students can ask themselves as they read, such as "Have I misunderstood a word that has caused me to become confused?", "Do I need to reread?", "What is the main idea?", "Is this a fact or an opinion?", or "Do I agree with this point?"

- Imagery, the ability to create a mental image from the words read, is taught by developing students' abilities to add details present in single sentences to ongoing events and descriptions that authors portray. Most often, less able readers have greater difficulty initiating this process than other comprehension processes. Many students require repeated instruction, using a wide variety of genres and hands-on manipulative exercises, before they can visualize concrete and, later, abstract concepts as they read.

- Relating to prior knowledge is the ability to integrate new information with previous life experiences and texts read. This mental process is taught as an important thought process that students use prior to, during, and after reading to improve retention and use of material read (Block, 1999). Teachers often help students develop this ability by performing think-alouds that demonstrate how key words in a text stimulate relevant prior reading and life events, so that the depth of an author's meaning can be understood, felt, valued, and retained.

- Monitoring one's reading is the ability to discern which types of text are most interesting, which authorial writing patterns one most enjoys, which environmental conditions can minimize distractions when one reads, and which processes are needed to increase one's motivation and comprehension when reading becomes difficult. Each of the meaning-making skills and thought processes involved in self-monitoring are usually introduced separately; then, students are asked to use more than one of these processes while reading.

- Seeking clarification requires that teachers demonstrate several methods of gaining meaning whenever confusion arises. Among the most frequently taught methods are the ability to reread; to question themselves, peers, and teachers; to use dictionaries; and to seek reference materials. Seeking clarification also requires that students possess the desire to achieve a complete understanding, to persist when difficulties arise and enjoy savoring subtle differences in exact word choices. Teachers know that motivational, volitional, and comprehension processes are interspersed (and often must be taught) before many students can learn to seek clarification while reading.

• Summarizing, a process that is assessed on many high-stake tests, is the ability to delete irrelevant details, combine similar ideas, condense main ideas, and connect major themes into concise statements that capture the purpose of a reading for the reader. Each of the abilities necessary to execute the summarizing process are usually taught separately and repeatedly practiced.

Regardless of the mental process taught, when students are unable to report that they are using it, teachers most often prompt them with statements such as the following:

"Make certain that you let us know what comprehension processes you are choosing and using." "Good readers are active when they read. I hope you choose to use several processes as you read." The teacher consistently sends the message that students should choose to be cognitively active, for the goal is self-regulated comprehension processes use. Self-regulation is all about students taking action on their own to comprehend, not about students responding to explicit prompts to use specific comprehension processes. Thus, in comprehension processes instruction the goal is for a teacher to never have to say to a student, "It is time to make images," or "This is where you should summarize."

Comprehension processes instruction is about encouraging young readers to be cognitively active as they read, just the way that mature, excellent readers are active cognitively. Consistent with a Vygotsky's (1978) perspective, it begins with input from a more knowledgeable other, the teacher, who models and explains use of comprehension processes. Then, students practice using processes with other students, with the many exchanges providing students practice in using processes and feedback about their use of mental comprehension processes (e.g., when a student makes an unjustified association to material in the text, other students in the group let her or him know). Gradually, students begin to use the processes on their own, both when they are reading with one another (e.g., during pair reading) and when they are reading on their own. Processes that were once carried out interpersonally are now carried out intrapersonally, consistent with the Vygotskian perspective on the internalization of cognitive processes.

What is new with respect to comprehension processes instruction? Quite honestly, there is less progress than we would like, although we were pleased that it was documented to be an effective research-based practice in both the National Reading Panel (2000) report and in the work of the RAND Reading Study Group (2002); that is, discerning researchers and practitioners have carefully reviewed this approach and the work supporting it, and have found it to be beneficial.

Summary

For children to become good comprehenders, they need to become fluent in word recognition processes, to acquire an extensive vocabulary, and to learn to be active in the ways that excellent, mature readers are active. Fortunately, word recognition, vocabulary, and comprehension processes can be taught. Fluent word recognition, extensive vocabulary development, and proficient use of comprehension processes depend very much, however, on young readers doing a great deal of reading. Extensive reading enables students to practice both word-level and above-word-level mental processing interchangably. The impact of extensive reading is likely to be maximally positive if children are reading the good stuff: stories and books that are excellent literature, informational texts that connect to important scientific, mathematical, and social scientific concepts. When that happens, children have prior knowledge that permits powerful predictions about what might occur in a text; their images are informed just as the visions of bright people are informed, and they are able to summarize text that connects interpretively to important ideas. In short, the cognitive activity stimulated by comprehension processes instruction is more mature and complete when the reader has extensive prior knowledge, developed in part through reading.

WHAT ELSE IS NEW? WHAT HYPOTHESES ARE EMERGING FROM OUR WORK?

During the last 5 years, we have visited numerous classrooms and interacted with thousands of teachers and educational decision makers across America and around the world. In a 2-year longitudinal study involving 400 teachers in Georgia, Texas, Maine, Florida, Colorado, Illinois, and New Jersey, researchers have examined changes that are occurring in schools, focusing on what happens when students are taught to read as excellent readers read (i.e., when they are taught sophisticated comprehension processes; Block, 2002d; Block & Johnson, 2003). An important aspect of the research is to measure the professional development required to create teachers who can help students automatize comprehension processes (Block, 2002d; Mangieri, 2002).

A lot of good news is emerging from this work:

• More teachers in this sample are teaching comprehension processes than when Wharton-McDonald, Pressley, and Hampston (1998)
observed teachers in the mid-1990s. For example, we have observed many
teachers doing think-alouds, relating to students how to look ahead, predict, clarify, and summarize as they read. As teachers think-aloud during
read-alouds, the role of prior knowledge in comprehension is salient, with
many reflections about how ideas encountered in new text relate to ideas
already known by the teacher–reader; that is, they are teaching students
how to make inferences by combining ideas in text with ideas in prior
knowledge. These teachers make it clear that students have goals when
they read. Sometimes, teachers display and explain graphics that portray
mental processes they want students to use during silent reading. In short,
teachers are letting students know that meaning is crafted through not
only activity, mostly cognitive activity, but also through overt activities such
as drawing pictures and making notes (Bakhtin, 1993; Block, 1999;
Bloome, 1986; Rosenblatt, 1978). This is not so much direct instruction
as it is modeling and explanation (see Duffy, 2003) of sophisticated response to literature (Block, 1999, 2002a, 2002b, 2002c, 2002d; Block,
Gambrell, & Pressley, 2003; Block & Johnson, 2003).
   • Professional development is necessary for the majority of teachers to begin comprehension processes instruction. For example, they require formal instruction about thinking aloud, as well as creating and
explaining graphic depictions of mental processes. In fact, the whole idea
of comprehension processes instruction playing a dominating role in reading instruction is so novel for most teachers that several days of professional instruction may be required (e.g., before beginning to use the
approach in the classroom, after beginning it, and as it becomes routine
during reading instruction but is still not being used throughout the
school day).
   • The students in the classrooms we observed seem to be learning
the comprehension processes their teachers are now modeling and teaching, as reflected by state tests and other assessments. This process of process internalization undoubtedly is helped initially by the many tips provided by teachers about when to use comprehension processes (e.g.,
"When there is a difficult part in a reading, I suggest you . . ."). It is also
helped by the many reminders to use processes (e.g., "What do you think
will be the most important comprehension processes you will use in reading this article?"). Perhaps a prime mover in students' actual use of these
processes is that the newer forms of instruction demand students' awareness and self-monitoring. In particular, students are often asked to describe to one another the processes they are using to comprehend text

(Block & Johnson, 2003), which encourages a great deal of metacognitive reflection about comprehension processing. As a result, students are often observed reporting their choices to use specific processes as they tackle new texts (i.e., they transfer the processes they are taught). Often, such processing seems natural and automatic, suggesting that active comprehension processing is becoming a habit of mind.

• Students in classrooms that use comprehension processes instruction seem to enjoy reading.

• More reading occurs in such classrooms, providing many opportunities for students to fall in love with quality literature (Block, 2002b).

• Buddy reading also seems to have increased in prominence in elementary classrooms in the past 4 years (Block & Dellamura, 2000/2001).

• Students are receiving a good deal of instruction about how to figure out the meaning of new words based on context clues.

All that said, we find ourselves hoping for more. We would like to see more student choice in reading lessons and greater encouragement of students to read a great deal, including many more communications to students that reading provides great pleasure, and that choosing to read is choosing to do something that is fun. We would also like to see more emphasis on students' choosing to be strategic, to be impressed more with the message than to be in charge of their reading and the processes they use during reading, that is, with the idea that they are to become self-regulated readers. Perhaps if that emphasis on self-regulation were heightened, there would be more automatic transfer of mental comprehension processes to novel texts, for there certainly is room for improvement with respect to transfer. Yes, we sometimes see evidence of it (Bogner, Raphael, & Pressley, 2002), but much more often, we have witnessed students carrying out processes only when prompted by the teacher to do so (Block, 2002d; Mangieri, 2002). What we have not seen inspires the closing for this chapter.

WHAT WE ARE WORKING ON NOW

We are convinced that students only become independent comprehension process users through opportunities and demands that they use comprehension processes on their own. One productive way for this to occur is that students read to each other in small groups, with the requirement that they think aloud as they read, that they report the comprehension processes they are using to understand text (i.e., teacher–reader groups in which students talk about the comprehension processes they are using; Block, 1999). In the context of a reading program with much instruction about effective comprehension processing, students often will have much to report about their own processing, especially once they become accustomed to thinking aloud during small-group reading. These groups are filled with metacognitive commentary. Students are asking each other questions about how they find main ideas, make inferences, construct predictions, draw conclusions, and overcome confusions (Block & Johnson, 2003). They talk about what goes on in their minds as they figure out where the author is going with a text and what unfamiliar words might mean (Block & Johnson, 2003). A lot of student self-initiated effort is expended in understanding what is being read (Block, 2002a).

A useful adjunctive activity is to teach students to use hand gestures to signal the various comprehension processes (see Figure 6.1). These gestures not only depict the mental comprehension processes (and hence, make them more comprehensibly concrete to the reader) but they also make salient to members of the group when the reader is making a prediction, drawing conclusions, visualizing, and so on. The hand signals enable students to depict the thought processes they are initiating, without their teacher prompting them to do so. These signals also make potentially abstract cognitive actions more concrete for children (e.g., students see that the mental activity of drawing conclusions is similar to the movement that occurs when hands spread apart come together as conclusions are reached). An added benefit is that the teacher gets a great deal of information about the type of cognitive processing in which individual students believe they are engaged, when they do so without prompting, which permits the teacher to provide corrective instruction, if needed, and to visualize when a specific comprehension is becoming automatic for a student.

Another approach to deepen students' processing of text is to encourage small groups of young readers to follow authors' trains of thought (Block, 2002c; Block & Johnson, 2003; Smolkin & Donovan, 2001). Students are taught to pay particular attention to the first two pages of a book, to determine how authors connect sentences and paragraphs, as well as how they construct summaries. The students make diagrams specifying the intratext connections after they become proficient in recognizing several authors' trains of thought. They also learn how to make and describe diagrams depicting how the content and writing style of the current text is similar in structure to other texts in the same discipline or content area. Of course, the goal is for the students to become facile in carrying out these processes on their own (see Figure 6.2 for a summary of the steps in such instructional lessons).

The research discussed illustrates that we are developing approaches to increase the active mental processing of students as they read text. The assumption is that as students learn how to be active in groups, they will

Upper Left: Clarify (Can you clarify the word that they author used)

Upper Center: Feelings (That page made me feel _____)

Upper Right: Connections (In my mind, I'm making a connection between what the author said and _____)

Lower Left: Prediction (I'm predicting that _____. My reasons for making this prediction are _____. I'm basing my decision on _____.)

Lower Center: Perspective (I've changed my perspective because _____)

Lower Right: Asking Questions (I've got this question in my mind: _____. That makes me wonder: _____)

FIGURE 6.1. Example of six comprehension process motions for the comprehension processes of (1) clarifying, (2) experiencing an affective response to a text, (3) making connections, (4) making predictions, (5) changing one's

- **Step 1:** Diagram sentence-to-sentence connections on first seven paragraphs.

- **Step 2:** Diagram paragraph-to-paragraph connections on first seven paragraphs.

- **Step 3:** Diagram summary method used by author.

- **Step 4:** Describe depth of author's style:

    Level 3: (very dense) Dense vocabulary; complex sentence structure; long paragraphs; many deep ideas.

    Level 2: (average density) Average vocabulary; compound sentence structure; average paragraphs; some deep ideas per paragraph.

    Level 1: (low density) Low vocabulary; simple sentence structure; short paragraphs; few deep ideas per paragraph.

- **Step 5:** Diagram intra- and intertext connections.

FIGURE 6.2. The first two pages are critical: Teaching students text-specific comprehension processes (teaching students to follow the author's train of thought as soon as they start to read).

begin to internalize the activities as individuals (Vygotsky, 1978) and use the processes practiced together as they read new texts alone. That said, much remains to be done, with great challenges.

An obvious challenge is that children read many more stories than expository texts, yet the world demands that readers be able to deal with informational texts that provide the vast amounts of new information entering the marketplace of ideas daily. People must do more and faster reading than ever before. Moreover, the information is being conveyed in both traditional media (e.g., books) and recently invented media (e.g., the Internet). The barrage of messages on the Internet alone demands new skills. For example, Internet texts are not vetted nearly as carefully as traditional print. Hence, readers must learn more and better discernment skills, which are necessary to help readers recognize what needs to be bookmarked later (e.g., with post-it notes, electronic and otherwise), for much information needs to be retrievable later, when it is needed, rather than read now! In short, the repertoire of comprehension processes being taught to students must expand as the repertoire of text types and processing demands increases. Much work needs to be done to invent ever more effective instructional approaches to assist students to effectively comprehend our ever-increasing variety of textual formats.

DISCUSSION AND ACTIVITIES

1. Readers of this chapter can rate their abilities to teach comprehension.
2. Readers of this chapter can begin to incorporate into their teaching some of the instructional suggestions in the chapter.
3. Readers can set their own agendas as to how they would like to improve their teaching of students' text processing. They might make pre- and postvideotapes or audiotapes of their teaching of comprehension, describe comprehension processes in action through think-alouds, diagrams, and hand signals. They can begin by demonstrating the comprehension process motion signals depicted in Figure 6.1. They can also begin to teach students to analyze authors' writing styles, by following the sequences of processing steps described in Figure 6.2. Readers are encouraged to work with other teachers to share ideas while attempting to implement the approaches covered in this chapter, such as engaging in a book study in which methods are taught and shared on a monthly basis at faculty meetings or in college courses.

REFERENCES

Anderson, V. (1992). A teacher development project in transactional strategy instruction for teachers of severely reading-disabled adolescents. *Teaching and Teacher Education, 8,* 391–403.

Bakhtin, M. M. (1993). *Toward a philosophy of the act* (V. Laipunov & M. Holquist, Trans.). Austin: University of Texas Press.

Block, C. C. (1999). Comprehension: Crafting understanding. In L. B. Gambrell, L. M. Morrow, S. B. Neuman, & M. Pressley (Eds.), *Best practices in literacy instruction* (pp. 98–118). New York: Guilford Press.

Block, C. C. (2002a, May). *New advancements in comprehension instruction.* Paper presented at the annual meeting of the International Reading Association. San Francisco, CA.

Block, C. C. (2002b, May). *New instructional strategies for non-fictional text.* Paper presented at the annual meeting of the International Reading Association, San Francisco, CA.

Block, C. C. (2002c). Helping children comprehend non-fiction: What we know, what we can do, and what we still need to learn. *California Reader, 35*(2), 3–11.

Block, C. C. (2002d, December). *Effects of professional development activities on students' reading achievement.* Paper presented at the annual meeting of the National Reading Conference. Miami, FL.

Block, C. C., & Dellamura, R. (2000/2001). Better book buddies. *The Reading Teacher, 54*(4), 364–370.

Block, C. C., Gambrell, L. B., & Pressley, M. (Eds.). (2003). *Improving comprehension instruction: Rethinking research theory and classroom practice.* San Francisco, CA and Newark, DE: Jossey-Bass and International Reading Association.

Block, C. C., & Johnson, R. (2003). Thinking process approach to comprehension instruction. In C. C. Block, L. Gambrell, & M. Pressley (Eds.), *Improving comprehension instruction* (pp. 54–80). San Francisco CA and Newark DE: Jossey-Bass and International Reading Association.

Block, C. C., & Mangieri, J. N. (1995). *Reason to read: Thinking strategies for life through literature* (Vol. 1). Boston, MA: Allyn & Bacon.

Block, C. C., & Mangieri, J. N. (1996a). *Reason to read: Thinking strategies for life through literature* (Vol. 2). Boston, MA: Allyn & Bacon.

Block, C. C., & Mangieri, J. N. (1996b). *Reason to read: Thinking strategies for life through literature* (Vol. 3). Boston, MA: Allyn & Bacon.

Bloome, D. (1986). Building literacy and the classroom community. *Theory Into Practice, 15,* 71–76.

Bogner, K., Raphael, L. M., & Pressley, M. (2002). How grade-1 teachers motivate literate activity by their students. *Scientific Studies of Reading, 6,* 135–165.

Breznitz, Z. (1997a). Effects of accelerated reading rate on memory for text among dyslexic readers. *Journal of Educational Psychology, 89,* 289–297.

Breznitz, Z. (1997b). Enhancing the reading of dyslexic children by reading acceleration and auditory masking. *Journal of Educational Psychology, 89,* 103–113.

Brown, R., Pressley, M., van Meter, P., & Schuder, T. (1996). A quasi-experimental validation of transactional strategies instruction with low-achieving second grade readers. *Journal of Educational Psychology, 88,* 18–37.

Collins, C. (1991). Reading instruction that increases thinking abilities. *Journal of Reading, 34,* 510–516.

Duffy (2003). *Expanded explanations: A resource for teaching concepts, skills, and strategies.* New York: Guilford Press.

Goswami, U. (2000). Phonological and lexical processes. In M. Kamil, P. B. Mosenthal, P. D. Pearson, & R. Barr (Eds.), *Handbook of reading research* (Vol. III, pp. 251–267). Mahwah, NJ: Erlbaum.

LaBerge, D., & Samuels, S. J. (1974). Toward a theory of automatic information processing in reading. *Cognitive Psychology, 6,* 293–323.

Mangieri, J. (2002, October). *Effective reading teachers.* Paper presented at the California State University Researchers Conference. Los Angeles, CA.

National Reading Panel. (2000). *Teaching children to read: An evidence-based assessment of the scientific research literature on reading and its implications for reading instruction: Reports of the subgroups.* Washington, DC: National Institute of Child Health and Human Development.

Pressley, M. (1999). Self-regulated comprehension processing and its development through instruction. In L. B. Gambrell, L. M. Morrow, S. B. Neuman, & M. Pressley (Eds.), *Best practices in literacy instruction* (pp. 90–97). New York: Guilford Press.

Pressley, M., & Afflerbach, P. (1995). *Verbal protocols of reading: The nature of constructively responsive reading.* Hillsdale, NJ: Erlbaum.

Pressley, M., El-Dinary, P. B., Gaskins, I., Schuder, T., Bergman, J., Almasi, J., & Brown, R. (1992). Beyond direct explanation: Transactional instruction of reading comprehension strategies. *Elementary School Journal, 92,* 511–554.

Pressley, M., Wharton-McDonald, R., Mistretta, J., & Echevarria, R. (1998). Effective beginning literacy instruction: Dialectical, scaffolded, and contextualized. In J. L. Metsala & L. C. Ehri (Eds.), *Word recognition in beginning literacy* (pp. 357–373). Mahwah, NJ: Erlbaum.

RAND Reading Study Group. (2002). *Reading for understanding: Toward an R&D program in reading comprehension.* Arlington, VA: RAND.

Rosenblatt, L. M. (1978). *The reader, the text, the poem: The transactional theory of the literary work.* Carbondale: Southern Illinois University Press.

Smolkin, L. B., & Donovan, C. A. (2001). "Oh, excellent, excellent question!": Developmental differences and comprehension acquisition. In C. C. Block & M. Pressley (Eds.), *Comprehension instruction: Research-based best practices* (pp. 140–158). New York: Guilford Press.

Tan, A., & Nicholson, T. (1997). Flashcards revisited: Training poor readers to read words faster improves their comprehension of text. *Journal of Educational Psychology, 89,* 276–288.

Vygotsky, L. S. (1978). *Mind in society: The development of higher psychological processes.* Cambridge, MA: Harvard University Press.

Wharton-McDonald, R., Pressley, M., & Hampston, J. M. (1998). Outstanding literacy instruction in first grade: Teacher practices and student achievement. *Elementary School Journal, 99,* 101–128.

Chapter 7

FLUENCY IN THE CLASSROOM: STRATEGIES FOR WHOLE-CLASS AND GROUP WORK

Melanie R. Kuhn

This chapter will:

- Review the role of fluency in the overall reading process.
- Discuss the components of fluent reading and how they contribute to reading development.
- Identify effective ways of integrating fluency instruction into the classroom literacy curriculum.
- Provide a simple measure for assessing the fluency of students in your classroom (the National Assessment of Educational Progress Oral Reading Fluency Scale [NAEP, 1995]).

When looking over those articles, chapters, and books that have dealt with fluency development over the past two decades, it becomes clear that their authors consider fluent reading to be a critical component of reading development (Allington, 1983; Chomsky, 1976; Dowhower, 1991; Optiz & Rasinski, 1998; Reutzel, 1996). This is due to the role of fluent reading in the overall reading process. There is a general consensus that fluent reading not only incorporates automatic and accurate word recognition and expressive rendering of text, but it is also likely to be a contributing factor to a reader's ability to construct meaning from what is being read (Kuhn & Stahl, 2000; National Reading Panel, 2000). Despite its importance to the reading process, however, these authors note that fluency development often has been overlooked as an instructional component of reading, both in the schools' literacy curricula and in the pre- and inservice courses designed for teacher development.

More recently, however, fluency has begun to be the focus of a greater amount of attention. A number of authors argue that it is not only deserving of instructional time within the classroom but that it is also an aspect of literacy learning that can make a significant difference in a student's success as a reader (Allington, 2001; Cunningham, 2000; Kuhn & Stahl, 2000; National Reading Panel, 2000; Rasinski & Padak, 2001). Furthermore, whereas previous research on fluency development has emphasized an increase in speed and accuracy, one unique component of this renewed interest has been the emphasis on expressive reading, or those aspects of reading that comprise prosody, as well as its connection to students' comprehension (Dowhower, 1991; Kuhn, 2000; Schreiber, 1991).

However, despite the recent renewal of interest in fluency instruction, one problem with a number of strategies designed to promote fluency development is that the approaches have been created for working with individual learners (see Kuhn & Stahl, 2000). These learners fall into two primary categories. The first consist of readers who experience difficulty making the transition from purposeful decoding, in which they need to work in order to identify virtually every word they encounter, to fluent reading. Such students are most often found in the second or third grade. The second category consists of older students who have been struggling with this transition for an extended period (Kuhn, 2000). One of the primary strategies designed to assist both categories of students is that of repeated readings (Dowhower, 1989; LaBerge & Samuels, 1974). In addition to repeated readings, there are a number of variations on this approach (e.g., Ash & Hagood, 2000; Herman, 1985; O'Shea, Sindelar, & O'Shea, 1985), as well as alternative strategies, including the Neurological Impress Method (Hollingsworth, 1970, 1978) and reading while listening (Carbo, 1978; Chomsky, 1976, 1978).

Although these strategies are highly effective in the development of fluent reading, they are not easily adopted as part of the classroom curriculum because teachers rarely have the opportunity to work extensively with individual students (Achilles, 1999; Nagel, 2001). Luckily, a number of highly effective strategies are designed for use with the whole class, pairs, or group work. Such literacy instruction includes paired repeated readings (Koskinen & Blum, 1986), fluency-oriented reading instruction (Stahl, Heubach, & Cramond, 1997), and the expressive rendering of texts through readers' theater (Allington, 2001; Bidwell, 1990; Henning, 1974; Optiz & Rasinski, 1998). In reviewing these strategies, my goals for this chapter are twofold. The central purpose is to identify effective ways for teachers in the primary grades to integrate fluency-oriented reading instruction into a broader literacy curriculum, while simultaneously emphasizing students' ability to construct meaning from text. However, before I outline effective ways to implement these strategies, it is necessary to explore the importance of fluency in the overall reading process as a means of determining the worth of such instruction.

FLUENCY'S ROLE IN THE READING PROCESS

Although there is no single definition of fluency (Ruetzel, 1996), there does appear to be a consensus regarding its primary components: accurate decoding; automatic word recognition; and the appropriate use of stress, pitch, and suitable phrasing, or the prosodic elements of language. Given that the ultimate goal of reading is the construction of meaning from text (e.g., Anderson, Hiebert, Scott, & Wilkinson, 1985), it is important to determine the role that fluency plays in a reader's comprehension. There are two primary ways in which fluency contributes to a reader's understanding of text (Kuhn & Stahl, 2000). The first focuses on the contribution of automatic word recognition, whereas the second incorporates prosody.

CONTRIBUTION OF AUTOMATIC WORD RECOGNITION TO COMPREHENSION

Proficient readers have certain features in common when it comes to word recognition; they not only identify words accurately, they also recognize them quickly. In other words, they have achieved automaticity and no longer need to spend time decoding the vast majority of words they encounter in text. Given that automatic word recognition is prerequisite to becoming a skilled reader, and skilled readers can construct meaning from text, the question becomes, in what ways does this automatic word recognition help lead to reading comprehension? According to several authors (Adams, 1990; LaBerge & Samuels, 1974; Perfetti, 1985; Stanovich, 1980), individuals have a limited amount of attention available for reading. This being the case, attention expended on one component of reading is, necessarily, attention that is unavailable for another. When reading, individuals necessarily perform two interdependent tasks: They must both decode the words present in a text and at the same time construct that text's meaning. Given that these two processes occur simultaneously, the greater the amount of attention expended on word identification, the less that remains available for comprehension. In order to ensure that readers have enough attention available to understand texts adequately, it is necessary for them to develop their decoding to the point that each word is recognized instantaneously. Once readers have established such automaticity, they will have freed up the attention necessary to focus upon meaning.

When considering this issue in terms of fluency development, the question that follows becomes, how do learners make the shift from decoding accurately but deliberately, to decoding automatically? According to a number of authors (e.g., Allington, 2001; Anderson et al., 1985; Cunningham, 2000; Rasinski & Padak, 2001), the most effective way to ensure that this transition occurs is through extensive practice. As with any skill that requires the coordination of a series of smaller steps to create a unified action, practice assists learners in becoming skilled readers. In the case of reading, this practice consists primarily in repeated exposures to connected text. In other words, the key to the development of students' automatic word recognition is the provision of extensive opportunities to read a wide variety of connected text. As words become increasingly familiar to the learner, less attention needs to be directed toward decoding them, with automatic word recognition as the result. However, there is an important and often overlooked (Dowhower, 1991; Schreiber, 1991) aspect of fluency that remains to be addressed, that of prosody.

CONTRIBUTION OF PROSODY

Although automatic word recognition accounts for accurate and effortless decoding, it does not account for the role prosody plays in fluent reading (Kuhn & Stahl, 2000). When discussing fluency, there is a tacit understanding that it involves more than simply reading the words quickly and accurately; it also involves reading with expression. Implicit in the term "reading with expression" is the use of those prosodic features that account for the tonal and rhythmic aspects of language (Dowhower, 1991; Schreiber, 1991). These prosodic features include pitch or intonation, stress or emphasis, tempo or rate, the rhythmic or regularly reoccurring patterns of language, and the use of appropriate phrasing.

Prosody's Role in Fluent Reading

It is commonly noted that children who are not fluent read either in a word-by-word manner or by grouping words in ways that deviate from the phrasing that occurs naturally in oral language (Allington, 1983; Dowhower, 1991; Rasinski, 1989; Reutzel, 1996; Schreiber, 1991). Conversely, appropriate phrasing, intonation, and stress are all seen as indicators of fluent reading (Chall, 1996; Chomsky, 1976, 1978; Dowhower, 1991; Rasinski & Padak, 1996; Schreiber, 1991). By incorporating such prosodic elements into their oral reading, readers are providing clues to an otherwise invisible process, that of comprehension. It is through their grouping of print into meaningful phrases that fluent readers make written text sound like oral language. Furthermore, their use of expression can be seen as an indicator of their understanding of what is being read because they can only begin to apply appropriate phrasing and expression to a text if they are able to make sense of it. It is this prosodic reading, in conjunction with accurate and automatic word recognition, that makes for a fluent rendering of a text.

INTEGRATING FLUENCY INSTRUCTION INTO THE LITERACY CURRICULUM

Given our understanding of the importance of fluent reading, the question then becomes how can we promote fluency development within the classroom. Reading with expression is something for which we always strive as part of our literacy instruction; however, it becomes a primary focus of reading development during the second and third grades (Chall, 1996; Stahl et al., 1997). Prior to this, emergent literacy behaviors and word recognition strategies are becoming established. It is important during this earlier period to provide extensive modeling of fluent reading for students and to provide them with numerous opportunities to practice the skills they are learning as part of their developing literacy. It is also essential that students be taught that reading is a meaning-making process, and that comprehension is the principal reason for reading any text. However, during the second and third grades, fluent reading becomes a primary focus. This emphasis provides students with the opportunity to gain comfort and familiarity with print and to establish their ability as automatic and expressive readers who can make sense of what they are reading. Although far and away the majority of fluency strategies were designed for individual learners, many classroom teachers face class sizes and time constraints that prevent them from viewing these approaches as practical (Achilles, 1999; Nagel, 2001). As a result, the strategies I present in the remainder of this chapter can be integrated into classrooms without demanding individualized instruction on the part of the teacher.

Paired Repeated Readings

The first strategy, that of paired repeated readings, was designed as a means of taking a successful approach to fluency development and making it more classroom-friendly. Repeated reading in its original form has proven to be a highly effective strategy for improving the fluency of readers. However, since it requires the teacher or tutor to record the students' rate and miscues, it is usually difficult for her or him to work with more than a few students over the course of the day. Koskinen and Blum (1984, 1986) had this in mind when they developed paired repeated reading as an alternative to the original. This strategy was designed so that students work with one another, rather than the teacher, to improve their reading fluency. As with repeated readings, students read a selection several times as a means of improving their word recognition. However, there are a number of variations derived from the original strategy. Most fundamentally, rather than working individually with the teacher, the students work with one another in pairs. To prepare the students for this work, the teacher spends time with them, explaining how to provide positive feedback for their partners. This training teaches the students to act as a coach for their partner and ensures that any comments are designed to assist in one another's fluency development. This includes teaching the students to respond positively to their partner's use of expression and improvements in her or his word recognition.

The students then select an approximately 50-word passage from the material they are currently reading as part of their classroom literacy curriculum. This material can be selected from either a basal reader or a trade book, and should have been introduced through an expressive oral reading by the teacher. However, Koskinen and Blum (1986) suggest that, if the students are using the same text, then each student in the pair selects different passages in order to minimize a "direct comparison of reading proficiency" (p. 71). Students should also decide who is to read aloud first, and creating an alternating schedule can be effective in minimizing disputes. For the initial reading, students are to read their passage silently. The first partner then reads her or his passage aloud to her or his partner a total of three times. During each reading, the partner listens carefully and, after the second and third attempt, he or she comments on ways in which the performance has improved. The partner also records the improvements on a listening sheet. After completing the passage, the reader also assesses her or his own performance, recording how well the rendition went on a self-evaluation sheet. After the first reader has completed her or his turn, the pair switches roles and the other partner reads her or his passage following the same format.

Because paired repeated reading can be used with the entire class or reading group, it is easy to integrate into the literacy curriculum. For example, it can take the place of independent seatwork or be used in a flexible grouping format. In order to optimize the pairings, I would suggest dividing the class in half according to reading ability and pair the strongest reader in the first half of the class with the strongest reader from the second half. This minimizes the discrepancy between the readers and maximizes the benefits for both partners. Paired repeated readings seems to have many of the benefits of the original procedure, with students improving in terms of both accurate and automatic word recognition, a key component of fluent reading. Furthermore, because reading with expression is part of the performance criteria, the students are likely to integrate this element into their reading of the passages. As with the original procedure, it appears that the improvements made on the practiced material transfer to previously unread text.

Reader's Theater

The next approach, that of reader's theater (Allington, 2001; Bidwell, 1990; Henning, 1974; Optiz & Rasinski, 1998), can be used with groups of students or the entire classroom. One advantage of this approach is that children really enjoy practicing material for performance. A second advantage is that it provides a real purpose for the repetition. Third, it is a method that can be used with virtually any reading material, including poetry and nonfiction (Hoyt, 2000), which tends to be under-utilized in the primary grades (Duke, 1999). There are two distinct ways to implement reader's theater in the classroom. The first is to have the students practice with plays that have been written specifically for children, examples of which are often available through the literature anthologies and basal readers used in many classrooms. Books of plays are often available through the school or public library as well. The second involves having the students rewrite a story or portion of a text as a performance piece. However, rather than creating an all-out performance, reader's theater pieces are meant to be ad hoc experiences. There is no need to create a set, use props, or design costumes in order to implement a reader's theater piece. In fact, students are not even required to memorize their parts! Instead, the students are expected to create their performance entirely through their expressive reading of the text. In order to achieve this, students need to practice their lines, while keeping in mind what it is that they wish to express through their role. Because they are not able to rely on props to assist them in telling their story, their performance is entirely dependent on their reading with appropriate expression.

As with paired repeated readings, reader's theater is designed to promote the automatic word recognition that is essential to fluency development. In addition, this method emphasizes the importance of appropriate expression as a means of relaying the text's meaning. The procedure involves a number of steps. To start with, it is important to select material that you believe can be adapted easily for reading out loud. Should you decided to have the students select the text, it is important to remind them that whatever they choose will be adapted into a script, and to bear in mind that it is something they will eventually perform. If you use material other than a play, it is possible for you to rewrite the text as a script. It is also possible to use a writing workshop as a venue for having the students rewrite the story in a script format themselves. Should you decide to do this, it is important to identify the elements that are required for a script and to guide students in their adaptation of the text. Next, the students should each be provided with a copy of either a play or a script. It is useful to read the text to the students, so that they can develop a sense of the story's rhythm before they begin practicing the script themselves. It is also helpful to have them read the story independently, in order to feel comfortable with the material.

The next step is for the students to begin practicing their parts. Depending on the length of the text, you may want to divide the students into groups, in order to ensure that each student has a role that he or she will be responsible for performing. Alternatively, you can have students read portions of the text in pairs or as a chorus, treating various sections as text for multiple voices. The students need to be provided with sufficient time to practice their parts by reading their passage(s) both silently and aloud. Furthermore, they should be encouraged to seek and provide positive feedback from/to their peers, in order to ensure that their rendition of the text is both expressive and appropriate for their character. Once the students have incorporated their peers' feedback and established fluency with the material, they should perform their interpretation of the role for their fellow classmates. As with paired repeated reading, it is important that the students have the opportunity for self-evaluation, in which they can critique their own performance with regard to the fluidity and expressiveness of their reading.

The Fluency Development Lesson

Another intervention intended for use with the whole class and easily incorporated within the existing literacy curriculum was developed by Rasinski, Padak, Linek, and Sturtevant (1994). The Fluency Development Lesson was designed as part of a 15-minute daily session that can be implemented either before or after the regular reading lesson. Its format is one that can complement basal programs, literature anthologies, or trade books. The method was developed around the notion that by having students repeatedly read a short passage or a poem, there would be growth in terms of both their automaticity and prosody. The procedure is quite simple. First, the teacher introduces a 50- to 150-word selection to the students by reading the passage aloud with expression. The students and teacher then discuss the text, in order to ensure that they have a shared understanding of the passage. By discussing the material prior to having the students read it themselves, the authors place an emphasis on comprehension. They considered this particularly important since young learners often develop the mistaken view that word recognition is the primary focus of reading instruction. The discussion is then followed by several choral readings of the selection, in which the class reads the passage aloud in unison. For the next component, the students complete paired repeated readings of the text using the previously outlined format. The students' own expressive interpretations of the text are encouraged. Students are also encouraged to take the selection home and practice reading it, in order to ensure that they have achieved fluency with the piece. Finally, they have the option of reading the passage aloud in front of their classmates, in order to share their interpretations. The teacher also has the option of assessing the students' reading individually to ensure that they are making adequate progress and to determine whether they need additional help. As is the case with the previously mentioned strategies, each component of the Fluency Development

Lesson places a significant emphasis on rate, accuracy, and expressive reading, while also ensuring a focus on comprehension.

A FLUENCY-ORIENTED LITERACY PROGRAM

In addition to the previously mentioned strategies that can be integrated into an existing literacy curriculum, the next method involves redesigning the overall literacy curriculum in order to ensure that fluency is one of the primary instructional components. Fluency-Oriented Reading Instruction (Stahl et al., 1997) was developed to assist second graders in becoming fluent readers. It was designed in response to a district mandate requiring schools to use grade-level basal material with all their students, no matter what their reading level. Given the wide range of reading levels in most classrooms, the authors developed the program to provide those students reading below grade level with enough support or scaffolding to ensure that they would be able to benefit from classroom instruction. In this way, they hoped that all the students would be able to access the instruction taking place within the classroom.

Using the Oral Recitation Lesson (Hoffman & Crone, 1985) as a model, Fluency-Oriented Reading Instruction was developed to provide students with a number of opportunities to read a particular text. At the same time, Stahl and his colleagues worked with the classroom teachers, in order to ensure that the program was straightforward and adapted to the students' needs. Because the schools were working with basal readers, the story selections for the initial program were predetermined. However, trade books or literature anthologies could easily be used instead. It took approximately 1 week to cover each story. The teacher began the first lesson with the type of prereading activities he or she would traditionally use to introduce a story, including things such as teaching key vocabulary words from the story or developing the students' background knowledge. The teacher would then read the text aloud while the students followed along in their copy by finger pointing to the words. Various procedures were then used to engage the students in a discussion of the story. These components focused the students' attention on two important elements of literacy learning: reading with expression and comprehension of the text. At this point, teachers had the option of conducting echo or choral reading(s) of the text, either with the entire class or with groups of students, as they considered it necessary. However, in practice, this regularly occurred since it provided the students with a means of guided practice before reading the text on their own.

The children were next required to read the story with a partner. Partner reading could take place at several points during the week, if the students were having difficulty with a given text. This procedure involved having each member of the pair read alternative pages of the text. Should the reader experience difficulty with the text, his or her partner would provide assistance, as necessary. If time allowed, a second partner reading of the story took place, with the children reading the pages opposite those they had read initially. For homework, the students were expected to read the story to a parent or another member of the household. Students who were still experiencing difficulty with the text after several readings were asked to take home the story for a second or even a third independent reading of the piece. Those students who were not experiencing difficulty with the text were expected to select alternative books for their at-home reading. In addition to the basal component of the story, the students were provided with a 15- to 20-minute daily free-reading period in which they could independently select books, in order to further develop their reading of connected text. The program was initially implemented over the course of 2 years; in the first, it was implemented with four classes of second graders, and in the second year, it was implemented with nine classes of second graders, both with great success. The authors chose to measure the students' reading, using an informal reading inventory that was administered in the fall and the spring. The results demonstrated that the program was extremely effective, with students making 1.88 years of growth on average in the first year, and 1.77 years of growth in the second year using an informal reading inventory as a measure of students' growth in terms of rate, accuracy, and comprehension. This indicates not only that the emphasis on fluency development in this program can lead to a generalized reading development, but also that the program is a highly effective alternative to a traditional basal curriculum.

Assessing Reading Fluency

Before leaving this discussion on developing fluent reading within the classroom, it is important to consider how students' reading fluency can be assessed. One easy-to-implement measure that can be used to address the fluency development of individual readers is the National Assessment of Educational Progress (NAEP) Oral Reading Fluency Scale (1995). This 4-point scale incorporates phrasing, smoothness, pace, and expression in a generalized measure of fluent reading. It assesses children's oral reading across a range of behaviors, starting with reading that is primarily word-by-word and lacks both a sense of expression and the appropriate use of grammar, and advances to reading that incorporates the previously mentioned attributes in a fluent rendering of the text (see Table 7.1). By using this simple scale, it is possible to decided whether

TABLE 7.1. National Assessment of Educational Progress's (1995) Oral Reading Fluency Scale

Level 4	Reads primarily in larger, meaningful phrase groups. Although some regressions, repetitions, and deviations from text may be present, those do not appear to detract from the overall structure of the story. Preservation of the author's syntax is consistent. Some, or most, of the story is read with expressive interpretation.
Level 3	Reads primarily in three- or four-word phrase groups. Some smaller groupings may be present. However, the majority of phrasing seems appropriate and preserves the syntax of the author. Little or no expressive interpretation is present.
Level 2	Reads primarily in two-word phrases, with some three- or four-word groupings. Some word-by-word reading may be present. Word groupings may seem awkward and unrelated to larger context of sentence or passage.
Level 1	Reads primarily word-by-word. Occasionally two- or three-word phrases may occur, but these are infrequent and/or do not preserve meaningful syntax.

students will benefit from a fluency-oriented instructional approach, or whether they have already achieved oral reading fluency and are ready to focus on another aspect of their reading development.

IMPLICATIONS FOR FUTURE RESEARCH

Although research indicates that these approaches all effectively promote fluent reading, there are still a number of questions that need to be answered regarding fluency development and its instruction. First, the exact nature of the relationship between prosody and comprehension is not entirely clear. Although we understand that, generally, as prosody improves, so does comprehension, it is less clear whether improvements in comprehension result from improvements in prosody, or whether there is an underlying factor that leads to improvements in both aspects of reading development. Because comprehension is the primary goal of reading, this is an important element for further study. Second, it is unclear whether improvements in fluency result specifically from the repetition of text and its resulting automaticity, or whether such automaticity could develop simply by increasing the amount of connected text students are responsible for reading. Studies that have compared repeatedly reading a small number of texts and actively engaging students in the reading of a larger number of texts without repetition have produced similar results (Kuhn & Stahl, 2000). If it is possible to ensure fluency development simply by increasing the amount of text that students read, then there may be other approaches that are as effective as those discussed here. Finally, it would be useful to create and assess fluency-oriented approaches specifically designed for flexible grouping. This would allow teachers to target instruction for students who have difficulty making the transition, even after their classmates have established themselves as fluent readers.

DISCUSSION AND ACTIVITIES

Each of the interventions discussed in this chapter has proven beneficial as a means of improving reading fluency. However, when looking across the approaches, several components can be identified as contributing to this success. First, all of the procedures reviewed provide a model for the learners in the form of an expressive initial rendering of each text. This provides students with a strong sense of how fluent reading sounds and what they should strive for in their own oral reading. Second, the interventions are designed so that students have repeated exposure to a number of connected texts. In other words, rather than expecting the learners to determine each word as they encountered it, the repetition provides students with scaffolding that serves to ease their transition to automatic word recognition. Third, several of these strategies focus on comprehension through a discussion of the story held early in the lesson; importantly, these discussions occur prior to the students' attempts to read the text independently. By discussing the material at the forefront of the lesson, children are more likely to identify the main purpose of reading as the construction of meaning from text rather than the provision of a word-perfect rendition of it. Fourth, in addition to the emphasis on accurate and automatic word recognition, the interventions all emphasize the use of expression, or prosody, as part of fluent reading development. Clearly, all of these aspects of literacy instruction are important to the development of fluent reading, and the consistency with which they appear across the various measures confirms their contribution to reading development. Although it is impossible to say which of these strategies will best fit within your literacy curriculum, it is clear that any of the methods can be used either in conjunction with your current reading approaches or as an alternative to your current oral reading practices. As such, I encourage you to adopt them as part of your reading instruction, in order to assist students in making the transition from the purposeful decoding of text to the fluent reading that is so crucial to overall reading success.

1. Select a text that your class will be reading. Have each of your students read a passage from the text out loud to you, without practicing it ahead of time. Using the NAEP Oral Reading Fluency Scale (1995), evaluate their oral reading level. This will give you a sense of which students in your class need to work on their fluency development.
2. Select a short poem or passage from a story. Pair up your students and have them practice repeatedly reading the text, using the paired repeating reading approach. Tell them to emphasis expression and their own interpretation of the piece. After the students have had the opportunity to practice the passage, ask for volunteers to perform their interpretation of the passage in front of their classmates.
3. Pick a play or plays from a literature anthology, or from your school or local library. Divide the class into groups. Allow your groups to practice their reading of the play(s) and then "perform" their text for one another by rendering their selection expressively.
4. Select a short text and follow the format outlined for Fluency-Oriented Reading Instruction for 1 week. This will allow you to become comfortable with an alternative to round-robin reading, while introducing your students to an effective approach to oral reading instruction.

REFERENCES

Achilles, C. M. (1999). *Let's put kids first, finally: Getting class size right.* Thousand Oaks, CA: Corwin Press.

Adams, M. J. (1990). *Beginning to read: Thinking and learning about print.* Cambridge, MA: MIT Press.

Allington, R. L. (1983). Fluency: The neglected reading goal. *The Reading Teacher, 36,* 556–561.

Allington, R. L. (2001). *What really matters for struggling readers: Designing research-based programs.* New York: Longman.

Anderson, R. C., Heibert, E. H., Scott, J. A., & Wilkinson, I. A. G. (1985). *Becoming a nation of readers.* Washington, DC: National Institute of Education, U.S. Department of Education.

Ash, G. E., & Hagood, M. C. (2000, May). *Improving struggling readers' oral reading fluency, meaning making, and motivation through Karaoke. "This song goes out to Miss Margaret and Miss Gwynne!": Creating a Karaoke club at your school.* Session presented at the annual meeting of the International Reading Association, Indianapolis, IN.

Bidwell, S. M. (1990). Using drama to increase motivation, comprehension, and fluency. *Journal of Reading, 34,* 38–41.

Carbo, M. (1978). Teaching reading with talking books. *The Reading Teacher, 32,* 267–273.

Chall, J. S. (1996). *Stages of reading development.* Orlando, FL: Harcourt Brace.

Chomsky, C. (1976). After decoding: What? *Language Arts, 53,* 288–296.

Chomsky, C. (1978). When you still can't read in third grade?: After decoding, what? In S. J. Samuels (Ed.), *What research has to say about reading instruction* (pp. 13–30). Newark, DE: International Reading Association.

Cunningham, P. M. (2000). *Phonics they use: Words for reading and writing*. New York: Longman.

Duke, N. (1999). *The scarcity of informational texts in first grade. Report No 1-007*. Ann Arbor, MI: Center for the Improvement of Early Reading Achievement (CIERA).

Dowhower, S. (1989). Repeated reading: Research into practice. *The Reading Teacher, 42*, 502–507.

Dowhower, S. L. (1991). Speaking of prosody: Fluency's unattended bedfellow. *Theory Into Practice, 30*(3), 158–164.

Henning, K. (1974). Drama reading, an on-going classroom activity at the elementary school level. *Elementary English, 51*, 48–51.

Herman, P. A. (1985). The effect of repeated readings on reading rate, speech pauses, and word recognition accuracy. *Reading Research Quarterly, 20*, 533–564.

Hoffman, J. V., & Crone, S. (1985). The oral recitation lesson: A research-derived strategy for reading basal texts. In J. A. Niles & R. V. Lalik (Eds.), *Issues in literacy: A research perspective* (34th Yearbook of the National Reading Conference, pp. 76–83). Rochester, NY: National Reading Conference.

Hollingsworth, P. M. (1970). An experiment with the impress method of teaching reading. *The Reading Teacher, 24*, 112–114, 187.

Hollingsworth, P. M. (1978). An experimental approach to the impress method of teaching reading. *The Reading Teacher, 31*, 624–626.

Hoyt, L. (2000). *Snapshots: Literacy minilessons up close*. Portsmouth, NH: Heinemann.

Koskinen, P. S., & Blum, I. H. (1984). Repeated oral reading and the acquisition of fluency. In J. A. Niles & L. A. Harris (Eds.), *Changing perspectives on research in reading/language processing and instruction* (33rd Yearbook of the National Reading Conference, pp. 183–187). Rochester, NY: National Reading Conference.

Koskinen, P. S., & Blum, I. H. (1986). Paired repeated reading: A classroom strategy for developing fluent reading. *The Reading Teacher, 40*, 70–75.

Kuhn, M. R. (2000, November). *A comparative study of small group fluency instruction*. Paper presented at the meeting of the National Reading Conference, Scottsdale, AZ.

Kuhn, M. R., & Stahl, S. (2000). *Fluency: A review of developmental and remedial strategies: Report No 2-008*. Ann Arbor, MI: Center for the Improvement of Early Reading Achievement (CIERA).

LaBerge, D., & Samuels, S. (1974). Toward a theory of automatic information processing in reading. *Cognitive Psychology, 6*, 293–323.

NAEP Oral Reading Fluency Scale. (1995). *Listening to children read aloud, 15*. Washington, DC: U.S. Department of Education, National Center for Education Statistics.

Nagel, G. K. (2001). *Effective grouping for literacy instruction*. Needham Heights, MA: Allyn & Bacon.

National Reading Panel. (2000). *Teaching children to read: An evidence-based as-*

sessment of the scientific research literature on reading and its implications for read-ing instruction: Reports of the subgroups. Bethesda, MD: National Institutes of Health. [Available online] *http://www.nichd.nih.gov/publications/nrp/*

Optiz, M. F., & Rasinski, T. V. (1998). *Good-bye round robin: 25 effective oral read-ing strategies.* Portsmouth, NH: Heinemann.

O'Shea, L. J., Sindelar, P. T., & O'Shea, D. J. (1985). The effects of repeated readings and attentional cues on reading fluency and comprehension. *Jour-nal of Reading Behavior, 17,* 129–142.

Perfetti, C. A. (1985). *Reading ability.* New York: Oxford University Press.

Rasinski, T. V. (1989). Fluency for everyone: Incorporating fluency instruction in the classroom. *The Reading Teacher, 42,* 690–693.

Rasinski, T., & Padak, N. (1996). Five lessons to increase reading fluency. In L. R. Putnam (Ed.), *How to become a better reading teacher* (pp. 255–265). Englewood Cliffs, NJ: Merrill.

Rasinski, T. V., & Padak, N. D. (2001). *From phonics to fluency: Effective teaching of decoding and reading fluency in the elementary school.* New York: Addison-Wesley/Longman.

Rasinski, T. V., Padak, N., Linek, W., & Sturtevant, E. (1994). Effects of fluency development on urban second grade readers. *Journal of Educational Research, 87,* 158–165.

Reutzel, D. R. (1996). Developing at-risk readers' oral reading fluency. In L. R. Putnam (Ed.), *How to become a better reading teacher* (pp. 241–254). Englewood Cliffs, NJ: Merrill.

Schreiber, P. A. (1991). Understanding prosody's role in reading acquisition. *Theory Into Practice, 30,* 158–164.

Stahl, S. A., Heubach, K., & Cramond, B. (1997). *Fluency-oriented reading instruc-tion* (Reading Research Report No. 79). Athens, GA: National Reading Research Center.

Stanovich, K. E. (1980). Toward an interactive–compensatory model of individual differences in the development of reading fluency. *Reading Research Quar-terly, 21,* 360–407.

Chapter 8

BUILDING A SOUND
WRITING PROGRAM

Karen Bromley

This chapter will:

- Explore writing theory, research, and issues related to instruction.
- Identify guidelines for effective K–8 writing instruction.
- Describe classroom writing practices.
- Suggest directions for future research and practice.

THEORY AND RESEARCH BASE

Writing is a complex interaction of cognitive and physical factors. It allows for the creation of ideas and information with written symbols and words. Writing can be a social process and is one way of communicating with others (e.g., a note to a friend, a letter to the newspaper, a paper for a professor, or a newsletter to a parent). Writing can also be a personal process done just for oneself (e.g., a grocery list, a "to-do" list, entries in a personal journal, or poetry). Many factors affect writing, including conceptual knowledge; vocabulary; knowledge of standard form; grammar, spelling, and punctuation; handwriting ease; small muscle development; and eye–hand coordination.

Although writing provides communication with others and introspection, it is more than transcribing meaning that already exists in one's head. The transaction that occurs as a writer writes and thinks can foster the creation of new knowledge (Smith, 1994). Also, rereading what is written can give a writer new ideas that did not occur before writing. Unlike spoken language that is limited by memory and attention, writing can be revisited and changed, thus liberating the imagination and providing new understandings and insights.

Theory and research in writing instruction suggest a view of the writing process that includes both social and personal aspects. Vygotsky (1978) proposed that writing is a way of communicating cultural understandings, and children learn to write when they have reasons that make it "relevant to life." Relevancy is also embedded in Cambourne's (1988) model of learning applied to literacy. He theorizes that authentic *engagement* accompanied by *immersion* and *demonstration* result in learning. Students learn to write when we surround them with examples and models, give them expectations, allow them to make decisions and mistakes, provide feedback, and give them time to practice in realistic ways.

Graves's (1983) research with young children resulted in a model of the writing process also based on relevancy and engagement in the recursive steps of *planning, drafting, revising, editing*, and *publishing* for a real audience. Casey and Hemenway (2001) conducted a 10-year study of third graders, up to their graduation from high school, and concluded that a balance between structure and freedom results in "more dynamic writers excited about their abilities" (p. 68). Atwell's (1998) research with middle school students and Murray's (1985) work with college students support the use of the writing process in a writing workshop. Hayes and Flower (1986) developed a similar process model based on evidence that college students monitor their writing as they move back and forth among the recursive steps.

However, research on isolating the teaching of grammar and mechanics from the writing process is not encouraging (Weaver, 1996). Studies show that teaching formal grammar to students has "a negligible or even harmful effect on improving students' writing" (Routman, 1996, p. 119). The only isolated skills teaching that does seem to show a positive effect on writing is teaching students how to combine sentences, and "a heavy emphasis on mechanics and usage results in significant losses in overall quality" (Hillocks, 1987, p. 74). But time spent actually engaged in the writing process that includes ". . . teaching and discussing word usage and sentence construction in the context of writing with intention for a specific audience" (Routman, 1996, p. 120) seems to help students most.

RESEARCH-BASED PRACTICE

Although a large body of theory and research informs the teaching of writing, new mandates challenge teachers to remain faithful to the relevant and authentic engagement practices supported by this theory and research. Higher standards, mandated assessments, and accountability issues cause some teachers to reduce time for writing, teach writing artificially, and fragment the curriculum (Strickland et al., 2001). In some classrooms, the focus may be away from the writing process, and toward skills and the written product. Proponents of a process approach to writing instruction are sometimes criticized for overlooking direct instruction, form, and legibility, although a skills–product approach, including grammar and punctuation practice, and teacher-provided prompts and rubrics is criticized for its teacher-centeredness that overlooks student motivation, purpose, and voice. But good writers need opportunities to engage in the process while learning the craft and skills of writing (Fletcher & Portalupi, 1998; Harwayne, 2001; Portalupi & Fletcher, 2001; Shanahan, 1997). Thus, this chapter offers glimpses into classrooms in one school where teachers use elements of both a process approach and a product–skills approach.

The five guidelines (depicted in Figure 8.1), drawn from the previous discussion of theory and research, reflect a balance between process and product-focused instruction. Using these guidelines to frame your writing program can help you think about ways to integrate writing with reading, science, and socials studies; avoid devoting writing time to test preparation; use formula writing sensibly; and blend writing skills with meaningful teaching.

Writing Goals That Guide Students, Teachers, and Schools

The following quote from Scott, a fourth-grade teacher, shows how he and his faculty are establishing goals and creating a writing curriculum to help their students develop into effective writers:

> "We have a school-wide commitment to writing. The writing curriculum we created helps every teacher know what students should be able to do when they leave their grade level. I feel more confident in my teaching because of the conversations we've had about writing. I know we're focused on those state assessments, and sometimes I think we pay too much attention to them. But right now, in education, accountability is forcing this focus.
>
> "I know I have better writers this year because I've changed my expectations and practices. For example, I'm more intentional now about helping kids analyze and think in science and social studies,

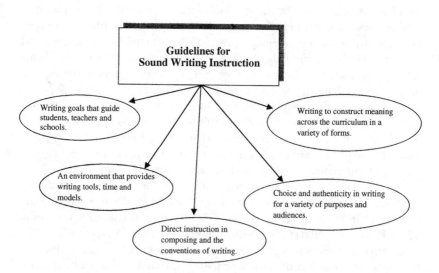

FIGURE 8.1. Use these guidelines to frame your writing program.

and then write about it. I often ask them to compare and contrast things like a poem and a report, and we write in different genres. We talk about what a good finished piece looks like. We create check-lists and rubrics students can use to guide their writing and self-evaluate after writing."

Scott and his faculty are responding to higher standards and mandated assessments with a focus on writing. They have identified school-wide goals for writing in light of the standards adopted by their state, and they continue to have dialogue about developing criteria and rubrics for good writing. They know that good instruction begins with goals and a vision of exemplary student performance. Good instruction also includes self-assessment by teachers and students.

Self-assessment can include answers to questions such as the following (Marino, 1997) which may help you examine and match your beliefs to your practices:

- How do students become good writers?
- For what purposes are students writing?
- Who are the audiences for their writing?
- Are they writing in a variety of forms in all content areas?
- Am I giving students choices in what they write?
- How am I using the writing process?
- What direct instruction am I providing?
- How am I using literature to inspire and model good writing?
- How am I helping students understand the effect of conventions on meaning?

Self-evaluation by students is important, too, because it helps students take responsibility for their writing progress. A writing attitude survey can provide information about how students feel about writing (Kear, Coffman, McKenna, & Ambrosio, 2000). Questions such as the following help students evaluate their skills and set goals for themselves (Hansen, 1996):

- What do I do well?
- What is the most recent thing I've learned as a writer?
- What do I want to learn next to become a better writer?
- What do I plan to do to improve?

As well as evaluating their writing progress, Scott often talks with his students before they write, to decide how a good finished product looks. For example, before writing letters to state Chambers of Commerce as part of a study of the United States, his students listed characteristics of a good letter and then organized them into categories. Scott added levels of use to his "rubric" to guide their writing (see Figure 8.2).

Creating rubrics and checklists of criteria with students before writing can have a dramatic effect on a finished product. It gives students goals for writing and the characteristics of a good report, essay, letter, or poem, for example, *before* they write, and it gives everyone an objective way to assess the finished product *after* writing. Rubrics and checklists can help you identify students' strengths and needs, so you know what to reteach, and they can help parents understand a student's grade. Of course, you will not use a rubric or checklist for every piece of writing, but this practice can take the mystery out of writing for students and improve the quality of key writing assignments and final projects.

An Environment That Provides Writing Tools, Time, and Models

A visitor to Jan's kindergarten and Farrah's sixth-grade class can tell that they recognize the value of environmental print for teaching reading and writing. In Jan's room, there are printed 5" × 8" labels on the *wastebasket*, the *pencil sharpener*, and other classroom objects. Around each child's neck is a nametag hanging from yarn. Jan finds opportunities daily to use these labels as tools in brief lessons to help build letter knowledge and sight

Letter Rubric

	Needs Work	Getting there	Almost there	Got it
Content				
Message /meaning				
Organization				
Details				
Complete sentences				
Word use				
Mechanics				
Inside address				
Date + greeting				
Body / paragraphs				
Closing + name				
Capitals + punctuation				
Neatness				
Spelling				

FIGURE 8.2. Rubrics guide writing and help make assessment objective.

vocabulary. She says that many of the printed words in the room find their way into the children's daily journals. In Farrah's room, there are large cans filled with pencils, felt-tip markers, calligraphy pens, colored pencils, and ball-point pens. This classroom also has labels affixed to objects, because Farrah uses labels and other environmental print as tools to help the five ESL students in her class learn English. She says Russell, a new immigrant from Russia, eagerly uses this print each day with a buddy, who helps him speak and write English as Russell teaches his buddy Russian.

Scott and other teachers set aside blocks of time when students can write on a topic of their choice during *writing workshop* (Atwell, 1998; Calkins, 1994; Graves, 1983, 1994). Calkins (1994) suggests use of the following components of writing workshop: minilessons, work time for writing and conferring, peer conferring and/or response groups, share sessions, and publication celebrations. Atwell (1999) spends an hour a day in writing workshop, about one-third of which is brief lessons focused on a demonstrated need of a group of students. She also spends time sharing and discussing well-written pieces of literature to help students improve their writing and learn to respond to each other's work.

Tonya, a third-grade teacher, organizes writing workshop differently each year. She listens to her students, reflects on what does and does not work, and modifies accordingly (Sudol & Sudol, 1995; Zaragoza & Vaughn, 1995). This year, Tonya uses writing workshop 3 days a week and begins with a 5- to 10-minute lesson on a skill, followed by 30 minutes writing and 10 minutes listening to someone share from the Author's Chair (Graves, 1994). Students sign up on a wall calendar to share a finished story twice a month. Student writing is displayed on bulletin boards, and wall posters are visible, such as the following T-chart that resulted from a class discussion about writing workshop and reminded students of good writing workshop behavior:

Writer's Workshop

Looks like	Sounds like
• People being polite	• Quiet but not silent
• Working not talking	• No put-downs
• Sharing ideas quietly	• Clean language
• Cooperation	• No unpleasant noises
• People writing	• Listening during sharing time
• People reading	• Asking good questions

Stefan's second graders typically spend 45 minutes a day in writing workshop. When he omits or shortens the workshop, students are disappointed. He says groans often accompany the signal to stop writing. In this school, parent volunteers manage a project called "Books from Boxes" that uses cereal boxes and other materials to make blank books. Students publish only their best work, and every piece of writing does not proceed through the entire writing process.

In her first year using writing workshop in third grade, Karen manages it with a chart that holds five tagboard pockets, one for each step of the process, and student names on tagboard strips (see Figure 8.3). Each day, students place their names in the pocket that shows where they are in the writing process. Then, Karen knows who is ready for a conference with

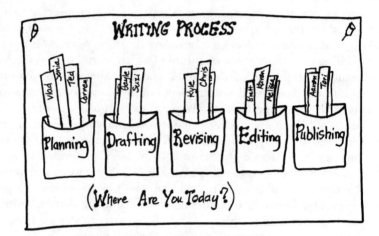

FIGURE 8.3. Charts like these help manage the writing workshop.

a buddy or her, or who is ready to share in an Author's Circle (Villaume & Brabham, 2002). At any point, Karen encourages students to use "buddy reading," so they can give each other feedback on their work (see Figure 8.3). Like Tonya's and Stefan's students, Karen's students write about topics they are researching in science and social studies, as well as fiction and poetry, as they learn to write across the curriculum.

Many teachers encourage buddy reading and collaborative writing, which can be particularly helpful for students who may have ideas to contribute but may not yet have the language skills, motivation, or confidence. Both ESL students and struggling readers are supported in their work and encouraged to develop their abilities when they work in pairs with English speakers who can learn about other cultures and languages from their buddies.

As well as tools and time, students need models, so that they know what good writing looks and sounds like (Calkins, 1994; Harwayne, 1992, 2000; McElveen & Dierking, 2001). Hearing and reading books read orally helps students think like writers and write with an audience in mind. Through literature, they can begin to see how authors hold the reader's attention and use conventions, and they can begin to use this knowledge in their own writing.

You might encourage your students to try *literary borrowing* (Lancia, 1997). For example, Jesse, a third grader, had read R. L. Stine's (2002) book, in which he uses "*THE END*" in the final sentence (e.g., "*It doesn't really matter in . . . THE END*"). Jesse borrowed this technique, concluding his nonfiction report on volcanoes with "*Volcanoes are very cool but when they erupt, it's . . . THE END.*" This example shows how reading all types of literature can have a positive impact on student writing.

Direct Instruction in Composing and Conventions of Writing

Experienced teachers of writing know that writers need direct, systematic instruction in writing, as well as time to write (Routman, 1996). They also need opportunities for enough instruction, guidance, and practice to allow them to become accomplished (Shanahan, 1997). Good writing teachers balance writing process and product as they celebrate and encourage individuality, creativity, meaning, standard form, and the conventions of language.

You can incorporate direct instruction in composing, and the conventions of grammar, spelling, form, and handwriting into writing workshop (Peterson, 2000). For example, teach terms such as *purpose, audience, form, voice, noun, verb, adjective,* and *voice,* which give students a common vocabulary for discussing and improving their writing (Bromley, 1998, 2002). Talking about sentence construction, grammar, and usage makes sense to students when they are writing for a specific audience that is real (Routman, 1996). You can also use "fix-the-error exercises" to teach specific grammar skills, with examples from real literature that students know (Kane, 1997). Teach minilessons using your own writing to show, for example, how quotations, commas, and periods should be used.

Like Tonya and Stefan, Karen begins writing workshop with a lesson on an aspect of writing, such as organization, run-on sentences, adjectives, verbs, or punctuation. She prefers the term *focus lesson* (Routman, 1996), because she believes the term *minilesson* may trivialize the direct instruction she provides in skills. Recently, she taught a focus lesson on common and proper nouns, after she noticed the overuse of pronouns in several students' stories. Part of the lesson included revising the work of a draft volunteered by a student.

To extend her students' writing beyond topics they choose themselves, Karen uses a *genre study*, in which students immerse themselves in a particular kind of literature and then write in this form (Calkins, 1994). For example, during recent writing workshops, and in conjunction with a social studies unit, Karen's students read nonfiction books about animals, gathered information from a CD-ROM encyclopedia, took an electronic field trip to a zoo, then created their own informative report about an animal. They compiled these reports into a book, which students shared with a first-grade class. Karen encourages students to co-author at least one story or report because she believes collaboration is a catalyst for learning.

Diane is a special education teacher whose students need direct instruction and modeling to support their writing. To teach persuasive writing, Diane first shared a paragraph she wrote to her husband, to convince him to try her favorite sport, roller blading. Next, she had students choose a hobby and someone to whom to write. Then, the students analyzed Diane's paragraph and identified the persuasive writing frame she used:

Persuasive Writing

Introduction (Position or Purpose)

Facts and Reasons
  1.
  2.
  3.

Conclusion (Restate Position)

Students planned their writing by using the frame, composed rough drafts, and self-checked to revise and edit (see Figure 8.4). Last, Diane used a volunteer's rough draft to model revising and editing, before students revised and edited their own work.

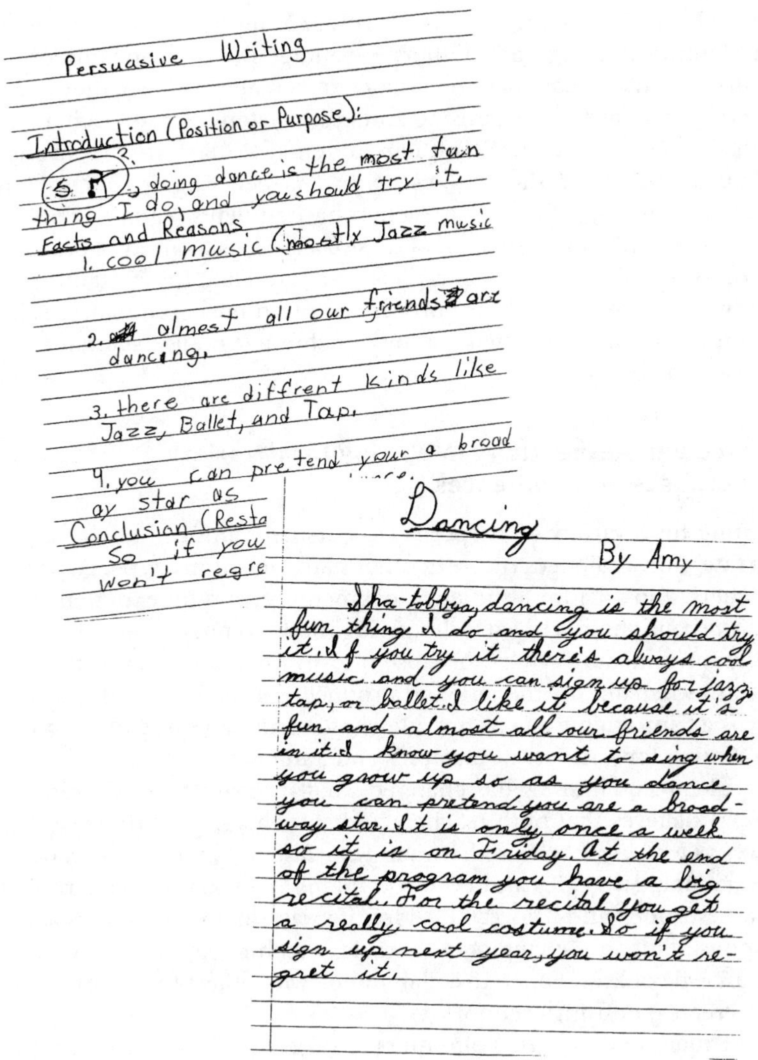

Persuasive Writing

Introduction (Position or Purpose):
(S.T.) doing dance is the most fun
thing I do, and you should try it.
Facts and Reasons
1. cool music (mostly Jazz music

2. almost all our friends are
dancing.

3. there are different kinds like
Jazz, Ballet, and Tap.

4. you can pretend your a broad
ay star as
Conclusion (Resta
So if you
won't regre

Dancing

By Amy

Sha-tobby, dancing is the most
fun thing I do and you should try
it. If you try it there's always cool
music and you can sign up for jazz,
tap, or ballet. I like it because it's
fun and almost all our friends are
in it. I know you want to sing when
you grow up so as you dance
you can pretend you are a broad-
way star. It is only once a week
so it is on Friday. At the end
of the program you have a big
recital. For the recital you get
a really cool costume. So if you
sign up next year, you won't re-
gret it.

FIGURE 8.4. A paragraph frame serves as a plan for persuasive writing.

Besides conferencing with students yourself, you can use peer conferences to give students a real and immediate audience for their work. Often, when students read their work to a peer, they discover what to revise. When you have students work in pairs or small groups to give each other feedback on writing, you can use PQS (P—Praise, Q—Question, S—Suggest) (Bromley, 1998). To help frame constructive feedback, have students respond with a sentence for each category.

What about spelling and handwriting? Many teachers teach spelling and handwriting together. Others encourage invented spelling on first drafts, so students can focus on fluency and creativity. Then, they require standard spelling in the revising and editing steps. Some teachers have set standards for neatness in their students' written work, refusing to accept a *sloppy copy*; rather, they use *rough draft*, believing sloppy copy sends the wrong message. Still other teachers have students regularly self-assess their own handwriting. In many of these classrooms, a variety of tools (e.g., colored pencils, pens, white-out, etc.) are available for student use, including the computer. Word-processing programs, grammar checkers, and spell checkers help many students achieve legibility, standard form, and accepted usage.

Choice and Authenticity in Writing for a Variety of Purposes and Audiences

Writing for a variety of purposes (to persuade, inform, entertain, and narrate) and audiences (those in other states or countries, peers, parents, teachers, and self) builds fluency, competence, and independence. Giving students choices in what they write builds competence as well, especially for reluctant writers, because it gives them a reason to write and builds ownership for the task and product. For many students, technology is an intriguing way to provide choice and authentic opportunities for writing for a variety of purposes and audiences.

Electronic literacy has changed what it means to be literate. Leu (1997) believes that both teachers and students should think of themselves as *becoming literate*, rather than *being literate*, as they learn to use the navigational strategies and critical thinking necessary for electronic literacy. Wepner and Tao (2002) identify ways that classroom teachers' responsibilities are changing as a result of technology. They urge teachers to be flexible and open to collaboration with others to support change and creative in using technology.

Today, students use computers to do research for written reports and presentations. Teachers use computers to gather information and prepare lessons. Both students and teachers engage in inquiry-based learning (Owens, Hester, & Teale, 2002) use CDROM encyclopedias, and primary sources on the World-Wide Web, such as historical documents or secondary sources such as museum or observatory websites. Viewing and evaluating hypertext (pictures, animation, and sounds) is necessary as students learn to search for information, interpret, and analyze it, and think critically about the validity of sources. Use a site such as *library.ucla.edu/libraries/college/instruct/critical.htm* to help students use criteria in evaluating web resources.

Research in K–6 classrooms indicates that teachers report an increase in their students' motivation to write when their work is published on the Internet (Karchmer, 2001). When students write for the Internet, as well as skills in viewing and analyzing, they build skills in keyboarding, word processing, and navigating with browsers and search engines. Some examples follow for using the computer to develop student writers:

- Many teachers establish electronic key pal exchanges with classes in other states or countries. Some exchanges are social and others are related to science or social studies.
- Classes take electronic field trips to places around the world, to extend learning in a content area. During these field trips, students can ask questions of experts and get answers that might not yet appear anywhere in print.
- Many teachers and students participate in collaborative projects with other schools. For example, you can create a virtual tour of a local historical landmark with electronic graphics and post it on the Historical Landmark site at *hilites@gsn.org.*
- Younger elementary school children, as well as older students, create classroom or school web pages, or their own personal web pages using web-based tools.
- Desktop publishing allows students to create professional-looking classroom newsletters that they can format and decorate with clip art.
- Students can publish their own original writing on *e-zines,* electronic magazines that include opportunities to write poetry, book reviews, and stories; enter contests; chat with others; and submit original artwork.
- A variety of Internet sites offer students choice in what they compose (see Table 8.1). These websites meet several criteria: appearance, ease of use, content, and K–8 suitability.

Writing to Construct Meaning across the Curriculum in a Variety of Forms

Arline, a fifth-grade teacher, believes it is important for teachers to be writers themselves. She keeps a personal journal, uses e-mail, and writes curriculum, lesson plans, and grant proposals for her classroom and school. She believes, as do Vacca and Vacca (2002), that writing regularly is a powerful strategy for learning subject matter. She says:

"From my own writing, I've learned that writing is a process of constructing meaning. I never realize what I know until I start writing.

TABLE 8.1. Websites for Writers

1. The Internet Public Library Youth Division—*www.ipl.org/youth/ HomePage2.html*
   In the "Reading Zone" at "Computers and the Internet," kids can view other kids' websites, post their own, and find links to online stories, favorite books, and authors.

2. Kids' Fun Online by Scholastic—*www.scholastic.com/kids/cards/*
   At "Card Factory," kids can write text and click-and-drag clip art to create and send their own unique online cards. Or, at *www.scholastic.com/ titles/ kids* can read tips from writers, find out about writers and illustrators' lives and post book reviews.

3. The Children's Book Forum—*faldo.atmos.uiuc.edu/BOOKREVIEW/*
   This "Internet Community Project" invites parents, kids, and teachers to submit reviews of children's books.

4. MidLink Magazine—*longwood.cs.ucf.edu/~midlink/*
   This electronic magazine for middle grades publishes kids' reviews of their favorite books.

5. Kidlink—*www.kidlink.org/index.html*
   This site is in English and 20 other languages, so kids from around the world can have discussions on Kidcafe, or be involved in Kidproj, which offers short- and long-term projects, and Kidforum listserves for discussions of specific topics.

6. Keypals Club—*www.mightymedia.com/keypals/*
   A place for kids to locate and correspond with other kids or classes around the world. Teachers can start a project with another class or just help kids create new friendships with kids on the other side of the world.

7. Blue Mountain Arts—*free.bluemountain.com/cdb/K/*
   In a section especially for kids, kids can design, send, and receive their own cards for all occasions.

8. Stone Soup—*www.stonesoup.com/*
   This international online magazine contains stories, poems, book reviews and artwork by kids.

9. Little Planet Times—*www.littleplanet.com/*
   This interactive, online newspaper publishes letters to the editor, movie reviews, stories, and creative ideas for and by kids.

10. Young Writers Clubhouse—*www.realkids.com/club.shtml*
    This site publishes *Global Wave*, a monthly, online magazine of writing by kids that includes story suggestions, stories to finish, book reviews, and more.

Then I make connections and come up with ideas that I didn't have before. When I understood the power of writing for me, I began to realize what it could do for my students. I make writing a conscious part of science, social studies, and math now. My students write in journals at different times of the day, for a lot of different reasons. I've found that it's pretty amazing what my students can relate about their thinking when they write. It's a totally personal, quiet time in our classroom when students write their insights about a unit we are studying or connect between math and social studies, or relate it to the world."

Arline and other teachers have discovered that when students do expository writing in a variety of forms in the content areas, they construct new meaning and demonstrate their science and social studies knowledge, too. Expository writing is writing to explain or share information. For example, after reading a story about the Cheyenne Indians, Arline asked groups to write what they had learned on a partially constructed web (see Figure 8.5). Arline's main categories were in bold print, and the student wrote what he remembered. Students added information to the web as they learned more about the tribe. Near the end of the unit, a student created the acrostic poem in Figure 8.5, showing what he had learned about the Cheyenne Indians' respect for the environment and their undeserved fate.

Expository writing across the curriculum takes many forms. In first grade, Jane linked math, social studies, and language arts in a unit called *Quilt Connections*. After students had read and heard many stories about quilts, researched other cultures' quilts in the library and on the Internet, visited a museum exhibit, and learned about shapes, equal parts, and fractions, a final activity involved creation of a classroom quilt. The finished quilt, made of special fabrics and designs contributed by each student, along with a journal, was taken home each day by a different student. Students and parents writing about the quilt in the journal gave parents an opportunity to be involved in their child's classroom learning.

Many teachers use graphic organizers to support student research and organize their ideas for expository writing (Irwin-DeVitis, Bromley, & Modlo, 1999) (see Figure 8.6). For example, in a second-grade study of Mexico, Rebecca's students read and gathered information using Venn diagrams (to show similarities and differences between two things) and data charts (to gather information from several sources). As part of a sixth-grade unit on Immigration, Michelle wanted her students to take the perspective of a character, or focus on particular relationships among characters. So she had them use character maps and character relationship maps (see Figure 8.7) to plan their expository writing about the feel-

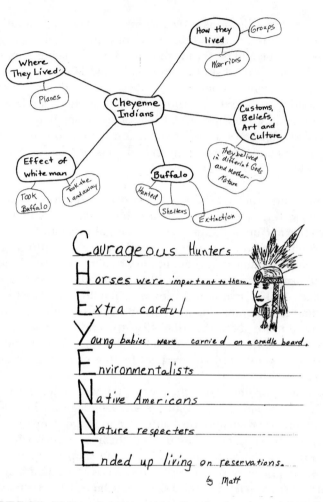

FIGURE 8.5. Webs and poetry writing have a place in social studies.

ings of characters in *How Many Days to America?* by Eve Bunting (1988), and *Molly's Pilgrim*, by Barbara Cohen (1998).

Today, expository writing is used in math class, a content area traditionally ruled by numbers. Gordon and Macinnis (1993) use dialogue journals in math to add a personal dimension to learning and provide "a window on students' thinking." Colleen regularly asks her eighth graders to write to her in their journals about what they enjoy and what gives them trouble (see Figure 8.8). Colleen also has students explain answers to incorrect test items for extra credit. This kind of expository writing lets

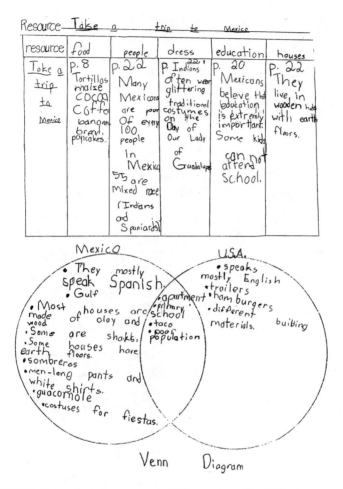

Resource— Take a trip to Mexico

resource	food	people	dress	education	houses
Take a trip to Mexice	p. 8 Tortillos maise cocoa Coffe bananm bread, pancakes.	p. 22 Many Mexicans are poor Of every 100 people In Mexica 55 are Mixed race (Indians and Spaniards)	p. Indions often wear glittering traditional costumes on the Day of Our Lady of Guadalupe	p. 20 Mexicans beleve that education is extremly important. Some kids can not attend school.	p. 22 They live in wooden huts with earth floors.

Mexico   USA.
• They mostly speak Spanish.
• Gulf
• Most houses are made of clay and wood
• Some are shakts,
• Some houses have earth floors.
• sombreros
• men-long pants and white shirts.
• guacornole
• costuses for fiestas.

apartment
• primary school
• taco
• poor population

• speaks mostly English
• trailers
• ham burgers
• different materials.

buiting

Venn   Diagram

FIGURE 8.6. Second graders use graphic organizers to aid their research and expository writing about Mexico.

her see students' reasoning, so she can reteach a concept, if necessary. For Colleen, writing is an assessment tool that shows math learning and misconceptions (see Figure 8.8).

Teachers of younger students use expository writing with math journals. Venita says that journals help her second graders clarify, extend, and document their thinking to show the results of research with their classmates (see Figure 8.9). Venita encourages her students to draw pictures to help them figure out problems and write their own problems as well. Sarah's third graders explain their computations to demonstrate

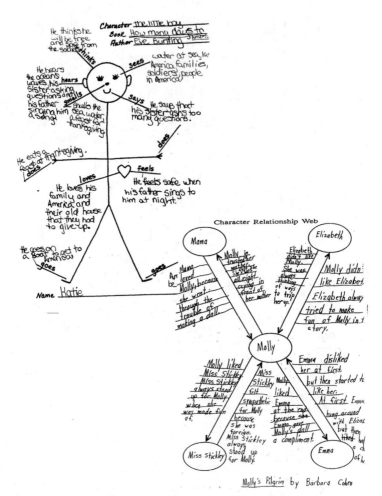

FIGURE 8.7. Graphic organizers help students gain insight into characters and their relationships.

understanding of a concept. From Kyle's expository writing, Sarah knows that he can teach long division to another student (see Figure 8.9).

IMPLICATIONS FOR FUTURE RESEARCH

The guidelines presented in this chapter and the classroom practices you have read about can help you frame a writing program that is based on theory and research. Blending both process and product approaches builds fluency, competence, and independence. A balanced approach

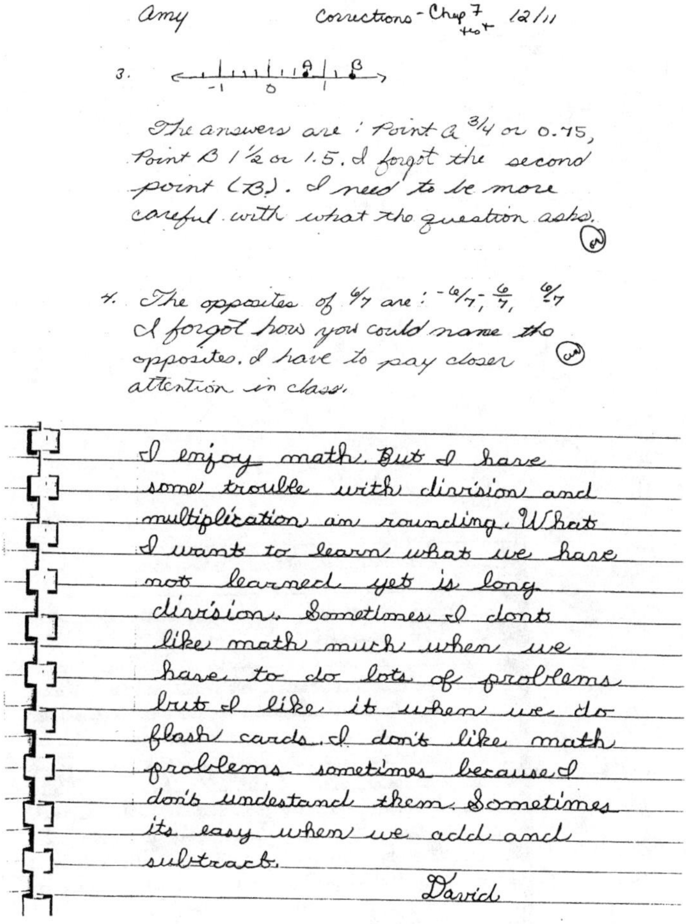

Amy   Corrections - Chap 7   12/11
                                        too t

3.   [number line diagram with points A and B between -1, 0, and 1]

The answers are : Point A ³/4 or 0.75,
Point B 1½ or 1.5. I forgot the second
point (B). I need to be more
careful with what the question asks.

4. The opposites of ⁴/7 are: ⁻⁴/7, ⁶/7, ⁸/7
I forgot how you could name the
opposites. I have to pay closer
attention in class.

I enjoy math. But I have
some trouble with division and
multiplication an rounding. What
I want to learn what we have
not learned yet is long
division. Sometimes I don't
like math much when we
have to do lots of problems
but I like it when we do
flash cards. I don't like math
problems sometimes because I
don't undestand them. Sometimes
its easy when we add and
subtract.
                              David

FIGURE 8.8. Math journal entries show students' math learning and misconceptions.

develops writers who enjoy and learn from writing as they write well in a range of forms, for a variety of purposes and audiences.

Writing instruction will undoubtedly change with findings from research and shifts in what it means to be literate. Accountability, mandates, assessment, technology, and the requirements of workplace literacy will undoubtedly continue to impact writing and how it is taught in schools. But research is needed to discover what the best balanced instruction looks like for students of different gender, cultural and ethnic backgrounds; ESL students; and students with learning disabilities and literacy difficulties.

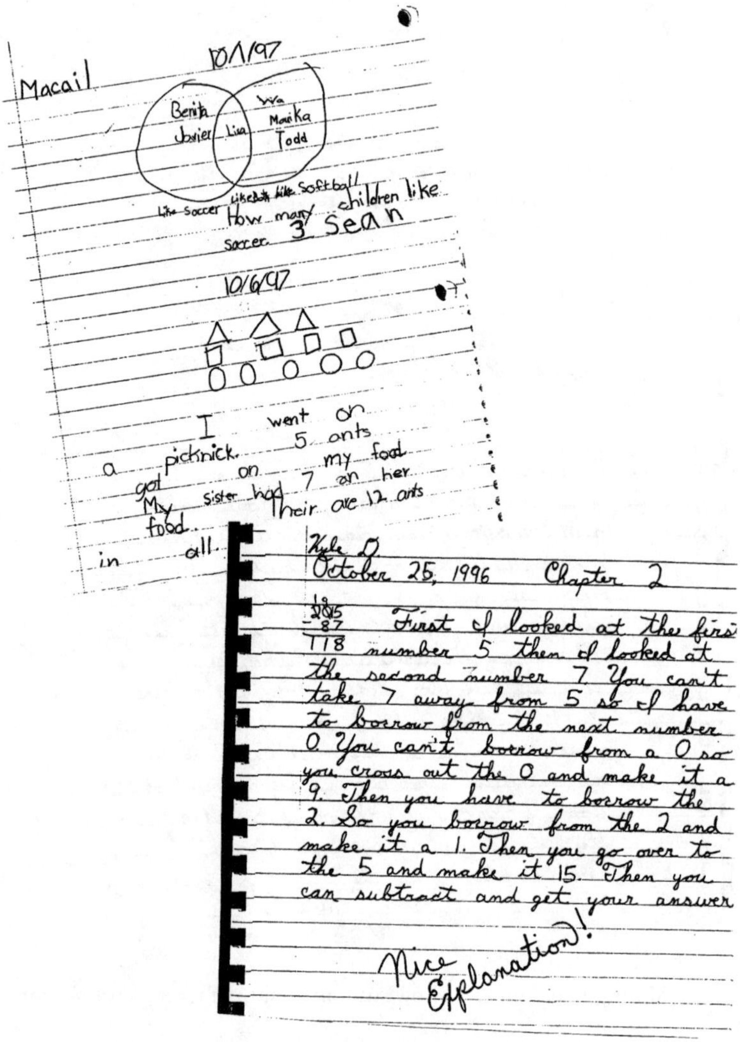

FIGURE 8.9. Entries in second- and fourth-grade journals show students' conceptual understandings.

DISCUSSION AND ACTIVITIES

1. Plato, one of the first great Greek writers, thought writing led to the deterioration of memory (Gee, 1996). He felt that writing discouraged people from speech that showed real learning, because the listener could ask "What do you mean?" and get a response. Socrates agreed, saying that

writing was open to inaccurate interpretations and was thus a dangerous endeavor. If you were debating them, what would your arguments be in favor of writing?

2. Create a rubric for the persuasive writing piece in Figure 8.4. How and why would you suggest making it, or one like it, with students in a real classroom?

3. Obtain a copy of *Craft Lessons: Teaching Writing K–8* by Ralph Fletcher and Joann Portalupi (1998; York, ME: Stenhouse) or *Nonfiction Craft Lessons: Teaching Information Writing K–8* by Joann Portalupi and Ralph Fletcher (2001; York, ME: Stenhouse). Review the lessons and determine whether the authors subscribe to a process, product, or balanced approach to teaching writing. Choose a lesson and teach it to a group of students. Evaluate the outcomes of the lesson, the students' response, and your delivery.

4. Visit the websites for writers found in Table 8.1 and use the criteria for evaluating websites discussed in this chapter. For what age/grade levels are they appropriate, and how effective do you think they would be in support of a classroom writing program?

5. Interview a reading teacher to find out his or her responsibilities in promoting effective writing instruction in his or her school. What is his or her background? Training? How does he or she assist teachers in teaching writing?

6. Visit *readingonline.org* and bookmark this electronic journal of the International Reading Association on your computer. Which articles show how teachers integrate reading and writing instruction? Which articles deal with some aspect of the writing process?

REFERENCES

Atwell, N. (1998). *In the middle: New understandings about writing, reading and learning* (2nd ed.). Portsmouth, NH: Boynton Cook.

Bromley, K. (1998). *Language arts: Exploring connections.* Boston: Allyn & Bacon.

Bromley, K. (2002). *Stretching students vocabulary.* New York: Scholastic.

Bunting, E. (1988). *How many days to America?* New York: Clarion.

Calkins, L. (1994). *The art of teaching writing.* Portsmouth, NH: Heinemann.

Cambourne, B. (1988). *The whole story: Natural learning and the acquisition of literacy in the classroom.* Auckland, NZ: Scholastic.

Casey, M., & Hemenway, S. (2001). Structure and freedom: Achieving a balanced writing curriculum. *English Journal, 90*(6), 68–75.

Cohen, B. (1998). *Molly's pilgrim.* New York: Beechtree.

Fletcher, R., & Portalupi, J. (1998). *Craft lessons: Teaching writing K–8.* York, ME: Stenhouse.

Gee, J. P. (1996). *Social linguistics and literacies* (2nd ed.). Bristol, PA: Falmer.

Gordon, C. J., & Macinnis, D. (1993). Using journals as a window on students' thinking in mathematics. *Language Arts, 70,* 37–43.

Graves, D. (1983). *Writing: Teacher and children at work.* Portsmouth, NH: Heinemann.

Graves, D. (1994). *A fresh look at writing.* Portsmouth, NH: Heinemann.

Hansen, J. (1996). Evaluation: The center of writing instruction. *The Reading Teacher, 50*(3), 188–195.

Harwayne, S. (1992). *Lasting impressions.* Portsmouth, NH: Heinemann.

Harwayne, S. (2000). *Lifetime guarantees: Toward ambitious literacy teaching.* Portsmouth, NH: Heinemann.

Harwayne, S. (2001). *Writing through childhood: Rethinking process and product.* Portsmouth, NH: Heinemann.

Hayes, J., & Flower, L. (1986). Problem-solving strategies and the writing process. *College English, 39,* 449–461.

Hillocks, G. (1987). Synthesis of research in teaching writing. *Educational Leadership, 12,* 71–82.

Irwin-DeVitis, L., Bromley, K., & Modlo, M. (1999). *50 graphic organizers for reading, writing and more.* New York: Scholastic.

Kane, S. (1997). Favorite sentences: Grammar in action. *The Reading Teacher, 51*(1), 70–72.

Karchmer, R. A. (2001). The journey ahead: Thirteen teachers report how the internet influences literacy and literacy instruction in their K–12 classrooms. *Reading Research Quarterly, 36*(4), 442–480.

Kear, D. J., Coffman, G. A., McKenna, M. C., & Ambrosio, A. L. (2000). Measuring attitude toward writing: A new tool for teachers. *The Reading Teacher, 54*(1), 10–23.

Lancia, P. J. (1997). Literary borrowing: The effects of literature on children's writing. *The Reading Teacher, 50*(6), 470–475.

Leu, D. J. (1997). Exploring literacy on the Internet: Caity's question: Literacy as deixis on the Internet. *The Reading Teacher, 51*(1), 62–67.

Marino, J. (1997). *Presentation to area educators.* Binghamton, NY: Board of Cooperative Educational Services.

McElveen, S. A., & Dierking, C. C. (2001). Children's books as models to teach writing. *The Reading Teacher, 54*(4), 362–364.

Murray, D. M. (1985). *A writer teaches writing* (2nd ed.). Boston: Houghton Mifflin.

Owens, R. F., Hester, J. L., & Teale, W. H. (2002). Where do you want to go today? Inquiry-based learning and technology integration. *The Reading Teacher, 55*(7), 616–641.

Peterson, S. (2000). Yes, we do teach writing conventions! (Though the methods may be unconventional). *Ohio Reading Teacher, 34*(1), 38–44.

Portalupi, J., & Fletcher, R. (2001). *Nonfiction craft lessons: Teaching information writing K–8.* York, ME: Stenhouse.

Routman, R. (1996). *Literacy at the crossroads: Crucial talk about reading, writing and other teaching dilemmas.* Portsmouth, NH: Heinemann.

Shanahan, T. (1997). Reading–writing relationships, thematic units, inquiry learning . . . in pursuit of effective integrated literacy instruction. *The Reading Teacher, 51*(1), 12–19.

Smith, F. (1994). *Writing and the writer* (2nd ed.). Hillsdale, NJ: Erlbaum.

Stine, R. L. (2002). *Beware: R. L. Stine picks his favorite scary stories.* New York: HarperCollins.

Strickland, D. S., Bodino, A., Buchan, K., Jones, K. M., Nelson, A., & Rosen, M. (2001). Teaching writing in a time of reform. *Elementary School Journal. 101*(4), 385–397.

Sudol, D., & Sudol, P. (1995). Yet another story: Writers' workshop revisited. *Language Arts, 72* (3), 171–178.

Vacca, R. T., & Vacca, J. L. (2002). *Content area reading: Literacy and learning across the curriculum.* Boston: Allyn & Bacon.

Villaume, S. K., & Brabham, E. G. (2001). Conversations among authors in Author's Circles. *The Reading Teacher, 54*(5), 494–496.

Vygotsky, L. (1978). *Mind in society.* Cambridge, MA: Harvard University Press.

Weaver, C. (1996). Facts: On the teaching of grammar. In C. Weaver, L. Gillmeister-Kraus, & G. Vento-Zogby (Eds.), *Creating support for effective literacy education* (section 12). Portsmouth, NH: Heinemann.

Wepner, S. B., & Tao, L. (2002). From master teacher to master novice: Shifting responsibilities in technology-infused classrooms. *The Reading Teacher, 55*(7), 642–661.

Zaragoza, N., & Vaughn, S. (1995). Children teach us to teach writing. *The Reading Teacher, 49*(1), 42–49.

Chapter 9

MATERIAL MATTERS: USING CHILDREN'S LITERATURE TO CHARM READERS (OR WHY HARRY POTTER AND THE PRINCESS DIARIES MATTER)

Douglas Fisher
James Flood
Diane Lapp

This chapter will:

- Provide a rationale for using children's literature in the elementary classroom.
- Identify instructional approaches for using children's literature.
- Explore the relationship between oral language and written language as these relate to literature instruction.
- Supply resources for teachers to identify quality children's literature.

In *Literature and the Child*, Cullinan (1989) notes that literature is both a window and a mirror to the world. It is through literature that students learn about people they might never meet and places they may never visit in their lifetimes. We believe that children must see themselves in books to affirm themselves, and must see others to expand their conception of the world. This is the purpose for using children's literature in the classroom; the focus of this chapter is as follows:

- Why teach literature?
- What types of literature are important to use?
- How does oral language development relate to literature instruction?
- How does written language development relate to literature instruction?
- How can literature affirm students' views of themselves and broaden their conceptions of the world?

Before we respond to these questions, we'd like to introduce you to Ms. Katz. Let's look into Ms. Katz's third-grade classroom. As she interacts with her students, it is easy to see the important role of literature in her classroom. Jessica, a student in Ms. Katz's class, tells us: "Everyone in my class reads a lot every day. Sometimes we all read different books about the same topic, and sometimes we read a book with Ms. Katz. She likes to ask us questions about what we have read. We also keep reflections in our journals, make our own books, and work on projects!"

Ms. Katz's 27 students come from a variety of backgrounds. Three students receive support from the resource specialist, and two students who speak Spanish receive services from a bilingual educator. Five other students receive bilingual services in Vietnamese. Ms. Katz's print-rich classroom is filled with Spanish, English, and Vietnamese words, phrases, books, and pieces of literature.

During the morning discussion, Ms. Katz encourages her children to share experiences about their families. As they do, she records the talk on a language chart that the children read and reread together, individually and in pairs. When the children return to their tables, Ms. Katz encourages them to write, illustrate, and share a story about a tradition that is a part of their family. Throughout this activity, her children are grouped heterogeneously, actively interacting with one another, sharing their family rituals and routines.

After they work for a while on their stories, she calls them to the rug to read *The Patchwork Quilt* (Flournoy, 1995), the target text in her unit on family. The day before, she had introduced several new vocabulary words in semantic maps that she knew the students would encounter, including *costume, recognized, realized, material, examined,* and *several.* Students were given time to respond to the text and to write questions about their responses in their journals (see Figure 9.1). After writing, students talked with a partner about their responses to the book. After several minutes of partner talk, Ms. Katz asks her students to share with the whole class. Justin excitedly tells the whole group that Cheyene has a great idea. Before Cheyene has a chance to speak, Justin tells the group that Cheyene thought that the class should look on the Internet for quilts from around the world. As we smile at their excitement, we glance at the classroom library and note that several theme extension books, both narrative and nonnarrative, are available: *Aunt Claire's Yellow Beehive Hair* (Blumenthal, 2001), *Grandma Francisca Remembers: A Hispanic-American Family Story* (Morris, 2002a), *The Raft* (La Marche, 2000), *Grandma Lois Remembers: An African-American Family Story* (Morris, 2002b), *Let's Talk about Living with a Single Parent* (Weitzman, 1997), and *Tea with Milk* (Say, 1999). After the children read and discuss *The Patchwork Quilt,* Ms. Katz invites them to go to their centers.

At one center, Kaila is working on her family quilt. She decorates the pieces of her quilt with a variety of family traditions that she had discussed with her mother. Ms. Katz had sent home a note to families about the upcoming theme, with a request that parents encourage a discussion between their child and relatives about family traditions, customs, and routines. Kaila's family is from the Pacific Islands, and her quilt highlights island life and her move to the mainland. During this time, Ms. Katz also meets with small, homogeneous groups of children who need explicit instruction in the vocabulary included in the story. She asks the children to create semantic maps, so that the literal meanings of words can be extended. For example, Allen tells her that a costume is a mask worn on Halloween. Through his semantic map and their discussion, he realizes that a costume can also be clothes or other personal effects, such as makeup, used to hide a person's identity, which can be worn at any time.

Response	Question

FIGURE 9.1. Student journal page.

Jessica is working in the Famous People center, where children look at the customs and traditions of their families. Jessica chose to write about Jackie Robinson. She loved the book, *In the Year of the Boar and Jackie Robinson* (Lord, 1984), which the class finished last month, and she found a biography about him, *Jackie Robinson* (Schaefer, 2002), in the school library. Muhammed decided to write about Helen Keller, because she was identified as a person who had a disability, during the class discussion on the book *True Confessions* (Tashjian, 1997). Muhammed read the biography *The Story of Annie Sullivan, Helen Keller's Teacher* (Selden, 1987) for his report. Dominique decided to write about Ryan White, the teenager who died of AIDS. Dominique's uncle had died the year before, and his mother had given the class a copy of *Losing Uncle Tim* (Jordan, 1989).

After the centers are completed, Ms. Katz gives her students time for free reading. Some children choose to read selections related to their morning centers. Others read about the experiences shared in the opening conversation, while others choose new themes. For example, Jeremy loves bicycles, and Ms. Katz is always looking at garage sales, bookstores, and library sales for informational books about bicycles. She encourages students to select books from the classroom library for this independent reading time, because her classroom library contains the best books, magazines, and newspapers available. She shares library books with other classroom teachers in order to provide variety for her students and to accommodate the wide range of reading ability of her students. The bilingual resource teacher also adds many materials to the classroom library. All of the children love bilingual books in which English is on one side of the page and the target language is on the other.

Later in the week, Ms. Katz explains to the class that they will be creating class books about their families. She tells them that the beauty of class books is that they contain the students' own words, and that they can read them over and over again.

Monique's group moves quickly to the floor near the classroom library, where they begin to look through previous class books to select one they would like to reread. After reviewing several, Erica has an idea for their book. She suggests that they write a book called "A Good Friend" and give the book to Ms. Katz, because the students consider her their friend. The students in the group take turns writing ideas about good friends. Erica wrote, "A good friend is someone you can walk on the beach and talk with." Jessica wrote, "A good friend is someone you care about and love." When each of the groups finish writing, illustrating, binding, and sharing their books, they are added to the classroom library for everyone to read.

As Ms. Katz teaches, assesses, groups, and regroups her students, we are constantly delighted with the importance she places on each child's literacy and literacy development. We know that she has carefully considered many questions in designing her reading/language arts program.

The next section of this chapter focuses on the questions about literature instruction that were raised in the introduction to this chapter.

THEORY AND RESEARCH BASE

Why Teach Literature?

Researchers (e.g., Huck, Hepler, & Hickman, 1993; Moss, 2003; Rosenblatt, 1990; Roser & Keehn, 2002; Roser & Martinez, 2000) indicate that teachers use literature as a significant part of the reading/language arts program for at least three reasons: modeling of language structures, connecting lessons to students' prior knowledge, and motivating readers. We believe that each of these reasons for using literature is important and worthwhile. Now let's turn to some of the research that has informed these three reasons for reading literature on classrooms.

Modeling Language Structure

When children are read to, they hear the sounds of the author's words. Over time, these exposures to the language structure of texts enable them to understand how different texts work (e.g., Power & Hubbard, 1996). "Stories told or read to children give them opportunities to hear words in use and, in the process, to support, expand, and stimulate their own experiments with language" (Cullinan, 1989, p. 15). Reading good literature encourages students to imitate language patterns and to create their own stories.

Literature also provides students with an appreciation of different genres, styles, and perspectives (Buss & Karnowski, 2000). When students in Ms. Katz's class were asked to create classroom books, Charise's group wrote about their grandparents. They used several words in their book that they had encountered while reading *The Patchwork Quilt*, such as *maternal* and *paternal, immigration*, and *generations*. The books from the classroom library on this topic included *Grandma's Latkes* (Druker, 1992), *Grandfather's Journey* (Say, 1993), and *Abuela's Weave* (Castaneda, 1993). Some children even brought in books from home. Lewis told the class how much he loved *Walk Two Moons* (Cheech, 1994), whereas Malik shared the informational book, *How My Family Lives in America* (Kuklin, 1992).

Accessing Prior Knowledge

Marshall (1996) maintains that all new knowledge is based on existing knowledge, and the previous experiences of students are central to completing the cycle. Children's literature can activate prior knowledge as an information source. Ms. Katz activated her children's prior knowledge when she asked them to talk about their family traditions, before introducing them to *The Patchwork Quilt*. The family quilt was one way that she encouraged her students to use information that they already knew, so that they could make connections between what they knew and what they were learning in the literature unit.

Motivating through Literature

Literature motivates readers, especially when readers see themselves living the life of a character. When children want to read, their attitude toward reading improves (Gambrell, 1996; Mazzoni, Gambrell, & Korkeamaki, 1999). A positive attitude toward reading usually results in more reading, and this, in turn, helps students develop fluency. The students in Ms. Katz's class gained a new understanding of their family's traditions by exploring the issues in *The Patchwork Quilt* (Flournoy, 1995).

What Types of Literature Are Important to Use?

Books chosen for children should cover a wide variety of genres, including folk tales, tall tales, fables, myths, legends, poems, fantasy, realism, and historical fiction, nonfiction, and science fiction. Books selected for use in classrooms must also be well written and include well-developed characters, interesting language, and engaging plots. We must also be aware of gender, racial, and ability stereotypes that might exist within the text. Like Ms. Katz, teachers should select books that depict a variety of family structures and perspectives on the world. We suggests that teachers should choose texts with (1) literary quality that has been demonstrated by reviews, awards, and trusted word-of-mouth recommendations; (2) aesthetic qualities that cover a wide array of genres that will elicit thoughtful responses from children; (3) concepts and ideas that children can grasp with guidance; and (4) opportunities to lead children to unique discoveries.

In choosing appropriate literature for the class, we may want to examine several book awards that are presented annually to newly published books worthy of distinction (see Table 9.1 for a list of award winners). Books that are selected for your classroom should depend on goals, themes, the languages spoken in the classroom, and the fluency of the students. In Ms. Katz's classroom, and in many other classrooms throughout the United States, basal reading programs (anthologies) that include the very best children's literature, as well as individual titles, make up a part of the classroom library.

How Does Oral Language Development Relate to Literature Instruction?

Literacy involves viewing, reading, writing, listening, and speaking. Among these, speaking is often forgotten or neglected in the literacy curriculum. Discussions about literature and performances of literature have been shown to affect literacy development positively (e.g., McDonald & Fisher, 2002; Roser & Hoffman, 1992; Worthy & Broaddus, 2002). One way to promote the development of oral language skills in the classroom is the implementation of literature circles. During literature circles, students have the opportunity to talk and share their ideas. Teachers use book clubs or literature circles in a variety of ways (Roser & Martinez, 1995).

In Ms. Katz's classroom, students are required to read a variety of works that provide an opening for discussion and examination of the multicultural world in which her children live. Seated in a large circle, students read, write, speak, and listen based on a process that is established during the first week of school (see Table 9.2). As a class, children

TABLE 9.1. Children's Literature Award Winners

Year	Title	Author

Newbery Medal Winners (1990–2003)

Year	Title	Author
2003	*Crispin: The Cross of Lead*	Avi
2002	*A Single Shard*	Linda Sue Park
2001	*A Year Down Yonder*	Richard Peck
2000	*Bud, Not Buddy*	Christopher Paul Curtis
1999	*Holes*	Louis Sachar
1998	*Out of the Dust*	Karen Hesse
1997	*The View from Saturday*	E. L. Konigsburg
1996	*The Midwife's Apprentice*	Karen Cushman
1995	*Walk Two Moons*	Sharon Creech
1994	*The Giver*	Lois Lowry
1993	*Missing May*	Cynthia Rylant
1992	*Shiloh*	Phyllis Reynolds Naylor
1991	*Maniac Magee*	Jerry Spinelli
1990	*Number the Stars*	Lois Lowry

Caldecott Medal Winners (1990–2003)

Year	Title	Author
2003	*My Friend Rabbit*	Eric Rohmann
2002	*The Three Pigs*	David Wiesner
2001	*So You Want to Be President?*	David Small
2000	*Joseph Had a Little Overcoat*	Simms Taback
1999	*Snowflake Bentley*	Mary Azarian
1998	*Rapunzel*	Paul O. Zelinsky
1997	*Golem*	David Wisniewski
1996	*Officer Buckle and Gloria*	Peggy Rathmann
1995	*Smokey Night*	Eve Bunting
1994	*Grandfather's Journey*	Allen Say
1993	*Mirette on the High Wire*	Emily Arnold McCully
1992	*Tuesday*	David Wiesner
1991	*Black and White*	David Mccaulay
1990	*Lon Po Po: A Red-Riding Hood Story from China*	Ed Young

TABLE 9.2. Guidelines for Moderators (Teachers or Students)

1. Have students write a journal response to the text being read (2–4 minutes; individually).

2. Share responses with a partner (2–4 minutes; pairs).

3. Lead discussion with the group (1–15 minutes; group).

    Begin by asking students to share thoughts based on their reading/ writing and discussion of text with their partner.

    Have content-specific questions ready to focus the discussion if it strays too far afield or becomes bogged down on a point that seems unresolvable.

4. Postdiscussion writing (4 minutes; individually).

5. Share responses with a partner (4 minutes; pairs).

6. Return to discussion with whole group (10 minutes; group).

    Invite responses based on the previous writing.

7. Write a journal entry (2–4 minutes; individually).

    Ask students to write about their response to the text as a result of reading, writing, and discussing with their peers.

agree on several general guidelines for operating a book club discussion (see Table 9.3).

In her classroom, students are accustomed to the Read, Write, Pair, and Share strategy (Flood, Lapp, & Fisher, 1999). Students expect to write in their journals after reading. By talking with their partners about their readings and writings, they have the opportunity to speak first with one person, before they are expected to share in a large group. This often makes them feel more comfortable and builds trust in the classroom. Children tend to see themselves and their partner as a team. For example, in one conversation, Justin said that Cheyene had a great idea about the book. He not only shared her idea with the class, but he also credited Cheyene with accolades that made her feel that her ideas were worth offering. Using the Read, Write, Pair, and Share procedures, Ms. Katz provides opportunities for both listening to student's ideas and having students listen to one another. She also uses choral reading and reader's theater as vehicles for enhancing her children's oral language skills through literature.

How Does Written Language Development Relate to Literature Instruction?

Children need to hear, see, and use language, so they can understand the connections between their thoughts, words, letters in printed words,

TABLE 9.3. Classroom Guidelines for Literature Discussion

- Be prepared to discuss your thoughts about the text by completing your reading and writing before the literature discussion begins.
- Be courteous by listening to everyone's comments.
- Be sensitive to people's feelings as you make contributions to the discussion.
- Wait until the speaker is finished before beginning your comments.
- Make your comments positive and constructive.
- Feel free to question and agree–disagree by clearly and calmly stating your opinion.
- Assume responsibility for your own growth.

and the way words sound. Children need to be exposed to a print-rich environment to become aware of sound symbol associations. This "print-rich environment" should reflect the range of languages represented in the class. As children interact with written and spoken languages, they begin to improve their vocabulary, decoding, and encoding, and to develop their reading comprehension and writing strategies (Salus & Flood, 2003).

Ms. Katz used shared reading, guided reading, and partner reading in her class to help children choose their topics. She selected vocabulary words from these readings and made these words her spelling words for the class. In this way, students had already encountered the word in context and could return to the text to find out more about the use of the word. In addition, Ms. Katz taught her students "word attack" strategies for situations in which they encountered unfamiliar words. Her students became quite familiar with using the Word Wall to identify word families and to spell words correctly. In addition, Ms. Katz integrated other elements of phonics, as needed.

Students also need explicit writing instruction from Ms. Katz. Most of the writing assignments in Ms. Katz' class extend over several days. Children in the class understand the writing curriculum for the class. Generally, this writing curriculum takes on the following form:

1. *Creating the writing assignment.* Students develop their topics as Ms. Katz guides and supports them. They often talk with partners about their ideas and answer questions about their topics.
2. *Planning the writing.* Students inform Ms. Katz of their role as the writer, their intended audience, and the format.
3. *Writing.* Students write at their desks, at centers, or in the media center based on the plan they have developed.

4. *Receiving feedback on written work.* Students meet with writing partners and Ms. Katz at a teacher editing table to share and respond to questions about their writing.
5. *Revising and editing.* With feedback in hand, students return to their desks, centers, or the media center to create a new draft of their texts. Students in Ms. Katz's class know that this step may be repeated several times to produce a quality work.
6. *Finalizing the writing.* When all the feedback has been considered and incorporated, students produce a display copy of their work. Some students use computers, whereas others handwrite. Everyone knows that illustrations are an important part of the writing process. They also know that they may choose to edit their work in the future as they learn more about a topic, but for now, it can be displayed for others to read.

During the unit on families, Ms. Katz provided students with specific feedback about their writing, spelling, editing, and grammar at the teacher editing table. She met with small groups of students while they discussed their papers with each other, and with her. Children also made decisions about which pieces to publish on the Writing Wall and which to add to their writing portfolios. Students also created visual representations of their writing, as Kaila did when she worked on her quilt.

How Can Literature Affirm Students' Views of Themselves and Broaden Their Conceptions of the World?

Students arrive in our classes with a number of assumptions about people. Often, these assumptions are stereotypes that result from lack of adequate information. Multiple literacy experiences in literature with children and adults from a variety of backgrounds enhances children's overall literacy development as it expands their worldview. Providing students with opportunities to discuss individual differences based on literacy experiences offers them new insights about people who are different from themselves (Katz, Sax, & Fisher, 1998). Discussing literature allows all children to look inward to examine their values, beliefs, and behaviors.

As teachers, choosing books may be our most important task. We suggest the selection of literature that is representative of the full range of human experiences found in our world. In Ms. Katz's classroom, students read about Maizon (Woodson, 1995), a girl who decides to leave a boarding school because she is unwilling to conform to the expectations of various cliques. Students also read narrative, biographical, and informational texts about children's lives, studies, habits, and hobbies in China, in books such as *City Kids in China* (Thomson, 1991) and *Look What Came from China* (Harvey, 1999). *Mother Jones and the March of the Mill Children* (Colman, 1994) provided students with opportunities to think about child labor, workers' rights, and the Chicago fire of 1871. As teachers, we must broaden our own perspectives so that our students are prepared for the diverse world in which we all live.

In Ms. Katz's class, students met people from all over the world in their exploration of the family. In Jessica's group, the children studied famous people and their families. She and her classmates learned about the families of Jackie Robinson, Helen Keller, and Ryan White. The impact that Ms. Katz's library of books has had on these students is inestimable.

The remainder of this chapter is devoted to instructional strategies that are useful in a literature curriculum. We use the following questions to guide our discussion:

- What is a balanced approach to literacy?
- What is the role of literature in beginning reading instruction?
- How should students be grouped for effective literature instruction?
- How do we assess students in a literature curriculum?

RESEARCH-BASED BEST PRACTICES

What Is a Balanced Approach to Literacy?

We believe that literature is essential in an effective, well-balanced program. We also think that explicit instruction is critical to a balanced approach. Every student is someplace on a nonhierarchial literacy continuum, and as Farnan, Flood, and Lapp (1994) note, "there is no point on the continuum that denotes too much literacy or, for that matter, not enough. There are no good or bad places to be, only places informed by children's previous knowledge and construction of literacy concepts" (p. 136). This perspective suggests that we should focus on what students know and are able to do, and build our literacy approach from there. The basis of this child-centered approach is the use of literature to access prior knowledge and provide students with information about the structure of their language.

Phonemic awareness, the awareness that words and parts of words are composed of sounds, has gained increased attention in recent years. We believe that one of the best ways to address phonemic awareness is through children's books that play with the sounds of language (Fisher & McDonald, 2001; Griffith & Olson, 1992). *Miss Spider's Tea Party* (Kirk, 1997) contains several word rhymes. For example,

> Some ants strode in, they numbered six,
> But ants with spiders will not mix.

She brewed them tea from hips of roses;
The proud platoon turned up their noses. (p. 12)

Books that encourage playing with sounds through the use of rhyme, rhythm, and repetition are especially good in a balanced literacy approach. Children see and hear words in context and also receive explicit instruction on the structure of language.

What Is the Role of Literature in Beginning Reading Instruction?

Emerging readers, like their middle- and upper-grade schoolmates, deserve a rich supply of the very best literature as the core to literacy–learning. Children need literature, because good stories help them make sense of the world, challenge their intellect, enlighten their imagination, nurture their desire to read, and heighten their awareness of self and others. Fortunately, by helping children develop all of their language skills— reading, writing, speaking, listening, and viewing—good literature also supports literacy achievement (Moss, 2003; Tunnell & Jacobs, 1989).

Allen (2000) maintains that books must be everywhere; they must be unavoidable in the classroom. Ms. Katz has her books propped against the fish tank, on the window ledges, and displayed prominently in her science, social studies, and math centers. She believes that books should announce their invitations to be read, talked about, laughed about, reread, inspected, referred to, reread, written about, enacted, and read one more time. When books permeate the classroom, literacy gains its surest foothold.

But especially for emerging and newly fluent readers, the supply of literature in the classroom must include another kind of text: decodable books that children can read themselves. These books should include all types of patterns, from rhyming to rhythmic. Although these books may not prove to elicit the deepest classroom discussion, they certainly entreat students to learn to read.

One effective way to teach literacy through literature is the use of big books or other shared reading experiences. These Big Books provide each student with the intimacy of an individual storytime, while allowing everyone visual access to the print and illustrations. Some teachers create their own big books and tape in the children's drawings, so they can be removed and returned to the artist. Using enlarged texts, young readers follow along as the teacher reads, using a pointer to indicate each word. Young readers may predict events or story language. Almost immediately, the children chime in, read along, and beg to "read it again." Reading repeatedly ensures familiarity and supports the children's own emergent reading of the stories. Through big books and shared reading, teachers help emerging readers work on the development of concepts of print—how books work, how print records and preserves language, how words travel on a page, and the significance of spaces marking them. Big books, along with the children's opportunities to write, support emergent reading and the development of understanding of the written language system (Roser, 1994).

However, all books are not created equally. Children need books that are inherently satisfying or meaningful as a story that can be "lived" through, such as *The Very Hungry Caterpillar* (Carle, 1979), or as rhythmical as *Engine, Engine, Number Nine* (Calmenson, 1997), or as instantly mastered as *It Looked Like Spilt Milk* (Shaw, 1947). Beginning reading is a very complex task that demands that children have opportunities to read great works and to learn and practice the skills that they are in process of achieving.

How Should Students Be Grouped for Effective Literature Instruction?

Traditionally, students have been grouped by their teachers' perception of their ability. This traditional grouping strategy has sometimes been a permanent assignment for each child. For much of their instructional day, students are grouped with others who teachers' believe have similar abilities. However, research over the past 25 years indicates that this type of grouping creates for students serious social problems that have lasting effects on their academic development (e.g., Flood & Lapp, 1997; Parratore & Indrisano, 2003). Students in the "low ability" groups are often required to complete more drill work in skills materials, are exposed to less literature, do far less silent reading than their peers in higher groups, and are frequently asked comprehension questions that do not require critical thinking skills (Lapp, Fisher, & Flood, 1999).

How, then, should teachers group students for effective instruction? Ms. Katz uses flexible grouping to meet the array of student needs within the class. Flexible grouping allows teachers to use a variety of grouping patterns to enhance student learning. These patterns include individual assignments, partners or pairs activities, cooperative groups with defined roles, on-to-one time with the teacher, cross-age groups that focus on themes, whole-class lessons, and learning centers.

In Ms. Katz's classroom, students are grouped and regrouped several times during the day. Some of the activities, such as the learning centers on Famous People, were completed in small heterogeneous groups. Other times, such as when she read *The Patchwork Quilt* (Flournoy, 1995), Ms. Katz provided instruction to the entire class. Still other times, her students worked individually and in pairs. Finally, recall that Ms. Katz met with a small group of students who needed specific skills instruction in one area. This group of students needed skills instruction in vocabulary, which Ms. Katz was able to provide during learning centers time. Ms. Katz uses the Center–Activity Rotation System (CARS) as her primary strategy for grouping students (Flood & Lapp, 2001). This system is based on three core beliefs:

1. Teachers use flexible groups that alternate membership efficiently.
2. Teachers work with individual students and small groups of students.
3. Teachers require students to participate in all activities, lessons, and units that have been designed.

When teachers use CARS, students are grouped heterogeneously for center activities. During the course of a weeklong lesson, students participate in one center per day. Throughout the week, each student meets several times with the teacher in a smaller group or individually. During this time, the teacher provides skills instruction, feedback on reading and writing strategies, and assessment information for her students. Flood and Lapp provide detailed information about the implementation of CARS in *Perspectives on Writing: Research, Theory, and Practice* (Indrisano & Squire, 2001).

How Do We Assess Students in a Literature Curriculum?

We believe that children need to have instruction in all the processes of literacy—reading, writing, speaking, listening, and viewing—and that this instruction should be based on assessments of student performance (Lapp, Fisher, Flood, & Cabello, 2001). However, assessments of literature knowledge have been restricted in the past to evaluations of students' knowledge of plot and characterization, or the information found directly in the text. Although such knowledge is critical, it is only a small piece of what needs to be assessed (Frey & Fisher, in press; Purves, 1994). New forms of assessment, including performance and portfolio assessment, need to be developed that will enable students and teachers to understand the ways in which students develop insights and interpretations. More specifically, new assessments that are compatible with response-based literature must be developed and used. To accomplish this, at least five different dimensions of literacy development must be considered as we design assessment instruments that will adequately measure our student's growth in literature:

- *Application of various kinds of knowledge.* Students should be able to use their knowledge from literature and apply it to their personal experiences, background, and culture. They should also be able

to apply knowledge to different genres, and to generalize terminology and theories.

- *Selection of material.* Students should not only select reading materials that develop their habit of reading, but they should also select materials that vary in format, genre, and complexity.
- *Articulation of a reasoned understanding of the text.* Reading literature
  is not done in isolation. Rather, students should display their understanding of texts in group discussions, during interactions with the
  teacher, and in their writing.
- *Reflection on the readings.* Students should develop an understanding of the distinctions between personal and public implications,
  and be able to place the text in the larger context of literature and
  culture.
- *Consideration of the role of literature in society.* Students should be able
  to distinguish between personal and public criteria for judging
  texts, and recognize levels and types of taste and quality.

With the use of these five dimensions, it should be possible to collect a variety of assessment materials, including reading logs, interviews,
performances, writing samples, speaking checklists, and other pieces that
inform us about students' skills and knowledge of literature—both narrative and non-narrative.

The Complete Picture

Many researchers believe that literature is the foundation for literacy development (e.g., Flood & Langer, 1994; Flood, Lapp, Squire, & Jensen, 2003;
Huck et al., 1993). Ms. Katz holds fast to this belief. Her classroom reflects
her strong belief that literature is the cornerstone of her literacy curriculum:

- She reads aloud pieces of great literature.
- She provides experiences in listening comprehension of impor-
  tant literary works.
- She encourages oral language development through discussion
  as a vehicle for understanding and appreciating literature.
- She models guided reading using literature.
- She uses literature that is socially sensitive and culturally specific.
- She provides a wide range of literary experiences, including the
  reading of many genres, topics, and difficulty levels.
- She models, encourages, and guides writing about each child's
  literary experiences.
- She provides time for students to choose books that they want to
  read.

The students in her classroom will remember the books they have read for a long time. We believe that these children have a much better chance at becoming lifelong readers because of their experiences with books in elementary school. We also know that access to good children's literature improves reading comprehension, oral language, and writing performance. We hope you will try some of these activities with your students.

DISCUSSION AND ACTIVITIES

1. *Theme Search.* Select a theme and find a targeted book for that theme. Ask your students to search the classroom and school libraries for books related to the theme. Once they have read several of them, discuss the differences and similarities in the texts. Using the same book from this activity, select a different message from that book and try the activity again. For example, a book may focus on families but also have information on cooking, fighting, or adoption. Doing this will teach children that books have many messages.
2. *Word Study Fun.* Find a book that has a rhyming pattern in which the words are spelled the same. Using the book, teach the students this pattern. Once they understand the onset and rime, ask them to identify additional words with this pattern, and to make their own story.
3. *Pair It.* Find a narrative book that you want to share with your students. As you share this book aloud, find a non-narrative text that can be paired with your narrative text and read parts from both books each day. Invite students to compare narrative and non-narrative text structures.
4. *Have a Genre Party.* Select a genre that you do not teach very often (e.g., poetry, biography, historical fiction, etc.), and collect different books from that genre and share them with students. Ask groups of students to read different books, then share information about the books and the genre with the whole class.

REFERENCES

Allen, J. (2000). *Yellow brick roads: Shared and guided paths to independent reading 4–12.* Portland, ME: Stenhouse.

Blumenthal, D. (2001). *Aunt Claire's yellow beehive hair.* New York: Dial Books for Young Readers.

Buss, K., & Karnowski, L. (2000). *Reading and writing literary genres.* Newark, DE: International Reading Association.

Calmenson, S. (1997). *Engine, engine, number nine.* New York: Hyperion.

Carle, E. (1979). *The very hungry caterpillar.* New York: Collins.

Castaneda, O. S. (1993). *Abuela's weave.* New York: Lee & Low.

Cheech, S. (1994). *Walk two moons.* New York: HarperCollins.

Colman, P. (1994). *Mother Jones and the march of the mill children.* New York: Millbrook.

Cullinan, B. E. (1989). *Literature and the child* (2nd ed.). San Diego: Harcourt Brace Jovanovich.

Druker, M. (1992). *Grandma's latkes.* New York: Harcourt Brace.

Farnan, N., Flood, J., & Lapp, D. (1994). Comprehending through reading and writing: Six research-based instructional strategies. In K. Spangenberg-Urbschat & R. Pritchard (Eds.), *Kids come in all languages: Reading instruction for ESL students* (pp. 135–157). Newark: DE: International Reading Association.

Fisher, D., & McDonald, N. (2001). The intersection between music and early literacy instruction: Listening to literacy. *Reading Improvement, 38,* 106–115.

Flood, J., & Langer, J. (Eds.). (1994). *Literature instruction: Practice and policy.* New York: Scholastic.

Flood, J., & Lapp, D. (1997, December). *Grouping: The unending story.* Paper presented at the National Reading Conference, Scottsdale, AZ.

Flood, J., & Lapp, D. (2001). Teaching writing in urban schools: Cognitive processes, curriculum resources, and the missing links—management and grouping. In R. Indrsano & J. R. Squire (Eds.), *Perspectives on writing: Research, theory, and practice* (pp. 233–250). Newark, DE: International Reading Association.

Flood, J., Lapp, D., & Fisher, D. (1999). Book clubs that encourage students to examine their cultural assumptions. In S. Totten, C. Johnson, L. R. Morrow, & T. Sills-Briegel (Eds.), *Practicing what we preach: Preparing middle level educators* (pp. 261–263). New York: Falmer.

Flood, J., Lapp, D., Squire, J. R., & Jensen (Eds.). (2003). *Handbook of research on teaching the English language arts* (2nd ed.). Mahwah, NJ: Erlbaum.

Flournoy, V. (1995). *The patchwork quilt.* New York: Puffin.

Frey, N., & Fisher, D. (in press). Linking assessments and instruction in a multilingual elementary school. In C. Coombe & N. Hubley (Eds.), *Assessment practices: Case studies.* Waldorf, MD: Teachers of English to Speakers of Other Languages.

Gambrell, L. B. (1996). Creating classroom cultures that foster reading motivation. *The Reading Teacher, 50,* 14–25.

Griffith, P., & Olson, M. (1992). Phonemic awareness helps beginning readers break the code. *The Reading Teacher, 45,* 516–523.

Harvey, M. (1999). *Look what came from China.* New York: Franklin Watts.

Huck, C., Hepler, S., & Hickman, J. (1993). *Children's literature in the elementary school* (5th ed.). Fort Worth, TX: Harcourt Brace.

Indrisano, R., & Squire, J. R. (Eds.). (2001). *Perspectives on writing: Research, theory, and practice.* Newark, DE: International Reading Association.

Jordan, M. (1989). *Losing Uncle Tim.* New York: Albert Whitman.

Katz, L., Sax, C., & Fisher, D. (1998). *Activities for a diverse classroom: Connecting students.* Colorado Springs, CO: PEAK Parent Center.

Kirk, D. (1994). *Miss Spider's tea party.* New York: Scholastic.

Kuklin, S. (1992). *How my family lives in America.* New York: Bradbury.

LaMarche, J. (2000). *The raft.* New York: HarperCollins.

Lapp, D., Fisher, D., & Flood, J. (1999). Does it matter how you're grouped for instruction? Yes! Flexible grouping patterns promote student learning. *California Reader, 33*(1), 28–32.

Lapp, D., Fisher, D., Flood, J., & Cabello, A. (2001). An integrated approach to the teaching and assessment of language arts. In S. R. Hurley & J. V. Tinajero (Eds.), *Literacy assessment of second language learners* (pp. 1–26). Boston: Allyn & Bacon.

Lord, B. (1984). *In the Year of the Boar and Jackie Robinson.* New York: Harper & Row.

Marshall, N. (1996). The students: Who are they and how do I reach them? In D. Lapp, J. Flood, & N. Farnan (Eds.), *Content area reading and learning: Instructional strategies* (pp. 79–94). Boston: Allyn & Bacon.

Mazzoni, S. A., Gambrell, L. B., & Korkeamaki, R. (1999). A cross-cultural perspective of early literacy motivation. *Reading Psychology, 20,* 237–253.

McDonald, N., & Fisher, D. (2002). *Developing arts-loving readers: Top 10 questions teachers are asking about integrated arts education.* Lanham, MD: Scarecrow Education.

Morris, A. (2002a). *Grandma Francisca remembers: A Hispanic-American family story.* New York: Millbrook.

Morris, A. (2002b). *Grandma Lois remembers: An African-American family story.* New York: Millbrook.

Moss, B. (2003). *25 strategies for guiding readers through informational texts.* San Diego: Academic Professional Development.

Parratore, J. R., & Indrisano, R. (2003). Grouping for instruction in literacy. In J. Flood, D. Lapp, J. Squire, & J. Jensen (Eds.), *Handbook of research on teaching the English language arts* (2nd ed., pp. 566–572). Mahwah, NJ: Erlbaum.

Power, B. M., & Hubbard, R. S. (1996). *Language development: A reader for teachers.* Englewood Cliffs, NJ: Prentice-Hall.

Purves, A. (1994). On honesty in assessment and curriculum in literature. In J. Flood & J. Langer (Eds.), *Literature instruction: Practice and policy* (pp. 153–169). New York: Scholastic.

Rosenblatt, L. M. (1990). Retrospect. In E. J. Farrell & J. R. Squire (Eds.), *Transactions with literature: A fifty-year perspective* (pp. 97–107). Urbana, IL: National Council of Teachers of English.

Roser, N. (1994). From literature to literacy: A new direction for young learners. In J. Flood & J. Langer (Eds.), *Literature instruction: Practice and policy* (pp. 71–108). New York: Scholastic.

Roser, N., & Hoffman, J. (1992). Language charts: A record of story talk. *Language Arts, 69,* 44–52.

Roser, N., & Keehn, S. (2002). Fostering thought, talk, and inquiry: Linking literature and social studies. *The Reading Teacher, 55,* 416–426.

Roser, N., & Martinez, M. (Eds.). (1995). *Book talk and beyond: Children and teachers respond to literature.* Newark, DE: International Reading Association.

Roser, N., & Martinez, M. (2000). What Alice saw through the keyhole: Visions of children's literature in elementary classrooms. *Journal of Children's Literature, 26,* 18–27.

Salus, P., & Flood, J. (2003). *Language: A user's guide.* San Diego: Academic Professional Development.

Say, A. (1993). *Grandfather's journey*. New York: Houghton Mifflin.

Say, A. (1999). *Tea with milk*. New York: Houghton Mifflin.

Schaefer, L. M. (2002). *Jackie Robinson*. New York: Pebble Books.

Selden, B. (1987). *The story of Annie Sullivan, Helen Keller's teacher*. New York: Dell Yearling.

Shaw, C. G. (1947). *It looked like spilt milk*. New York: Harper & Row.

Tashjian, J. (1997). *True confessions*. New York: Scholastic.

Thomson, P. (1991). *City kids in China*. New York: HarperCollins.

Tunnell, M. O., & Jacobs, J. S. (1989). Using "real" books: Research findings on literature based reading instruction. *The Reading Teacher, 42,* 470–477.

Weitzman, E. (1997). Let's talk about living with a single parent. New York: Powerkids.

Woodson, J. (1995). *Between Madison and Palmetto*. New York: Delacorte.

Worthy, J., & Broaddus, K. (2002). Fluency beyond the primary grades: From group performance to silent, independent reading. *The Reading Teacher, 55,* 334–343.

Chapter 10

ADOLESCENT LITERACY

Lisa Patel Stevens
Thomas W. Bean

This chapter will:

- Explore dichotomies between secondary school–sanctioned literacies and literacies used by adolescents outside of school contexts.
- Provide a brief review of the literature on content area and adolescent literacy.
- Describe compelling adolescent literacy instructional practices for a shifting economic, political, and social landscape of the 21st century.
- Engage readers to explore implications for their practices and for future instruction.

You are in Mrs. Azner's 10th-grade Algebra II and Trigonometry II class. It is Wednesday, third period, and today's topic from Chapter 7 of your textbook, *Algebra and Trigonometry: Structure and Method*, Book 2 (Brown, Dolciani, Sorgenfrey, & Kane, 1990) will be introduced in the typical fashion.

Mrs. Azner, standing by the whiteboard at the front of the room, says, "Today we'll be dealing with quadratic functions and their graphs. We'll start by learning how to graph parabolas where equations have the form $y - k = a(x - h)^2$, and how to find the vertices and axes of symmetry." She writes the equation $y - k = a(x - h)^2$ and the vocabulary terms "vertices" and "axes of symmetry" on the whiteboard.

You concentrate on copying down whatever Mrs. Azner writes on the board. If you can stay awake, you can figure out parabolas. So far, you have got a solid C going in Mrs. Azner's honors class and, at this point, you'd just like to maintain it. Mrs. Azner allows no talking during her lecture and most of the class time. She drones on in a dull monotone, and you hope that reading the textbook, the only book used in the class, will help you understand these new formulas tonight, when you get home after swimming practice. You are not sure what parabolas are good for, but you know that someday you would like to be an engineer and design power plants. Mrs. Azner references the book by telling the class what chapter is about parabolas and mentions that "on page 65, it explains that the y axis is called the axis of symmetry, or the axis of the parabola."

Time passes, and some students daydream. Others, like you, take notes on the upcoming problems for tonight's homework. The textbook is used largely for its seemingly endless store of practice problems. In Mrs. Azner's class, reading and understanding mathematics is tantamount to replicating her blackboard examples with different sets of numbers.

Your friend Kyle wakes up from a catnap and says, "Mrs. Azner, I don't get it. What's a parabola do?" Your other friends giggle at Kyle, and Mrs. Azner's deep-creased frown gets even more dour as she replies, "I already explained that, Kyle. If you were awake you'd know. Just make sure you understand this material by next Monday when we have the chapter test."

You cringe, knowing that the chapter test will consist of a series of problems like those from the book, and all you can do is go home and practice solving them. You also know that when you get home, you'll need to surf the Net to find information for a history paper on the Holocaust and to find information on chaos theory for biology class. You know your textbooks cover this information, and your science teacher even gave the class a bibliography of books in the library that address microorganisms. However, from experience, you have found that it is much easier to download the information from the Net and quickly modify it for your school purposes. You know that you may have to prove to one of your teachers that you did not plagiarize the information, but this is part of the game, because your teachers do not seem to use their computers for anything other than recording students' grades.

The preceding scenario describes a familiar but unfortunate experience in today's secondary schools: one in which the curriculum and the texts are less than engaging and the teacher's role is more that of central locuter than facilitator of rich pedagogical practices, crucial curriculum, and timely texts. Literacy in secondary schools often gets bogged down in dry practices revolving around weighty textbooks and "remedial" classes, perpetuating rudimentary definitions of literacy and reading at the elementary level. In this chapter, we briefly review the literature on adolescent literacy and best practices, then illustrate our view of best practices in adolescent literacy by providing examples of how rich pedagogies might be addressed in a dynamic secondary school context. Following this example, we discuss implications of this model and offer additional resources designed to help other content teachers and literacy professionals develop classrooms that truly exemplify best practices.

THEORY AND RESEARCH BASE

Secondary literacy instruction typically comes in one of two forms: One is remedial classes, with strict attention to direct instruction and guided practice of word study skills such as phonemic awareness, phonics, and spelling. These skills are typically taught through mastery learning exercises that most often are not tailored to the meet the specific needs of students (Vacca, 1998). The other form, content area literacy, did not come into its own as a discipline until the advent of the 20th century (Moore, Readence, & Rickelman, 1983). Early influence and direction was provided by one of the prominent leaders of early content area instruction, William S. Gray. Gray was instrumental in promoting the slogan, "Every teacher a teacher of reading," which embodied a bold recognition of the variety of skills demanded by reading subject matter at all levels (Moore et al., 1983). Although this statement reflected a grand and progressive notion that literacy instruction should be integrated across subject areas, it received considerable backlash as secondary content area teachers perceived and resisted ideas of additional instructional responsibilities, which became an enduring affective stance among content area teachers to this day (Moore, Bean, Birdyshaw, & Rycik, 1999).

Changing Views of Content Area Literacy

Content area literacy was defined in the mid- and late 20th century by experimental and quasi-experimental investigations of cognitively based strategies for more efficient negotiation of content area texts (Alvermann & Moore, 1991; Bean, 2000). For example, perhaps the most widely known of textbook strategies, Scan Question Read Review Reflect (SQ3R), became widespread, at least in reference, if not in practice, in schools during this time. This strategy asks students to follow a five-step sequential process in previewing, reading, and rereading content area texts. Researched in laboratory settings, the strategy sought to use methods originally developed by the military to help students negotiate textbooks. As might be expected, the overtly linear strategy was not widely embraced by students, although it is still widely known and referenced as a current textbook reading strategy (e.g., Readence, Bean, & Baldwin, 2001; Walker, 1976).

In fact, in a comprehensive review of early 1980s research in the field of content area literacy, Alvermann and Moore (1991) found that many of these teaching strategies had (1) limited ecological validity, (2) limited teacher input, (3) limited texts, and (4) limited instruction in actual strategy use. In other words, content area literacy instruction had spent too many years in the "atheoretical guise of methods and materials . . . more or less, a bag of tricks" (Vacca, 1998, p. xvi). Antithetically, this perceived guise would play a role in secondary teachers' resistance to integrated infusion of literacy strategies into their instruction.

This "bag of tricks" approach had not only not fallen somewhat short of showing adolescents effective ways of reading content texts, but it had also been met with significant resistance from content area teachers to the infusion of these strategies into their practices. As mentioned before, secondary content area teachers resisted these strategies for many com-

plex and interwoven reasons, including the social, political, and historically situated structures of secondary schools that ran contrary to student-
centered pedagogies (Hinchman & Moje, 1998; O'Brien, Stewart, & Moje,
1995). Instead, these practices have historically supported a cognitive
stance that has helped to perpetuate the secondary school structure formulated in a postindustrial quest to equip students with vocational and
academic knowledge to become part of the workforce (O'Brien et al.,
1995). Furthermore, the separation of subjects in secondary schools has
marginalized the locus of literacy practices in both teachers' and students'
lives; that is, one does science in science, and writing and reading in
English.

In the 1990s, secondary literacy research shifted to qualitative investigations into both particular uses of content area literacy strategies and
resistance from secondary teachers (Bean, 2000). These qualitative studies shed considerable light on why so many of the strategies developed
and validated in experimental and quasi-experimental settings in the
1970s and 1980s were not being infused into teachers' practices and were
therefore not supporting students' literacy learning.

Recent researchers have studied the effective use of content area
literacy strategies, but in specific contexts, with corresponding sociocultural aspects. In general, these studies have highlighted content area literacy strategies that support and work against classroom dynamics. Arising from these studies have been both more integrated strategies for
supporting adolescents' literacy learning, and wholly integrated textbooks
and inservices.

Strategies arising from the 1990s also reflect an integrated approach,
which considers the prior knowledge that each adolescent brings to any
instructional context. For example, Ogle's (1992) KWL provided a structure for students to access prior knowledge, set a purpose for reading, and
monitored comprehension in a flexible format suited to myriad scenarios.
By guiding students through what they *know*, what they *want* to know, and
what they *learned*, the seemingly simple strategy represents the integrated
and flexible approach to literacy that has proved much more amenable to
secondary content teachers (Ogle, 1992). Strategies such as this one were
also explored and fueled by research in actual secondary classrooms, further validating and texturizing knowledge of the strategy.

As content area literacy in the 1990s began both to question past
didactic approaches and to support contemporary integrated and flexible approaches, many qualitative studies arose that revealed how actual
teachers and students made sense of these strategies. These studies explored both overall approaches to content area literacy by teachers and
students and more specific applications of single strategies. Endemic to
these studies was a sociocultural framework, which maintained that lit-

eracy learning and instruction are intertwined with the cultural, epistemological, and historical background of the participants and of the classroom as a discourse community (Au, 1998; Vygotsky, 1978).

For example, Elizabeth Moje's (1996) 2-year ethnography of how a veteran high school science teacher and her students used content area literacy in the science classroom demonstrated that the classroom climate and the teacher's and students' past experiences played inherent roles in the unfolding of literacy practices. Using qualitative designs of symbolic interactionism and hermeneutic phenomenology, Moje found that, in this particular classroom, literacy was "practiced as a tool for organizing thinking and learning in the context of a relationship built between the teacher and her students" (p. 173). Strategies included textbook preview, SQ3R, concept mapping, graphic organizers, notebooks, Venn diagrams, and portfolios. Obviously, this high school classroom represented an integrated approach to literacy learning; however, Moje found that students did not transfer use of these strategies to other classrooms. Although the integration and application of these strategies occurred at a high level in the science teacher's classroom, this was the result of the unique, sociocultural makeup of this discourse community. Studies such as these have also begun to mark a gentle shift from the pervasive notion of the adolescent as little more than a bundle of hormones (Finders, 1998).

No longer seeking to find a one-size-fits-all approach to strategies, the field of content area literacy has been able to highlight specific examples of integrated literacy learning that engage both students and teachers in specific contexts. However, an enduring tension is that between a reverence for the text as the center of instruction and the purpose of learning, and the student at the center of learning. A nominal and theoretical shift to adolescent literacy in the late 1990s marked a purposeful desire to bring the adolescent back into focus as central to any and all secondary literacy activity.

Adolescent Literacy

In 1998, the International Reading Association (IRA) formed the Adolescent Literacy Commission, whose ensuing position statement called particular attention to the marginalized position of adolescent literacy in education (Moore et al., 1999). This statement has underscored the need for schools first to acknowledge, recognize, and utilize the multiliteracies that dominate workplaces functioning under globalization and the multiliteracies in which adolescents engage. Hinchman and Moje (1998, p. 121) called for literacy practitioners in secondary schools to "look more closely at particular students' literacy practices, find out what they think about school, about different content areas, and about how their outside-of-school lives influence and merge with their in-school lives." Texts, viewed from a social constructivist stance are far from neutral sources. "They are cultural tools for establishing belongingness, identity, personhood, and ways of knowing" (Moje, Dillon, & O'Brien, 2000, p. 167).

Throughout all of these recent appeals is the notion that literacy instruction for adolescents must continue to not only refine content area literacy strategies but also consider other forms of literacy events in which adolescents and adults engage. The shift in moniker from content area literacy to adolescent literacy, at least in part, symbolizes a desire to bring the adolescent into focus as the centerpiece of instruction.

For example, while the formation and negotiation of identities is a lifelong endeavor, it is strongly associated with young people. These often difficult, fluid, and transformational journeys have been at the center of much young-adult fiction (Bean, 2001). When fiction and nonfiction texts are carefully considered from a critical literacy perspective, silenced voices and marginalized groups come into sharper focus. Adolescents function as social actors and creators of their identities within often fluid virtual spaces and a fast-paced global economy that destabalizes home and school life (McDonald, 1999). In many young-adult novels, adolescents are taking on adult roles, helping support their families when one or more parents are out of work (e.g., *Danger Zone*, Klass, 1996; *Fighting Ruben Wolfe*, Zusak, 2000). By expanding the scope of adolescent literacy to encompass critical literacy, identity issues, social justice concerns, and questions surrounding how race, class, and gender are treated in a postmodern world, all become possible considerations. Noting how characters are positioned based on identity, gender, ethnicity, and culture opens untapped horizons for considering issues of social justice. Similarly, making intertextual connections between social studies events (e.g., globalization) and fiction illuminates inequities, silenced voices, and simplistic essentialist views.

Although some debate ensues on whether content area literacy is a subsection of adolescent literacy (D. G. O'Brien, personal communication, April 29, 1999), appeals for researchers and teachers to approximate more closely the multiliteracies of not only adolescents but also a fast-paced, globally mediated economy are consistent. Other studies involving middle school students have also called for expanded, systematic reform efforts (e.g., Lipka, 1998). Although the governments of the United Kingdom and Australia have begun to appropriate some aspects of critical literacy into curricular frameworks (Luke, 2000), research in the United States is just beginning to bring issues of adolescent literacy to the surface.

A few action research projects have begun to examine the implications of this type of framework in school settings. The study by Lewis and Fabos (2000) of one Midwestern girl's use of Instant Messaging (IM; a brief, real-time, online form of communication) and other Internet uses speaks volumes about the complex, dynamic ways in which adolescents use literacy. In stark contrast to the adolescent's sophisticated, often simultaneous, use of IM, chat rooms, and e-mailing, the simple linearity of many school-sanctioned reading and writing strategies holds little value for her. Lewis and Fabos point out that, as educators, whether of adolescents or preservice teachers, we have the responsibility to bring these types of multiliteracies into our instruction, using them as texts to inform our pedagogical framework. This stance is supported by several studies into the use of popular culture as potential texts in classrooms (e.g., Alvermann, Moon, & Hagood, 1999; Stevens, 2001).

To explore and explicate research-based practices in adolescent literacy in the early 21st century, we describe a secondary classroom in which a new type of pedagogical framework, described by the New London Group in 1997, positions the teacher and students as active conegotiators of texts, as both critical consumers and producers. This pedagogical framework includes (1) situated practice (taking into account the unique and specific sociocultural context for specific practices), (2) overt instruction (including a presence in the instruction for direct guidance and scaffolding of students' metacognitive and metalinguistic awareness), (3) critical framing (act of positioning texts and information within its social, cultural, and historical, and political contexts), and (4) transformed practice (reconstructing meanings, breaking down established frames of reference, and constructing new meanings in new social spaces). Enacted with all components together, this pedagogical framework provides an epistemology and a methodology for literacy in content classrooms (in fact, in all secondary classrooms, because expanded notions of text include the ascription to various discourse communities) to build a dynamic two-way bridge between students' home and school multiliteracies, support students in their meaning making of various forms of text, and position students and the learning community at the forefront of instruction. The following secondary classroom scenario is a narrative based on Stevens's work with high school teachers in the western United States.

RESEARCH-BASED PRACTICE

Frank Owens teaches 10th-grade U.S. history in an urban high school. His students come from mostly low- and middle-class backgrounds, are widely diverse in ethnic and religious backgrounds, and have been learning to develop and apply critical literacy skills in their language arts and reading classes. On a spring day in 2002, Frank opens his fifth-period tenth-grade social studies class by asking his students what current events have been in the news lately. Several students shout out, "The war on terrorism." Several others name the conflict in the Middle East between Israel and Palestine as a key news topic as of late.

Frank asks his students to consider whether they think the media coverage of the war on terrorism and the Israeli–Palestinian war has been fairly covered. After a lull in the classroom, Monica, an African American girl, responds by saying, "Fair to who?"

"Great question, Monica. Does it make a difference if I say fair to the United States? Or maybe fair to the Middle East?" Frank responds.

"A little bit," says Isaac, an Arab American student, "but not much. I come from both of those countries, so it's not just one or the other."

"Well, what do you think of the articles about the Israeli–Palestinian war, Isaac?" probes Frank.

"Um, I'm not really sure. I haven't read all the articles, but I know my dad gets really PO'ed every time he watches the evening news."

"OK, anybody else?" Frank asks. A few other students offer opinions that the media coverage is just confusing, for example, Amanda's comment:

"Well, I just don't get it. I mean aren't we fighting a war on terrorism? If we are, then why doesn't President Bush want the Jews to fight the war on the terrorists from Palestine? I mean, isn't it all the same thing—terrorism?"

"Yeah, but that doesn't count, because it's not against the right terrorists," quips Jordan, a Japanese American male student.

Frank leads the students to focus their discussion on the Israeli–Palestinian war and how it is represented in U.S. media coverage. He acts as scribe for a whole-class brainstorm on the board, eliciting any and all information the students already know or suspect about the situation.

He then introduces the class's next project.

"We're going to investigate this a bit more using the critical literacy techniques you've been using in your language arts classes. I'd like you to begin by obtaining some samples of media coverage of this war, and we're going to pay attention to who is represented and who is not, how, and why in these articles. Depending upon what you find, we'll end by creating our own coverage of the war and making the adjustments we think are appropriate."

Frank hands out several resources to students, including a recommended starting point for print and electronic texts, a list of critical literacy questions, and a primer on Hallidayan grammar, which embeds critical literacy into language analysis by identifying the agent, action, and object, instead of neutralized subjects, nouns, and verbs.[1]

The students spend the next week investigating sources. They consult the Internet, print newspapers, magazines, nonmainstream websites and magazines, and they videotape and examine several TV clips from major network and cable stations. When the students share what they have found, the examples provided are diverse in their representation of the conflict.

Colin, a European American male, and Lindsey, a Jewish American female, share a *New York Times* article with the following headline: "Unusually Unified in Solidarity with Israel, but Also Unusually Unnerved" (Wilgoren, 2002).

"Well, this article is about Jewish people, this group in Chicago especially, and how they feel about the Israel and Palestine War," explains Colin.

"Yeah, but look at the headline," Lindsey says to Frank and the other class members. "They don't even identify the agent. It's all assumed, like the reader should automatically know that the article is about Jewish people, and not Arab people."

"What do you think about that?" asks Frank.

"Well, we think it's not very fair, because not everyone who reads the *New York Times* is Jewish," offers Colin.

"Yeah, even though I'm Jewish, even I know that the article is biased in my favor," says Lindsey.

Another pair of students, Jessica and Mary, use Frank's computer and projector to share a nonmainstream website they found, entitled "Electronicintifada" (Available: *electronicintifada.net*). Jessica explains that the website claims to be a network providing pro-Palestinian media coverage of the conflict.

Ben, a Latino male, shares the resources he found on a website created by a political science professor.

"I really liked the parts where he talks about political cartoons. Here, look," Ben says as he clicks on the hyperlink to political cartoons. "See, I never thought about how they draw the noses bigger to make stereotypes about people."

As the students offer examples of both mainstream and nonmainstream representations, they note in their discussion that the media coverage is not a simple "one way or the other." There are lots of interpretations, and one discussion point is whether it is possible to have a "fair" representation.

"I don't think so," says Colin. "It's always going to have some biases."

1. For more information on Hallidayian grammatical analysis, see Halliday (1998).

"Well, what if they interview both Arabs and Jews for the story?" offers Lindsey.

"Nah, not even then, because not all Arabs think the same thing about this," says Colin.

Frank directs the students to consider the possible neutrality of texts. He helps to restate and clarify students' positions, offers alternative viewpoints, and asks the students to refer back to their deconstruction of the media texts for examples. Frank brings in a media text sample from the bombing of Pearl Harbor and asks students to consider the similarities and differences in the media coverage of this still heartfelt incident in U.S. history in Hawaii.

As the discussion develops, it becomes clear to both the students and to Frank that whereas a neutral text is neither obtainable nor desirable for a deeper understanding of the nature of texts, crafting texts to portray diverse viewpoints is essential. With that, the students spend the next week creating their own texts about the Israeli–Palestinian conflict. Colin and Lindsey conduct interviews of Arab Americans, write a text similar to the style and genre of the *New York Times* article, and send a copy to the journalist who wrote the original article. Jessica and Mary construct a website for other students investigating the conflict and purposefully provide a guide that explains the slant and positionality found in the other hyperlinked websites. Ben drafts a political cartoon for the school newspaper, using satire to show stereotypes of teenagers (skateboarders, surfers, nerds, jocks) alongside ethnic stereotypes of Jews and Arabs. His headline reads, "This Is Your Brain on Stereotypes. Just Say No."

This classroom scenario briefly explores the present and future possibilities of adolescent literacy, a field that has the ability to transcend the text-centered privilege (Cope & Kalantzis, 1993) that content area textbooks have enjoyed since the dawn of American secondary schooling. In this snapshot, the teacher uses the New London Group's pedagogical framework to guide a dynamic exploration and creation of texts that capture the intersection of textual practices, culture, ideology, and the world.

The teacher situates the practice of media texts within the particular contexts of the western United States, asking students to compare and contrast a seemingly far-removed conflict and the most salient military incident to occur on Hawaiian soil in the 20th century. He also uses clear and overt instruction to guide the students toward their retrieval, reading, and critique of media texts. By drawing on Hallidayian grammar analyses, Frank provides explicit tools for the students to consider complicated questions of representation, identity, power, and ideology. As a function of the overt instruction and the general format of the inquiry, Frank uses critical framing to position the texts within the local contexts of the adolescents' lives (information about parents' views is sanctioned) and the larger social, historical, economic, and political realms of the world. Finally, Frank provides the crucial opportunities for transformed practices. To stop his students' inquiry at the point of text deconstruction would have created the very real possibility of a group of adolescents who were little more than nihilistic about the media and its representations. Instead of throwing up their hands at the lack of neutrality in any texts, Frank's students are provided with space and opportunities to explore how this lack of neutrality can be made to work for different kinds of purposes. This classroom scenario offers a synergistic description of the possibilities when textual practices in schools are transformed to resemble both the dynamic, hybrid multiliteracies found outside of most schools and the hybrid ways that literacies work to position us in the world.

IMPLICATIONS FOR FUTURE RESEARCH

Most secondary teachers, and content area teachers in particular, come to their vocations through the development of an expertise in English, science, social studies, math, and so on. Through this expertise, they implicitly and explicitly are acculturated to position the content, and therefore the content textbook, at the center of their instruction. However, New Times (Luke & Elkins, 1998) characterized by the global marketplaces, shifting economic planes, and unprecedented and dizzying dominance of electronic text forces the question of not only what is relevant to adolescents today but also what will be relevant tomorrow? In the classroom scenario, Frank opted to cover his curriculum of current events, but in such a way that quickly left behind flat goals of the students being able to summarize the who, what, when, where, and why of a mainstream front-page article. As a result, his students gained a sense of advocacy, power, and identity as consumers and creators of text that is rarely seen in the typical secondary history classroom.

Future research into adolescent literacy must tackle the difficult questions of how to reconcile and negotiate the multiliterate lives of adolescents and of the marketplace, with content-heavy secondary curricula, tests, and traditions.

DISCUSSION AND ACTIVITIES

1. How can critical literacy perspectives be encouraged in secondary schools that traditionally position factual explorations of content?

2. In what ways and to what extent does your local curriculum include critical literacy, multimediated texts, and intertextual connections?
3. As facets of globalization and multimediated texts become more pervasive, how can secondary schools help to prepare students for possible future worlds?

REFERENCES

Au, K. H. (1998). Social constructivism and the school literacy learning of students of diverse backgrounds. *Journal of Literacy Research, 30,* 297–319.

Alvermann, D. E., Moon, J. S., & Hagood, M. C. (1999). *Popular culture in the classroom: Teaching and researching critical media literacy.* Newark, DE: International Reading Association.

Alvermann, D. E., & Moore, D. W. (1991). Secondary school reading. In R. Barr, M. L. Kamil, P. B. Mosenthal, & P. D. Pearson (Eds.), *Handbook of reading research* (Vol. II, pp. 951–983). White Plains, NY: Longman.

Bean, T. W. (2000). Reading in the content areas: Social constructivist dimensions. In M. Kamil, P. D. Pearson, R. Barr, & P. Mosenthal (Eds.), *Handbook of reading research* (Vol. III, pp. 631–644). Mahwah, NJ: Erlbaum.

Bean, T. W. (2001). Exploring the intergenerational dialogue journal discussion of a multicultural young adult novel. *Reading Research Quarterly, 36,* 232–248.

Brown, A. G., Dolciani, T., Sorgenfrey, M. L., & Kane, G. (1990). *Trigonometry: Structure and Method, Book 2.* New York: Steck Vaughn.

Cope, B., & Kalantzis, M. (Eds.). (1993). *The powers of literacy.* London: Taylor & Francis.

Finders, M. (1998). Raging hormones. *Journal of Adolescent and Adult Literacy, 42,* 252–263.

Halliday, M. A. K. (1998). *Introduction to functional grammar* (2nd ed.). London: Routledge.

Hinchman, K. A., & Moje, E. B. (1998). Locating the social and political in secondary school literacy. *Reading Research Quarterly, 33,* 117–128.

Klass, D. (1996). *Danger zone.* New York: Scholastic.

Lewis, C., & Fabos, B. (2000). But will it work in the heartland? A response and illustration. *Journal of Adolescent and Adult Literacy, 43,* 462–469.

Lipka, R. P. (1998). Implications for educational research and evaluation. In R. P. Lipka, J. H. Lounsbury, C. F. Toepfer, Jr., G. F. Vars, S. P. Alessi, Jr., & C. Kridel (Eds.), *The eight-year study revisited: Lessons from the past for the present* (pp. 57–92). Columbus, OH: National Middle School Association.

Luke, A. (2000). Critical literacy in Australia: A matter of context and standpoint. *Journal of Adolescent and Adult Literacy, 43,* 448–461.

Luke, A., & Elkins, J. (1998). Adolescent literacy for new times. *Journal of Adolescent and Adult Literacy, 48,* 525–530.

McDonald, K. (1999). *Struggles for subjectivity: Identity, action and youth experience.* New York: Cambridge University Press.

Moje, E. B. (1996). "I teach students, not science": Teacher–student relationships as contexts for secondary literacy. *Reading Research Quarterly, 31,* 172–195.

Moje, E. B., Dillon, D. R., & O'Brien, D. (2000). Reexamining roles of learner, text, and context in secondary literacy. *Journal of Educational Research, 93,* 165–180.

Moore, D. W., Bean, T. W., Birdyshaw, D., & Rycik, J. A. (1999). Adolescent literacy: A position statement. *Journal of Adolescent and Adult Literacy, 43,* 97–112.

Moore, D. W., Readence, J. E., & Rickelman, R. J. (1983). An historical exploration of content area reading instruction. *Reading Research Quarterly, 18,* 419–438.

New London Group. (1997). A pedagogy of multiliteracies: Designing social futures. *Harvard Educational Review, 66*(1), 60–92.

O'Brien, D. G., Stewart, R. A., & Moje, E. B. (1995). Why content literacy is difficult to infuse into the secondary school: Complexities of curriculum, pedagogy, and school culture. *Reading Research Quarterly, 30,* 442–463.

Ogle, D. (1992). KWL in action: Secondary teachers find applications that work. In E. K. Dishner, T. W. Bean, J. E. Readence, & D. W. Moore (Eds.), *Content area reading: Improving classroom instruction* (3rd ed., pp. 270–282). Dubuque, IA: Kendall/Hunt.

Readence, J. E., Bean, T. W., & Baldwin, R. S. (2001). *Content area literacy: An integrated approach* (7th ed.). Dubuque, IA: Kendall/Hunt.

Stevens, L. P. (2001). *South Park* and society: Instructional and curricular implications of popular culture in the classroom. *Journal of Adolescent and Adult Literacy, 44,* 548–555.

Vacca, R. T. (1998). Foreword. In D. Alvermann, D. Moore, S. Phelps, & D. Waff (Eds.), *Toward reconceptualizing adolescent literacy* (pp. xv–xvi). Mahwah, NJ: Erlbaum.

Vygotsky, L. V. (1978). *Mind in society: The development of higher psychological processes* (M. Cole, V. John-Steiner, S. Scribner, & E. Souberman, Eds.). Cambridge, MA: Blackwell.

Walker, J. E. (1976). The case of SQ3R: Tried or tired? *Illinois Reading Council Journal, 41*(4), 24–25.

Wilgoren, J. (2002, April 22). Unusually unified in solidarity with Israel, but also unusually unnerved. *New York Times.* Available: *http://nytimes.com/search/article-page.html?res=9colE1D91131A15757coA9649c8B63*

Zusak. M. (2000). *Fighting Ruben Wolfe.* New York: Scholastic.

Chapter 11

BEST PRACTICES IN LITERACY ASSESSMENT

Peter Winograd
Leila Flores-Dueñas
Harriette Arrington

This chapter will:

- Examine the political and conceptual thinking that influences current assessment practices.
- Discuss the guidelines that teachers should follow in the ethical and constructive use of assessments for all of the students in their classrooms.
- Describe some important assessment strategies, including contextual and cultural surveys, student observation, portfolios, and conferencing.
- Analyze some of the trends that will affect the assessment of literacy in the future.

THEORY AND RESEARCH BASE

All, regardless of race or class or economic status, are entitled to a fair chance and the tools for developing their individual powers of mind and spirit to the utmost.

—*A Nation at Risk*, 1983

These reforms express my deep belief in our public schools and their mission to build the mind and character of every child, from every background, in every part of America.

—PRESIDENT GEORGE W. BUSH, January 2001

We begin our chapter with these two quotes because they provide much of the political and practical context for many of the assessment efforts currently under way in schools throughout the United States. We believe that understanding the politics of assessment is as important as understanding the theoretical and research base of assessments themselves, because teachers, particularly teachers who teach literacy, often find themselves caught by conflicting demands when it comes to the best practices in literacy assessment.

What are the best practices in literacy? One way to answer this question is by placing literacy assessment within the larger context of the national debate on the need to reform the entire system of public education in the United States.

In 1983, *A Nation at Risk* was published. Almost two decades later, the No Child Left Behind Act was passed. As our two quotes indicate, these reform efforts focused on two related crises in American education. The first is the low levels of academic achievement of American students in general, and the need for higher, "world-class" standards of learning, so that the United States can remain economically competitive in the future. The second crisis is the continued low academic achievement of many black, Hispanic, Native American, inner-city, and poor rural students, and the importance of helping *all* children obtain an equitable and effective education.

Over the last 7 years, national attention has also focused on the crisis in the teaching profession. The National Commission on Teaching and America's Future (NCTAF; 1996), for example, examined the uneven and often dismal quality of the teaching profession, and argued eloquently for the need to improve teacher preparation, teacher recruitment, teacher induction, professional development, and the ways that schools are organized. The NCTAF also argued that, next to the family, what teachers know and are able to do is the most important influence on what students learn, and that recruiting, preparing, and retaining good teachers is the central strategy for improving the nation's schools. The seriousness of this issue becomes apparent when one considers that approximately 2 million teachers will need to be hired in the next 7 to 8 years.

In an attempt to address these crises in education, policy makers, educators, and other stakeholders have engaged in a variety of reforms since the mid-1980s. In the last few years, we have witnessed a more comprehensive and systemic approach to education reform. Systemic reform, in this context, refers to efforts that include several key components: (1) the promotion of meaningful goals and standards for all students; (2) the increased focus on accountability and assessment of students, teachers, and schools; (3) the alignment of policy approaches and the coordination of a wide variety of educational, economic, social, and health institutions, and stakeholders to support student achievement; (4) the restructuring and aligning of public education governance to support student achievement; (5) the increase in the funding and other resources needed to support student achievement; and (6) the increased focus on the role of the classroom teacher.

The most recent effort to improve public education has been the passage of Elementary and Secondary Education Act, 2001. This act, known as "No Child Left Behind," is probably the most significant federal legislation dealing with education in the last 20 years. The Act contains a number of sweeping provisions, including many with a particular focus on assessment, teacher quality, and reading. The Act has both its advocates and detractors (who refer to the legislation as "The No Child Left Untested Act"), but it remains to been seen how this federal legislation will actually impact the practice of teachers in schools. One thing is for certain, however. The political aspects of literacy assessment are likely to increase.

Let us consider, for a moment, some of the latest evidence behind the concerns over excellence, equity, and the importance of teachers. These data come from a number of crucial sources, including the 2000 and 2001 Quality Counts Reports published by *Education Week* (*www.edweek.org*), *Kids Count Data Book* (2002; *www.aecf.org*), the Education Trust (*www.edtrust.org*), the U.S. Department of Education (2002; *www.ed.gov*), and the National Assessment of Educational Progress (2000; *www.nces.ed.gov/naep*).

The following are some of the national statistics related to reading and writing:

- Thirty-two percent of fourth-grade students performed at or above the proficient level in 2000. The proficient level is the level identified by the National Assessment Governing Board (NAGB) that all students should reach.
- The reading performance of the nation's fourth graders has remained relatively stable across assessment years. In 2000, the national average scale score of 217 was similar to that in 1992.
- Although the reading performance of the nation's fourth graders has become relatively stable, significant changes are evident at the upper and lower ends of the performance distribution. Higher performing students' scores in 2000 were significantly higher than in 1992. In contrast, lower performing students' scores in 2000 was significantly lower than in 1992.
- In 2000, students who were eligible for the free/reduced-price lunch program had a lower average score than students who were ineligible for the program; 14% of eligible students performed at or above the *proficient* level in comparison to 41% of noneligible students.
- An overall pattern of declining performance is evident in the average writing scores of 11th-grade students from 1984 to 1996.
- The writing performance of eighth-grade and fourth-grade students did not change significantly from 1984 to 1996.

But some other statistics, which are equally important, let us take a look at the larger picture:

- Seventeen percent of children were in poverty in 2000.
- Eleven percent of teens (1. 6 million teenagers ages 16–19) were high school dropouts in 2000.
- Nationally, school districts with the highest child poverty rates have $1,139 fewer state and local dollars to spend per student compared

with the lowest-poverty districts. That translates into a total $28,475 for a typical classroom of 25 students.

- Nationally, school districts with the highest minority enrollments have $979 fewer state and local dollars to spend per student compared with the lowest-minority districts. That translates into a total $24,475 for a typical classroom of 25 students.
- Some 43% of minority children attend urban schools. Most of them attend schools in which half of the students are poor and predominately, often completely, minority.
- In about half of the states with large cities, a majority of urban students fail to meet even minimum standards on national tests.
- The poorest students are at greatest risk. In urban schools in which most of the students are poor, two-thirds or more of children fail to reach even the "basic" level on national tests.
- Twenty-two percent of the classes in high-poverty schools were taught by teachers without a major or minor in the relevant field in 1993–1994.
- Twelve percent of all newly hired teachers enter the workforce without any training at all, and another 15% enter without having fully met state standards.
- Twenty-three percent of all secondary school teachers do not have a college minor in their main teaching field.

These statistics, and those from other reports produced by national, state, or local organizations, are powerful tools in helping us understand what education is about, and what our priorities should be. We see the debates about meaningful goals and standards, the use of multiple indices to measure progress, the disagreements about what these measures really mean, the arguments over resources, and the struggles to reform teaching and learning as a sign of health in American education. Although the process can be frustrating, it does show a country coming to grips with the reality of public education. One way to measure best practices in assessment at the national level, then, is to see how well they motivate and guide us in improving the lives of all our students.

We can also argue that the best practices in literacy assessment are those that help us understand the larger issues, frame important goals, gather multiple kinds of evidence, and engage in rich discussions about how to help children become better readers, writers, listeners, and speakers. To put it another way, no particular assessment is a best practice in and of itself; rather, the quality of assessments lies largely in how wisely they are used. Here are some thoughts about using assessment wisely.

The most effective practices in literacy assessment are those that occur in the classroom between a competent teacher and a confident student. The most effective practices in literacy assessment occur when teachers and students can work side by side in a trusting relationship that focuses on growth, nurturance, and self-evaluation. The problem we face, however, is nurturing these kinds of trusting relationships in a educational world dominated by the pressures to raise student achievement, as measured by high-stakes accountability systems.

Let us consider these challenges in more detail. One of the most difficult challenges is ensuring that there is an adequate supply of teachers who are well-prepared in the instruction and assessment of literacy, and that these teachers work in contexts that enable them to focus on meeting the needs of their children. This is no small problem when we consider the nation's need for so many new teachers and that, in too many states, prospective teachers may take only one course in reading. What is even more frightening is that some teachers who enter the classroom through alternative routes may take no classes in reading. Professional organizations such as The International Reading Association, the American Federation of Teachers, the National Council on Measurement in Education, and the National Education Association have developed thoughtful standards about what teachers should know and be able to do in terms of evaluation and assessment, but it will take serious revision of teacher preparation programs and professional development opportunities to ensure that the majority of teachers can meet these standards.

Moreover, we need to ensure that when new teachers obtain their licenses, they begin work in schools that are better organized for and more supportive of student and teacher success. Asking teachers who have heavy workloads and too little time to engage in more intensive evaluation and instruction with individual children is unrealistic and unfair. We want to stress that we are not blaming teachers. We are fortunate that the majority of teachers are competent, caring, and committed. What we are saying is that if we truly believe that teachers should engage in the assessment of literacy, then we must strengthen the ways teachers are prepared and improve the ways schools are organized.

Another challenge we face is to think more wisely about how to meet the needs of the children in the classrooms. For example, we must understand that when teachers teach reading or writing, they often face issues that are not just educational in nature. The fact that 68% of America's fourth-graders scored below the proficient level on the 2000 National Assessment of Educational Progress (NAEP) reading exam is a social, political, economic, *and* educational problem. Keeping this context in mind is vital, because the best practices in literacy assessment are those that help us understand these broader issues and how to deal with them systemically, so that all students receive an excellent and equitable education. Assessments that focus on a narrow or isolated aspect of literacy are not as effective as those that give us a richer picture of the whole child and the world in which he or she lives.

We must also understand that assessments are a very limited tool in dealing effectively and fairly with children and the world they live in. Madaus (1994, p. 79) makes this point most eloquently when he cautions us about becoming too enchanted with assessments and overlooking the needs to attend to student health, nutrition, and living conditions; teacher training; and other critical components in the system of education: "There is a danger that technological solutions, such as alternative educational assessment, will blind policymakers and the public to the reality that we Americans cannot test, examine, or assess our way out of our educational problems (National Commission on Testing and Public Policy, 1990)."

The National Council on Educational Standards and Testing (NCEST; 1992, p. 6) raises a similar point when it states, "Particularly for children, who have historically experienced less success in schools, such as the poor, ethnic minorities and students with disabilities, schools should ensure the opportunity to learn as a critical condition for valid and fair use of assessment results." It is important to note that this is not just concern voiced by a few advocates in the field; rather, it is a specific standard for the fair use of educational and psychological tests developed by the American Educational Research Association (AERA), the American Psychological Association (APA), and the National Council on Measurement in Education (NCME) (1985; AERA, 1999). The issue of fairness in assessment, especially for students whose first language is other than English, is of critical importance that has yet to be addressed in any systematic fashion across the nation (e.g., King, 1993; LaCelle-Peterson & Rivera, 1994; Linn, 1994; Valdés & Figueroa, 1994; Winograd, Benjamin, & Noll, 2001).

We need to understand the larger issues in education and educational reform, because we often find ourselves torn between the demands for assessment for accountability and the need for assessment to improve instruction. We need to understand why there is such a demand for assessment for accountability and how to deal with that demand in a constructive fashion. We find it useful to think about assessment by identifying what kinds of audience it can serve. For example, assessment can help

- Students become more self-reflective and in control of their own learning.
- Teachers focus their instruction more effectively.
- Educators determine which students are eligible for Title 1, programs for the gifted, or special education.
- Parents understand more about their children's progress as learners.

- Administrators understand how groups of students in their schools are progressing.
- Legislators and citizens understand how groups of students across the state or nation are progressing.
- Policy makers and stakeholders monitor the implementation and effectiveness of various reform initiatives, including those that deal with school finance and resource allocation, governance and policy issues, or changes in curriculum.

The best practices in literacy assessment, then, are those that use a variety of appropriate indices to address the needs of different audiences. Thus, the choice does not have to be assessment for accountability versus assessment for instruction. Some states, such as Vermont, Kentucky, and Maryland, have attempted to develop assessments systems that are performance-based, linked to clear standards, support important curricular goals, and are useful for both accountability and instructional purposes. In addition, these assessments are viewed as part of an overall approach to reform that includes professional development, curricular development, and other key changes to the system. As Darling-Hammond (1994, p. 7) notes, the fundamental question "is whether assessment systems will support better teaching and transform schooling for traditional under served students or whether they will merely reify existing inequalities."

Unfortunately, too many states, districts, and schools continue to use assessments in ways that do reify existing problems and inequalities. The misuse of tests continues despite the large body of research that indicates traditional forms of assessments are based on outdated and inappropriate models of learning; narrow the curriculum in destructive ways; provide results that are misinterpreted and misused; and often produce invalid results that vary widely for individuals and reflect confounded effects related to socioeconomic status, home experiences, or testing conditions (e.g., Darling-Hammond, Ancess, & Falk, 1995; Haney & Madaus, 1989; Winograd, Paris, & Bridge, 1991).

Fortunately, the large body of research on assessment has produced some principles for using assessments wisely. Here are some of our favorites drawn from a number of sources including the National Center for Fair and Open Testing (1998; *www.fairtest.org*), Fowler and McCallum (1998); Harp (1996); Johnston, 1991; Stiggens (1997); Tierney (1998); and Winograd and Perkins (1996).

The best practices in literacy assessment do the following:

- Focus on important goals and support meaningful student learning.
- Are based on our most current and complete understanding of literacy and children's development.

- Are based in the classroom rather than imposed from outside.
- Involve students in their own learning and enhance their understanding of their own development.
- Use criteria and standards that are public, so that students, teachers, parents, and others know what is expected.
- Start with what the students currently know.
- Involve teachers (and often students) in the design and use of the assessment.
- Empower teachers to trust their own professional judgments about learners.
- Nourish trust and cooperation between teachers and students.
- Focus on students' strengths rather than just reveal their weaknesses.
- Provide information that is used to advocate for students rather than to penalize them.
- Support meaningful standards based on the understanding that growth and excellence can take many forms.
- Are integral parts of instruction.
- Gather multiple measures over time and in a variety of meaningful contexts.
- Provide educators and others with richer and fairer information about all children, including those who come from linguistically and culturally diverse backgrounds.
- Are part of a systemic approach to improving education that includes strengthening the curriculum, professional development for teachers, and additional support for helping those children who need it.
- Provide information that is clear and useful to students, teachers, parents, and other stakeholders.
- Continually undergo review, revision, and improvement.

The increased use of large-scale, standardized testing for accountability has sparked a large and ever-growing body of literature on the principles for using standardized tests wisely. Given the current political and educational climate, testing for accountability is likely to increase, so the importance of these principles is also likely to increase.

The best single source for appropriate guidance in this area comes from the AERA, APA, and NCME 1999 Standards for Educational and Psychological Testing (AERA, 1999). Here, for example, is AERA's position (based on the 1999 Standards) on the appropriate and fair use of high-stakes testing in pre-K–12 education. This is a long quotation, but it is vitally important that teachers understand these standards given the increased use of high-stakes testing, particularly in the field of reading.

It is the position of the AERA that every high-stakes achievement testing program in education should meet all of the following conditions:

Protection against High-Stakes Decisions Based on a Single Test
Decisions that affect individual students' life chances or educational opportunities should not be made on the basis of test scores alone. Other relevant information should be taken into account to enhance the overall validity of such decisions. As a minimum assurance of fairness, when tests are used as part of making high-stakes decisions for individual students such as promotion to the next grade or high school graduation, students must be afforded multiple opportunities to pass the test. More importantly, when there is credible evidence that a test score may not adequately reflect a student's true proficiency, alternative acceptable means should be provided by which to demonstrate attainment of the tested standards.

Adequate Resources and Opportunity to Learn
When content standards and associated tests are introduced as a reform to change and thereby improve current practice, opportunities to access appropriate materials and retraining consistent with the intended changes should be provided before schools, teachers, or students are sanctioned for failing to meet the new standards. In particular, when testing is used for individual student accountability or certification, students must have had a meaningful opportunity to learn the tested content and cognitive processes. Thus, it must be shown that the tested content has been incorporated into the curriculum, materials, and instruction students are provided before high-stakes consequences are imposed for failing examination.

Validation for Each Separate Intended Use
Tests valid for one use may be invalid for another. Each separate use of a high-stakes test, for individual certification, for school evaluation, for curricular improvement, for increasing student motivation, or for other uses requires a separate evaluation of the strengths and limitations of both the testing program and the test itself.

Full Disclosure of Likely Negative Consequences of High-Stakes Testing Programs
Where credible scientific evidence suggests that a given type of testing program is likely to have negative side effects, test developers and users should make a serious effort to explain these possible effects to policy makers.

Alignment between the Test and the Curriculum
Both the content of the test and the cognitive processes engaged in taking the test should adequately represent the curriculum. High-stakes tests should not be limited to that portion of the relevant curriculum that is easiest to measure. When testing is for school account-

ability or to influence the curriculum, the test should be aligned with the curriculum as set forth in standards documents representing intended goals of instruction. Because high-stakes testing inevitably creates incentives for inappropriate methods of test preparation, multiple test forms should be used or new test forms should be introduced on a regular basis, to avoid a narrowing of the curriculum toward just the content sampled on a particular form.

Validity of Passing Scores and Achievement Levels

When testing programs use specific scores to determine "passing" or to define reporting categories like "proficient," the validity of these specific scores must be established in addition to demonstrating the representativeness of the test content. To begin with, the purpose and meaning of passing scores or achievement levels must be clearly stated. There is often confusion, for example, among minimum competency levels (traditionally required for grade-to-grade promotion), grade level (traditionally defined as a range of scores around the national average on standardized tests), and "world-class" standards (set at the top of the distribution, anywhere from the 70th to the 99th percentile). Once the purpose is clearly established, sound and appropriate procedures must be followed in setting passing scores or proficiency levels. Finally, validity evidence must be gathered and reported, consistent with the stated purpose.

Opportunities for Meaningful Remediation for Examinees Who Fail High-Stakes Tests

Examinees who fail a high-stakes test should be provided meaningful opportunities for remediation. Remediation should focus on the knowledge and skills the test is intended to address, not just the test performance itself. There should be sufficient time before retaking the test to assure that students have time to remedy any weaknesses discovered.

Appropriate Attention to Language Differences among Examinees

If a student lacks mastery of the language in which a test is given, then that test becomes, in part, a test of language proficiency. Unless a primary purpose of a test is to evaluate language proficiency, it should not be used with students who cannot understand the instructions or the language of the test itself. If English language learners are tested in English, their performance should be interpreted in the light of their language proficiency. Special accommodations for English language learners may be necessary to obtain valid scores.

Appropriate Attention to Students with Disabilities

In testing individuals with disabilities, steps should be taken to ensure that the test score inferences accurately reflect the intended construct rather than any disabilities and their associated characteristics extraneous to the intent of the measurement.

Careful Adherence to Explicit Rules for Determining Which Students Are
to Be Tested
> When schools, districts, or other administrative units are compared
> to one another or when changes in scores are tracked over time, there
> must be explicit policies specifying which students are to be tested and
> under what circumstances students may be exempted from testing.
> Such policies must be uniformly enforced to assure the validity of score
> comparisons. In addition, reporting of test score results should accu-
> rately portray the percentage of students exempted.

Sufficient Reliability for Each Intended Use
> Reliability refers to the accuracy or precision of test scores. It must be
> shown that scores reported for individuals or for schools are sufficiently
> accurate to support each intended interpretation. Accuracy should
> be examined for the scores actually used. For example, information
> about the reliability of raw scores may not adequately describe the
> accuracy of percentiles; information about the reliability of school
> means may be insufficient if scores for subgroups are also used in
> reaching decisions about schools.

Ongoing Evaluation of Intended and Unintended Effects of
High-Stakes Testing
> With any high-stakes testing program, ongoing evaluation of both
> intended and unintended consequences is essential. In most cases,
> the governmental body that mandates the test should also provide
> resources for a continuing program of research and for dissemina-
> tion of research findings concerning both the positive and the nega-
> tive effects of the testing program. (AERA, 1999, adopted July 2000;
> *www.aera.net/about/policy/stakes.htm*)

These principles are important for classroom teachers to understand.
Often, the best practices in literacy assessment mean being an informed
and effective advocate for the fair, limited, and reasonable use of tests in
today's schools.

RESEARCH-BASED PRACTICE IN CLASSROOM ASSESSMENT

The term "research-based practice" covers a great deal of territory, including everything from high-stakes standardized testing to a range of
classroom-focused evaluation strategies. For example, at the national level,
using the NAEP to assess the reading achievement of large groups of students is based on solid psychometric research. These scores are used by
policy makers to evaluate the effects of large-scale educational initiatives.
At a more local level, individual teachers use a variety of research-based
practices to learn about their particular students and their own teaching,

including surveys, portfolios, observations, and conferences. These assessments are the primary focus of this chapter, so we turn our attention to classroom-focused, research-based practices that teachers should use to improve daily instruction.

Trying to identify which classroom-based literacy assessments are "best" in some absolute sense is a task fraught with perils, because the field of literacy has a huge array of classroom assessment methods and strategies that can be used either effectively or inappropriately. For example, we have informal reading inventories; running records; concepts about print tests; assessments for emergent literacy; tests for book-handling knowledge; miscue analysis; portfolios; conference guides; anecdotal records; guides for evaluating metacognitive awareness; holistic and analytic evaluations of writing; interview, attitude, and disposition surveys; retellings; basic skills tests; decoding skills tests; comprehension checklists; spelling checklists; vocabulary tests; student self-assessments of reading and writing; observational checklists for reading and writing; checklists and surveys for parents; literacy profiles; language records; developmental scales for emergent reading and writing; performance tasks, rubrics, and benchmarks for literacy; instruments for placing students in programs; instruments for taking students out of programs; and methods for teachers to evaluate the teaching of literacy.

And, of course, the general field of education has all kinds of performance-based assessments, standardized tests, diagnostic tests, norm-referenced tests, criterion-referenced tests, constructed response tests, psychoeducational batteries, achievement tests, minimum-competency tests, group tests, individual tests, graduation examinations, or college entrance examinations, all of which involve the assessment of literacy. Please note that we have not even mentioned issues such as report cards, computer-based assessments, assessments for special populations, or many of the other assessment-related topics. (Here is an interesting factoid: The National Center for Fair and Open Testing (*www.fairtest.org*) estimates that more than 100,000,000 standardized exams are administered in America's public schools each year, including IQ, achievement, screening, and readiness tests. Clearly, one best practice would be to reduce the amount of testing that takes place, especially for young children!)

Because of the critical importance of achieving educational excellence for *all* students, it is worth asking what some of the best assessment strategies are for working with culturally and linguistically diverse students. In 1990, approximately one-third of school-age children in this country were considered to be at risk for academic failure, the majority of whom were non-native speakers of English (Scarcella, 1990). Garcia (1992) associates this failure with lack of literacy development in English for language-minority students. Although some gains in reading development have been made by language-minority students, educators in the United States remain challenged by the low academic achievement of a great number of these students.

From the time that second language learners enter school, they score consistently and significantly lower than other minorities in reading and writing (Applebee, Langer, & Mullis, 1989). Disproportionate numbers of culturally and linguistically diverse students are placed in lower reading groups and special education programs in U.S. schools (Oakes, 1985). Once these students are placed on a slower track, they remain behind their peers in reading throughout their elementary school years (Barr, 1989; Goodlad, 1984). Other problems associated with the reading achievement or the literacy development of these students have been attributed to the organization and content of instruction in U.S. classrooms (Beck & McKeown, 1984; Langer, 1984; Purves, 1984). In attempting to explain the role that society and school plays in creating the disparities between the reading development of language-minority students and white European American students, Au (1993) emphatically states:

> Schools function primarily to maintain the status quo, not to provide all students with high-quality education. The familiar old patterns of instruction that prevent students from diverse backgrounds from achieving high levels of literacy, such as assessment that devalues their home languages and instruction that violates the values of students' own cultures, result from the power dominant groups have to impose their values and standards upon subordinate groups. (p. 10)

Although many educators may not intend to discriminate against students whose cultural and linguistic backgrounds are different from their own, Spindler and Spindler (1990) document teachers' practices of unconsciously selecting those students who are from higher status, mainstream backgrounds (like their own) to succeed in academic areas. This selection process is often part of teachers' informal and formal ongoing assessments of the child's literacy development. This type of discrimination can be seen in the treatment of students who have weak English skills and who attend all-English classrooms. These children are often sent out of the classroom for remedial reading instruction or are placed in low reading groups that follow transmission models of instruction that focus on oral reading, isolate skills, and rote learning (Allington, 1991). These students, then, fail to progress well in developing reading and writing skills, and they often demonstrate negative attitudes toward school, and toward using literacy skills (Au, 1993).

Because our space is limited, we focus on a few assessment strategies that we find particularly helpful for students, teachers, and parents. These strategies grow out of the national debates about excellence and equity, and the concerns surrounding the limitations of traditional, multiple-choice tests. A number of researchers have attempted to develop forms of assessment that are based on current models of learning, enhance and strengthen the curriculum, are easily understood by stakeholders, and produce valid results and positive educational consequences for all children. The class of approaches, loosely labeled "alternative assessments," performance assessments, or authentic assessments, is the results of these efforts (U.S. Congress, 1992; Wiggins, 1989).

Alternative assessment is assessment that occurs continually in the context of a meaningful learning environment and reflects actual and worthwhile learning experiences that can be documented through observation, anecdotal records, journals, logs, work samples, conferences, portfolios, writing, discussions, experiments, presentations, exhibits, projects, performance events, and other methods. Alternative assessments may include individual as well as group tasks. Emphasis is placed on self-reflection, understanding, and growth rather than responses based only on recall of isolated facts. Alternative assessments are often called performance-based or authentic assessments, because they are intended to involve learners in tasks that require them to apply knowledge faced in real-world experiences rather than a test given after, and disconnected from, instruction. Alternative assessments are also intended to enhance teachers' professional judgment rather that weaken it, and to provide teachers with systematic opportunities to engage in linguistically and culturally appropriate evaluation and instruction.

In the remainder of this chapter, we examine four recommended authentic assessment strategies for use in classrooms:

1. Contextual and cultural surveys
2. Observation strategies: literature discussions, anecdotal records, and developmental checklists
3. Portfolios
4. Student–teacher conferences

It is important to note from the beginning that these strategies are interrelated. Surveys will provide the importance context for the information contained in portfolios, gathered during observations of daily student work, and the conversations that take place between students and teachers. Portfolios will contain, among other things, evidence of the students' performance in writing and reading, records of the teacher's observations, and conferences with students. Portfolios, anecdotal records, and developmental checklists provide important starting points for conferences between teachers and students.

It is also important to note that our discussion of these strategies in only an introduction to what is available. The field of literacy has benefited from a long list of outstanding educators and researchers who have made, and are making, critical contributions to the field of assessment. Here are a few sources of assessment instruments and approaches that will provide you with a sample of what is available: Clay (1985); Darling-Hammond et al. (1995); De Fina (1992); Gambrell and Almasi (1996); Goodman, Goodman, and Hood (1989); Harp (1994, 1996); Hill and Ruptic (1994); Johnston (1991); Morrow and Smith (1990); Rhodes (1993); Rhodes and Shanklin (1993); Sharp (1989); Stiggens (1997); Tierney, Carter, and Desai (1991); and Valencia, Hiebert, and Afflerback (1994).

Contextual and Cultural Surveys

Constructive evaluations for all students, but particularly for diverse learners, require that teachers, students, and parents work together to improve the child's literacy learning. The learning environment, the tasks and processes students are expected to perform and master, and the culture of the learner's household must all be considered when assessing the literacy skills of these students (Crawford, 1993). In order to respond adequately to the literacy needs of diverse student populations, educators must begin developing a sound knowledge base about histories, contributions, and values of the cultural and linguistic groups that represent diverse students in our classrooms.

Furthermore, our literacy teaching must clearly reflect this knowledge, so that all students are able to see the value of their own experiences and to mobilize their "funds of knowledge" (Moll & Díaz, 1985) through a variety of forms of literacy. In other words, students should be able to read and write about familiar topics that they understand well. This enables these students to express themselves in a coherent manner and to use all of the specialized vocabulary they might already have. If students write about what they know, they can become increasingly sophisticated in their expressive forms. For example, they may write about their parents' occupations or family rituals (Moll, 1992). Helping students to build on this knowledge is crucial to developing students' self-confidence in communication skills.

Knowing who your students are and what your classroom setup (e.g., curriculum, assignments, and ways to interact) may mean for each one of them is often difficult to fully understand. People (particularly from different cultures) often understand or interpret language and communication in different ways. Cumulative folders from former teachers and standardized test scores may indicate some important information about the child's literacy learning, but they may not provide a full picture of the child and his or her literacy development. In fact, it is possible that context may have greatly affected how the student performed on each of the assessment samples. The point is, context always matters, and we should be able to investigate, for ourselves, what context we are providing for the children's literacy learning in our classrooms.

The surveys illustrated in Figures 11.1 and 11.2 include a rich range of questions that teachers can use to better understand who the children in their classrooms are and how the outside world affects their literacy learning.

Classroom Interaction

A number of important studies were published in the 1980s about classroom discourse (what is talked about, who gets to talk, and when) and its role in teachers' assessment of minority students' literacy learning (e.g., Carrasco, 1984; Cazden, 1988; Heath, 1981; Michaels, 1981). These studies showed us that cultural and linguistic communication differences between teachers and students could have a positive or negative effect on how a teacher assesses and teaches a particular child during literacy instruction. These studies also suggested to us that teachers have the responsibility

1. What is the general socioeconomic and ethnic makeup of the community and school? Are there adequate resources (e.g., grocery stores, parks, banks, religious institutions, medical facilities) for the community to thrive?
2. What are some of the parents' occupations within the community? How are these related to students' funds of knowledge?
3. In general, how many years have most families lived within this community?
4. In general, what it the nature of the family structures of the children in your classroom? For example, are the children from single-parent homes, two-parent homes, multiple-family homes?
5. What is the primary language of the students at home and in the community? Do they speak the same or a different language with their brothers and sisters? (In many bilingual homes, the children often speak to siblings, who are at a third-grade level or higher, in English, while speaking to their parents in another language.)
6. What evidence of parental interest and support of the school do you see? What has been communicated to you about this? In general, what is the feeling about parents and their ability and willingness to participate in their child's education?
7. Try to observe the treatment of parents in the office of the school. How are parents talked to? Is the treatment fairly equal for most parents you observed? Are they treated as though they communicate well?
8. What is your attitude about the parents? How do you demonstrate this attitude to your students?

FIGURE 11.1. General community and classroom survey.

1. Describe, in general, the literacy levels of the students in your classroom?
2. How were reading levels determined? Were various forms and texts used for assessment? What was really measured by the assessment instrument, decoding or comprehension skills, or both?
3. Take a look at the materials being used in the classroom. What cultures are represented? Are there any books on the shelves or in reading book baskets that are "culturally familiar" to your students? How many? List the titles? Does each English language learner have books in the classroom collection that he or she can read?
4. Do you require students to write in daily journals? What other kinds of assignments require students to use their funds of knowledge?
5. Do students get a substantial silent-reading period? Do you model this procedure? What kinds of materials are used for silent reading?
6. What kind of grouping strategies do you use? Do second-language learners have the opportunity to practice speaking?
7. Is literature infused in most lessons? How do you do this?
8. Is there evidence of reading and writing for every subject, every day?
9. Do you use an integrated approach to the curriculum? For example, do your students use the science text during your reading/language arts block?
10. Do you regularly allow for "sharing time" to listen carefully to student voices and to allow them to process their thinking out loud or on paper? Do the children use examples of experiences from their home lives?
11. Are *all* students required to be "on-task" during lessons? Who is off-task and why? Who is not communicating or engaging in learning? How might the classroom structure or your beliefs and expectations be related to the students' lack of participation?

FIGURE 11.2. Literacy survey.

to understand their own communication expectations and those of their students (Au, 1993).

Figure 11.3 is an example of a self-observation guide that teachers can use to examine their own classroom interactions during a lesson. Teachers should also do their to part to understand, accept, and build on their students' communication styles.

Surveying Home Literacy

Understanding how different families use and value literacy practices at home can greatly help us contribute to our understanding of such communities. We define literacy broadly; in other words, we see it as all of the forms of communication that have been modeled for the child at home. Literacy learning at home includes listening, speaking, reading, and writing in a particular sociocultural context. For example, if a child comes from a home where storytelling plays a major role in learning morals and values, then it is likely that he or she will be able to under-

FIGURE 11.3. Classroom interaction self-observation guide.

1. What is the procedure for calling on students? Do all get spoken to, and do all speak? How much?
2. Do you accept the contributions from all students? Is anyone left out or cut off?
3. What levels of talking are accepted? Who gets to talk? Who is asked to talk or read aloud?

To answer these questions, you will need to make a drawing of the classroom. Next, label each desk with "G" or "B" for "girl" or "boy" or label each desk with the child's name. During a teacher-directed lesson, put a dot on the space of each child who is talked to, asked a question, listened to, or responded to in any way by the teacher. Do this for at least a 30-minute period when the teacher is direct teaching. Take a tally, explain in detail the patterns you see. Who gets called on or talked to by the teacher? Who does not? Why?

CLASSROOM INTERACTION OBSERVATION

Materials needed: classroom map, video camera, or observer
Instructions:
1. Label each desk on the map with the student's name.
2. Label each student's desk with a "G" (girl) or "B" (boy).
3. Indicate differences/special needs/ethnicity of children with abbreviations—for example, sn (special needs), hi (hearing impaired), ell (English-language learner), asa (Asian American), etc.
4. Teach a 30- to 60-minute teacher-directed lesson and videotape it, making sure that the teacher and all the students can be seen throughout the lesson, *or* have someone else observe the lesson.
5. On the map, mark or have the observer mark the student's desk as the student speaks or is spoken to by the teacher.
6. Tally the number of marks for each student and analyze the patterns you see.
7. Commit to an action plan to improve classroom interactions.

SAMPLE CLASSROOM MAP AND TALLY SHEET

T—teacher; G—girl; B—boy; ell—English-language learner; sn—student with special needs

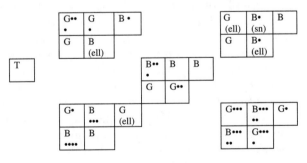

Girls: ☓☓☓ ☓☓☓ ☓☓☓ 15,   Boys ☓☓☓ ☓☓☓ ☓☓☓ ☓☓☓ /// 23

(*continued*)

FIGURE 11.3. *continued*

Initial Patterns I See

- I called on students who sit on my right side; they are mostly my "high" kids.
- I mostly called on boys. I did a lot of behavior corrections; boys call out a lot.
- I only called on one English-language learner, one time.
- I asked yes/no, low-level questions of my "low kids."
- I only praised girls for good, quiet behavior.

Plan of Action to Improve Classroom Interaction

Questions for Self-Reflection:

1. What procedure do you use for calling on students? Do all students get spoken to, and do all get to speak? Who gets to? Who does not? Why?

    Suggestion: Survey the students to ask how they feel about your system for calling on students.

2. Do you repeat all student's contributions or just some? Is anyone left out?

3. What volume levels of talk do you accept? Do second-language learners have enough time to practice speaking?

4. Who is asked to talk or read aloud? Why?

5. Do you speak to one side of the room more often than the other?

6. How much "wait time" is given to students? Do some get more than others?

7. Are there differences in how you respond to girls as opposed to boys? Who is praised for behavior? Who is not?

8. Do you talk differently to students from particular ethnic groups? If so, how?

stand the main ideas of stories. Having the child use home stories to illustrate comprehension of stories would be another way to understand his or her comprehension skills.

Gender, age, and topics of discussion play a major role in how language in used in various situations including the classroom. Understanding the role(s) of the child may help the teacher to make better judgments about how to interpret the child's literacy interactions in the classroom. Teachers can learn how to relate the contributions of the family to the child's needs in school literacy learning (e.g., storytelling, humor, musical, etc.). Visiting the homes of all children in a classroom can prove to be extremely worthwhile for the teacher, the family, and the student. Making home visits with children from unfamiliar cultural groups may require that the teacher visit with a fellow teacher or friend, and make clear the intention of the visit (e.g., to learn about the family history and literacy practices to better serve the interests of their child).

Because cultural differences can have powerful effects on student achievement in literacy, it is useful to gather some systematic information about children and their families. The Home Literacy Survey presented in Figure 11.4 provides teachers with a useful and appropriate tool for gathering such information.

Contextual surveys are invaluable for learning more about how the outside world influences your students' literacy behaviors. Now, we turn our attention to ways that you can focus your observations even more precisely on the ways students read and write.

Observation Strategies: Literature Discussions, Anecdotal Records, and Developmental Checklists

Most of the information that teachers gather about their students comes from observation. Yetta Goodman (1978) coined the term "kid watcher," and it is clear that good teachers are constantly watching their kids. Kid watching can take many forms, from informal observation on the play-

Inquire about the family and child's demographic/historical information. For example, if appropriate, learn about the following topics:

- The number of household members
- The occupations of the household members
- Number of years in this country (for newer immigrants)
- What brought them here
- Ethnicity of family members
- Languages that are spoken and by whom
- Language the child speaks and to whom—since birth and today
- How the child learned to communicate (stories, songs, rhymes, etc.) and in what language
- Formal education of grandparents, parents, siblings, and child
- Perception of the role of school in the household
- Family's view of the child's current school
- How the family communicates (talking, storytelling, writing notes, etc.)
- Who in the household reads and writes
- The role of talking
- The child's history of literacy learning (when the child started to speak, when it is appropriate for children in the family to speak)
- The role of gender as related to literacy use in the family
- Who helps the child with schoolwork
- What resources (books, games, etc.) are available in the home
- The appropriate titles, names, of people in the home

FIGURE 11.4. Home literacy survey.

ground to systematic keeping of anecdotal records, to more structured observations using checklists. In this section, we examine how teachers can use anecdotal records and developmental checklists to assess students growth in literacy.

The use of observation as a means of assessment has a number of advantages. For example, anecdotal records, developmental checklists, and other forms of observation

- Provide teachers with a way of assessing how students interact with a complex environment, both in and out of classroom.
- Provide teachers with an efficient method of assessing students in many different situations over longer periods of time, thus increasing the reliability of the assessment data.
- Focus the teacher's attention on what the student can do rather than on what the student has yet to learn.
- Provide a relatively stress-free form of evaluation for students, especially those students who become anxious when they take standardized tests.

Literature Discussions with a Focus on Student Reading Processes

1. Have students read a short story or a chapter from a trade book written in English and underline the parts of the story that they did not understand.

2. When the students finish reading the selection, they retell the story in writing. This activity allows them to formulate their thoughts before participating in the group discussion. They are reminded to write everything they can remember about the story (before and during this activity, there is no discussion).

3. Once all retellings are turned in, discussion about the story takes place. Ask students to tell what they noticed about the story, how the story made them feel, what the story reminded them of in their own lives, and how difficult was it for them to understand the text. Probe further to get them to elaborate on their thoughts and on the parts of the story that they underlined when they initially read the text. Encourage them to use examples from the text to explain what they mean.

4. After each discussion about the story takes place, a related topic associated with reading should be discussed. During these discussions, students often refer back to the texts they read together in the past to clarify their explanations. Using open-ended questions, such as, "What do good readers do when they read stories?" Probe for more discussion on the following general topics:

- Good readers versus poor readers
- Student and family reading practices
- Understanding some stories versus other stories
- Silent reading versus reading aloud
- Personal choices in reading selections
- Use of voice in stories (e.g., first person)
- Unknown vocabulary (strategies used)
- Pronunciation in English
- The kind of "talk" used in books
- Influence of bilingualism on students' English reading

Anecdotal Records

Anecdotal records are informal observations about what students are learning, how they are responding to instruction, or any other student behaviors, actions, or reactions that might provide teachers with some insight. The best time to take anecdotal records is while observing the students, and it is often helpful to focus on the following questions:

- What can this child do?
- What does this child know?
- How does this child read, write, work on projects, work with others, or deal with other important aspects of the school curriculum?
- What kinds of questions does the child have about his or her work?
- What does the child's attitude reveal about his or her growth and progress?

In addition, anecdotal records often include teacher comments and questions that are particularly useful in helping teachers become more reflective about their teaching. Experienced teachers record their observations of a student over time and then analyze their anecdotal records for patterns of what the student knows and can do. This information is then used to plan appropriate instruction.

Occasionally, some teachers find anecdotal records a bit overwhelming and difficult to keep. In our experience, this happens when teachers are making anecdotal records more complex than they need to be. The purpose of anecdotal records is to provide teachers with a tool for sharpening their professional judgments. Fowler and McCallum (1998) suggest using a focused approach to anecdotal records:

- Select a focus for your anecdotal record keeping. In reading, for example, the focus may be on fluency, comprehension, response, or interests. In writing, the focus may be on voice, organization, or mechanics.

- Develop a simple form that includes space for the date of the observation, the names of the students being observed, and the focus of the observation.
- Observe the students you are most concerned about, and take notes about what you see in terms of the focus area.
- Use the anecdotal records, along with any other evidence you have gathered, to plan instruction. As you work with the students, continue to observe how they perform and grow in the areas you identified.

Fowler and McCallum (1998) suggest a simple anecdotal record (see Figure 11.5) for keeping track of anecdotal records for individual students.

Developmental Checklists

Checklists are a common and useful way to evaluate students' growth in literacy. A major reason for their appeal is that they can be used in a wide variety of instructional contexts. Teachers interested in looking at examples of checklists will find lots of good ideas in the literature on assessment (e.g., Clay, 1985; Goodman et al., 1989; Harp, 1994, 1996; Kemp, 1989; Routman, 1988, 1991; Sharp, 1989).

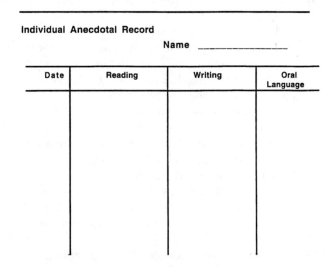

Individual Anecdotal Record

Name _____

Date	Reading	Writing	Oral Language

FIGURE 11.5. Fairfax County Public Schools' individual anecdotal record. Reprinted with permission of Fairfax County Public Schools.

Figures 11.6–11.8 are checklists for observing student's use of reading strategies before, during, and after reading. Figure 11.6 comes from some of our earlier work, whereas Figures 11.7 and 11.8 are from Fowler and McCallum (1998).

Reading Strategies Assessment

Name _____ Date_____

Directions: As you observe each student, place a check mark beside each behavior in the appropriate column: Most of the Time, Working On, or Not Yet. You may wish to note the circumstances or activity in which observation occurred, write in additional criteria or notes about the evaluation, and write ideas for next instructional steps.

Circumstances or Activity				
Behavior	Most of the Time	Working On	Not Yet	Notes/Next Steps
THINK AHEAD				
Previews the reading text				
Recalls prior knowledge				
Sets purposes for reading				
Understands different ways of reading				
THINK WHILE READING				
Checks and clarifies comprehension				
Understands different kinds of meaning				
THINK BACK				
Reviews comprehension				
Applies different kinds of reading				
Additional Criteria:				

FIGURE 11.6. Checklist for evaluating the use of reading strategies before, during, and after reading.

Reading Name: _____ Individual Checklist:		
	Date	Comments
Before Reading:		
Chooses reading as a free-time activity		
Has book ready during reading workshop		
Chooses appropriate reading material		
Previews text before reading		
During Reading:		
Connects background knowledge to information in the text		
Predicts and confirms or revises predictions		
Discusses explicit and implied information		
Stops and reviews reading with longer texts		
Reads familiar material with clarity, using punctuation appropriately		
When confronting unfamiliar words:		
Cross-checks one cue with another (phonics, language structure, and meaning)		
Rereads		
Uses chunks within multisyllable words to read		
Skips, reads on, and goes back to check word		
Asks another person for help		
Self-corrects to preserve meaning		
Uses features of informational text to aid comprehension		
Uses the context to determine meaning of new or unfamiliar vocabulary		
After Reading:		
Retells, including important information or events		
Relates what is read to personal knowledge		
Makes comparisons		
Categorizes and classifies appropriately		
Summarizes		
Draws conclusions based on reading		
Shows understanding using graphic organizer		
Uses information in the book to justify a response, confirm a prediction, or discuss elements of fiction or important information		
Written response shows evidence of critical thinking and a reflective stance towards reading		
Evaluates use of author's craft		

FIGURE 11.7. Fairfax County Public Schools' individual checklist for evaluating the use of reading strategies before, during, and after reading. Reprinted with permission of Fairfax County Public Schools.

Portfolios

Portfolios come in a variety of forms, and each serves a different purposes. One of the most popular types of portfolios is a *best-pieces* portfolio, which contains examples of work that students (sometimes with help from the teacher) consider to be their best efforts. Best-pieces portfolios are popular because they encourage students to become more reflective about and involved in their own learning. Indeed, a number of writers argue that what makes a portfolio a portfolio is that these collections include "student participation in selecting contents, the criteria for selection, the criteria for judging merit, and evidence of student self-evaluation" (Paulson, Paulson, & Meyer, 1991, p. 60). Tierney et al. (1991) also stress

Reading Group Checklist:	Names							
Before Reading: Dates→								
Chooses reading as a free time activity								
Has book ready during reading workshop								
Chooses appropriate reading material								
Uses text structure to preview								
Connects background knowledge to information in the text								
During Reading:								
Predicts and confirms, or revises predictions								
Stops and reviews reading with longer texts								
Reads familiar material with clarity, using punctuation appropriately								
When confronting unfamiliar words: Cross-checks one cue with another (phonics, language structure, and meaning)								
Rereads								
Uses chunks within multisyllable words to read								
Skips, reads on, and goes back to check word Asks another person								
Self-corrects to preserve meaning								
Uses features of informational text to aid comprehension								
Uses the context to determine the meaning of new or unfamiliar vocabulary								
After Reading:								
Retells, including important information or events								
Relates what is read to personal knowledge								
Makes comparisons								
Categorizes and classifies appropriately								
Discusses explicit and implied information								
Summarizes								
Draws conclusions based on reading								
Shows understanding using graphic organizer								
Uses information in the book to justify a response, confirm a prediction, or discuss elements of fiction or important information								
Written response shows evidence of critical thinking and a reflective stance towards reading								
Evaluates use of author's craft								

FIGURE 11.8. Fairfax County Public Schools' group checklist for evaluating the use of reading strategies before, during, and after reading. Reprinted with permission of Fairfax County Public Schools.

that portfolios are not objects; rather, they represent the students' abilities to engage in the processes of selecting, comparing, self-evaluating, sharing, and goal setting.

Setting the criteria for selection, setting the criteria for judging merit, and showing evidence of student self-evaluation are perhaps the most important aspects of best-pieces portfolios. One of the most powerful strategies in the teacher's repertoire for developing these crucial self-assessment skills in students is pairing portfolios with rubrics such as those described in the previous section.

The following is a step-by-step introduction to using best-pieces portfolios and rubrics in your classroom:

- Start by identifying some of your most effective instructional activities in literacy. Do you teach the students the writing process; have them develop neat stories; engage them in literature-response groups, oral presentations, sustained silent reading, literary analyses, and the other best practices in literacy instruction? Pick one instructional strategy that really works well for you and your students.

- After students have gained some experience with this particular instructional activity, begin to discuss what make a good piece of work in this context. For example, after students have written some stories, ask, "What makes a good story?" After making presentations, ask them, "What makes a good presentation?" Other key questions include "What makes someone a good writer?" or "What makes someone a good reader?"

- During these discussions, the teacher and the students develop a set of criteria for what makes a good piece of work. These criteria should be recorded on charts on the wall or other public places and used as the basis for rubrics that students will use (and revise) to help them internalize standards of quality.

After the students have become comfortable with discussions about what makes a good piece of work, move on to the next set of steps:

- Introduce the concept of portfolios to the students. Discuss with students why they are creating portfolios—so that the students, their teachers, and their parents can see how they have grown as readers and writers.

- Work with the students to identify what kinds of work samples should be included in the portfolios, and how those materials will be stored. Student work samples that might be included in portfolios include literature response logs, writing samples, story retellings, drawings, and so forth. Ways of storing these samples include large envelops, notebooks, folders, boxes, or baskets.

- Develop some simple forms for helping students evaluate the pieces of work they include in their portfolios. Many teachers produce a simple form that asks students the following questions:

> What does your portfolio show that you can do?
> What is your favorite piece in your portfolio? Why?
> Which pieces show that you have made improvement?
> What changes would you like to see in your portfolio?

This is also a good time to have students develop a table of contents for the portfolio.

• Work with students to set up a regular schedule for making additions to their portfolio. Make sure there are regular times in class when students can select the work samples, evaluate, and record why they have been chosen as best pieces, and update their portfolios.

• Use the portfolios regularly to inform classroom discussions about what makes a good piece of work. Take time for students to compare their earlier work samples with later ones in order to reflect on how they have grown as readers and writers.

• Use the portfolios for student–teacher conferences, as well as for student–parent–teacher conferences. Enjoy!

Helping children reflect on their own work forms the crucial interplay between assessment and instruction. Consider this example from an experienced first-grade elementary school teacher who had her class come up with ideas of what they thought makes a piece of writing a "best piece." Her students generated the following list:

• Uses imagination.
• The words make good pictures in your mind.
• Uses things that happen in your own life.
• Uses writing rules such as periods and capitals.
• Has spaces between words.
• Makes you want to keep on reading.

The teacher reported, "After writing down these ideas, the children were able to evaluate the work in their portfolios with some focus. The audience for this best piece was their own classmates. When they realized that their best pieces would truly circulate among their friends, they became very self-motivated and diligent in their efforts to present their best pieces to their friends in the best possible light. Now, when students read their best piece in the classroom, the authors aren't satisfied unless they are getting laughs, gasps, or smiles from the audience. We now choose a best piece about once every 2 months, which has added a lot of enthusiasm to our writing workshops."

Experienced teachers understand that the ability to engage in self-reflection does not just appear fully developed in children. They need to see teachers and other students modeling self-assessment. Students also need support and structure as they learn to evaluate themselves as learners.

Student–Teacher Conferences

Conferences between teachers and students are another powerful tool in the repertoires of teachers adept at authentic assessment. Conferences can be quick and informal or a bit more structured and systematic. Informal conferences may last from 3 to 4 minutes and may focus on something interesting that the teacher has seen or overheard. More structured conferences may take a bit longer and follow a predictable pattern in which students have a good idea of what is expected of them. For example, if the conference is about books read or papers written, then students are familiar with the kinds of questions that will be asked. The important point with conferences of all sorts is that they should be conducted in a safe and comfortable manner, so that students feel encouraged to take risks and share their ideas.

Student–teacher conferences are an important method of authentic assessment, because they provide information about the following:

- What the student is learning.
- The student's understanding about reading, writing, mathematics, and other aspects of the primary program curriculum.
- The student's interests.
- Areas where the student needs help.
- What things the teacher is doing that the student feels are particularly helpful.
- What things the student would like to learn next.

Conferences are often centered around something specific—a book being read, a paper being written, a performance task being developed, a project being completed. Here are some examples of different kinds of conferences and the kinds of information that teachers can learn.

Reading Conferences

The teacher can listen to the student read, discuss a book that has been previously read, or talk about the student's book log. These activities enable a teacher to learn about

- The strategies that the student uses
- Whether the student reads for meaning
- Whether the student is developing fluency
- The student's interests
- Whether the student selects reading materials of appropriate difficulty
- Whether the student is reading a variety of genres
- The student's progress in comprehending and retelling what has been read
- The student's ability to justify an opinion about what has been read

Writing Conferences

The teacher can help the student brainstorm topics to write about, discuss early drafts, listen to a student read a paper, or talk about which piece of work the student considers his or her best work and should be included in the best-pieces portfolio. These activities enable teachers to learn

- How the student is progressing in the use of the writing process
- What the student knows about organization, topic development, mechanics, and spelling
- Whether the student can effectively verbalize opinions, ideas, and feelings
- Whether the student can write for a variety of purposes
- Whether the student can edit drafts to a point that others can understand them

Clearly, conferencing can be a useful form of assessment in any aspect of the curriculum. As students talk about mathematics, social studies, art, and other activities and projects, then teachers can learn

- What students need to learn next
- Whether students can communicate what has been learned
- Whether students can use appropriate terminology
- Whether students can use strategies to solve real-life situations
- Whether students can provide reasonable explanations for solutions and strategies

Paris (1995) suggests a very useful framework that works well with reading and writing conferences, as well as conferences that take place around portfolios. He suggests that teachers ask questions about performance, processes, and perceptions. Performance questions focus on the actual work the student has completed. Process questions focus on reading and writing strategies. Perception questions focus on the students' motivational and affective perceptions about literacy and include the dimensions of effort, confidence, independence, and self-evaluation.

Sample performance questions
- What do you like about this paper?
- Tell me why you included this piece in your portfolio?
- What books did you read this last month?
- Did you meet your writing (reading, learning) goals this month?

Sample process questions

- How did you get the idea for writing this?
- What do you do when you read something you don't understand?
- How did you change your writing as you made drafts?

Sample perception questions

- What is the hardest part about reading (writing) for you?
- Who are your favorite authors?
- What kinds of books do you read at home?
- What is the best part of your writing?
- What makes you a good reader? A good writer?
- What should we work on this year to make you a better reader (or writer)?

Paris (1995) also reminds us of the key guidelines to keep in mind about conferences. Do not ask too many questions; let the student do most of the talking. Be interested, enthusiastic, and brief. Celebrate the student's strengths and be constructive about areas of growth. Record pertinent comments that will be useful information for later review. Remember that the goal of the conference is student self-reflection.

IMPLICATIONS FOR FUTURE RESEARCH

When we identify any practice as a "best practice," we run the risk of assuming that the particular practice has reached the peak of its development. Nowhere is this risk more dangerous than in the area of assessment. Although we have made major progress in terms of improving assessment, we have so much farther to go (e.g., Darling-Hammond, 1994; Linn, 1994; Winograd, 1994; Worthen, 1993). The following are some questions that face educators interested in continually improving the assessment of literacy:

- How do we ensure that literacy assessments are viewed as an integral part of a systemic approach to educational reform rather than as a panacea to cure all of education's ills?
- How do we ensure that literacy assessments meet rigorous standards of validity, reliability, authenticity, relevance, responsiveness, and flexibility?
- How do we ensure that literacy assessments meet rigorous standards for fairness, particularly for those students with diverse language or cultural backgrounds?

- How do we ensure that the consequences of literacy assessments are positive for all students?
- How do we set standards of student performance that are clear, fair, and achievable, and then ensure that assessment and instruction are integrated in constructive ways that improve teaching and learning?
- How do we ensure that all teachers receive adequate initial preparation and continued professional development in the ethical, technical, and instructional uses of educational assessments?
- How do we involve parents, school board members, legislators, and other stakeholders in the process of changing assessments from a process of ranking and sorting students to one of helping all students reach their full potential?

Given American education's love–hate relationship with testing in general, the long history of literacy assessment in particular, the large number of approaches for literacy assessment, the broad range of functions these assessment serve, and the number of issues to be solved, it is important to ask, "What is the future of literacy assessments?"

We believe that the future of literacy assessments can be positive, and we are cautiously optimistic. Educators, researchers, and policy makers interested in literacy have shown a willingness to explore new forms of assessment, because we do recognize the limitations and problems inherent in our traditional and current approaches. We are making a genuine effort to reconceptualize the purpose of assessment from a process of classifying children into winners and losers, to a process for providing students with opportunities to gain ownership of and insight about their own learning, and providing teachers with a rich basis for making professional judgments about instruction. Many of the forms of literacy assessment that have been developed recently do have the capacity to provide rich, descriptive evidence of students' literacy understandings and growth, and the potential to provide educators with ways to engage in linguistically and culturally appropriate evaluation and instruction, particularly for students whose knowledge is poorly reflected in traditional, standardized testing.

But we must be realistic. The overuse and misuse of testing and evaluation is still a major problem, and the current national emphasis on accountability is likely to exacerbate the problem. This situation is not going to change until Americans have more trust and confidence in teachers and in public schools.

In summary, our current practices in literacy assessment have the potential to strengthen or weaken the ways we teach reading and writing in schools. Whether the effects of literacy assessment will be positive or negative depends on our ability and willingness to ask the right questions about our priorities, our schools, our teachers, our students, and ourselves.

DISCUSSION AND ACTIVITIES

1. Work with another teacher as a partner and use the Home survey. Complete the general community and classroom survey for your students. Survey each other's classroom interaction with the Classroom Interaction Worksheet. Work together to identify possible themes or patterns.
2. Use different kinds of literature, including multiethnic stories, with the same assessment strategies (e.g., reading conference) to learn how the same student performs differently depending on the kind of literature.
3. What kinds of long-term, ongoing literate actives (i.e., journal writing, etc.) in which your students are engaged will provide a rich record of student growth over time?
4. What are the different perspectives about testing and assessment voiced by school administrators, school board members, legislators, parents, and teachers? What are the areas of agreement? Of disagreement? What kinds of evidence (other than just test scores) can a teacher gather to help these other groups feel confident about how students are progressing?

REFERENCES

Allington, R. L. (1991). Children who find learning to read difficult: School response to diversity. In E. H. Hiebert (Ed.), *Literacy for a diverse society: Perspectives, practices, and policies* (pp. 237–252). New York: Teachers College Press.

American Educational Research Association (AERA). (1999). AERA position statement concerning high-stakes testing in preK–12 education. Retrieved *www.aera.net/about/policy/stakes.htm.*

American Educational Research Association, American Psychological Association, and National Council on Measurement in Education. (1985). *Standards for educational and psychological testing.* Washington, DC: American Psychological Association.

Applebee, A. N., Langer, J. A., & Mullis, I. V. S. (1989). *Crossroads in American education.* Princeton, NJ: Educational Testing Service.

Au, K. H. (1993). *Literacy instruction in multicultural settings.* Fort Worth, TX: Hartcourt Brace College.

Barr, R. (1989). The social organization of literacy instruction. In S. McCormick & J. Zutell (Eds.), *Cognitive and social perspectives for literacy research and instruction* (38th Yearbook of the National Reading Conference, pp. 19–33). Chicago: National Reading Conference.

Beck, I., & McKeown, M. G. (1984). Application of theories of reading in instruction. In N. Stein (Ed.), *Literacy in American schools: Learning to read and write* (pp. 63–84). Chicago: University of Chicago Press.

Carrasco, R. L. (1984). *Collective engagement in the "segundo hogar": A micro-ethnography of engagement in a bilingual first grade classroom.* PhD dissertation, Harvard University, Cambridge, MA.

Cazden, C. B. (1988). *Classroom discourse: The language of teaching and learning.* Portsmouth, NH: Heinemann.

Clay, M. (1985). *The early detection of reading difficulties* (3rd ed.). Portsmouth, NH: Heinemann.

Crawford, L. W. (1993). *Language and literacy learning in multicultural classrooms.* Boston: Allyn & Bacon.

Darling-Hammond, L. (1994). Performance-based assessment and educational equity. *Harvard Educational Review, 64,* 5–30.

Darling-Hammond, L., Ancess, J., & Falk, B. (1995). *Authentic assessment in action: Studies of schools and students at work.* New York: Teachers College Press.

De Fina, A. (1992). *Portfolio assessment: Getting started.* New York: Scholastic.

Education Trust. (2002). Retrieved from *www.edtrust.org.*

Education Week. (2000). Quality counts. Retrieved from *www.edweek.org.*

Education Week. (2001). Quality counts. Retrieved from *www.edweek.org.*

Educational Resources Information Center (ERIC). Clearinghouse on Assessment and Evaluation. (1998). Retrieved from *www.ericae.net/main.htm.*

Fowler, D., & McCallum, S. (1998). *Assessing: Expanding expectations.* A language arts resource guide published by Fairfax County Public Schools, Fairfax, VA.

Gambrell, L., & Almasi, J. (1996). *Lively discussions!: Fostering engaged reading.* Newark, DE: International Reading Association.

Garcia, E. E. (1992). Linguistically and culturally diverse children: Effective instructional practices and related policy issues. In H. C. Waxman, J. Walker de Felix, J. E. Anderson, & H. P. Baptiste, Jr. (Eds.), *Students at risk in at-risk schools: Improving environments for learning* (pp. 65–86). Newbury Park, CA: Corwin Press.

Goodlad, J. (1984). *A place called high school.* New York: McGraw-Hill.

Goodman, K., Goodman, Y., & Hood, W. (1989). *The whole language evaluation book.* Portsmouth, NH: Heinemann.

Goodman, Y. (1978). Kidwatching: An alternative to testing. *Journal of National Elementary Principals, 57*(4), 41–45.

Haney, W., & Madaus, G. (1989). Searching for alternatives to standardized tests: Whys, whats, and whithers. *Phi Delta Kappan, 70,* 683–687.

Harp, B. (1994). *Assessment and evaluation for student centered learning.* Norwood: MA: Christopher-Gordon.

Harp, B. (1996). *The handbook of literacy assessment and evaluation.* Norwood, MA: Christopher-Gordon.

Heath, S. B. (1982). Questioning at home and at school: A comparative study. In G. Spindler (Ed.), *Doing the ethnography of schooling: Educational anthropology in action* (pp. 102–131). New York: Holt, Rinehart & Winston.

Hill, B., & Ruptic, C. (1994). *Practical aspects of authentic assessment: Putting the pieces together.* Norwood, MA: Christopher-Gordon.

Johnston, P. (1991). *Constructive evaluation of literate activity.* White Plains, NY: Longman.

Kemp, M. (1989). *Watching children read and write: Observational records for children with special needs*. Portsmouth, NH: Heinemann.

Kids Count Data Book. (2002). Retrieved from *www.aecf.org*

King, D. (1993). Assessment and evaluation in bilingual and multicultural classrooms. In B. Harp (Ed.), *Assessment and evaluation in whole language classrooms* (pp. 159–176). Norwood, MA: Christopher-Gordon.

LaCelle-Peterson, M., & Rivera, C. (1994). It is real for all kids? A framework of equitable assessment policies for English language learners. *Harvard Educational Review, 64*, 55–75.

Langer, J. A. (1984). Literacy instruction in American schools: Problems and perspectives. In N. Stein (Ed.), *Literacy in American schools, learning to read and write* (pp. 111–136). Chicago: University of Chicago Press.

Linn, R. (1994). Performance assessment: Policy promises and technical measurement standards. *Educational Researcher, 23*(9), 4–14.

Madaus, G. (1994). A technological and historical consideration of equity issues associated with proposals to change the nation's testing policy. *Harvard Educational Review, 64*, 76–95.

Michaels, S. (1981). Sharing time: Children's narrative styles and differential access to literacy. *Language in Society, 10*(3), 423–442.

Moll, L. (1992). Literacy research in community and classrooms: A sociocultural approach. In R. Beach, J. L. Green, M. L. Kamil, & T. Shanahan (Eds.), *Multidisciplinary perspectives on literacy research* (pp. 211–244). Urbana, IL: National Council of Teachers of English.

Moll, L., & Díaz, S. (1985). Ethnographic pedagogy: Promoting effective bilingual instruction. In E. Gracía & R. V. Padilla (Eds.), *Advances in bilingual education research* (pp. 127–149). Tucson, AZ: University of Arizona Press.

Morrow, L., & Smith, J. (1990). *Assessment for instruction in early literacy.* Englewood Cliff, NJ: Prentice-Hall.

National Assessment of Educational Progress. (2000). Retrieved from *www.nces.ed.gov/naep*

National Center for Fair and Open Testing. (1998). Retrieved from *www.fairtest.org*

National Center for Research on Evaluation, Standards, and Student Testing. (1998). Retrieved from *www.cresst96.cse.ucla.edu*

National Commission on Excellence on Education. (1983). *A nation at risk: The imperative for educational reform.* Washington, DC: Government Printing Office.

National Commission on Teaching and America's Future. (1996). *What matters most: Teaching for America's future.* New York: Columbia University Press.

National Commission on Testing and Public Policy. (1990). *From gatekeeper to gateway: Transforming testing in America.* Chestnut Hill, MA: Boston College.

National Council on Education Standards and Testing (NCEST). (1992). *Raising standards for American education: A report to Congress, the Secretary of Education, the National Education Goals Panel, and the American people.* Washington, DC: Government Printing Office.

National Education Goals Panel. (1998). Retrieved from *www.negp.gov*

Oakes, J. (1985). Keeping track: How schools structure inequality. New Haven, CT: Yale University Press.

Paris, S. (1995). *Coming to grips with authentic instruction and assessment.* Presentations sponsored by The Education Center, Torrance, CA.

Paulson, F., Paulson, P., & Meyer, C. (1991). What makes a portfolio a portfolio. *Educational Leadership, 48,* 60–64.

Purves, A. C. (1984). The potential and real achievement of U.S. students in school reading. In N. Stein (Ed.), *Literacy in American schools, learning to read and write* (pp. 85–110). Chicago: University of Chicago Press.

Rhodes, L. (1993). *Literacy assessment: A handbook of instruments.* Portsmouth, NH: Heinemann.

Rhodes, L., & Shanklin, N. (1993). *Windows into literacy: Assessing learners K–8.* Portsmouth, NH: Heinemann.

Routman, R. (1988). *Transitions: From literature to literacy.* Portsmouth, NH: Heinemann.

Routman, R. (1991). *Invitations: Changing as teachers and learners K–12.* Portsmouth, NH: Heinemann.

Scarcella, R. C. (1990). *Teaching language minority students in the multicultural classroom.* Upper Saddle River, NJ: Prentice-Hall.

Sharp, Q. (1989). *Evaluation: Whole language checklists for evaluating your children.* New York: Scholastic.

Spindler, G., & Spindler, L. (1990). The American cultural dialogue and its transmission. London: Falmer Press.

Stiggens, R. (1997). *Student-centered classroom assessment.* Upper Saddle River, NJ: Merrill.

Tierney, R. (1998). Literacy assessment reform: Shifting beliefs, principled possibilities, and emerging practices. *The Reading Teacher, 51,* 374–391.

Tierney, R. J., Carter, M. A., & Desai, L. E. (1991). *Portfolio assessment in the reading-writing classroom.* Norwood, MA: Christopher-Gordon.

U.S. Congress, Office of Technology Assessment. (1992). *Testing in American schools: Asking the right questions* (OTA-SET-519). Washington, DC: U.S. Government Printing Office.

U.S. Department of Education. (2002). *National Center for Educational Statistics.* Retrieved from *www.ed.gov*

Valdés, G., & Figueroa, R. (1994). *Bilingualism and testing: A special case of bias.* Norwood, NJ: Ablex.

Valencia, S., Hiebert, E., & Afflerbach, P. (1994). *Authentic reading assessment: Practices and possibilites.* Newark, DE: International Reading Association.

Wiggins, G. (1989). A true test: Toward authentic and equitable forms of assessment. *Phi Delta Kappan, 70,* 703–713.

Winograd, P. (1994). Developing alternative assessments: Six problems worth solving. *The Reading Teacher, 47,* 420–423.

Winograd, P., Benjamin, R., & Noll, E. (2001). Alternative assessment: High hopes, grave concerns. In D. Wagner, B. Street, & R. Venesky (Eds)., *Literacy: An international handbook.* New York: Garland.

Winograd, P., Paris, S., & Bridge, C. (1991). Improving the assessment of literacy. *The Reading Teacher, 45,* 108–116.

Winograd, P., & Perkins, F. (1996). Authentic assessment in the classroom: Principles and practices. In R. Blum & J. Arter (Eds.), *Handbook for student performance assessment* (pp. 8:1–8:11). Alexandria, VA: Association for Curriculum Development.

Worthen, B. (1993, February). Critical issues that will determine the future of alternative assessment. *Phi Delta Kappan, 74,* 444–454.

Part III

SPECIAL ISSUES

Chapter 12

ORGANIZING EFFECTIVE LITERACY INSTRUCTION: GROUPING STRATEGIES AND INSTRUCTIONAL ROUTINES

D. Ray Reutzel

This chapter will:

- Review current research on the effects of various grouping strategies.
- Explain the implementation, benefits, and limitations of a variety of classroom grouping strategies.
- Describe the effect of classroom instructional routines on successful literacy instruction.
- Identify aspects of effective classroom literacy instructional routines.

It is the first day of school for 20 excited and somewhat frightened first graders. Like most young children, they arrive fully expecting that this is the year, perhaps even the day, when they learn to read and write! Ms. Songi, first-grade teacher at Sunset Elementary School, greets each child with a warm smile as the children rambunctiously enter a classroom carefully crafted to support a variety of literacy teaching and learning situations.

The classroom is organized into several areas—each thoughtfully designed to meet the needs of whole-class, small-group, and individual learning opportunities. The classroom is filled with print—labeled objects, posters, charts, daily schedules, message centers, books, word walls, word chunks, environmental print collections, signs, work board or classroom routine displays, and so on. A multicolored carpet with a black square for each child is located in the front of the room near the dry-erase whiteboard. Close by, there is an electronic music keyboard and an easel stocked with large chart paper, readied for whole-class instruction. A small horseshoe-shaped table in a distant corner of the classroom awaits a variety of instructional activities organized for small groups of children.

Learning centers are placed around the perimeter of the classroom. A publishing center runs along one side of the room, opposite the windows; on a cupboard top in this area, a full line of writing tools and materials awaits anxious but willing hands for writing and publishing. A small, carpeted reading nook, complete with a large rocking chair for one-to-one reading and several beanbag chairs for independent reading by children, is neatly organized in a quiet area of the room. Near the front is a play office area, complete with typewriter, adding machine, telephone, desk, writing tablets, pencils, pens, erasers, markers, rubber stamps, dictionary, speller, liquid White-Out, and a dry-erase board for business planning and messages. Across the room, a small center, stocked with everything from stencils and magnetic letters to Alpha-Bits cereal, is designed to enable children to explore letters of the alphabet and engage in word play, exploration, sorting, and study. Near the classroom door is a listening center, complete with cassette tape recorder, headphones, audiocassette tapes of books, six-pack copies of selected children's book titles, and a computer and monitor loaded with children's books on compact discs (CDs). A storage area with 20 large plastic trays is located on the other side of the classroom door. The classroom has no desks, only tables and chairs organized into many interesting and exciting learning areas. Each child is instructed to find a chair with his/her own nametag carefully written in manuscript on a cartoon bookworm character—a nametag to be pinned to each child's shirt. Each child writes a duplicate nametag and places his or her nametag on a tray to be used for storing books and personal supplies. School is ready to start.

If permitted, Ms. Songi would tell us that much study, reading, planning, thought, and preparation have preceded this momentous day. It is common knowledge that effective classroom environments, use of grouping strategies, and planning and implementing of effective classroom organizational structures do not occur by accident. These organizational components, like so much of effective literacy instruction, are the products of teacher knowledge, skill, and ingenuity.

THEORY AND RESEARCH BASE: THE EFFECTS OF GROUPING ON LITERACY LEARNING

Because teachers' experience and expertise in managing the complexity of classrooms vary greatly, and because students' needs are equally complex and challenging, the question of grouping for instruction is of critical importance for all teachers—novice and experienced alike. When teachers determine to use a variety of grouping plans, they consciously or unconsciously add to the complexity of managing the classroom environment and at the same time provide necessary accommodations to meet individual student needs. This tension between increasing management complexity and meeting student needs is a tenuous balancing act for many teachers. For example, let us assume a teacher has chosen to use only whole-class instruction to reduce the complexity of management in a classroom. The potential moral consequences of such a choice may be that individual student needs are not met or, worse yet, that selected children, often the most needy, may be denied access to knowledge, instruction, and an opportunity to learn (Goodlad & Oakes, 1988; Oakes, 1986, 1988; Opitz, 1998a; Worthy & Hoffman, 1996). Thus, a teacher's decision to use a particular grouping strategy must be made in full appreciation of the potential social, instructional, psychological, and moral outcomes of such a choice on children, not just for the ease or convenience of the teacher. On the other hand, an overtaxed, stressed out teacher with too many small groups or individual learning activities may not be as emotionally available to respond sensitively to the needs of all children. A workable model for many teachers is to begin with a simple, limited, and manageable grouping plan and gradually expand toward using a wide range of grouping strategies effectively to provide intensive, extensive, teacher-guided instruction to allow for individual differences and free choice, foster collaboration, provide access to knowledge, support individual readers as they develop, and encourage social interaction.

Organizing classrooms into smaller groups of children fills the moral imperative often felt by teachers to meet individual student needs. However, somewhere between meeting individual needs and managing a classroom filled with children lies an expansive chasm to be bridged by grouping strategies and organizational plans. Individualized instruction in classrooms filled with 20–30 children, although desirable as the ideal, is also impractical and virtually impossible. On the other hand, the exclusive use of whole-class grouping fails to address students as individuals whose needs, skills, performance, and dispositions differ greatly. It is through the use of a variety of whole, small, and individual grouping strategies that teachers effectively address students' needs, skills, and motivations in learning literacy. Positive and negative effects of whole-class and ability grouping on student learning and engagement are discussed next. Following this, I suggest a variety of small-group strategies that provide classroom teachers workable and effective alternatives to whole-class and ability grouping.

Whole-Class Instruction

Whole-class instruction can be used effectively to address the *general developmental* needs of a group of children in a given classroom. No attempt is made to subdivide the group into smaller or more focused instructional groups along any dimension of learning, need, or skills.

Whole-class grouping is a popular organizational format for providing explicit, direct, systematic skills and strategy instruction, as well as for literature study using a core books approach, or for shared reading (Reutzel & Cooter, 2000, 2003; Cox & Zarillo, 1993; Fisher & Medvic, 2000). It is an effective means to safety-net young learners as they develop conventional and increasingly sophisticated literacy learning strategies. Whole-class instruction shields the individual within a community of learners from potentially harsh emotional and psychological consequences that may result from the risks associated with *solo reading*. Whole-class instruction can also reduce some of the negative effects of labeling young learners as "below average," "slow," "special needs," or "disabled."

Because becoming literate is both a social and a cognitive endeavor, whole-class instruction engages teachers and children in a community of socially shared literacy activities and discussions. Shared literacy learning activities generally provided in whole-class instruction need to be a regular and integral part of every literacy classroom (Cunningham, Hall, & Defee, 1998; Flood, Lapp, Flood, & Nagel, 1992; Wilkinson & Townsend, 2000). Just a few examples of potentially effective literacy learning activities that can be used in connection with whole-class instruction include the following: telling stories; dramatizing; reading books aloud and sharing student-authored stories, poems, and songs; reading big books together; reading the enlarged texts of songs, poems, raps, and jingles; participating in an experiment or some other active-learning experience; and creating language-experience charts. On the downside, whole-class instruction used exclusively clearly fails to meet the needs of individual children, especially those with learning disabilities (Schumm, Moody, & Vaughn, 2000). Flexibility in grouping seems to be a key element of successful reading instruction (Opitz, 1998a; Wilkinson & Townsend, 2000).

Ability Grouping

Ability grouping places children in several homogeneous groups, typically, three groups, for instruction as determined by their performance on a reading achievement test or some other form of norm- or criterion-referenced measurement (Hiebert, 1983; Pallas, Entwisle, Alexander, & Stluka, 1994; Opitz, 1998b; Slavin, 1987). Typical ability grouping has resulted in establishing three achievement groups: high, medium, and low. These groups are often given names to mask the leveled nature of the grouping scheme. But children often uncover the meaning of being in the Eagles, the Robins, or the Buzzards group—or in the Roses, the Daisies, or the Weeds group—as the case may be! Ability grouping has often been characterized by some of its critics *as running a three-ring reading circus.*

Although most teachers have relied heavily upon standardized reading achievement test scores in assigning children to an ability group, other factors such as personality attributes, general academic competence, work habits, and home background are also weighed in the decision (Haller & Waterman, 1985; Wilkinson & Townsend, 2000). Also, ability grouping has been associated with the use of graded basal readers, workbooks, and skills lessons designed to follow a published scope and sequence of skills development (Moody, Schumm, Fischer, & Jean-Francois, 1999).

Interestingly, one survey of teacher opinions on grouping strategies revealed that regular education teachers preferred whole class and mixed-ability grouping for reading instruction, whereas special educators preferred same-ability grouping for reading instruction (Moody, Vaughn, & Schumm, 1997). Teachers' continued reliance upon ability grouping has likely been rooted in the worthwhile goal of attending to individual student needs. According to Kletzien (1996), ability grouping for reading instruction is still used in 50% of the nation's "blue ribbon" or top elementary schools! Unfortunately, very often, the instruction offered to students in ability groups has failed to meet student needs and, in some cases, has been harmful to both teachers and students.

Numerous negative outcomes have been associated with the use of ability grouping despite its intuitive appeal and longevity. For example, children in low-ability groups spend more time in oral *round-robin* or *barbershop* reading and reading workbook assignments than do their peers in high-ability groups (Allington, 1983; Harp, 1989a, 1989b; Leinhardt, Zigmond, & Cooley, 1981; Pallas et al., 1994). Teachers tolerate more outside interruptions in low-ability groups than in high-ability groups (Allington, 1980). In the spring of the school year, children assigned to low-ability groups for reading instruction exhibited three times the number of inattentive behaviors exhibited by their counterparts assigned to high-ability groups (Felmlee & Eder, 1983). Children in low-ability groups tend to have lowered academic expectations and self-concepts (Eder, 1983; Hiebert, 1983; Rosenbaum, 1980). Time devoted to decoding instruction and practice is fully double for low-ability group readers as compared to high-ability groups (Gambrell, Wilson, & Gnatt, 1981). Teachers tend to interrupt low-ability readers more often than they do high readers for miscues while reading (Allington, 1980). In a more recent study, however, students with learning disabilities assigned to mixed-ability groups complained that pacing, embarrassment, and working conditions were drawbacks to heterogeneous grouping for them (Elbaum, Moody, & Schumm, 1999).

Weinstein (1976) found that as much as 25% of the variation in reading achievement at the end of first grade could be attributed to group assignment. Kulik and Kulik (1982) analyzed the results of 52 studies and determined that (1) ability grouping generally has small effects on achievement, (2) high-ability readers profit from ability grouping in terms of achievement, and (3) the effects of ability grouping on average- and low-ability children's achievement is only trivial. On the other hand, children's friendships tend to be increasingly influenced by continuing membership in an ability group (Hallinan & Sorensen, 1985; Sorensen & Hallinan, 1986). Eder (1983) showed that even 1 year in an ability group caused some children to begin to question the reasons underlying their group membership. Thus, reading achievement may be minimally affected by ability grouping, but children's self-images and social circles appear to be profoundly affected (Harp, 1989a, 1989b; Oakes, 1988; Wuthrick, 1990).

In short, the use of traditional ability grouping is not recommended to promote effective literacy instruction. In defense of ability grouping, there are those who suggest that its negative effects are largely associated with the static nature of the groups and the teacher's attitudes and expectations. They also maintain that if groups were changed at least monthly, and the teacher were aware of and resisted the expectations often invited by ability grouping, the ability-grouping strategy might not constitute as harmful a practice to teachers and children as has been suggested (Worthy & Hoffman, 1996). Wilkinson and Townsend (2000) indicate that flexibility of grouping is not the only key to success, that ability grouping can be used successfully *if* three conditions are met: (1) teachers view ability as incremental and malleable rather than fixed, (2) teachers ensure a close fit between students and texts, and (3) ability grouping is only one of many organizational arrangements used by teachers to group students for instruction and other classroom activities.

However, given the pervasive use of ability grouping in the past, which has given way to the pervasive use of whole-class grouping of late, many teachers are prompted to ask, "If whole-class instruction is insufficient to meet student needs and ability grouping is or can be harmful, just what do we put in the place of ability grouping?" The discussion that follows is intended to provide an answer to this question by suggesting multiple grouping alternatives for organizing effective classroom literacy instruction.

ALTERNATIVE GROUPING STRATEGIES

Flexible Grouping

Flexible grouping is a partial answer to the looming question for many teachers about what to put in the place of whole-class instruction or ability grouping (Wilkinson & Townsend, 2000). In flexible grouping, children are placed into *temporary* groups based on their level of independence as learners and their personal interests that sustain independence. Optiz (1998a) describes flexible grouping as allowing "students to work in differently mixed ability groups depending upon the learning task at hand" (p. 10). There are several key differences between ability- and flexible-grouping strategies. Some of these are summarized in Table 12.1.

TABLE 12.1. Comparing Characteristics of Flexible and Ability Grouping Strategies

	Ability grouping	Flexible grouping
Forming groups	Test scores	Ability to manage leveled books
Nature of groups	Static	Dynamic, changing
Instructional tasks	Given low-level tasks	Given high-level tasks
Reading practice	Oral round-robin	Oral guided and silent reading
Reading materials	Basal selections chosen by teacher	Trade and leveled books chosen by teacher and students
Typical assessment	Test scores	Observations, informal checklists, performance of authentic reading tasks

Flexible groups are formed and reformed on the basis of a set of principles. Some of these summarized principles are well articulated by Unsworth (1984, p. 300):

1. There are no permanent groups.
2. Groups are periodically created, modified, or disbanded to meet new needs as they arise.
3. At times, there is only one group consisting of all pupils.
4. Groups vary in size from 2 or 3 to 9 or 10, depending on the group's purpose.
5. Group membership is not fixed; it varies according to needs and purposes.
6. Student commitment is enhanced when students know how the group's work relates to the overall program or task.
7. Children should be able to evaluate the progress of the group and the teacher's assessment of the group's work.
8. There should be a clear strategy for supervising the group's work.

It is clear from these principles that flexible-grouping strategies can be used to accommodate student interests, learning styles, and social needs, such as friendship groups, in addition to meeting instructional needs and goals. For flexible grouping to function effectively, the organization, purpose, and tasks must be clearly understood by students.

Concerns such as what is to be accomplished and how it is to be accomplished must be clearly stated and understood by students. The potential for unproductive chaos is high in flexible-grouping arrangements if the teacher has not carefully prepared the learning tasks and the environment for success. For example, a classroom in which flexible grouping is used to provide for participation in multiple centers or stations might operate something like the one described next.

This hypothetical classroom has six literacy learning centers, established in various locations around the classroom. The first center is an alphabet and word-building station, where children use magnetic letters and word pattern cards (rimes/word families) to build words, sort words, and store words in personalized word banks. A second center houses listening stations, where students have multiple copies of a single title to be read with a read-along cassette tape. A third center provides a quiet, comfortable area for reading self-selected books, magazines, comics, and so on. A fourth center seats children around a horseshoe-shaped table for guided reading and interactive writing sessions with the teacher. A fifth center is a writing workshop, where students can have peer conferences, get and give editing assistance, and prepare student-authored products from greeting cards, recipes and calendars, to newspaper ads, books, and story murals. Finally, there is a center for individual student conferences that are scheduled in advance with the teacher.

Flexible groups of children are formed to participate in these six designed center activities. Each flexible group includes a mix of reading and writing ability levels, called heterogeneous grouping, to avoid the pitfalls associated with ability grouping. Flexible groups may also have an elected or appointed group leader to oversee cleanup of centers, operation of necessary equipment, management of supplies, and other tasks. In any case, these groups have assigned tasks to complete in each center. Behavioral and instructional guidelines and goals are clearly established and communicated to each group prior to center time. And most importantly, students are helped to know what they may do as follow-up work should they finish before the others. All of this requires extraordinary instructional planning and management skills on the part of the teacher, but the busy and productive activity and learning that come from the flexible grouping strategy make it well worth the effort!

Visiting Basal Reader Selection Groups

In visiting basal reader selection groups, students are invited to spend about 20 minutes browsing through the basal reader table of contents, looking at the pictures throughout the book, and scanning the stories. This requires that teachers and students think about the basal reader as an anthology of literature to serve as a resource. Following this browsing time, the teacher might read each title in the table of contents aloud. Students indicate their interest in each story title read aloud by raising their hands, and the teacher records interest levels in the teacher's manual table of contents. This process provides a quick means of gauging interest for each selection in the basal reader. Following this initial interest assessment, the teacher looks at selection titles in the table of contents for common themes or topics, so that basal stories can be grouped by theme, genre, or author to provide several related units to organize visiting basal reader selection groups.

To get the visiting basal reader selection groups launched, the teacher describes the themes or topics for groups of selections, as well as each selection related to the theme or topic. Students pick their first or second basal selection choices for group membership. The remaining steps for forming visiting basal reader selection groups are the same as those described in the next subsection outlining literature circles. Some teachers like to start with whole-group instruction on a common skill or strategy lesson and then use small-group instruction such as visiting basal reader selection groups (Wiggins, 1994). If all or parts of basal stories are to be read aloud, I suggest using the "Tag Reading" strategy, in which one student (or the teacher) starts reading and then tags another student at random to continue the reading (Hoeck-Buehler, 2001). Visiting basal reader selection groups, recommended by the Commission on Reading in the report *Becoming a Nation of Readers* (Anderson, Hiebert, Scott, & Wilkinson, 1985), represent a potentially effective grouping strategy to be used in conjunction with published basal reading programs.

Literature Circles

In literature circles, teachers and children use trade books or literary books, both narrative and expository, as the core for reading instruction. To form literature circles, the teacher has children look through several selected titles of trade books available for small-group instruction. (This will mean that multiple copies of each book or title will be needed! It is recommended that teachers purchase about eight copies of each book rather than purchasing classroom sets. Opitz [1998b] recommends that books with a common topic or element called "text sets" be used in literature study groups.) At the conclusion of this exploration period, the teacher reads available book titles aloud and asks how many students would like to read each book. In this way, teachers can get a quick idea of which available books seem to interest the students most, and which engender no interest. The teacher selects from the high-interest trade books three to four titles, depending on how many literature circles he or she can reasonably manage, and how many copies of each book are available. Next, the teacher works up a "book talk" on each of the selected books to present to the students the following day. A book talk is a short, interesting introduction to the topic, setting, and problem of a book. After presenting a book talk on each of the books selected, the teacher asks older children to write down the titles of their first two choices. The teacher asks the younger children to come to the chalkboard and sign their names under the titles of the two books they like best of those presented. Only one literature circle meets each day with the teacher to discuss and respond to a chapter or predetermined number of pages to be read in a trade book. It is best if the teacher meets with each literature circle, after children have indicated their choices, to determine how many weeks will be spent reading the book, and how many pages per day need to be read to reach that goal. The remaining steps for organizing literature circles are summarized as follows:

1. Select three or four books children may be interested in reading from the brief interest inventory of literature available in the school or classroom, as described.
2. Introduce each of the books by giving a book talk on each.
3. Invite children to write down the titles of their two top choices.
4. Depending on the number of multiple copies of trade books available, fill each group with those children who have indicated the book as their first choice. Once a group is filled, move the remaining children to their second choice, until all children have been invited to attend the group of their first or second choice.
5. Decide how many days or weeks will be spent reading this series of book choices.
6. Meet with each of the literature circles and determine the following:
   a. How many pages per day will need to be read to complete the book in the time allowed.
   b. When the first group meeting will be held. (The teacher meets with only one group per day.)
   c. How children will respond to their reading. This may involve a reading response log, character report cards, or wanted posters.
7. Help children understand when the first or next meeting of their literature-response group will be, how many pages in the book will need to be read, and which type of response, such as group retellings, wanted posters, a story map, and so on, to the reading will need to be completed before the meeting of the literature-response group (Wood & Jones, 1998).
8. Near the completion of the book, the group may discuss possible extensions of the book to drama, music, art, and other projects.

Peterson and Eeds (1990), in their book *Grand Conversations*, suggest a checklist that may be used by teachers to track student preparation for and participation in literature response groups. I have modified this form to be used with literature circles, as shown in Figure 12.1.

When the literature-circle book has been completed, literature circles are disbanded and new groups are formed for selecting and reading a new series of books. Thus, students' interests are engaged by encouraging choice, and the problem of static ability-grouping plans can be avoided.

Cooperative Learning Groups

Another grouping strategy for effective reading and writing instruction, called cooperative learning, makes use of heterogeneous groups ranging

---

Name _____   Date _____

Author _____   Title _____

Preparation for Literature Study

- Brought book to the literature circle.   Yes ___ No ___
- Contributed to developing group reading goals.   Yes ___ No ___
- Completed work according to group goals.   Yes ___ No ___
- Read the assigned pages, chapters, etc., for the goals.   Yes ___ No ___
- Noted places to share (ones of interest, ones that were
  puzzling, etc.)   Yes ___ No ___
- Completed group response assignments before coming
  to the day's discussion.   Yes ___ No ___

Participation in the Literature Circle Discussion

- Participated in the discussion.   Weak ___ Good ___ Excellent ___
- Gave quality of verbal responses and
  contributions.   Weak ___ Good ___ Excellent ___
- Used text to support ideas and assertions. Weak ___ Good ___ Excellent ___
- Listened to others.   Weak ___ Good ___ Excellent ___

FIGURE 12.1. Record of goal completion and participation in literature circles. Adapted from Peterson and Eeds (1990). Copyright 1990 by Scholastic Canada. Adapted by permission.

from two to five children working together to accomplish a *team task* (Harp, 1989a; Johnson & Johnson, 1999; Opitz, 1992; Slavin, 1987). Harp (1989a) indicates four characteristics of cooperative learning groups. First, each lesson begins with teacher instruction and modeling. Second, the children in the group work together to accomplish a task assigned by the teacher to the group. Third, children work on individual assignments related to a group-assigned task. Each student must be willing to complete his or her part of the group-shared assignment. Finally, the team is recognized by averaging each individual grade and assigning one grade to the group.

Much research indicates that children in cooperative learning groups have consistently shown greater achievement than those who participate in traditional grouping schemes (Johnson, Maruyama, Johnson, Nelson, & Skon, 1981; Jongsma, 1990; Opitz, 1992; Radencich, 1995; Slavin, 1988; Stevens, Madden, Slavin, & Farnish, 1987a, 1987b; Topping, 1989; Webb & Schwartz, 1988; Wood, 1987). In a synthesis of research on cooperative learning, Slavin (1991) found that cooperative learning not only increased student achievement but also improved student self-concept and social skills.

Manarino-Leggett and Salomon (1989) and Wood (1987) describe several different grouping alternatives that can be applied with the concept of cooperative learning. A few of these group alternatives are briefly described in Table 12.2.

Needs Grouping

Needs groups are determined by careful observation as teachers assess and work with children in a variety of literacy learning activities. Through the use of assessment strategies such as running records, anecdotal records, group participation records, and observation, teachers determine individual students' learning needs. Needs groups are formed when this careful assessment and observation process indicates several children with similar learning needs, whether these needs be skills, content, or strategy based. Typically, a needs group will include as few as two students or as many as half the class, 10–15 students. The purpose of a needs group is to teach a temporary group of students a particular procedure, literary stylistic device, skill, or strategy they have yet to learn and apply. The vehicle for instruction within needs groups is minilessons.

Minilessons can occur with an entire class or with small needs groups. They are not always meant to be lessons for which outcomes are required. Sometimes minilessons are simply invitations to engage in some literate behavior or process. Hagerty (1992) describes three types of minilessons that may be taught in a needs group setting: (1) *procedural*, (2) *literary*, and (3) *strategy/skills*.

TABLE 12.2. Alternative Grouping Plans for Encouraging Cooperative Learning

Dyads

Wood (1987) assigns roles to each student in a dyad or pair of readers. Each student reads two pages of text silently, or in some cases the two students read orally in unison. After reading these two pages, one student acts as the recaller and verbally recounts what the two have read. The other student acts as listener and clarifier for the recaller. Dyad reading is an effective means for supporting young children's reading development, especially for at-risk readers (Eldredge & Quinn, 1988).

Focus trios

Children may be randomly assigned or may form social groups of three students for the purposes of summarizing what they already know about a reading selection and developing questions to be answered during reading. After reading, the trio discusses answers to the questions and clarifies and summarizes their answers.

Group retellings

Students read different books or selections on the same topic. After reading, each student retells to the other group members what he/she has read. Group members may comment on or add to the retellings of any individual.

Groups of four

Groups of four are randomly assigned task completion groups. Each individual is given a responsibility to complete some phase of a larger task. For example, when writing a letter, one student might be the addresser, another the body writer, another the checker, etc. In this way, all students contribute to the successful completion of the task. Roles should be exchanged regularly to enable students to experience all aspects of task completion.

Jigsaw

Students in a group are each assigned to read a different part of the same selection. After reading, each student retells to the others in the group what he/she has read. A discussion usually ensues in which students may interview or question the reteller to clarify any incomplete ideas or correct misunderstanding. After this discussion concludes, students can be invited to read the rest of the selection to confirm or correct the retellings of other group members.

Metacomprehension pairs

Students alternate reading and orally summarizing paragraphs or pages of a selection. One listens, follows along, and checks the accuracy of the other's comprehension of the selection.

(*continued*)

TABLE 12.2. (*continued*)

<hr>

Problem-solving/project groups

Having children work together cooperatively in pairs or small groups to solve reading or writing problems is another effective classroom practice involving the collaboration of children to enhance classroom instruction. Small problem-solving groups are initiated by children who wish to work collaboratively on a self-selected reading or writing problem.

In project groups, children are encouraged to explore a wide variety of possible reading and writing projects (e.g., plays, puppetry, reader's theater, research, student-authored books, poetry, lyrics to songs, notes, invitations, or cards). The products resulting from project groups are to be of publishable quality. The culmination of a project group is sharing the project or product with an authentic audience.

Think–pair–share

Lyman (1988) recommends that students sit in pairs as the teacher presents a reading minilesson to the class. After the lesson, the teacher presents a problem to the group. The children individually think of an answer; then with their partners they discuss and reach a consensus on the answer. A pair of students can be asked to share their agreed-upon answer with the class.

Turn-to-your-neighbor

After listening to a student read a book aloud, share a book response, or share a piece of published writing, students can be asked to turn to a neighbor and tell one concept or idea they enjoyed about the presentation. They should also share one question they would like to ask the reader or author.

<hr>

A procedural reading minilesson, for example, might involve the teacher and students in learning how to care for new books to be placed into the classroom library, as well as how to repair worn older books already found there. The teacher may demonstrate how to break in a new book's binding by standing the book on its spine and opening a few pages on either side of the center of the book, carefully pressing them down. Cellophane tape and staplers may be used to demonstrate how to repair tears in a book's pages or covers. A heavy-duty stapler can be used to reattach paperback book covers in another demonstration on caring for books.

Another example of a literary minilesson might involve a child presenting the teacher with a small written-at-home booklet in the shape of a puppy, that retells favorite parts from the book *A Taxi Dog Christmas* (Barracca & Barracca, 1994). This may present an opportunity for the teacher to share the book with his or her students as one demonstration of how another student shared ideas using the writing process.

A typical strategy/skills minilesson might occur during the reading of a big book entitled *Who's in the Shed?* (Parkes, 1986), with the teacher making note of the fact that many of the words in the book rhyme, but the rhymes are not spelled the same (*shed* and *said*). Noticing this irregularity in the text, the teacher draws the children's attention to these words and to the fact that these words rhyme but are spelled differently. For example, while rereading the big book the next day, the teacher may cover the words "shed" and "said" with small, self-adhesive notes. During the group rereading of the book, the teacher reveals the *covered words*. On subsequent readings, the teacher invites students to join in the reading, while emphasizing the target words. Children use the /ed/ rime to produce rhyming words written on cards to be displayed on the Word Wall. They add other rhyming words to the Word Wall as they think of them.

A minilesson for more advanced readers might pertain to patterns used by nonfiction writers to make abstract information easier to understand (e.g., cause–effect, description, problem solution, or comparisons). The lesson could involve (1) describing the patterns used; (2) searching for examples in science, mathematics, and social studies materials; then (3) having students write/create their examples of these patterns pertaining to a topic of choice.

In summary, needs groups are formed to achieve specific learning outcomes formulated through careful observation and assessment by the classroom teacher. These groups are not simply formed to teach a skill or strategy to a group of children because it appears in the curriculum guide or the scope and sequence chart of the basal reader; rather the groups are only formed specifically to address student needs discerned through careful teacher assessment.

Dynamic Grouping for Guided Reading Instruction

Guided reading is an essential part of an effective reading program. The practice of guided reading focuses on reading *with* and *by* children when texts would present too many challenges if children were to take full responsibility for the initial reading. Thus, the purposes of guided reading are (1) to develop reading strategies and (2) to move children toward independent silent reading (Booth, 1998; Fountas & Pinnell, 1996, 2001; Mooney, 1990; Opitz & Ford, 2001).

At first, the use of dynamic grouping for guided reading looks somewhat similar to those grouping practices previously described as ability grouping. Because ability grouping has already been discussed, it is appropriate to examine the practices of dynamic grouping for guided reading and contrast these with ability grouping.

Dynamic grouping to provide guided reading instruction is begun by placing children into small, homogeneous reading groups reflecting developmental levels and a range of competencies, experiences, and interests (Mooney, 1990; Fountas & Pinnell, 1996). The most important consideration centers on the child's ability to handle and process leveled books successfully. Developmental guided reading groups are composed of six to eight children, who will be working together for a period of time with the assistance of the teacher. Groups change as children make progress during the year—usually changing in months rather than in weeks or days.

Prior to guided reading, great care is taken to match a leveled book and child to ensure that children can enjoy and control the book throughout their first reading. Texts chosen for each level should present children with not only a reasonable challenge but also a high degree of success. Typically, children should be able to read 90–95% of the words correctly in a leveled book chosen for use in a guided reading group. During guided reading, teachers use questions and comments to help children employ strategies and resources available to them from within themselves and the text.

Children should *not* be placed in guided reading groups until they have had ample opportunities to listen to stories, poems, songs, and so on, and to participate in shared or community-based whole-class reading experiences. A gradual release of responsibility from teacher to child for the first reading of a guided reading book generally occurs as teachers observe that children understand basic print concepts and have acquired a basic sight-word vocabulary. As teachers work with children in guided reading groups, they lead them to understand and use strategically three important cuing systems that good readers use to unlock text: the meaning and organization of text, grammatical elements, and visual/letter–sound cues. Guided reading groups provide a context for systematic skills instruction related specifically to the language, literary devices, and content of each leveled book read in the group. Guided reading is a time to focus instruction directly on student reading skills development rather than on appreciating and responding to superb literature. In fact, the use of leveled books in guided reading does not always allow the use of recognized literature of enduring quality; rather, it necessitates use of books written to support individual readers in their development of self-extending reading strategies.

SCAFFOLDING CLASSROOM READING INSTRUCTION (K–2): THE PRIMARY GRADES LITERACY WORKSHOP

Children develop a sense of security when the events of the school day revolve around a sequence of anticipated activities. Although variety is the spice of life for children too, they find comfort in familiar instructional routines in a well-organized classroom (Holdaway, 1984). There are any number of ways to organize the activities and instruction of the school day. However, it is important that children experience a variety of interactive settings in the whole class, in small groups, and individually each day. Groups should be flexible, meet the needs of the students, and involve the "best practices" of literacy instruction.

One such approach that has been widely used to organize the school day is the *Reading Workshop* (Atwell, 1987; Calkins, 1994, 2001; Fountas & Pinnell, 2001; Reutzel & Cooter, 1991). Reutzel and Cooter (2003) have adapted the traditional Reading Workshop for the primary grades, called the *Primary Grades Literacy Workshop*. The organizational framework of the Primary Grades Literacy Workshop is a functional and flexible instructional scaffolding to provide primary grade interactive, shared, guided, and independent reading and writing experiences similar to other reading organizational plans, such as the four blocks plan authored by P. M. Cunningham (Cunningham et al., 1998).

The Primary Grade Literacy Workshop consists of five parts: (1) Reading and Writing Together, (2) Working with Words and Strategies, (3) Guided Reading, (4) Fluency Development, and (5) Independent Center Study and Individual Assessment. The five components of the Primary Grade Literacy Workshop incorporate elements of reading instruction recommended in several recent national reading research reports, including decoding instruction, fluency development, vocabulary and comprehension strategy instruction, and guided oral reading (Snow, Burns, & Griffin, 1998; National Reading Panel, 2000). The Primary Grades Literacy Workshop is designed to run for 150–180 minutes daily during an uninterrupted instructional time block. The structure of the Primary Grades Literacy Workshop is outlined in Figure 12.2.

Reading and Writing Together (35–40 Minutes)

During this group instructional time, teachers engage young readers in three sequenced reading and writing experiences: (1) Interactive Read-Aloud, (2) Shared Reading, and (3) Interactive and/or Shared Writing.

Working with Words and Strategies (30 Minutes)

The purpose of the *working with strategies* instructional block is to develop children's emerging decoding, spelling, vocabulary, and comprehension strategy awareness and use. During this time, children are taught how to select the appropriate strategy for a language problem-solving task and apply it in a variety of reading situations and contexts. I cannot emphasize enough the importance of providing students with direct, explicit instruction. This means that teachers do not rely on discovery approaches;

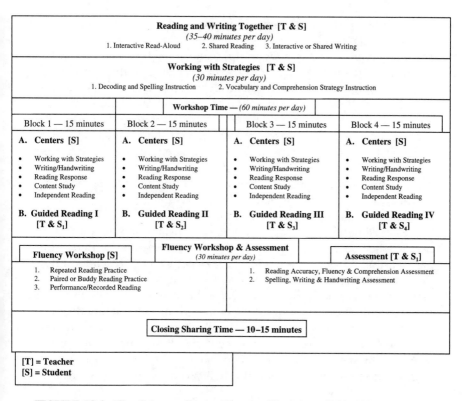

Reading and Writing Together [T & S]
(35–40 minutes per day)
1. Interactive Read-Aloud   2. Shared Reading   3. Interactive or Shared Writing

Working with Strategies   [T & S]
(30 minutes per day)
1. Decoding and Spelling Instruction   2. Vocabulary and Comprehension Strategy Instruction

Workshop Time — *(60 minutes per day)*

Block 1 — 15 minutes	Block 2 — 15 minutes	Block 3 — 15 minutes	Block 4 — 15 minutes
A. Centers [S]	**A. Centers [S]**	**A. Centers [S]**	**A. Centers [S]**
• Working with Strategies • Writing/Handwriting • Reading Response • Content Study • Independent Reading	• Working with Strategies • Writing/Handwriting • Reading Response • Content Study • Independent Reading	• Working with Strategies • Writing/Handwriting • Reading Response • Content Study • Independent Reading	• Working with Strategies • Writing/Handwriting • Reading Response • Content Study • Independent Reading
B. Guided Reading I **[T & S₁]**	**B. Guided Reading II** **[T & S₂]**	**B. Guided Reading III** **[T & S₃]**	**B. Guided Reading IV** **[T & S₄]**

Fluency Workshop & Assessment
(30 minutes per day)

Fluency Workshop [S]
1. Repeated Reading Practice
2. Paired or Buddy Reading Practice
3. Performance/Recorded Reading

Assessment [T & S₁]
1. Reading Accuracy, Fluency & Comprehension Assessment
2. Spelling, Writing & Handwriting Assessment

Closing Sharing Time — 10–15 minutes

[T] = Teacher
[S] = Student

FIGURE 12.2. The Primary Grades Literacy Workshop (150–180 minutes).

rather, they model how a task is done, explain, demonstrate, guide, and engage students in directly applying the strategies taught. I also strongly recommend that daily lessons focus on both decoding/spelling and vocabulary/comprehension instruction. This provides children a comprehensive collection of strategies to enable successful reading performance and growth throughout their elementary school years and beyond.

Workshop Time (60 Minutes)

Workshop time is divided into four blocks of 15 minutes each. The structure of workshop time is fairly rigid in the beginning as students learn to rotate from center to center, use their time wisely in completing center tasks, and manage themselves so as to minimize off-task behaviors. Within each 15-minute block of time, two major types of activities dominate: *guided reading* and *learning centers*. The teacher is stationed in the guided reading area of the classroom and is prepared to offer guided reading instruction. The children, on the other hand, are called to their guided reading group (homogeneous group) from an assigned "center rotation" group (mixed-ability group). *Centers* (i.e., learning centers) are teacher selected, designed, and provisioned. Learning centers should focus on decoding, spelling, handwriting, the writing process, content area studies, reader response, and independent reading. Management of centers is a primary concern for teachers; centers must be designed so that the activities and tasks are clearly understood, independent of teacher supervision, and able to be completed within the time allowed. It is also important that tasks completed in learning centers have a component of accountability and performance. Figure 12.3 shows two possible approaches for managing learning center group rotations.

Managing the workshop is a complex effort for most teachers. I caution teachers against the creation of too many learning centers. In the early part of the year, fewer centers are easier for both teachers and students to handle. As the year progresses, adding a few new centers, especially optional centers, can add variety to the workshop. I have also found that very little flexibility is desirable in the group rotation schedule early in the year. As time progresses and children acquire more experience with the rotation between learning centers, I have found it better to assign children specific tasks to be completed during this time period rather than a time-controlled rotation through various learning centers.

Fluency Workshop and Assessment (30 Minutes)

This 30-minute period of the Primary Grades Literacy Workshop is divided into two separate sets of activities for teacher and students: fluency development learning centers, and individual reading and fluency assessment. For the teacher, the bulk of this time is devoted to meeting individually with five students, 5 minutes each, to hold an individual reading/writing assessment conference. Five students per day sign up for a reading/writing assessment conference on their own or at the urging of the teacher. Children who are scheduled for a reading/writing assessment conference are instructed to bring (1) an assigned "benchmark" book or graded text to read aloud for assessment purposes, or (2) a completed writing project to be assessed for style, structure, coherence, handwriting, form, spelling, punctuation, and so on, depending on what has been emphasized in current or past instruction. Information garnered in these assessment conferences is used to shape later *working with strategies* instruction. If a child brings a piece of writing to the assessment conference, it is evaluated for handwriting legibility, conventional spelling, appropriate presentation, and general readability.

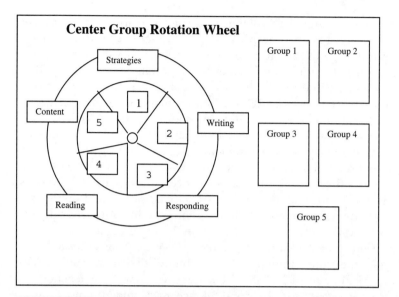

FIGURE 12.3. Learning center group management/rotation plans.

For students, this period of time is devoted to a variety of center-based activities (mixed-ability groups) designed to increase reading fluency. Children engage in repeated readings by going to a listening center, where books on audiocassette tapes are available, along with multiple copies of a single title. Or children can go to the computer center to read a book presented on a CD-ROM. Children may read with a partner by reading around the room, rereading big books together, practicing sight words on word cards in pairs, rereading charts of poems and songs, or rereading sentence strips or interactive writing strips in pocket charts. Other children will be in a drama center practicing the reading of a play or a reader's theater script for performance. Another area of the classroom is stocked with individual audiocassette tapes for children to place into a cassette recorder and record their own reading. After reading into the tape recorder, children rate their own fluency using an adapted student version of the *Multidimensional Fluency Scale* (Zutell & Rasinski, 1991). They may erase the audiocassette recording of their first reading. The repeated reading recording should be rated again, with the teacher noting any improvements in their oral fluency. Each student must come to the final class-sharing session from the fluency development period prepared to perform a reading selection for the whole class, a small group, or a peer.

Student Sharing Time (10–15 Minutes)

As a daily closing activity for the Primary Grades Literacy Workshop, the teacher calls the class together to share a reading selection that each child has prepared previously. The idea here is to bring closure to the day's work and give children a chance to share their reading with the group or a friend. Children can read aloud their own writing products or perform reader's theater productions, puppet shows, individual reading recitations, reader's/author's chair read-alouds, and plays. I have found that there is only one problem with sharing time: keeping it to the time frame of 10–15 minutes.

IMPLICATIONS FOR FUTURE RESEARCH

Grouping children for instruction has always been grounded in a teacher's desire to accommodate individual student needs. Throughout the history of classroom literacy instruction, several variations on ability grouping and whole-class instruction have persisted despite a large body of relevant research pointing to several negative outcomes for students and teachers related to these grouping strategies. In recent years, a number of alternative grouping strategies have emerged, including flexible groups, visiting basal reader selection groups, literature circles, cooperative learning groups, needs groups, and guided reading groups; these strategies offer teachers a wider array of possibilities.

More research is needed to determine the effects of alternative grouping strategies on students' reading growth, engagement, motivation, and achievement. For example, we do not know how homogeneous grouping for guided reading affects students' achievement, motivation, engagement, or reading growth compared with whole-class or heterogeneous grouping strategies, singly or in combination. Also, we need to know more about how flexible grouping strategies interact to ameliorate the effects of ability grouping for students with varying needs and abilities.

DISCUSSION AND ACTIVITIES

1. Discuss why students with learning disabilities seem to dislike mixed-ability grouping strategies, when the research also seems to point to many negative effects for same-ability grouping on struggling students.
2. Observe several levels of dynamic guided reading groups in classrooms and take field notes. Then, interview four or five children in various levels of dynamic guided reading groups about their perceptions. Do the typical issues associated with ability grouping seem to be present in the observations and interview responses of the children in varying levels of guided reading groups?
3. For children given a reading task to perform individually or in a cooperative learning group, what is the result on student performance? Is quality higher or lower? Do individuals or groups use learning time more efficiently? Is the performance or product given to individuals or cooperative learning groups higher or lower? How do children of varying abilities and skills levels feel about the group processes and products?
4. Discuss whether it is important for teachers to know what children are learning from time spent in learning centers. If it is important, how can teachers require accountability from children for learning activities found in typical, independent learning centers?
5. Although children often have rich discussions of trade book literature in literature circles, do these arrangements produce better comprehension abilities, larger vocabularies, and greater motivation to read than do basal reader ability groups or visiting basal reader selection groups?

REFERENCES

Allington, R. L. (1980). Teacher interruption behaviors during primary grade oral reading. *Journal of Educational Psychology, 72,* 371–372.

Allington, R. L. (1983). The reading instruction provided readers of differing reading ability. *Elementary School Journal, 83,* 255–265.

Anderson, R. C., Hiebert, E. F., Scott, J. A., & Wilkinson, I. A. G. (1985). *Becoming a nation of readers: The report of the commission on reading.* Washington, DC: National Institute of Education.

Atwell, N. (1987). *In the middle: Writing, reading, and learning with adolescents.* Portsmouth, NH: Heinemann.

Barracca, D., & Barracca, S. (1994). *A taxi dog Christmas.* New York: Dial.

Booth, D. (1998). *Guiding the reading process: Techniques and strategies for successful instruction in K–8 classrooms.* York, ME: Stenhouse.

Calkins, L. (1994). *The art of teaching writing* (rev. ed.). Westport, CT: Heinemann.

Calkins, L. (2001). *The art of teaching reading.* Boston: Allyn & Bacon/Longman.

Cox, C., & Zarillo, J. (1993). *Teaching reading with children's literature.* Englewood Cliffs, NJ: Merrill/Prentice Hall.

Cunningham, P. M., Hall, D. P., & Defee, M. (1998). Nonability-grouped, multilevel instruction: Eight years later. *The Reading Teacher, 51*(8), 652–664.

Eder, D. (1983). Ability grouping and student's academic self-concepts: A case study. *Elementary School Journal, 84,* 149–161.

Elbaum, B., Moody, S. W., & Schumm, J. S. (1999). Mixed-ability grouping for reading: What students think. *Learning Disabilities Research and Practice, 14*(1), 61–66.

Eldredge, J. L., & Quinn, D. W. (1988). Increasing reading performance of low-achieving second graders with dyad reading groups. *Journal of Educational Research, 82,* 40–46.

Felmlee, D., & Eder, D. (1983). Contextual effects in the classroom: The impact of ability groups on student attention. *Sociology of Education, 56,* 77–87.

Fisher, B., & Medvic, E. F. (2000). *Perspectives on shared reading: Planning and practice.* Portsmouth, NH: Heinemann.

Flood, J., Lapp, D., Flood, S., & Nagel, G. (1992). Am I allowed to group? Using flexible patterns for effective instruction. *The Reading Teacher, 45*(8), 608–616.

Fountas, I., & Pinnell, G. S. (1996). *Guided reading: Good first teaching for all children.* Exeter, NH: Heinemann.

Fountas, I. C., & Pinnell, G. S. (2001). *Guiding readers and writers (Grades 3–6): Teaching comprehension, genre, and content literacy.* Portsmouth, NH: Heinemann.

Gambrell, L. B., Wilson, R. M., & Gnatt, W. N. (1981). Classroom observations of task-attending behaviors of good and poor readers. *Journal of Educational Research, 74,* 400–404.

Goodlad, J. I., & Oakes, J. (1988). We must offer equal access to knowledge. *Educational Leadership, 45*(5), 16–22.

Hagerty, P. (1992). *Reader's shop: Real reading.* New York: Scholastic.

Haller, E. J., & Waterman, M. (1985). The criteria of reading group assignments. *The Reading Teacher, 38*(8), 772–781.

Hallinan, M. T., & Sorensen, A. B. (1985). Ability grouping and student friendships. *American Educational Research Journal, 22,* 485–499.

Harp, B. (1989a). What do we know now about ability grouping? *The Reading Teacher, 42*(6), 430–431.

Harp, B. (1989b). What do we put in the place of ability grouping? *The Reading Teacher, 42*(7), 534–535.

Hiebert, E. H. (1983). An examination of ability grouping for reading instruction. *Reading Research Quarterly, 18*, 231–255.

Hoeck-Buehler, S. (2001). Let's play tag!: A technique for successful mixed-ability group reading. *The Reading Teacher, 54*(5), 477–478.

Holdaway, D. (1981). Shared book experience: Teaching reading using favorite books. *Theory Into Practice, 21*, 293–300.

Holdaway, D. (1984). *Stability and change in literacy learning.* Portsmouth, NH: Heinemann.

Johnson, D. W., & Johnson, R. T. (1999). *Learning together and alone: Cooperative, competitive, and individualistic learning* (5th ed.). Boston: Allyn & Bacon.

Johnson, D. W., Maruyama, G., Johnson, R. T., Nelson, D., & Skon, L. (1981). Effects of cooperative, competitive and individualistic goal structures on achievement: A meta-analysis. *Psychological Bulletin, 89*, 47–62.

Jongsma, K. S. (1990). Collaborative learning (questions and answers). *The Reading Teacher, 43*(4), 346–347.

Kletzien, S. B. (1996). Reading programs in nationally recognized elementary schools. *Reading Research and Instruction, 35*(3), 260–274.

Kulik, C., & Kulik, J. A. (1982). Effects of ability grouping on secondary students: A meta-analysis of evaluation findings. *American Educational Research Journal, 19*, 415–428.

Leinhardt, G., Zigmond, N., & Cooley, W. (1981). Reading instruction and its effects. *American Educational Research Journal, 18*, 343–361.

Lyman, F. (1988). Think-pair-share, wait time two, and on. . . . *Mid-Atlantic Association for Cooperation in Education Cooperative News, 2*, 1.

Manarino-Leggett, P., & Salomon, P. A. (1989, April–May). *Cooperation vs. competition: Techniques for keeping your classroom alive but not endangered.* Paper presented at the 34th Annual Convention of the International Reading Association, New Orleans, LA.

Moody, S. W., Schumm, J. S., Fischer, M., & Jean-Francois, J. (1999). Grouping suggestions for the classroom: What do our basal reading series tell us? *Reading Research and Instruction, 38*(4), 319–331.

Moody, S. W., Vaughn, S., & Schumm, J. S. (1997). Instructional grouping for reading: Teachers' views. *Remedial and Special Education, 18*(6), 347–356.

Mooney, M. E. (1990). *Reading to, with, and by children.* Katonah, NY: Owen.

National Reading Panel (NRP). (2000). *Report of the National Reading Panel: Teaching children to read.* Washington, DC: National Institute of Child Health and Human Development.

Oakes, J. (1986). Keeping track, Part 1: The policy and practice of curriculum inequality. *Phi Delta Kappan, 68*(1), 12–17.

Oakes, J. (1988). Beyond tracking. *Educational Horizons, 65*(1), 32–35.

Opitz, M. F. (1992). The cooperative reading activity: An alternative to ability grouping. *The Reading Teacher, 45*(9), 736–738.

Opitz, M. F. (1998a). *Flexible grouping in reading: Practical ways to help all students become better readers.* New York: Scholastic.

Opitz, M. F. (1998b). Text sets: One way to flex your grouping—in first-grade, too! *The Reading Teacher, 51*(7), 622–624.

Opitz, M. F., & Ford, M. P. (2001). *Reaching readers: Flexible and innovative strategies for guided reading.* Portsmouth, NH: Heinemann.

Pallas, A. M., Entwisle, D. R., Alexander, K. L., & Stluka, M. F. (1994). Ability-group effects: Instructional, social, or institutional? *Sociology of Education, 67*(1), 27–46.

Parkes, B. (1986). *Who's in the shed?* Crystal Lake, IL: Rigby.

Peterson, R., & Eeds, M. (1990). *Grand conversations: Literature groups in action.* Ontario, Canada: Scholastic Canada.

Radencich, M. C. (1995). *Administration and supervision of the reading/writing program.* Boston: Allyn & Bacon.

Reutzel, D. R., & Cooter, R. B., Jr. (1991). Organizing for effective instruction: The reading workshop. *The Reading Teacher, 44*(8), 548–555.

Reutzel, D. R., & Cooter, R. B., Jr. (2000). *Teaching children to read: Putting the pieces together* (3rd ed.). Upper Saddle River, NJ: Merrill/Prentice-Hall.

Reutzel, D. R., & Cooter, R. B., Jr. (2003). *Strategies for reading assessment and instruction: Helping all children succeed* (2nd ed.). Upper Saddle River, NJ: Merrill/Prentice-Hall.

Rosenbaum, J. (1980). *Making inequality: The hidden curriculum of high school tracking.* New York: Wiley.

Schumm, J. S., Moody, S. W., & Vaughn, S. (2000). Grouping for reading instruction: Does one size fit all? *Journal of Learning Disabilities, 33*(5), 477–488.

Slavin, R. E. (1987). Ability grouping and student achievement in elementary schools: A best-evidence synthesis. *Review of Educational Research, 57*(3), 293–336.

Slavin, R. E. (1988). Cooperative learning and student achievement. *Educational Leadership, 45*(2), 31–33.

Slavin, R. E. (1991). Are cooperative learning and "untracking" harmful to the gifted? *Educational Leadership, 48*(6), 68–71.

Snow, C. E., Burns, M. S., & Griffin, P. (1998). *Preventing reading difficulties in young children.* Washington, DC: National Academy Press.

Sorensen, A. B., & Hallinan, M. T. (1986). Effects of ability grouping on growth in academic achievement. *American Educational Research Journal, 23*(4), 519–542.

Stevens, R. J., Madden. N. A., Slavin, R. E., & Farnish, A. (1987a). *Cooperative integrated reading and composition: A brief overview of the CIRC program.* Baltimore: Johns Hopkins University, Center for Research on Elementary and Middle Schools.

Stevens, R. J., Madden, N. A., Slavin, R. E., & Farnish, A. M. (1987b). Cooperative integrated reading and composition: Two field experiments. *Reading Research Quarterly, 22*(4), 433–454.

Topping, K. (1989). Peer tutoring and paired reading: Combining two powerful techniques. *The Reading Teacher, 42*(7), 488–494.

Unsworth, L. (1984). Meeting individual needs through flexible within-class grouping of pupils. *The Reading Teacher, 38*(3), 298–304.

Webb, M., & Schwartz, W. (1988, October). Children teaching children: A good way to learn. *PTA Today,* pp. 16–17.

Weinstein, R. S. (1976). Reading group membership in first grade: Teacher behaviors and pupil experience over time. *Journal of Educational Psychology, 68,* 103–116.

Wiggins, R. A. (1994). Large-group lesson/small group follow-up: Flexible grouping in a basal reading program. *The Reading Teacher, 47*(6), 450–460.

Wilkinson, I. A., & Townsend, M. A. R. (2000). From Rata to Rimu: Grouping for instruction in best practice New Zealand classrooms. *The Reading Teacher, 53*(6), 460–471.

Wood, K. D. (1987). Fostering cooperative learning in middle and secondary school classrooms. *Journal of Reading, 31*(1), 10–19.

Wood, K. D., & Jones, J. (1998). Tips for teaching: Flexible grouping and group retellings include struggling learners in classroom communities. *Preventing School Failure, 43*(1), 37–38.

Worthy, J., & Hoffman, J. V. (1996). Critical questions. *The Reading Teacher, 49*(8), 656–657.

Wuthrick, M. A. (1990). Blue jays win! Crows go down in defeat! *Phi Delta Kappan, 71*(7), 553–556.

Zutell, J., & Rasinski, T. (1991). Training teachers to attend to their students' oral reading fluency. *Theory Into Practice, 30*(3), 211–217.

Chapter 13

SEE IT CHANGE: A PRIMER ON THE BASAL READER

Nancy L. Roser
James V. Hoffman
Norma J. Carr

This chapter will:

- Provide a historical look at basal readers.
- Recount some historical criticisms leveled against basals' form, content, and use.
- Summarize changes in basal readers over time.
- Examine the balance that effective teachers work for as they teach children first, and manage materials secondarily.

THEORY AND RESEARCH BASE

By examining the materials of instruction, historians (e.g., Mathews, 1966; Smith, 1934/2002) attempted to determine prevalent instructional practices across time. Although a materials-use retrospective provides a less than perfect vantage point on instruction-past, it is nonetheless at least a defensible way to infer practice. More recently, surveys and comparative analyses have been used to (1) judge the pervasiveness of use of basal materials in instruction and (2) compare the contents of those basals across editions.

Use of Basal Readers

When Austin and Morrison (1963) surveyed practices of teaching reading in all U.S. communities with populations over 10,000, they found that "despite discordant views over its value, the basal reader is unquestionably the predominant tool of instruction in most of the school systems sampled throughout this study . . ." (p. 54). In fact, during their original field study, Austin and Morrison visited only one school system in which basal readers were the dominant material. The researchers discovered that administrators who were most committed to basals were those most convinced that use of a basal series was the only way to ensure that all skills would be developed and a progression of vocabulary instruction ensured.

Twenty-six years later (1989), the National Council of Teachers of English (NCTE), through its Commission on Reading, issued "Basal Readers and the State of American Reading Instruction." The statement began by noting that basal readers dominate reading instruction in roughly 90% of the elementary school classrooms in the United States. In a 1988 resolution, "On Basal Readers," the NCTE expressed concerns about the tendency across the United States to view and promote basal readers as complete systems for teaching reading (Goodman, Shannon, Freeman, & Murphy, 1988). Their resolutions reflected a call for a move toward the use of alternative materials and methods in reading instruction in the United States.

Such a move is evident in the results of a study reported by Baumann, Hoffman, Moon, and Duffy-Hester (1998). They conducted a modified replication of Austin and Morrison's 1963 study of reading instruction. The results of the replication study indicated that teachers were moving away from sole reliance on basal reading programs toward instruction that included the use of trade books *and* basal readers. Only 2% of the teachers reported using basals exclusively, while 16% reported using trade books exclusively in their reading program. The majority of the teachers (83%) reported using the basals supplemented by trade books (56%), or trade books supplemented by basal readers (27%).

Content Comparisons of Recent Basals

Hoffman and his colleagues (Hoffman et al., 1994) compared student texts from the most popular (in terms of sales and marketing) literature anthologies (1993) with more traditional, older (1986/1987) programs. The total number of words in the 1993 programs was considerably fewer than in the older programs, but the newer programs contained substantially more unique words than the old. Evidence of vocabulary control and repetition had been significantly reduced, if not abandoned, in the basal programs of the early to mid-1990s. In contrast with the series from the 1980s, adaptations of trade literature for these "literature anthologies" was minimal. Further, the materials for beginners were judged substantially more predictable on features such as repeated patterns, rhyme, and rhythm.

However, the literature anthologies presented more decoding demands for young readers, challenging those who needed more support from the text. In partial response, the recent series have once again provided constructed texts for young readers, including a plethora of "little books," short (8–16 pages), "decodable" leveled texts that offer focused sound/spelling patterns, practice with recurring words, and a promise of steady buildup in difficulty (Hoffman, 2001).

Across recent decades, there are increasingly fewer basal publishing houses and programs, and those remaining major producers have come under great scrutiny both for the accessibility of their contents and their match with "research-based" strategies. But shifts and changes in basic instructional materials did not begin yesterday. Across America's history, a combination of societal, political, religious, economic, and personal forces have resulted in changes in the texts our children are offered in schools.

The Birth of Basals

The First Instructional Materials

Since (at least) the late 1960s, it has been almost a badge of honor to be a critic of "basal readers." In a decade awakened by civil rights, student unrest, and the questioning of almost every icon, midcentury basals were found wanting. They "wanted" in their representation of diversity, in rich language, in flexible teaching plans, and even in effect sizes when compared with other "approaches." For example, in *The First Grade Studies*, a series of comparative investigations conducted in the late 1960s, basals "plus" almost anything showed greater gain in beginners' classes than did basals alone—when reading scores were the dependent variable (Bond & Dykstra, 1967). Yet, to paraphrase Richard Nixon, "There weren't always basal readers to kick around." The ancient Greeks might have wished for some. William Harris (1989), in his exploration, *Ancient Literacy*, noted that "if we may judge from a third-century Greek collection of school-texts from Egypt, there were . . . apparently no readings for children between single words on the one hand and Homer on the other" (p. 137). There were no "readers" or "leveled texts" for most of human history. The most prevalent teaching materials (in recorded history) were a set of alphabet letters and, when available, scriptures. According to John Locke, born in 1632, the first English schoolbooks for children were the horn book, primer, psalter, testament, and Bible (Venezky, 1997).

Colonial American children met their letters on a hornbook as well. The hornbook was a paddle-shaped piece of wood just a few inches across, with a card of print tacked to it containing letters, syllables, and the Lord's Prayer. A thin sheet of transparent horn protected the letters from smudges (Huey, 1908/1968). The first "primers" for American children, according to Nila Banton Smith's *American Reading Instruction* (1934/2002), were actually church books. The dominant text in our colonial history, the *New England Primer*, presented the alphabet, syllables, and lists of words increasing in length, all introductory to the simple prayers and religious material that followed (see also Venezky, 1987). The purpose of this primer was to instill religious doctrine and build character, as reflected in the preface to a latter edition of the *New England Primer* (1841):

> The *New England Primer*, with its original contents as printed nearly a hundred years ago, was esteemed as the best little book that could be put into the hands of children, when first beginning to learn their letters; and in their progress to the spellings and other reading, they found such easy lessons, instructive verses, hymns, and other useful matter, as always had a

tendency to leave a durable impression on their infant minds, and imbue them with such moral and religious principles as were rarely eradicated during their lives. (p. 2)

Following the colonial period, children's reading texts were called "spellers." That may have been in reference to the way children learned to read, first by spelling and then pronouncing the words. The best-selling speller for about a half-century was Noah Webster's famous Blueback, nicknamed for its pale blue cover. The Blueback not only had word lists organized by number of syllables but also reading selections with decided moral and patriotic tones. Webster's goal was to standardize the pronunciations and spellings of words in the young, diverse, and disconnected America (Roser, 1984).

The First Graded Series

Smith (1934/2002) cites the 19th century as the first time "authors" began to prepare series of books for students, with each book intended to be more difficult than the one preceding it. Field (1918) notes that Lindley Murray's three-book series, *The English Reader* (1800), *Sequel to The English Reader* (1809), and *Introduction to The English Reader* (1810), all published in the first half of the 19th century, was the first graded series ever printed. By the end of the Civil War, Venezky (1987) describes the graded series much as it began to appear in modern times, with five or six books preceded by a primer. So perhaps basal readers were "born" over 150 years ago. The 20th century brought the assignment of graded readers to grade levels, the introduction of the preprimer to teach the vocabulary of the primer, and, eventually, the kind of basal reader that persisted for many decades: five or six books at first grade, and books for each semester thereafter. From the outset, the books produced for beginners tried to make the text "manageable" by introducing fewer words, providing repetition, and illustrating more profusely. Books for older students carried information, speeches, and other pieces of literature useful for oral interpretation or elocutionary performances. The most popular readers in terms of sales were the *McGuffey Eclectic Readers*, which offered students rules for reading, pronunciation guides, comprehension questions, and words for spelling (Venezky, 1987).

Perhaps from the beginning, publishers of school texts, fighting for a market share, swayed with the times. For example, the early McGuffey readers, prepared for a post–Civil War southern market, avoided mention of Abraham Lincoln and slavery. Other basals, touting their strengths, pridefully announced their superiority, such as, for example,

The School Reader: Second Book (Sanders, 1840b), which proclaimed in the preface:

> These works have called forth unqualified expressions of approbation from Teachers, Superintendents, and all others who have become best acquainted with them from use. They have been fully tested by experience, and they have been the means of securing that permanent uniformity, so long desired, wherever they have been adopted. (p. i)

The publishers of *The Normal Course in Reading* (Todd & Powell, 1895) boldly noted:

> It is confidently believed that a careful examination of the plan and subject-matter of the *The Normal Course in Reading* will at once reveal its *raison d'être*, and that a practical use of these books in the school-room (which is, after all, the supreme test of excellence) will demonstrate their superiority to those hitherto published for the same work. (p. 3)

Teacher Guides and Directives

Directives for teachers that accompany children's materials have evolved from one-page prefaces in individual texts to simple lesson outlines or questions tucked in the margins, to a single manual for an entire series of readers, to multiple manuals per grade level. An early example is found in a two-page preface to *The Primary School Primer* (1840a), in which the author, Charles Sanders, offered instructional advice:

> The teacher will then pronounce each sentence in the most easy and natural manner, directing the child to follow him. Let this be repeated, till the child succeeds in giving the required ease and accuracy of enunciation. When this is effected, then—and not till then—let the child see and read it. Should he then depart from his previous accuracy, withhold the book again, and repeat the previous exercise. (p. 5)

William Swinton provided an eight-page introduction to his *Swinton's Primer* (1883). Titled "Author to Teacher," Swinton admonished:

> The more successful you are in teaching primary reading, the less will you be disposed to make a fetish of any so-called "method." Children have been taught to read by every method and by no method—and it would puzzle the wisest to tell exactly how a child does learn to read our anomalous mother tongue. (p. 4)

Over the decades that followed, guidebooks and manuals for teaching reading expanded considerably. Venezky (1987) noted wryly that as teacher education and opportunities for professional growth have increased, so too have the unabashed sizes of teacher guides, with some 500-page manuals available for guiding the teaching of a single text. According to Hoffman et al. (1994), teachers' guides for literature-based basals seemed less prescriptive (if not thinner), moving from the "teacher-as-technician" model toward the "teacher-as-decision-maker" model. Basal publishers would no doubt contend that guides would be slimmer volumes if basals were called on to do only what they did in McGuffey's day: present the orthography, list the vocabulary, provide comprehension questions, and offer principles of elocution.

How Basals Are Developed

Suzanne Singleton (1997), a former vice president of Macmillan/McGraw-Hill School Division, described the creation of basal readers as a process of collaboration involving hundreds of people in multiple roles, including program authors, consultants, editors, writers, teacher advisors, student advisors, designers and artists, technology developers, sales' representatives, as well as public input. According to Singleton, the complex process of constructing a basal program takes approximately 3 years. Typically, a diverse author team selected based on "curricular expertise, gender, geographical location, and cultural background" (p. 869) helps to shape the program's pedagogical framework. Experts in many areas, ranging from multicultural literature to cooperative learning, provide input. Teacher users and student advisors register needs and wishes, and react to prototype offerings along the way. The process of basal building includes field-testing instructional designs, as well as the lengthy process of reviewing, selecting, and field-testing literature selections. A team of artists and designers work to ensure that the instructional materials have usable and appealing layouts. Other teams may develop technology or work to obtain permission to reprint trade books.

Publisher Roger Rogalin (1997) contends that major adoption states have great impact on the preparation of basals. For example, because California has 11% of the U.S. student population, basal publishers both listen to and comply with state demands. As mentioned earlier, recent demands for "accessible text" in California, Texas, and other states has meant publishers are producing more "decodable" books—especially for beginning readers. "Decodable" is defined in various ways, but in Texas, for example, for a text to be judged decodable, 80% of its words can be decoded "through the application of phonic rules taught explicitly up to that point in the program" (Hoffman, 2001, p. 5). These strictures provide extraordinary challenge for producing engaging texts for a broad market.

Basal Readers and Their Critics

In 1908, Edmund Huey criticized the language used in early readers: "The language used often shows a patronizing attempt to 'get down to the child's level,' and results in a mongrel combination of points of view and of expression that is natural neither to an adult nor to a child" (p. 279). He pointed out that one basal author insisted that reading should reflect talking, yet Huey noted, "How a child could talk such stuff naturally is beyond comprehension, and reading it can scarcely help developing that drawling, wooden monotone so generally found in reading classes" (pp. 279–280).

Admittedly, early "readers" had contrived and insipid real-life adventures, and offered a grammar of "Go. Go. Go." and "Funny, funny Sally." These oft-lampooned patterns of "preprimerese" fed the pens and pockets of cartoonists and T-shirt designers for the decades that followed. In addition, Flesch (1955) produced a popular-press attack on the "whole-word" methodologies promulgated by these basals.

But there were other serious criticisms: Basals of the 1960s were chastised for their flatness in depicting the world of readers. Children and adults depicted in the readers of the 1950s were only white. In a kind of flurry to rectify this lack of diversity, one basal publisher rushed into print with a new series that literally imported children of color into existing illustrations. Others quickly "tinted" the faces; settings and plots were not immediately affected. While discussing the "bland and Pollyannaish" themes found in first-grade readers, Busch (1972) noted,

> There is evidence that attempts to overcome these deficiencies in the more recent "multi-ethnic" readers have not met with any greater success. That bland stories with little relevance to the experiences of first graders are also uninteresting to them is shown in studies of children's free choices of library books to read. Here one finds a marked discrepancy between the story content children choose to read and the content of first grade readers. (p. 216)

In her "Introduction" to the special "basal reader" issue of the *Elementary School Journal* (1987), Jeanne Chall wrote from a 20-year vantage point on her own basal inspection (Chall, 1967/1983). She summarized the mid-1980's discomfort and antipathy against basals as questioning the following: the methodology (whether their suggested practices are true to existing research and true to principles of effective learning and teaching); the degree of use (or overuse, as critics argued) of basals; their complexities (e.g., length, detail, number of components); and their "sameness" within historical periods. Among Chall's recommendations was a challenge to consider both the content and literary quality of basals' selections. It was this concern, echoed broadly across the country, that changed basals in decided ways.

Toward the end of the 1980s came a demand for "real" (meaning well-crafted, published, recognizable trade) literature with which to teach children. Researchers who analyzed the content of basals (e.g., Flood, Lapp, & Flood, 1984), made recommendations for increased breadth and quality of selections. Others argued that "real" texts promoted literacy as well as, or better than, basals (Tunnell & Jacobs, 1989). Criticism of basals included antipathy toward adaptations, revisions, and excerpts as destructive of a legitimate art form—children's literature—and of the natural language patterns that support children's efforts to read (Babbitt, 1990; Goodman, Maras, & Birdseye, 1994). Venezky (1987) argued that textbooks today "as they have since textbook publishing began in this country, tend to be conservative, representing a narrow, sterilized view of society and the child's role in it" (p. 248).

Other critics have charged basals with sustaining the status quo by encouraging teachers to do what they have always done, "deskilling" teachers by undermining their voice and power (Shannon, 1989). Shannon suggested that teachers had become the support system for the basals, instead of the basals supporting thoughtful, instructional decision making by teachers. "As commercial reading materials become more prominent and persuasive in reading programs, teachers become less important in the process of reading instruction in America" (p. 80).

In the past 25 years, basals have been analyzed for their depiction of the elderly; inclusion of Native Americans; representations of characters displaying literacy, proffered values, gender roles, and sexism; as well as the more predictable analyses of genre breadth, vocabulary demands, content appeal, theoretical shifts, adaptations, skill traces, readability, attention to phonics and phonemic awareness, and more. Hoffman and his colleagues (1994) contend:

> Publishers must anticipate changes in teaching practices if they are to remain viable; they must walk the fine line between not offering a product that is so new and different that it appeals only to the high "risk-takers" and something that is so conservative and traditional that it is viewed as outdated. In the past, the safe position for most of the successful publishers has been to take a rather conservative stance toward change. (p. 48)

Currently, a new set of concerns about children's understanding of their written language system, whether emanating from governmental policy, national reports, or curriculum mandates, are influencing decisions about content and adoption of assessments and textbooks, making selection of materials even more removed from communities, classrooms, and students.

RESEARCH-BASED PRACTICE

Changes in basal reading programs have come in response to a number of factors, including (1) a changing political climate in which policy makers have assumed a bolder stance in prescribing pedagogy; (2) new theoretical directions in reading, as well as findings from research on reading acquisition, reading instruction, and teacher development; and (3) changes in the resource needs for teachers in planning for instruction. It would be impossible to sort out the degree of these influences on change, if for no other reason than they interact directly with one another.

However, we focus our discussion on the last point: Teachers are changing in terms of teaching practices and demanding changes in the materials they need to support this instruction. The challenge for basal publishers is to develop materials that meet these needs insofar as they represent or project the future. The question for all of us to ponder is what teachers need as they represent the future of reading instruction.

Who are these cutting-edge teachers that basals must consider? We describe three representatives of this group. One has never used a basal series in her classroom; another abandoned the basal after several years of frustration; and still another uses a basal but diverges from it. We describe them in terms of the challenges they face in everyday teaching and the innovations they are exploring. Finally, we discuss the issue of can/ should/will basals serve a range of teachers who think, explore, create, weigh, and inquire?

Rosa Hernandez

Rosa Hernandez is a fourth-grade teacher in an urban school district that serves an ethnically diverse, working community. Rosa is one of those teachers who lives in her classroom. She arrives by 7:00 in the morning and seldom leaves before 7:00 in the evening. Her district recently instituted a year-round school calendar, although anyone who knows Rosa believes that year-round is the only way she has ever worked. When she is not teaching or getting ready to teach, she volunteers, serving meals at shelters, building houses for low-income families, or pinch hitting in her church's nursery.

Her classroom is a special place. Each time we visit, it has changed. On one visit, for example, we found that the room had been transformed into a cave with stalagmites and stalactites "growing" strategically. Multiple copies of *Trapped in Death Cave* (Wallace, 1988) sat near a display of information books, evidence of book clubs that had spawned inquiry. Additional evidence of reading, writing, and learning abounds: models, projects, displays, photos, articles, experiments, graphs, notebooks, charts, reports. On the next visit, we found ourselves in a Mayan village, and then a space station. The environment never stops changing.

Rosa uses the basal unit themes to center her cross-curricular planning. She finds unit titles such as "Viewpoints," "Communities," and "Challenges" broad enough and ambiguous enough to be interpreted in multiple ways. The space station followed children's interests but fits within a theme of "Exploration" she selected (out of "sequence") from the basal. She relies on basals for multiple copies of good literature. She uses basal selections to illustrate a host of understandings about language use. She treats basals as an instructional choice that opens a further set of instructional decisions. Rosa's use of basals reminds us of an observation made by Jeannette Veatch in 1978, when she noted that it was not the books of the basals that were objectionable, but the "insistence that all use them in the same way" (p. 377). Rosa's use of basals illustrates flexible decision making based on the interests and needs of the students.

Not long ago, Rosa received a teaching award. During the awards ceremony, each teacher acknowledged appreciation to friends, family, and coworkers in the misty-eyed audience. They commented on their dedication to children and the privilege of touching the future. Rosa was the last to be recognized that day, and her message was different. She confessed her embarrassment at not being able to join with the other teachers in attributing her quest for excellence in teaching to her dedication to children. She explained her driving force in terms of a selfish motivation, what she labeled her "addiction." "I am addicted to learning," she explained. "It is in my nature to wonder, question, and inquire. The quest for knowledge has become a habit for me that I cannot break. It is only in teaching that I find my habit satisfied. I learn with my students. That is my reward, and my challenge. When I cease to be excited about learning, I will cease to be a teacher."

Pam Stillwell

Pam Stillwell teaches first grade. We have observed in her classroom and have had many long chats with her about teaching. Several years ago she "threw out" (her words) the basal from her classroom. She told us she decided that if she had to teach one more idiotically contrived story, she was going "to get sick right there on the floor." And so she made a plan. First, she sat down with her principal to arrange a teaching schedule that would allow her 3 hours of uninterrupted instructional time every morning with her students—no "pullouts," no "specials," no services—just Pam and her class from 8:30 to 11:30 A.M., focusing on the hard work and great joys of becoming literate. Second, she went to work to make it happen. Pam understood that she could teach her students to read without basal readers because they are not an essential element in systematic reading instruction (Betts, 1946).

Fortunately, a renewed focus on instruction didn't place a ban on quiet observers. We observed Pam orchestrating her students through 3 hours of integrated reading/language arts/social studies instruction. Now, she uses only trade books in her classroom. As we watch, we are caught up in the new "routines"—the rhythms of journal writing and sharing, the entrenchment of skills through "warmups" for reading, the discussions of old favorites and new stories, the problem solving and inquiry that lead children into information texts.

Pam is "direct" and "explicit" in her teaching, without disrupting the flow of activity and experience. She has a "meta" lexicon all her own for the written code of language that never fails to get giggles and attention: She points out "garbage words" (words that have vowel combinations that are irregular) or "peanut butter and jelly words" (those with vowel combinations that kids can count on because they "stick" together). At work with new texts, she consistently models and makes reading strategies explicit. All of this is done without distracting or distorting the experience of message or story or text. In addition, she focuses the students' attention on code at every turn—in reading and in writing and across the curriculum. By challenging her students to look more carefully, to search for patterns, and to share their insights, she ensures that they determine how their writing system works. The code of written language is internalized by students and used with great enthusiasm.

New literature enters Pam's classroom daily. The first experience with a new piece of literature is typically under storytime conditions—but this is only the first experience. The story (or whatever text) is read again and again under different types and degrees of support and for different purposes—shared reading, repeated reading, dramatization, small-group guided reading, pocket-chart work, paired reading, and so on. Gradually, students gain independence with the text. Eventually, it will become part of the classroom library for independent reading time, and part of the take-home library for family sharing.

Pam favors literature that causes her children to laugh. She loves the theatrical and hardly ever shares a book aloud without adding some dramatic flair. Music is a key part of Pam's teaching. The students sing the traditional rhymes and popular children's songs, as well as Pam's creations of new lyrics to popular "rock" songs that fit whatever theme they are exploring.

Observations in her classroom reveal the "intake" and "output" periods of a day described by Sylvia Ashton Warner in *Teacher* (1964), or the intensity and rhythms of Vivian Paley's classroom (see, for example Paley (1997), *The Girl with the Brown Crayon*)—as though the instructional day is synchronized with the heartbeats of the children.

There is a sense of "flow" (Csikszentmihalyi, 1990) in Pam Stillwell's first-grade language arts period, described by psychologists as those moments of intensity and engagement that sweep us up and almost take over consciousness—children and teacher at work.

Cathy Cichantek

Step outside a classroom such as Pam's, however, and you often find this synchrony in conflict with a different set of expectations and realities. Cathy Cichantek is another teacher who "teaches against the grain." She does things differently than do most of her colleagues. Already an innovative teacher in an urban setting, Cathy was recruited by a new principal in a suburban district. Committed to change, the new principal wanted the kindergarten teachers to break away from traditional forms of instruction and offer more integrated language instruction. But change was to be slow. The extant kindergarten team took comfort in teaching the same content every day. Their lesson plans were exactly the same. The letter of the week was exactly the same. There were uniform expectations for the art projects and products. Even bulletin boards were the same. Cathy was told by her new team that the thematic units of instruction were already established for the year by the basal plan.

The message from her new team was clear: Join us. Every variation or deviation on Cathy's part was viewed as undermining what the team had developed over the years. Even so, Cathy initiated an experience-oriented kindergarten in which the need for literacy was "critical." In her classroom, print was unavoidable. Print on chart tablet began the day with class stories, songs, and rhymes; print made magical announcements ("Gina has a surprise to tell us!"), print communicated the important business of school ("M-m-m-m. Soup for lunch today!"); it directed the rabbit's feeding, recorded the hamster's weight, compared the children's favorite foods. Print announced, invited, and remembered in her classrooms. Pam's children were given time for just reading and just writing. Book publishing was so heroic that it competed with construction and gardening. During the first year, she was forced to defend (1) her choices of read-alouds ("But *Charlotte's Web* is a fourth-grade book"), (2) her investigative projects ("But hatching eggs is for second grade"), (3) her views on instruction ("But opportunities to write 'real messages' don't prepare children adequately for first grade penmanship"), and (4) her views on learning ("But children's reversed letters indicate referral for dyslexia intervention").

Cathy has been at the school for 3 years now. Things have changed. She has moved into a multiage teaching setting, with a combined group of kindergarten and first-grade students. Three of her colleagues have joined with her in considering the primacy of children rather than curriculum, but it has been a struggle. Step inside the classroom, though, and you cannot feel the heat. The students are excited and engaged and learning about their world through language. And they don't use basals.

IMPLICATIONS FOR FUTURE RESEARCH:
THE BASAL DILEMMA

Pam, Cathy, and Rosa, collectively, have read more books, attended more conference sessions, conducted more inservices than imaginable. They struggle to solve the problems of teaching. None sees the current basals as a solution. They want something else, something that provides greater flexibility for them to use in a responsive teaching environment.

Do these three teachers represent the future? Or do these teachers represent the exceptions who will always be teaching against the grain? What (if anything) can basals provide them? Is it possible for a basal series to assist teachers who want to redefine the instructional paths in their classrooms? Can a basal series capture and transmit the strategies of the best teachers without codifying and rendering those strategies lifeless?

Traditionally (and typical even today), basals provide a sequential lesson plan that includes background information, vocabulary, purposes for reading, skills instruction, and writing activities that flow from the reading assignment. Some teachers attend to the suggestions provided in basals, while others view the basals simply as multiple copies of appropriate reading material for students. No matter how a teacher utilizes the basal, it should be noted that, like a classroom library, paper and pens, math manipulatives, and science materials, the basal is intended as a tool for teachers to interpret and apply knowingly and skillfully in providing effective reading instruction.

It is unlikely that any set of instructional materials—including basal readers—will ever again have to carry the entire weight of the past. Given the prevalence of print, the basal is no longer the protector/transmitter of the mores/norms/culture. Perhaps it never was. Some of our friends and contemporaries tell us they never "identified" with the basal that looked like our Midwest 1950s world. Laughingly, they recall that their basal's depiction of suburban settings with its pale-skinned and light-haired populace, its picket fences and unleashed dogs, was never their world. Its stories were never theirs.

But if one role of the basal may be to continue to reflect society's memories, to hold onto a "communal past" through which novitiates are inducted both into literacy and culture, another role may be to point at the present. Today's basal has much help: There are approximately 90,000 children's books in print, about 6,000 additional titles published each year, as well as periodicals and online sources. Martinez and McGee (2000) identified five areas in which trade books are meeting critical needs in literacy instruction, including books that invite beginning readers, that sustain beginning readers, that transition readers from picture books to chapter books, that address children's interests in history and nature, and that reflect diverse cultural experiences.

But the issues are never even as simple as what book, for whom, and when. In his *A History of Reading*, Manguel (1996) contends that the methods (and by implication, the materials) with which we learn to read embody the conventions of a society's stance on literacy, including the "channeling of information, the hierarchies of knowledge and power, [and the] . . . ways in which [the] ability is put to use" (p. 67). Manguel, himself, muses that in the Argentina of his youth, learning to read was neither for pleasure nor for knowledge, but merely for instruction.

Singleton (1997), writing from the perspective of a producer of basal materials, describes the difficult task that basals are expected to perform:

> Teachers ask for the latest research translated into manageable classroom practice. They ask for instructional designs that are clear, concise, and easy to follow, and for options that allow them flexibility and decision-making power. The publisher's job is to create instructional plans that translate theory into practice effectively. (p. 870)

Given that basals are primarily designed and selected by those who may not actually use them, the question may be whether basals can serve well the teachers who strive to move beyond them. What do the best and most effective teachers want them to do? Cathy wants nothing at all. Her children, though, have a wealth of materials to learn from, supplied by her own budget, the school's resources, and willing parents. Pam needs more multiple copies of books that the children can and want to read from the beginning of the year, but she is not so worried about a slow and steady buildup of sound–symbol patterns. She feels competent to take care of code instruction through the myriad ways she works with her children to make all texts manageable. The state in which she teaches, however, has, in its most recent call for new textbooks, the expectation that publishers provide her first graders with "decodable texts." Rosa wants broad, inviting themes, more complete texts, and easily implemented strategy lessons not embedded in hundreds of pages of summary, guide, adaptation suggestions, and questions. She would be happier with a thin guide.

Textbook selection committees, charged with the serious task of making recommendations for classrooms and children, determine how competing basal series measure up against agreed-upon criteria. Ultimately, basals are private enterprise. They follow the "proclamations" and "initiatives." Because expense prohibits (currently) basals being produced for regions or states, the largest state adoption sites have advantages over those states with local adoptions, in that the features and factors that big states call for are passed on. As basal series grow fewer in number, as the expenses of production escalate, and the survival of the publishing houses depends upon marketing, publishers walk the line, with most arguing for a "balanced perspective" (Pearson, 1996).

Yet as we wonder about the future of basals, we return to a prediction made by Nila Banton Smith in 1934:

> The great majority of public schools undoubtedly are not yet ready to dispense with a basal reader. The techniques of teaching through functional activities must undergo further development and refinement; new materials must be prepared; administrative difficulties must be overcome; and teachers must be better trained. In the meantime, many schools have gone far enough in introducing this type of reading instruction to lend assurance to the conviction that the basic set of readers eventually will disappear. It may continue to wield its power for fifteen years or for fifty years, but in time it will march silently out of the classroom and be relegated to dusty attics along with its progenitor, the hornbook. (1934/2002, pp. 266–267)

More than 50 years have come and gone since Smith's prediction and basals (albeit changed) remain a presence in classrooms. However, whether or not they avoid the dusty attics rests on their ability to balance needs, trends, and practice—and continue to evolve.

DISCUSSION AND ACTIVITIES

1. In 1987, Chall noted, "And we know that basal readers are perhaps the most effective way to improve students' reading achievement" (p. 244). Discuss her statement, keeping in mind the increasing trend by teachers to use textbooks, trade books, and leveled texts in the teaching of reading.
2. Based on your experiences as teachers (and those of Pam, Cathy, and Rosa), produce a list of qualities of effective literacy instruction. Then, returning to that list, consider: To what degree is each quality in the list dependent on the instructional material I choose?

REFERENCES

Austin, M. C., & Morrison, C. (1963). *The first R: The Harvard report on reading in elementary schools.* New York: Macmillan.

Babbitt, N. (1990). Protecting children's literature: On preserving the fragile medium of fiction. *Horn Book Magazine, 66*(6), 696–703.

Baumann, J. F., Hoffman, J. V., Moon, J., & Duffy-Hester, A. M. (1998). Where are teachers' voices in the phonics/whole language debate? Results from a survey of U.S. elementary classroom teachers. *The Reading Teacher, 51*(8), 636–650.

Betts, E. A. (1946). *Foundations of reading instruction*. New York: American Book Company.

Bond, G. L., & Dykstra, R. (1967). The cooperative research program in first-grade-reading instruction. *Reading Research Quarterly, 2,* 1–142.

Busch, F. (1972). Basals are not for reading. In S. L. Sebesta & C. J. Wallen (Eds.), *The first R: Readings on teaching reading* (pp. 215–224). Chicago: Science Research Associates.

Chall, J. (1983). *Learning to read: The great debate.* New York: McGraw-Hill. (Original published 1967)

Chall, J. (1987). Introduction. *Elementary School Journal, 87,* 243–245.

Csikszentmihalyi, M. (1990). *Flow: The psychology of optimal experience.* New York: HarperCollins.

Field, W. T. (1918). *Fingerposts to children's reading.* Chicago: McClurg.

Flesch, R. (1955). *Why Johnny can't read and what you can do about it.* New York: Harper & Row.

Flood, J., Lapp, D., & Flood, S. (1984). Types of writing included in basal reading programs: Preprimers through second-grade readers. In J. A. Niles & L. A. Harris (Eds.), *Changing perspectives on research in reading/language processing and instruction* (pp. 5–10). Rochester, NY: National Reading Conference.

Goodman, K., Maras, L., & Birdseye, D. (1994). Look! Look! Who stole the pictures from the picture book?: The basalization of picture books. *The New Advocate, 7*(1), 1–24.

Goodman, K. S., Shannon, P., Freeman, Y. S., & Murphy, S. (1988). *Report card on basal readers.* Katonah, NY: Richard C. Owens.

Harris, W. V. (1989). *Ancient literacy.* Cambridge, MA: Harvard University Press.

Hoffman, J. V. (2001). Decodable texts for beginning reading instruction: Leadership or politics in California and Texas? *The California Reader, 34*(3), 2–8.

Hoffman, J. V., McCarthey, S. J., Abbot, J., Christian, C., Corman, L., Curry , C., Dressman, M., Elliott, B., Matherne, D., & Stahle, D. (1994). So what's new in the new basals? *Journal of Reading Behavior: A Journal of Literacy, 26*(1), 47–73.

Huey, E. B. (1968). *The psychology and pedagogy of reading.* Cambridge, MA: MIT Press. (Original published 1908)

Manguel, A. (1996). *A history of reading.* New York: Viking.

Martinez, M. G., & McGee, L. M. (2000). Children's literature and reading instruction: Past, present, and future. *Reading Research Quarterly, 35*(1), 154–169.

Mathews, M. M. (1966). *Teaching to read: Historically considered.* Chicago: University of Chicago Press.

National Council of Teachers of English. (1989). Basal readers and the state of American reading instruction: A call for action. *Language Arts, 66*(8), 896–898.

New England Primer. (1841). Concord, NH: Roby, Kimball & Merrill.

Paley, V. G. (1997). *The girl with the brown crayon.* Cambridge, MA: Harvard University Press.

Pearson, P. D. (1996). Reclaiming the center. In M. F. Graves, P. van den Broek, & B. M. Taylor (Eds.), *The first R: Every child's right to read.* New York: Teachers College Press.

Rogalin, R. (1997). The changing face of literacy: A publisher's perspective. In J. Flood, S. B. Heath, & D. Lapp (Eds.), *Handbook of research on teaching literacy through the communicative and visual arts* (pp. 864–866). New York: Macmillan.

Roser, N. L. (1984). Teaching and testing reading comprehension: An historical perspective on instructional research and practice. In. J. Flood (Ed.), *Promoting reading comprehension* (pp. 48–60). Newark, DE: International Reading Association.

Sanders, C. W. (1840a). *The primary school primer.* New York: American Book Co.

Sanders, C. W. (1840b). *The school reader: Second book.* New York: Newman & Ivison.

Shannon, P. (1989). *Broken promises.* Granby, MA: Bergin & Garvey.

Singleton, S. (1997). The creation of a basal program: A collaborative effort. In J. Flood, S. B. Heath, & D. Lapp (Eds.), *Handbook of research on teaching literacy through the communicative and visual arts* (pp. 869–871). New York: Macmillan.

Smith, N. B. (2002). *American reading instruction.* Newark, DE: International Reading Association. (Originally published 1934)

Swinton, W. (1883). *Swinton's primer.* New York: American Book Co.

Todd, E. J., & Powell, W. B. (1895). *The normal course in reading: First reader.* New York: Silver, Burdett, & Co.

Tunnell, M. O., & Jacobs, J. S. (1989). Using "real" books: Research findings on literature-based reading instruction. *The Reading Teacher, 42,* 470–477.

Veatch, J. (1978). *Reading in the elementary school* (2nd ed.). New York: Wiley.

Venezky, R. L. (1987). A history of the American reading textbook. *Elementary School Journal, 87,* 247–266.

Venezky, R. L. (1997). The literary text: Its future in the classroom. In J. Flood, S. B. Heath, & D. Lapp (Eds.), *Handbook of research on teaching literacy through the communicative and visual arts* (pp. 528–535). New York: Macmillan.

Wallace, B. (1988). *Trapped in death cave.* New York: Holiday House.

Warner, S. (1964). *Teacher.* New York: Bantam.

Chapter 14

STRATEGIES FOR LITERACY DEVELOPMENT FOR STUDENTS WITH DISABILITIES

Kim Baker
Richard L. Allington

This chapter will:

- Discuss how most children experiencing reading difficulties can have their literacy development accelerated when they have access to sufficient appropriate instruction.
- Discuss how teachers who provide personalized, interactive lessons, skills instruction within context, and substantial reading and writing opportunities are most effective.
- Discuss how a comprehensive system with three components—prevention, acceleration, and long-term support—is needed in schools to meet the needs of students experiencing literacy difficulties.

THEORY AND RESEARCH BASE

Not all children, unfortunately, acquire literacy easily. There has been a steady increase in learning disability and dyslexia research shifting the definition and naming of reading difficulties to learning disabilities (Allington & McGill-Franzen, 1996; Lyon & Moats, 1997). As Sack (1999) notes, the number of children identified as learning disabled rose from 120,000 in 1968 to 2.7 million in 1997. Although there has always been much debate as to just why some children struggle to become readers and writers, in this chapter, we focus on how exemplary instructional support might be provided to such children and leave the issue of etiology of learning difficulties for others to discuss. In our view, children who find learning to read and write more difficult are best served not by identifying some label for them, but by designing and delivering sufficient and appropriate instruction and substantial opportunities to actually engage in real reading and writing activity. Thus, we draw on our experiences in two long-term, school-based research projects to offer detailed descriptions of interventions that we consider exemplary in nature and outcomes.

In our view, efforts to intervene productively begin in the general education classroom. Providing all children with exemplary classroom literacy instruction is an essential first step in addressing the needs of children who find learning to read and write more difficult. In our studies of exemplary first-grade teachers (Pressley, Allington, Wharton-McDonald, Block, & Morrow, 2001), for instance, we found that the greatest impact of the exemplary teachers we studied was on the development of reading and writing proficiency in the lowest-achieving children. In other words, in the classrooms of the exemplary first-grade teachers, there were far fewer children who ended first grade still struggling with reading and writing. Likewise, Mendro, Jordan, and Bembry (1998) studied the effects of 3 consecutive years of high-quality teaching on student reading development. They compared the achievement of children placed in high-quality classrooms with that of students who were unfortunate enough to have attended lower quality classrooms over the same period. Although the children's average standing on national norms rose consistently year after year in the high-quality classrooms, the standing of children in the lower quality classrooms dropped each year. After 3 years, the achievement of children who had similar initial achievement now differed by almost 40 percentile ranks! The results of this large-scale study have led to similar findings with respect to the impact of quality classroom instruction on reading development (Allington & Johnston, 2001; Pressley et al., 2001; Taylor, Pearson, Clark, & Walpole, 2000).

Now, it would not have seemed necessary, in some senses, actually to conduct studies showing that access to high-quality teaching is important—essential, in fact. Who would argue against providing high-quality classroom instruction? But then, who argues for it? How often are resources allocated to improving classroom instruction from funding provided by either the Title 1 program of the No Child Left Behind Act (NCLB) or special education under the Individuals with Disabilities Education Act (IDEA)? How often are such funds allocated for the purchase of needed classroom instructional materials, for instance, to purchase a classroom supply of trade books of an appropriate level of complexity for use by students with learning disabilities? Or how often are funds allocated to provide professional development opportunities for classroom teachers to learn how to better document the development of children who are struggling with literacy learning?

Instead, these programs more often fund additional personnel, including specialist support teachers (reading teachers, learning disabilities teachers, speech and language teachers), school psychologists, social workers, or paraprofessional personnel. There may be a role for any and all of these extra personnel, but in our view, a necessary first step is ensuring that children have access to high-quality classroom instruction regardless of their label or participation in a special program. One question that we now routinely pose is whether there is evidence that specialized personnel enhance the quality of classroom instruction. In other words, what evidence is available that points to the ways that the school psychologist has improved classroom teaching? The same question might be asked about the roles of the social worker, the learning disability specialist, the reading teacher, or the paraprofessional. If the presence of specialized personnel is not improving classroom instruction, at the very least we should reconsider the role demands for such positions, so that improving the quality of classroom teaching becomes a central attribute of each specialist's role (Walmsley & Allington, 1995).

However, even exemplary classroom teachers cannot do it all. Although such teachers dramatically reduce the incidence of reading difficulties, a few children typically continue to struggle even in these exemplary classrooms. Some children have enormous instructional needs that simply cannot be met in the day-to-day bustle of the classrooms. Their needs for close and personalized teaching simply exceed the capacity of even exemplary teachers. It seems to be both a quantity and quality problem. Most of these children simply need closer and more explicit teaching than can be accomplished by a teacher with the responsibility for a classroom filled with 25 children. These children need, for instance, more guided reading opportunities. Most will need a supply of books at appropriate levels of difficulty—typically, levels different from those used in the daily classroom lessons and activities. And some will need particularized instruction—an emphasis on hearing sounds in words, for instance—that may require not only more time to provide than the classroom teacher has available but also a particular instructional expertise that classroom teachers do not routinely acquire, even exemplary classroom teachers (Allington, 2001). Thus, another feature of exemplary intervention efforts is the useful and targeted deployment of special support teachers and personnel who provide the intensive and personalized instruction that those few children need in order to thrive in school.

Unfortunately, it is common today also to find that a school employs paraprofessional staff in attempting to meet the instructional needs of children who find learning to read difficult, usually funding such personnel with monies allocated by Title 1 or IDEA. In other words, huge numbers of paraprofessionals are employed in remedial and special education programs (International Reading Association, 1994). There is substantial evidence that students gain little academic benefit when paraprofessionals deliver intervention instruction (Achilles, 1999; Allington & Cunningham, 2002; International Reading Association, 1994). In fact, the use of paraprofessionals in classrooms of any sort of school has been shown to have no positive effect on student achievement (Boyd-Zaharias & Pate-Bain, 1998). The key to understanding these findings is located in the need children have for access to expert instruction. Too often, it seems, school programs are designed such that children who find learning to read difficult are paired with paraprofessional staff for instruction and practice. Paraprofessionals should not be criticized for their failure to offer expert instruction; they are the least expert of all school personnel when it comes to providing appropriate instruction. The criticism should fall on those who design programs that place paraprofessionals in the untenable position of being the person least well prepared to work with children with the greatest instructional needs. Instead, schools need to develop longer term instructional support plans that respond to the needs of children in comprehensive, flexible ways (Allington & Cunningham, 2002).

So, what might an exemplary intervention program look like? It would, of course, begin with exemplary classroom teaching. Support for exemplary classroom teachers would be available in the form of expert specialists, who provide appropriate and intensive services for children in need of such added attention. This support might be offered during the school day, after school, or during the summer. It might be offered in the classroom or in another location. There might be paraprofessional support for either the classroom teacher or the specialist teacher, or for both. But the efforts of the specialist and any paraprofessionals would be targeted at fostering student success on the classroom curriculum and enhancement of classroom instruction in as short a period of time as possible.

A grand scheme, you say, but what exactly would it look like in practice? In the following sections, you will meet (1) an exemplary first-grade teacher and spend a day in her classroom, and (2) an exemplary support teacher—certified and experienced in both reading and special education—and spend a day with her as she goes about supporting teachers and children as they learn to read and write.

RESEARCH-BASED PRACTICE

Exemplary Classroom Instruction for Children Who Find Learning to Read and Write Difficult

Georgia teaches in a small, rural district in northern California. Nearly two-thirds of the children come from low-income families, and one-sixth of them are members of ethnic minority groups. Seasonal employment in agriculture supports a mobile, low-wage workforce in this community. Because of the transient nature of agricultural work, Georgia's class membership had a 50% changeover during the last school year.

However, when you walk into Georgia's first-grade classroom, the mood is one of a community that is actively engaged and interested in what it is doing. Students are working in groups and alone, reading and writing, sharing and exchanging ideas and information. Georgia integrates reading and writing throughout the day and across subjects. Print surrounds the students on all four walls, including students' stories, students' artwork with labels, charts of songs and poems, and a pocket board for sentences about the basal story from guided reading.

Georgia's language arts program involves a weekly schedule of varied reading and writing activities, not the more common daily schedule.

At least three times a week, the students have independent reading time, while Georgia holds individual reading conferences. A literature-based basal reader is used twice weekly for guided reading, supplemented with appropriately leveled little books at these sessions for more guided reading. The class is divided by reading ability into four groups for these twice weekly sessions, but it is heterogeneously grouped for daily independent reading time. While Georgia meets with guided reading groups, the other students have center activities. Friday is an independent reading day for all groups. Each day after lunch, the students have leisure reading time. Georgia also reads aloud daily, offering a chance for predictions, sharing of personal knowledge and experiences, and vocabulary building. Often, she chooses books that enhance a math, science, or social studies concept on which the class is working. Writers Workshop is a vital component in the planned weekly literacy program. Twice a week, students are composing for at least 45 minutes. Other writing assignments, responses to their reading, personal journals, and whole-class generated big books offer diverse writing opportunities. The students have cubbies and are encouraged to write notes to each other.

A Day in First Grade

Students enter school at 8:20 A.M., quickly hang up their jackets, put away lunches, and group on the rug. On Mondays, there is oral sharing time, when students have the opportunity to participate in telling an experience or not. Georgia quickly takes lunch count, attendance, and has two helpers who write the day of the week and the date. (At the beginning of the school year, she modeled this and, by January, handed it over to students to do on their own.) While this is going on she engages the rest of the class in "reading the room"—reading words from the Word Wall and from the poems and songs around the room. When the students finish their calendar information, the class reads it silently and then in unison. Then, the pledge is said and a patriotic song is sung, with a student pointing to the large printed words on a chart. Again, an activity that Georgia did at first has been taken over by the students. This usually takes 15 minutes, and by 8:35 A.M., the class is engaged in guided reading and centers, independent reading, or Writers Workshop. Georgia has organized a time block of 90 minutes for literacy activities. Over two-thirds of this period involves students daily in individual reading and writing. Writing Workshop, guided reading and centers, independent reading, and conferences are included throughout the week.

Guided reading revolves around a basal selection for the week. Georgia has all the students gather on the rug as she performs a prereading activity. With this week's story, *Over in the Meadow* (Keats, 1993), she has the children close their eyes and think about animals and plants in a meadow. She tells them, "There is a creek, not as big as our local creek, and a tree trunk nearby, with ants crawling on it. Up in the blue sky are clouds. If you were sitting back in this meadow, you would be smelling things, seeing things, and hearing things." Georgia then directs the students to the story, illustrated by Ezra Jack Keats. A discussion ensues about the fact that this is an old story—Keats did not write it—and how they have read other retold stories. Georgia reads it aloud from a big book edition, and the students comment that it is a counting book, a rhyming book, and a repeating book. *Muskrat, snug,* and *chirp* are discussed as vocabulary as she reads, because they are hard words to determine from the pictures. Georgia asks questions about the muskrat; she has just elaborated on *snug* by saying, "I like snug. It reminds me of being warm and comfortable." She demonstrates "chirping" when asked, "What is chirp?" by a student.

Georgia had the written numbers *one* through *ten* on cards and arranged them, using a pocket chart, in a column and placed blank cards across from them in another column. As the students worked on remembering which animal matched which number, they flipped the cards to reveal the correct names. Georgia also used this exercise to stress sounds and words. She used the word numbers *one* and *eight* to talk about how *one* starts with the *w* sound, not *o*, and how *e* and *i* says *a* in eight. As students matched the animals to the number from the story, they silently—in their heads—read. Then in unison they read it again, with all the students appearing to be able to read. At their seats, using the table of contents, they all found the story in individual books and read chorally.

Then, Georgia directed her students to write in their journals about their favorite baby animal, and why it was their favorite. During this time, Georgia and her aide circulated, helping students sound out words. With *cheetah,* Georgia directed a student to look at her mouth as she said the word, stretching it out. The student said, and then wrote *ch- - -e- - -ta.* This sound stretching was a common feature in the classroom during writing. Both Georgia and her aide linked the students' sound spelling to developing phonemic segmentation by modeling word stretching in segments and encouraging the students to do this on their own.

The next day, in the students' smaller guided reading groups, Georgia worked with the pocket board using sentences from the story, but leaving blank the animals and their activity. The students filled in these missing words by reading the sentence in their head, talking with each other, and deciding what should fit. Afterward, they read it silently or whisper-read, then read aloud together. Finally, Georgia directed the students to read from individual books, loud enough for her to hear when she moved around, but not loud enough to disturb their neighbors.

The reading teacher, who provides instruction to five students in a pullout program, did so at this time. The reading teacher coordinates what she is working on with Georgia. Next, she pulls one student for a lesson geared toward the difficulties the child is having. She has trained Georgia's aide to work with another student, using one-on-one daily instruction. This understanding of reading strategies and decoding is helpful when the aide works with any student in the Writing Workshop, when working with students who are practicing for Author's Chair, in literacy activities at the centers, and during independent reading time. The aide is there all morning and spends most of her time working with students individually, while Georgia monitors her interactions and offers bits of advice about each student. Next, the students who have been with the reading teacher have a discussion with Georgia about what they heard in the story and saw outside (the class went for a walk in the meadow to observe and gather data the day before). Georgia shares pages from several books about bees. Then she introduces the Storybox book, *The Bee*, by Joy Cowley (1990), preparing the students by activating their background information about bees, previewing the cover and the following pages, and setting the readers up to whisper-read successfully on the first try. She then had them reread two times, stressing that the sentences make sense. Next, she did a minilesson on the double *ee* sound, starting with *bee* and making a list with *see, meet, beet,* and *bees,* all words from this story and a recently read book. The students thought of sentences about what bees can do: *Bees can sting. Bees can collect nectar. Bees can drink.* Although they knew only the beginning letter of *collect,* the students spelled everything else as Georgia wrote. As Georgia wrote *collect,* she modeled stretching out the sounds of the word to better be able to hear and spell them. Students whisper-read the chart, read all the sentences together, and then each student picked a sentence to read alone.

Guided reading is alternated with independent reading of books chosen from the baskets. The baskets are filled with teacher-selected books that the students have encountered during previous lessons. This is a quiet reading time, but students share with each other or sometimes read with partners, taking turns. With the groups heterogeneously mixed and a variety of leveled books available, students model good reading strategies and fluency for each other. During this time, Georgia has individual reading conferences, takes running records, jots down notes, and offers personal instruction in reading strategies to encourage self-monitoring, multiple strategy use, and independence. In one reading conference with a student, Georgia encourages his use of multiple strategies: self-monitoring, decoding, and—most importantly—meaning making. *Apples and Pumpkins* by Anne Rockwell (1994) is a new book for this reader, so Georgia encourages talking about it a little bit, looking at the title, and discussing the opening illustration and what he thinks is going on. When the student reads "country farm" instead of "Comstock Farm," Georgia praises the attempt, saying it was a really good word that made sense. She then claps out the syllables in *Comstock*, directing the student to look closely at the letters, and he is able to sound it out by syllables. Early in the story the student reads "greens and chickens" for "geese and chickens." Georgia draws attention to the mistake, asking, "Does that make sense?" The student quickly rereads the phrase correctly. She then encourages the use of multiple strategies, using picture cues, making sense, use of letter–sound relationships, and reading on to find out what happens. The student slowly but successfully reads, "The geese and chickens and a big fat turkey walked with us on our way to the . . . where the apples grow." The word skipped is *orchard*. Georgia builds upon the student's knowledge, asking "Where do apples grow? What do we call a lot of trees? What parts of the word look familiar?" until the student uses existing prior knowledge and the word structure to correctly pronounce "orchard." As the student reads on he becomes more fluent. Another mistake, "for me vine"/ "for the vine"/ "from the vine" is a quick succession of readings. The student is self-correcting as Georgia asks, "Does that make sense?" Another self-correction leads Georgia to ask, "How did you figure out that it was 'carry'?" The student does not know how to verbalize what strategies he used, so Georgia suggests some: "Did you look at the pictures? Did you go on?" For a final mistake, "fake" for "face," Georgia again stresses making sense: "Read it again and see if that makes more sense to you, from the beginning." Thus, she encourages another strategy, rereading along with meaning making, in cross-checking. The student successfully reads, "At home we carve a jack-o-lantern face on our big orange pumpkin." Georgia praises him for his use of multiple strategies and for sticking to the reading even though the book has many hard words.

The days that students have reading for 30 minutes from the literature baskets are also Writing Workshop days. The teacher and the aide give individual attention and encouragement to the writers. Checklist cards for editing encourage final punctuation, capitals, and spelling. Most of the students spell phonemically, sounding out words and stretching the sounds. Back in January, Georgia added a priority word list of 25 nonphonemic and high-frequency words. The students have a list of them on their tables and are expected to refer to it whenever they need to use these words in writing. After 3 months, students were spelling them correctly without looking at the lists. Today, there is much use of the Word Wall for spelling other words. A typical example is a boy adding to a story on giant sea turtles. He is reading from a book about sea turtles to gather new information. He has already written two drafts that have been revised and edited. As he writes, he uses the Word Wall, and the information and spelling from the book he is using as a resource. Another student is working on a chapter book about animals, because she has decided to combine two works in progress, one on horses and one on dogs.

After recess, Georgia has a math lesson on telling time on the hour and the half hour. It begins as a whole-class discussion on the rug as Georgia models the time for reading, for recess, and for leisure reading using a large yellow clock with movable hands. Again literacy is stressed. To tie in with this unit on telling time, she reads aloud *The Bear Child's Book of Hours* by Anne Rockwell (1987). Students then proceed to more individualized work back at the tables, each writing their own *My Book of Hours and Half Hours*. Each student fills in clocks and composes sentences that match personal experiences with the assistance of Georgia and her aide, scaffolding when necessary. Lunchtime and another recess end this busy morning.

When students return from lunch, they settle down for an independent leisure reading time. Crates of books of different reading levels are available, including many easy ones, as well as magazines and student-published books. Students share responses with each other, partner read, or read segments to each other from the books they have chosen. There is a very low hum to this reading time. Twenty-five minutes later, students go to the gym. When Georgia picks them up from the gym she comes prepared, with clipboards, paper, and pencils. They discuss the various sights and smells they envisioned earlier on the rug, before reading *Over in the Meadow*. Then, Georgia directs them to write down anything they observe as they go on their meadow walk. Students are busy, talking, smelling, looking, and sharing ideas as they gather data and write their own observations.

This day, the students have written in response journals, in their individual "book of hours," and now on clipboards about their trip to the meadow, writing in their own words everything they have seen, smelled, or heard. Georgia teaches both reading and writing skills explicitly, typically in the context of a reading or writing activity. She is opportunistic, selecting multiple occasions daily to provide explicit skills information, during whole-group, small-group, and individual meetings. But Georgia is also systematic, incorporating much of her strategy and skills instruction into her guided reading lessons, Writing Workshop conferences, and reading conferences. All of these activities offer students instruction on a personalized basis.

Exemplary Instructional Support for Children Who Find Learning to Read and Write Difficult

Joyce is a reading teacher in an old mill town on a river in the Northeast. The school serves a significant number of at-risk students, with 40% of the children eligible for free or reduced-price lunch. Joyce starts her day at 8:30 A.M., snatching small conferences with the various teachers whose rooms she pushes into, getting plastic baskets ready with books for the various first-grade rooms she enters, and setting up her small, cozy room for the two pullout sessions she does each day. At 9:00, she enters the first of five first-grade classrooms she visits on a daily basis.

The "warm-up" involves 10 students who come over immediately as Joyce spreads multiple copies of eight little books. These are all rereads in which students quickly engage, with comments such as "I can read this one" (e.g., *The Ghost*; Cowley, 1990) or "Let's read this one together" (e.g., *In a Dark, Dark Wood*; Ross, 1990). Joyce works with and listens to each student read in a whisper, their silent reading. As they finish one book, students take or trade for another. After 10 minutes, Joyce collects those texts and gives each child a copy of *Where's the Halloween Treat?* (Ziefert, 1985), introduced yesterday.

Joyce starts the guided reading with "Where are your eyes going to be?" The students chime, "On the words." Working on the title, one student knows the word *the*, another, *Halloween*; still another guesses *trick*. Noting that *trick* makes sense, Joyce asks, "Is that trick or treat?" The student answers, "Treat because of the *t* at the end." Students read the text together, misreading *us* for *me*. When asked, "Is that *us*?" they reread, saying that it starts with an *m*, and self-correcting to *me*. Joyce points out, "I hear a rhyme. Listen for two words," and rereads the pages. Students quickly pick out and say "Eat/treat." Detective eyes are asked to find more rhyming words as the story progresses. Joyce picks up the pace; so does the group, self-correcting individually as they go along. When they finish the story, Joyce has them turn back to page 6, finding the words *good*, *eat*, and *six*. She cues each word with "What's it going to start with?" This reread with a minilesson on rhymes takes 10 minutes.

For the final 10 minutes, Joyce introduces a new book, *Going Up?: The Elevator Counting Book* (Cummins, 1995). Finger pointing to the first word, she asks, "What does it say?" As she covers the *ing*, students quickly chant *go*; then, they chant *going* as she uncovers the word. From the title, students predict where the character is—in an elevator. Joyce asks the students, "Why is this a good name for a book about an elevator, and how does it know when to stop?" Students have various responses, which are all accepted positively. Then, they begin to read as Joyce finger-points to each word. The elevator stops at floor number five. She then asks them to predict what will happen next: The numbers go down as the elevator goes down. Then, they all read the rest of the text together. Before leaving, Joyce tells the students that they will work on writing books tomorrow.

Joyce quickly goes back to her small room, where she picks up the next basket of books and hurries on to her second first-grade class. In this class, students start their warm-up with *Jack-O'-Lantern* (Frost, 1990). Each student has his or her own copy. Joyce has extra copies for those children who took the book home and forgot to bring it back. Joyce spreads out other books for warm-up, with the instruction, "Everyone find one page to read to me. When I have heard you read your page, take a different book." Joyce encourages rereading, thinking of a word that makes sense, and starts with the beginning sound and voice-print match. One student, who picked the first page of *Scarecrow* (Bacon, 1993), reads. Joyce asks him how the book ends, which he does not know. She tells him to find the end of the book and together they read the last pages, working on self-correcting and understanding. After the 12-minute warm-up, the students are directed to put the books in the middle and are told they can keep *Jack-O'-Lantern* and take it home.

In this group, she introduces *Where's the Halloween Treat?* Looking at the title, students are directed to the *H* and asked, "What sound does it make?" Students all say /h/ and start thinking of a word that makes sense with the cover picture. They offer *haunt, house, Halloween.* Another student reads, "Where's the" and everyone choruses, "Halloween." Joyce begins the book, finger pointing to the words as she goes along. By the second page, students are chiming in and predicting a good thing to eat behind the door. *Sandwich* and *apple* are accepted; the word *skeleton* prompts, "Is that something good to eat?" By the third page, the students are using the repetition and their knowledge of numbers to read with no assistance. When asked how they know it is *seven*, students say it starts with an *s*, and another adds that it ends with *n*. Near the end of the book, Joyce asks the students to predict: "What do you think they did when the ghost said Boo?" Answers varied from "They stayed," to "They ran," to "They were afraid." They finished the story to see what would happen and revised their predictions as needed.

With 5 minutes left, Joyce has the students begin writing their own book, modeled after the book they just read. The classroom teacher allows them to continue writing as Joyce leaves.

Joyce's third first-grade class does a warm-up reading time for 10 minutes. Then *Where's the Halloween Treat?* is read chorally, a reread for three students and new to two others. With this group, Joyce takes from her basket *My Journal* books, with each child's name at the bottom of the covers. In the book, they are working on patterns and words they can make from them to use in writing. The students are directed to make a box, then a *u* in the box, then a wall, and then an *s*. Joyce asks, "What's that word?" Students respond, "Us." After writing it under the box, Joyce asks, "What would rhyme with us?" Students think of *bus*. Joyce models on a pad writing *us* and putting a *b* in front of it, while she thinks aloud, "If we can write *us*, we can write *bus*. We need to put the *b* first, then *us*." Students are now directed to write *give* on the bottom of their page; the students and Joyce spell it. Next they are asked to write *us* from above, read the two words, and add a number, *Give us 7*. Then, together they spell *good things to eat,* with the students spelling the beginning and ending sounds and the *ing.* Joyce ends her half-hour by telling the students, "When I come back tomorrow, we will cut up these sentences and do a new book."

It is now 10:30 A.M. and time for Joyce's fourth first-grade class. Six students in this group quickly dive into the warm-up books Joyce brought in a plastic basket. As she comments positively to one student, "I like the way you are finger pointing," other students start finger pointing. Joyce works individually with each student. Then, a new book for this group is introduced, *Jack-O'-Lantern.* The end of the lesson revolves around the word *made.* "We are going to write the word *made.* Think about it. How big a box?" Joyce asks. She uses a small easel blackboard to model a box with three spaces, the last divided with a dotted line. The students fill in *m, a, d,* as Joyce ends by saying, "There is a letter we don't hear at the end." Students predict *n* or *t,* and Joyce tells them *e.* They add the *e,* commenting that there are three sounds but four letters. This leads to students writing in their journals about the kind of face they would make on a pumpkin. Joyce has each student say the sentence he or she wants to write, concentrating on adjectives. Students quickly write, "I made a", then Joyce helps them sound out *vampire, scary, wolf, happy,* or *mad.* She then directs them to the word *face* in their book. On a blank piece of paper, she writes each sentence, cuts it up, and puts it and a copy of *Jack-O'-Lantern* in a Zip-loc bag for each student to take home.

Joyce is a little behind schedule, arriving in the fifth classroom at 11:10. They do warm-up reading and then Joyce holds up the new book, *Jack-O'-Lantern,* saying, "Look at the cover. What do you see?" Students say, "Pumpkin." Joyce responds, "Do you think that word says *pumpkin?*" The students reply, "No." Her "Why?" is answered with "Because it starts with a *j.*" Joyce prompts them: "What is another name that starts with *j?*" They answer "jack-o'-lantern." Different students take turns finger pointing and reading with Joyce. Then, the students read in pairs from their own copies of the book. Joyce then has each student pick one page to read out loud to her after first practicing it in pairs.

Joyce now has a prep time and lunch, which she spends preparing the different baskets for the five first-grade lessons tomorrow. Over lunch, she talks with the fourth-grade teacher in whose room she will be for an hour.

Joyce is giving daily intensive tutoring to the two first graders who are struggling most with reading. At 12:30 she provides a one-on-one pullout session with one of the first graders. She picks up the student, quickly walking with her to her small tutoring room. Out of a packet kept in the reading room, the student picks a copy of *The Monster's Party* (Cowley, 1990) with her name on it. She reads it, finger pointing as Joyce listens. Then Joyce picks *Sing a Song* (Melser, 1990) out of her packet. As the student reads it, she takes a running record. When she gets stuck on the word *about*, Joyce prompts, "What can you do if you don't know it?" The student says, "Read on," and she does. Although she does not self-correct here, she does so later on when reading *together* for *bed* and *tuck* for *us*. In both cases, she appears to use both letters and meaning to help self-correct. As the student completes the book, Joyce asks, "Can you tell me one thing in this story you liked?" The girl likes the splashing. Joyce continues: "What else happened in the story?" The student replies, "They got out." Joyce asks, "How did they get out?" The student answers, "Jump." She is asked to find the word and does. The next book they read is *Hairy Bear* (Cowley, 1990). They discuss that *we* and *together* mean more than one tiger. Up on the blackboard Joyce and the student work on the word *out*, making a box with one wall and one segment divided with a dotted line. The student fills in the *t*, Joyce the *o* and *u*. They then work on a box for *about*, the word the student missed in her reread for the running record. The student hears and writes each sound, then practices writing *about*. Then, she writes *out* and *about* on 3" × 5" cards that will be added to her word box, a recipe box. For 2 minutes, they practice words from the box. Then, while the student picks another story to read, Joyce writes a sentence on jumping from *Sing a Song*: "Out, Out, Out we jump." The student reads the sentence. Joyce cuts it up, has her assemble it, and read again. Into a bag go the cut-up sentence, the book, and the 3" × 5" cards *out* and *about* to go home for practice. In the last 3 minutes, they discuss real and make-believe as a new book, *Dan the Flying Man* (Cowley, 1990), is introduced. Joyce begins reading, with the book in front of the student, and has the student finger point to the words. Joyce leaves blanks at the end of the sentence, and the student correctly supplies *trees* and *train*. Halfway through, the student takes over. Joyce joins in again at the ending, which has a change of wording. The student goes back to her room as Joyce goes on to the fourth-grade class.

The fourth-grade teacher has requested that Joyce work with her to enhance her writing instruction. In September, Joyce had modeled the writing process, brainstorming, rough drafts, revising, conferencing, editing, and publishing. She and the teacher worked on modeling peer conferences that sensitively gave feedback, constructive criticism, and specific ideas to the writer. With the writing process smoothly working in late October, Joyce continued to help with writing conferences but also was available for reading conferences and small heterogeneously grouped work. Language arts time was structured so that remedial aid included students with special needs who were working on reading and writing material at their independent and instructional levels. More frequent conferences in reading and writing were provided for them.

Joyce enters the room as the teacher is reading the beginning of *The Eerie Canal* (Reber, 1991). The introduction to the book had taken place earlier. Joyce points out at the end of the chapter, "I met a lot of characters. They keep mentioning Tom. I think he will be important." A student adds that another character, Sandy, is being described in detail and must be important too. As the teacher reads, Joyce and the children discuss the opening chapters, and inferences and predictions flow. Questions such as "I'm getting a funny feeling," "What do you think right now?", " What do you feel?", "Can you picture that?", and "What made you think it?" all encourage response, sharing of different ideas, and predictions. Both teachers then lead the discussion to important characters and significant events that happen to them. In groups of two or three, they discuss, share ideas, and write about the two main characters and important events they experienced in the opening chapters. Joyce and the teacher circulate among the students, listening, prompting, and asking questions to expand ideas and encourage examples. In the return to whole-class discussion and a composite list of events, the conversation also includes the author's style, and how he pulled the reader right into the story. They contrast it to Cynthia DeFelice's style in *The Light on Hogback Hill* (1992), the current read-aloud, which has a much slower beginning and drew the reader in slowly. As this discussion continues, Joyce leaves.

It is now 2:00 P.M. and time to pick up the other first grader for intensive one-on-one tutoring. After this, Joyce has a prep period, which she uses to prepare for the individualized tutoring she will do tomorrow and further preparation for the five first-grade classes she pushes into.

Joyce and her school have participated in a variety of studies with a nearby university for 10 years. Organizational support from a former administration allowed and even encouraged change involving teachers and their ideas. Earlier, some 12 years ago, when Joyce was a special education teacher, she started pushing into the classrooms. She started with one teacher:

> "It was contagious. People were upset I couldn't come into their room. Part of it was that they were getting something back. They were learning how to teach with literature, and they really wanted to have their special education kids with them more of the time. We were learning together how to best do this."

When she became a reading teacher 9 years earlier, the program was completely pullout. At that time, an administrator wanted to start a brand new kindergarten and first-grade reading program that was a push-in model.

"The K–1 teachers never had exposure to working with someone in their rooms before. They might not have invited me in, but I just couldn't feasibly do a pullout in K–1. Plus it was really successful with the way my special ed program was operating. . . . I don't think people like to see you come in with a halo of authority. I would always say we should sit and talk. First, we had discussion time. I would say to them, 'I need to know what I'm doing, when I'm in the room, so let's decide what your goals are and what you want to accomplish, and I'll talk about some of my goals and what I want to accomplish. Then let's figure out how we can do this together in the room at the same time.' Every person was different."

One teacher and Joyce worked on flexible grouping, with students rolling in and out between them. For another teacher, she modeled read-alouds and having the children respond to stories. "I had to give her something concrete, something predictable, something she could do every day by herself."

In the subsequent years Joyce's role changed

"The teachers have gotten comfortable with literature-based instruction and teaching it themselves. I don't have to spend much time giving whole-class lessons. I'm spending more time with students, individualizing more. I try to do a lot more things quickly—quicker than I used to. I make sure they read lots of books when I'm with them. I'm seeing the kids more often. The real secret has to be that the classroom teachers really know how to do instruction, and that we figure out a plan, where some days I'm integrated in everything, and other days maybe I'm not integrated. I'm working with my kids, but also I'm pulling out other kids that have that same problem."

Joyce and the teachers she works with feel "that we are both responsible for all of the kids in that room," yet she works primarily with the kids that really need the additional instruction.

The remedial program has become very collaborative. Several days throughout the year, substitutes come in, rotate, and relieve the classroom teachers so that they can attend roughly hour-long conferences with Joyce. Planning focuses on the very specific needs of certain children and how those needs will be addressed. Joyce has changed from a complete push-in model to primarily a push-in model, with two periods a day in which she pulls out students for one-on-one tutoring. One positive outcome of all these changes is a large reduction in the number of children being labeled and placed in special education.

IMPLICATIONS FOR FUTURE RESEARCH

Certainly more studies that continue the research into exemplary teachers and their instructional practices are needed. Studies should focus on measuring children's accelerated progress with fluency in reading; higher level thinking; and summarizing, analyzing, and responding to texts. Another area in which there is little or no research involves looking at comprehensive intervention programs that include long-term support. This crucial component needs to be better understood, so schools can offer professional development, create budgets, and coordinate instructional support that will provide exemplary support programs for children throughout their schooling.

DISCUSSION AND ACTIVITIES

Exemplary early literacy interventions begin with an emphasis on ensuring that all children have access to high-quality classroom instruction. But classroom teaching is complex, and classroom teachers will likely never to be able to meet the substantial demands on time and expertise that some children pose. This suggests, then, two roles for special program personnel. The first involves working with classroom teachers to enhance the quality of literacy instruction offered as part of the general education experience. This might occur in any number of ways, but in the cases that we observed, the specialists offered training, advice, information, and appropriate materials to classroom teachers, in order to enhance classroom instruction. The second role is to provide direct instruction to children who find learning to read difficult, but instruction that extends classroom lessons and is offered in a more intensive and personalized manner. Delivering such instruction requires working with classroom teachers over a period of time, but the benefits suggest that the effort paid substantial dividends.

1. Examine several individualized education plans (IEP). Look for coordination of the individualized goals with classroom instruction and district curriculum standards.
2. Interview an elementary school principal and ask about the school's literacy program. How does it meet the needs of all students? What components are in place for preventing reading and writing difficulties? What support is there for intervening and accelerating the progress of students who struggle with reading and writing?
3. How many fourth-grade students in your district will need additional support in middle school and high school?
4. Find out about preventive, accelerated, and longer term support plans in place in your school district. Are there clear links between preschool and elementary school programs, and elementary and middle school programs?

ACKNOWLEDGMENTS

The development of the case studies reported in this chapter was supported in part under the Educational Research and Development Program (Grant Nos. Rll7GIOO15 and R305A60005), and the National Research Center on English Learning and Achievement, as administered by the Office of Educational Research and Improvement, U.S. Department of Education. However, the contents of this chapter do not necessarily represent the positions or policies of the sponsoring agencies.

REFERENCES

Professional Literature

Achilles, C. M. (1999). *Let's put kids first, finally: Getting class size right.* Thousand Oaks, CA: Corwin Press.

Allington, R. L. (2001). *What really matters for struggling readers.* Boston: Allyn & Bacon.

Allington, R. L., & Cunningham, P. M. (2002). *Schools that work* (2nd ed.). New York: Longman.

Allington, R. L., & Johnston, P. H. (2001). What do we know about exemplary fourth-grade teachers and their classrooms? In C. Roller (Ed.), *Learning to teach reading: Setting the research agenda* (pp. 150–165). Newark, DE: International Reading Association.

Allington, R. L., & McGill-Franzen, A. (1996). Individual planning. In M. Wang & M. Reynolds (Eds.), *Handbook of special and remedial education* (pp. 5–35). Elmsford, NY: Pergamon.

Boyd-Zaharias, J., & Pate-Bain, H. (1998). *Teacher aides and student learning: Lessons from Project STAR.* Arlington, VA: Educational Research Service.

International Reading Association. (1994). Who is teaching our children? Implications of the use of aides in Chapter 1. *ERS Spectrum, 12,* 28–34.

Lyon, G. R., & Moats, L.C. (1997). Critical conceptual and methodological considerations in reading intervention research. *Journal of Learning Disabilities, 30,* 578–588.

Mendro, R. L., Jordan, H., & Bembry, K. L. (1998, April). *Longitudinal teacher effects on student achievement and their relation to school and project evaluation.* Paper presented at the annual meeting of the American Educational Research Association, San Diego, CA.

Pressley, M., Allington, R. L., Wharton-McDonald, R., Block, C. C., & Morrow, L. (2001). *Learning to read: Lessons from exemplary first-grade classrooms.* New York: Guilford Press.

Sack, J. (1999, March 17). Report charts rise in special education enrollment. *Education Week,* p. 40.

Taylor, B., Pearson, D., Clark, K., & Walpole, S. (2000). Effective schools and accomplished teacher: Lessons from primary grade reading instruction in low-income schools. *Elementary School Journal, 101,* 121–165.

Walmsley, S.A., & Allington, R. L. (1995). Redefining and reforming instructional support programs for at- risk students. In R. L. Allington & S. A. Walmsley (Eds.), *No quick fix: Rethinking literacy programs in America's elementary schools* (pp. 19–41). New York: Teachers College Press.

Children's Literature

Bacon, R. (1993). *Scarecrow.* Crystal Lake, IL: Rigby.

Cowley, J. (1990). *The bee.* Bothell, WA: Wright Group.

Cowley, J. (1990). *Dan the flying man.* Bothell, WA: Wright Group.

Cowley, J. (1990). *The ghost.* Bothell, WA: Wright Group.

Cowley, J. (1990). *Hairy bear.* Bothell, WA: Wright Group.

Cowley, J. (1990). *The monster's party.* Bothell, WA: Wright Group.

Cummins, P. (1995). *Going up?: The elevator counting book.* Glenview, IL: Celebrations Press.

DeFelice, C. (1992). *The light on Hogback Hill.* New York: Scribner.

Frost, M. 1990). *Jack-O'-lantern.* Bothell, WA: Wright Group.

Keats, E. J. (1993). *Over in the meadow.* New York: Scholastic.

Melser, J. (1990). *Sing a song.* Bothell, WA: Wright Group.

Reber, J. (1991). *The eerie canal.* Unionville, NY: Trillium Press.

Rockwell, A. (1994). *Apples and pumpkins.* New York: Aladdin Paperbacks.

Rockwell, A. (1987). *The bear child's book of hours.* New York: Crowell.

Ross, C. (1990). *In a dark, dark wood.* Bothell, WA: Wright Group.

Ziefert, H. (1985). *Where's the Halloween treat?* New York: Viking Press.

Chapter 15

EFFECTIVE USE OF TECHNOLOGY IN LITERACY INSTRUCTION

Michael C. McKenna
Linda D. Labbo
David Reinking

This chapter will:

- Examine research-based classroom practice using technology.
- Describe how the instructional use of technology relates to learning theory.
- Dispel myths concerning technology use by elementary-school-age children.
- Suggest how best practice can (and must) successfully embrace technology.
- Identify activities for self-reflection and planning.

The advent of computer technology presents literacy educators with an ever-expanding array of possible applications. Some, such as utilities for producing materials and maintaining records, are used behind the scenes. These have obvious value in terms of convenience, flexibility, and time saved. Other applications entail student use of computers in classroom settings. Such uses continue to be proposed and employed by creative teachers, and research into their effectiveness has steadily accumulated. In this chapter, we explore some of the major classroom applications shown to be effective to date, applications that offer the brightest promise to literacy teachers.

COMPUTER APPLICATIONS WITH BEGINNING READERS

It is now commonplace to see students in the upper elementary grades and higher using classroom-based computers productively for a variety of applications. It is far less common, in our experience, to observe primary-grade children similarly engaged, and work products on display in schools rarely involve computer applications (Labbo, Montero, & Eakle, 2001). What accounts for the reluctance of many primary grade teachers to embrace computer technology as a means of fostering the literacy growth of their students? We believe that two popular myths play a role in constraining their thinking.

Myth 1: Computers Are Too Hard for Young Children to Use

According to this myth, the basic operation of a computer is too difficult for most children in kindergarten and grade one to master. Although computers are sophisticated machines, to be sure, and some applications require considerable expertise, a range of available software invites use by the very young. Granted, a certain level of fine motor development is needed for tasks such as the operation of a mouse, but our experience is that this level has been reached by most children in early kindergarten. Indeed, in some cases, fine motor skills needed for computer use develop before the corresponding skills needed for conventional literacy tasks. For example, it is far simpler for children at this age to create a letter of the alphabet by pressing a key than by moving a pencil. Whereas this first myth might have been plausible during the advent of microcomputers in the early 1980s, there is no longer a defensible reason for deferring technology use until the upper elementary grades. Seymour Papert (1993), in *The Children's Machine*, employs the metaphor of a virus invading the body in order to describe how teachers and schools sometimes react to the "invasion" of microcomputers. They are often relegated to labs and the corners of classrooms, places where they can least interfere with conventional operations. We suspect that some teachers may rely on Myth 1 in order to avoid integrating technology into their early literacy instruction.

Myth 2: You Must Be Able to Read to Read with a Computer

The limited reading skills of K–1 students, as this myth implies, prevent any meaningful interaction with text displayed on a computer. To be sure, the need to decode unfamiliar words might indeed prohibit successful reading on the part of many beginners. This is true, however, only if their decoding is not supported by the software. If it is displayed on screen in a static way, as it would appear in a book, then, of course, there would be little chance of independent reading. On the other hand, when electronic text is supported by digitized pronunciations available on a point-and-click basis, children are presented with a tool that is unavailable to them in print environments. Pronunciation support has the potential to erase the difference between a child's frustration and independent reading levels (McKenna, 1998). In effect, such support makes it possible for a child to read materials at or near the listening level, with minimal teacher assistance. In our studies at the National Reading Research Center, we have found that children learn a substantial number of new sight words through incidental exposure, while reading electronic books equipped with pronunciation support. The only prerequisite is that certain emergent literacy skills (alphabet recognition, left–right orientation, and knowledge about word boundaries) must have been attained.

These two myths can be summarized in a single, dismissive statement: Young children lack the skills to use computers, and even if they possessed them, they could not read what they see on the screen. We hope that we have begun to dispel these myths. The classroom scenarios we discuss further suggest how best practice in beginning reading instruction must now embrace the integration of technology.

Scenarios from Two Effective Classrooms

The scenarios that follow illustrate the range of effective computer applications that are possible with beginning readers. This first set of scenarios provides insights into a classroom community of kindergarten children who are as comfortable with reading and writing on a computer screen as they are with reading and writing on paper. When the children work at the computer with another child or with an adult, they have occasion socially to construct concepts about print (e.g., directionality, speech-to-word match), gaining insights into functions and forms of literacy, composing with a word-processing program, and even enhancing their social status with their classmates. In part because the centrally located computer adjoins other areas of high activity, the computer is part of the classroom culture (Haughland, 1992). The second set of scenarios explores the uses of electronic text in a first-grade classroom. Here, children find that they can "read" material that far exceeds their decoding ability because of the support the computer offers them.

Ms. Martin's Kindergarten Class

It is 9:20 A.M. on a cold October morning in Ms. Martin's kindergarten class, and the room is filled with the sounds of children working at various centers. Patrick and Dartrell sit side by side in the computer center, which adjoins the sociodramatic play center and the classroom library. They are contemplating a color monitor that displays information about bats (see Figure 15.1). Earlier, during rug time, the boys had listened to their teacher introduce the unit for the week, "Creatures That Fly in the Night Sky." After hearing the text on the screen read aloud to them, the boys decide how to interact with the computer to receive additional information, in this instance, an audio rereading of a definition, pronunciations of words highlighted in blue, digital drawings that pop up in boxes over the text, or various sound effects. They confer briefly and click on an illustration that also provides the sound of a feeding bat. As Kelly, a classmate, walks by the computer, she stops, looks at the screen, and asks them a question.

KELLY: How did you do that? Get that up there [on screen]?

PATRICK: All you do is . . . wait (*closes the application*). Like Ms. Martin did. All you do is . . . this (*demonstrates how to click the mouse and get access to the CD*).

KELLY: You're so smart, Patrick. You should be in college.

a b c d e f g h i j k l m n o p q r s t u v w x y z

bat

Other meaning

A bat is a small, furry animal with wings. Bats hang upside down to sleep during the day, and hunt for food at night.

Surprise me   Backtrack   Games   Quick search   Options   Quit
© 1995 Dorling Kindersley Multimedia

FIGURE 15.1. Patrick and Dartrell learn about bats.

Word of Patrick's expertise quickly spreads throughout the classroom; soon, other children ask him for a demonstration of how this application works from the CD inserted in the CD-ROM drive of the computer. Patrick's computer ability seems to enhance his social standing with several of his peers, who seek him out for the first time as a reading partner during buddy reading.

At 9:50 A.M., Aerial and Jasmine sit in the computer center and compare a storybook version to an electronic book version of *Stella Luna* (Cannon, 1993). As a "page" of the text is highlighted and read aloud on the computer screen, Aerial points at the corresponding text on a page in the book. Jasmine delights in using the mouse to click on a screen illustration of one of the main characters, a lost baby bat's mother. The girls watch the animation of the mother bat flying over trees, calling, and looking for her baby, who is lost but safely snuggled in a nest with baby birds. Later, when the girls use a *Stella Luna* bat puppet and a bird puppet to retell the story in the sociodramatic play center, they are joined by three other children, who serve as an audience. The story innovation they enact is filled with plot twists, melancholy dialogue, humorous events, and voices that sound a great deal like the characters from the electronic book.

At 1:30 P.M., during afternoon center time, JaMaris brings an informational book about bats and the *Stella Luna* puppet with him. He props the book on a small, book-size easel that has been placed beside the computer monitor and holds the puppet on his lap. He has decided to contribute to a class book of collected stories on bats. His assignment is to draw and write something about bats using *KidPix2* (Hickman, 1992). As JaMaris begins, he is joined for a few minutes by his teacher, who crouches by his side.

Ms. Martin: So what's your story going to be about?

JaMaris: It's gonna be a story about a really cool bat named Spidey and his super powers.

Ms. Martin: OK. So how do you want to begin? With "Once upon a time?"

JaMaris: No . . . my name first (*selects the keyboard function and types in the letters of his name using the hunt-and-peck method*) . . . and I want to draw Spidey.

Ms. Martin: That's not a bad idea. If you draw that bat, you might get some good story ideas. So, what does this old bat look like—like Stella Luna?

JaMaris: Sorta like this one but with big green eyes (*pointing to the photograph of a bat on the book cover*). How do I get green?

Ms. Martin: Remember how I showed you the other day, during rug time? (*Before leaving the computer center, Ms. Martin demonstrates how to access the color option from the program's menu.*)

JaMaris uses electronic artist tools to draw a bat with big green eyes, large fangs, and a crooked "B" on the chest (see Figure 15.2). He then writes a two-line story that consists of strings of letters and a word copied from the book cover. He makes two printouts. One is placed in a folder of children's stories that will be bound into a class book, and the other goes into his backpack, so he can show it to his mother.

A classroom visitor, witnessing the children's computer work, might assume that they are all remarkably gifted or that they come from affluent homes, where they have daily access to computers. However, quite the reverse is true. None of the six children mentioned in these vignettes

FIGURE 15.2. JaMaris's bat story.

has a computer at home; all qualify for free or reduced-price lunches and have average or below-average literacy ability. The primary reason the children are adept at using technology is because their teacher consistently plans inviting, enriching, and appropriate computer-related experiences. In Ms. Martin's classroom, computer-related learning is meaningful and purposeful.

Mr. Saunders's First-Grade Class

Our second set of scenarios explores the uses of electronic text in Mr. Saunders' first-grade classroom. Here, children find that they can "read" material that far exceeds their decoding ability because of the support the computer offers them. By October, Mr. Saunders' first graders already represent a wide range of literacy development. Most of them know the alphabet and have mastered basic concepts about print. Some have begun to acquire a store of sight words, and a few have become accomplished decoders. One or two students already read with relative proficiency, whereas others will challenge his resourcefulness as a teacher.

Mr. Saunders makes use of well-designed decoding software, such as *Reading Mansion*, that embodies research underlying effective instructional practice (see Fox & Mitchell, 2000; McKenna, 2002). However, he also makes a point of engaging the children with electronic text. He does so by using his four computers as centers, giving the children a variety of experiences that complement conventional print-based activities. He uses electronic text in two basic ways.

Sometimes he presents a commercially prepared electronic book, such as one of the Living Books developed by Broderbund. Because these books contain hidden seek-and-find features that he regards as engaging but distracting (see Labbo & Kuhn, 2000), he allows the children first to explore the book thoroughly in a spirit of play. Later, they return to the book in a "read only" manner. Mr. Saunders has learned from experience that he cannot rely on the computer to engage the children and lead the way to productive results. Clear expectations must be communicated, and careful monitoring must follow (Labbo, Sprague, Montero, & Font, 2000). He therefore makes his expectations clear, namely, that a child visiting the center will read every word of the book, even if it is necessary to click on all of the words. Because there is no built-in comprehension follow-up, Mr. Saunders tries to engage his young center visitors in a brief postreading discussion that focuses on inferential and critical questions that provoke thought, while ensuring that the children have read the book.

All of the books have paper versions, and Mr. Saunders calls his students' attention to them on his bookshelf, though he stops short of situating the print versions near the computers, as Ms. Martin does. Many of the children choose one of these books during self-selected reading time; the books provide an opportunity for repeated reading after an initial supported reading via computer. Mr. Saunders occasionally asks the children which version they prefer, and nearly all of them indicate that they like the computer versions better. All but Sarah, that is, who complains that the mouse "makes my hand sweat."

The second way in which Mr. Saunders makes electronic text available to his students is through brief passages that he composes himself. He uses a text-to-speech program called *Write Out Loud,* produced by Don Johnston, Inc. The software automatically provides pronunciations for any of the words Mr. Saunders has written. As with the commercially prepared books, all the children need to do is point to a troublesome word and then click to hear it pronounced. (See *www.donjohnston.com*)

One morning, as Jarrell visits the computer, he discovers to one side a copy of Mr. Saunders's class roster. On the screen is the following paragraph:

Find your name on the list beside the computer. Count the number of letters in your first name. Write this number next to your name. Then go back to your seat.

It has taken Mr. Saunders only a minute or two to compose and enter this paragraph. Note that this particular paragraph combines both a built-in comprehension check and a timely math link. Some of these first graders take far longer than others to accomplish the task and return to their seats, because they must access a greater number of pronunciations in order to interpret the message. Nevertheless, most of the children are eventually able to accomplish the task successfully. A few of them need Mr. Saunders's help, and he monitors the center while he works with children elsewhere in the room.

Mr. Saunders occasionally varies the use of *Write Out Loud* by entering a brief passage from a trade book they have studied. He then follows it with a brief question that he later uses to ground a short discussion at the end of center time. He sometimes uses stories the students themselves have written, after receiving their permission to share, and after making a few touch-ups with respect to spelling and syntax. For example:

Toby's Story

My favorite food is chocolate. I love to eat it at Easter and Halloween. I also like it at other times. It is my favorite food.

To monitor his students' comprehension of stories like Toby's, Mr. Saunders does not ask for critical reactions to the writing but concentrates rather on whether students remembered Toby's favorite food, whether they shared his opinion, and so forth. Mr. Saunders has found that posting student work for others to read is a highly popular activity, one that would have been impossible without the support offered through technology. These applications by a resourceful teacher are representative of a wide variety of effective strategies for implementing electronic text in classroom-based computer centers (for others, see Labbo, 2000).

BROADENING THE CONCEPT OF LITERACY

Although we still have much to learn about effective technology and literacy instruction in primary classrooms, research over the last decade (e.g., see Fatorous, 1995; Labbo, 1996) provides insights into how to plan appropriate computer-related learning experiences that foster children's literacy development. In this chapter, we draw on relevant research and underlying sociocognitive theory (Vygotsky, 1978) to offer suggestions for establishing a classroom environment that promotes demonstration, collaboration, and other forms of social interaction. We do so by describing how teachers can use technology to support children's conventional literacy development and the development of what has been called "electronic literacy" (Reinking, 1994).

Conventional literacy development refers to language arts processes of listening, speaking, reading, and writing that are related to traditional typographic features of linear text, such as print, illustrations, and graphics. Electronic literacy development expands conventional literacy to include digital and multimedia materials with these fundamental processes. Others have referred to this expanded view of literacy in other ways. For example, Flood, Heath, and Lapp (1997) refer to the "visual and communicative arts," and the Vanderbilt Learning and Technology Group refers to "representational literacy," which includes a variety of new media that can be integrated with conventional texts to create meaning. (For a range of perspectives on the notion of multiple literacies and how to address them in classroom settings, see Richards & McKenna, 2003). Conventional approaches to literacy instruction are being revisited and modified accordingly. Labbo, Eakle, and Montero (2002), for example, have successfully adapted the language-experience approach to include both multimedia and text.

INTEGRATING TECHNOLOGY INTO THE SOCIAL ENVIRONMENT OF THE CLASSROOM

The evidence is clear that the social environment of the classroom will always play a central role in determining how a computer is used by children in schools (see Kamil, Kim, & Intrator, 2000; Leu, 2000). It is our belief that if computers are to adequately support both conventional and electronic literacy development of children, then computer-related activities must be woven into the fabric of daily classroom routines through planned activities in areas such as (1) teacher interactive demonstration, (2) thematic integration and innovation, (3) diverse collaboration, and (4) attention to special needs.

Teacher Interactive Demonstration

Our research (Labbo, Phillips, & Murray, 1995–1996) suggests that integration of technology can be achieved when teachers demonstrate the use of a classroom computer during whole- and small-group lessons; however, the makeup of the demonstrations should not consist only of the teacher explaining or modeling the use of a computer. Rather, demonstrations should combine teacher modeling with opportunities for children to become involved. For example, Mr. Saunders uses a projector to demonstrate how to point and click on the words in electronic text to hear them pronounced. He asks one or more of the children to assist him in this demonstration. Teachers can also solicit children's input during demonstrations of how to use the computer to maintain a calendar of events, to compose and print out notes to parents, to write and print out individual copies of the morning message and daily news, to make lists of things to do, and to create signs for classroom events. By socially negotiating the form, content, and context of the demonstrations, teachers can help children create a rich schema for employing technology in ways that quite naturally involve many literacy-related activities. Thus, the perspective we advocate implies much more than perfunctory uses of technology that place computers outside the mainstream of literacy activities in classrooms.

For example, from a sociocognitive perspective, we posit that children who observe and interact with teachers during whole- and small-group technology demonstrations will internalize relevant vocabulary, develop approaches to problem solving, and encounter action schemes—all of which enable them to use the computer as a tool for thinking, learning, and communicating. As Papert (1980) suggests, children will use a computer in ways that they see the adults in their lives make use of computers. Adult modeling of literacy activities is a major factor in children's acquisition of conventional literacy. It is no less so in the acquisition of electronic, or digital, literacy.

Other benefits of interactive demonstrations are evident when children dictate personal news to add to the morning message, watch their words typed on the screen, and thereby have opportunities to become aware of graphophonemic aspects of print. Additionally, when children receive an individual printout of the morning message and are invited to circle words, letters, or letter-sounds they recognize, they then have an opportunity to enrich or refine their conventional literacy knowledge.

Thematic Integration and Innovation

Creative teachers who put a classroom computer to its best use seem consistently to discover natural connections between curricular themes, learning objectives, and innovative uses of technology. The scenarios given earlier in this chapter provide concrete instances of four guidelines that we have discovered to be instrumental in designing technology-related units, such as "Creatures that Fly in the Night Sky":

1. Collect, display, and demonstrate themed children's books and software related to the theme.
2. Design computer-based learning center activities connected to the theme.
3. Enhance sociodramatic play that connects the theme and computer-based activities.
4. Provide occasions for celebrating children's computer experiences and products.

First, collections of thematically related children's books and software are displayed, shared, and discussed. Just as books are selected to provide a variety of genres and perspectives on a theme, software can be selected to provide various types of literacy experiences related to the theme. Appropriate software for young children should be easy to open, easy to use, highly interactive, responsive to student choices, and, ideally, related to the other forms of classroom literacy experiences and skills instruction.

Some of the materials for Ms. Martin's unit consist of several fictional and informational books; two puppets, with a puppet staging area; and three software programs that are displayed on a bookshelf close to the computer center. Her daily routine includes shared reading of one of the books or shared viewing of one of the software applications. On one day, she reads aloud the book *Stella Luna* (Cannon, 1993). Children discuss the story plot, the characters, and ways that the author of this fictional story helps them to explore their feelings about bats.

On another day, she conducts a shared viewing of the CD-ROM *My First Incredible Amazing Dictionary* (1995). Ms. Martin has a large monitor that allows her to display the computer output to all of her students. Much as a big book is recommended for sharing stories and concepts about print with a large group of children, a large monitor or a projector is recommended for shared viewing of software. Ms. Martin's shared viewing consists of the following steps:

• She begins by briefly introducing the title and general purpose of the software and then stating a specific purpose for interacting with the program. In our example, her purpose is to find definitions and see illustrations related to unit topics. This activity helps her students understand that different software has different purposes and must be approached strategically, depending on one's intentions. In other words, the decisions made before using the software will depend upon the intent. In this instance, the teacher shows students how to access definitions through an alphabet index or a search-and-find function. Mr. Saunders encourages a somewhat different purpose—to read for pleasure and understanding, while decoding all of the words—and makes his purpose clear to the children.

• Next, Ms. Martin reads or clicks on audio messages and animation that appear on the screen. While navigating through the program, she briefly explains how selecting particular options helps to meet the previously stated goal of learning more about vocabulary related to the unit. While navigating through the program, children may be invited to take turns operating the software or offering opinions about the importance of various types of information included in the program. This activity allows children to develop strategies for making decisions, while using the program on their own later.

• Last, after a shared viewing, Ms. Martin encourages the children to discuss critically the information, presentation of the content, and the operation of the program itself. This activity helps students develop the ability to analyze the software critically and to take a critical stance in using digital material, just as we hope they will in using conventional printed materials. Mr. Saunders likewise engages his students in brief discussions, and one of his motives is to monitor their comprehension.

Second, center activities include computer-related options aimed at accomplishing various literacy objectives. Ms. Martin's students all worked in the same computer center on the same day, yet they all selected different activities. By being provided with choices, Ms. Martin's children learn how to select an activity that they find interesting and meaningful. They are also given occasions for making sense of topics across various classroom activities that include computer explorations. When children bring objects with them to the computer center, they may use the objects to inspire stories and illustrations, to focus them on the topic, and to help them acquire information from different sources. As Schwartz (1985) has pointed out, three-dimensional objects such as a stuffed animal or a book may help children connect to a similar, two-dimensional object they see on the computer screen.

For example, after hearing Ms. Martin read *Stella Luna*, Aerial and Jasmine interact in what we have called a "screen and book read-along" (Labbo & Ash, 1998) in the computer center; that is, children connect the audio, text, and animation on the screen with the print and illustration of the book by turning the virtual pages on the screen and the real pages in the book simultaneously. They point to words in the book as they are read on the screen. Whether children choose to listen to an electronic book, echo read, or chorally read, our research suggests that the listening version of an electronic story can help children develop a sense of story, extend their vocabulary, increase knowledge of words, and enrich concepts about print (McKenna, 1998).

In Mr. Saunders's class, when beginning readers click on unfamiliar words and hear them pronounced, they make substantial gains in sight-word acquisition, provided they can already name letters and recognize word boundaries (McKenna & Watkins, 1994, 1995, 1996). We have obtained the same results with older, struggling readers (McKenna, Cowart, & Watkins, 1997; McKenna & Shaffield, 2002).

Third, sociodramatic or dramatic play is related to the unit theme and to the use of technology. In Ms. Martin's classroom, the sociodramatic play center was transformed into a puppet theater equipped with puppets related to the characters in the books and software. Reenacting and often extending the story through dramatic puppet play gives children additional occasions for trying out characterizations, reinforcing story structure, and reliving story plots.

When sociodramatic play centers are enriched with literacy props, including a computer or even a cardboard model of a computer, children gain insights into the role of technology and literacy in various cultural and workplace settings (see Labbo & Ash, 1998; Neuman & Roskos, 1992). For example, if a unit theme focuses on various ways to travel, the sociodramatic play center may be transformed into an imaginary travel agency. Children may make tickets, time tables, maps, travel posters, destination booklets, and passports to use in their play scenarios. The office may be set up with a cardboard model of a computer, available at local office supply stores, a play telephone, notepads, nameplates on desks, credit card facsimiles, and brochures. An interview with a travel agent or a field trip to a travel agency can help children understand how the office works, the role of literacy in the work that takes place there, what types of conversational discourse are appropriate in that setting, and how computers are an integral part of the environment. By playing in the center, children have opportunities to enrich their schemas about workplace forms and functions of literacy.

Mr. Saunders employs a different approach to play, encouraging his students to explore the hidden features of e-books. They do so with partners and delight in taking turns with the mouse. This use of play is not sociodramatic, to be sure, but it is certainly social and affords an enjoyable opportunity for students to learn from one another in concert.

Fourth, children's computer experiences and work are celebrated. When children learn how to use a computer to accomplish their communicative tasks, teachers can invite them to demonstrate and explain their newfound knowledge to their classmates. Collections of students' theme-related work may be bound into a class book, exhibited as artwork, or displayed in a computer presentation, such as an electronic slide show. As is the case with printed materials, celebrating accomplishments and finished products involving digital materials enhances motivation and engagement. One example is Mr. Saunders's use of text-to-speech software to allow his students' to share written work with one another. Doing so apprises the children at an early age that reading and writing are reciprocal processes in which literate people engage for meaningful purposes. With adaptations, teachers can easily apply these approaches with children in the upper elementary school grades.

Another example involves our work with students in the upper elementary school grades. We found that involving teachers and students in creating multimedia book reviews on the computer had far greater benefits for reading and writing than did conventional book reports. Students were much more engaged in creating the multimedia book reviews, and we found that their use of technology to respond to their reading involved them in a much richer socially interactive process. These benefits were derived partly from the fact that, unlike conventional book reports, the multimedia book reviews were stored in a searchable database that was easily accessible to other students looking for books to read and to parents who visited the school at various times (including a school technology fair). Inevitably too, students' interactions about the books they were reading took place incidentally, in the context of celebrating their accomplishments in mastering the technology. For example, when one student eagerly explained to another, who was an equally avid listener, how he had added sound effects to his book review, the latter student incidentally discovered an interest in the book that was the subject of the review. This example also illustrates how celebrating accomplishments in one medium can enhance involvement in another medium.

Our work (Reinking & Watkins, 2000) suggests that when teachers make children's multimedia book reports accessible through a networked framework that is authored and presented on hypertext, students electronically share book titles, exchange information about authors, and consider various responses to books. Additionally, children can make intertextual links, or electronic connective paths, between information in their own book reports that is related to information in the reports of their classmates. Having easy access and tools to make such links gives students a capability to manage the exchange of information that is unique to an electronic environment.

DIVERSE OPPORTUNITIES FOR COLLABORATION

Children who collaborate while working on the computer have opportunities to construct conventional and electronic literacy knowledge. Traditional writing processes employing traditional paper-and-pencil tools are enhanced by the malleable screen, the keyboard, and the cutting and pasting tools of technology. Additionally, Internet and e-mail interactions foster unique forms for students' socially constructed learning experiences.

For example, a process-writing approach to composition, such as Writing Workshop, can be enhanced by computer-based collaborations. When children brainstorm, write drafts, revise, edit, and publish with a word-processing program, they can focus more on managing and organizing their ideas and less on tedious or mechanical aspects of writing (Jones, 1994). When writing is supported by a word-processing program, the computer may be viewed as an interactive partner in the writing process. Such a view is especially warranted when a child's communicative intentions involve multimedia, such as audio and video. Creating high-quality final drafts is also facilitated by desktop publishing capabilities such as formatting text, incorporating graphics, and selecting typefaces. Wild and Braid (1996) note that collaborative or cooperative computer-related word-processing experiences foster children's cognitively oriented talk that is focused on the task of writing.

We believe that it is crucial for teachers to provide enough time for children to be able to compose on the computer, and not just type in a handwritten draft, so they can print out their work. To reap the benefits of technology, and, indeed, to prepare children to use the tools of contemporary writing, word processing must be integrated into all phases of the writing process. Students may keep an electronic file of their work, such as a reflective journal, topic ideas, responses to books, works in an early draft stage, works to be edited or spell-checked, or works to be read and responded to by a peer. In these instances, the computer is used as an organizer, a manager, and an electronic writing folder, similar to a conventional portfolio. However, unlike a conventional portfolio, an electronic one reinforces the idea that electronic writing is never a final product. Each electronic file awaits future modification.

Paired keyboarding occurs when one child who has knowledge about computer operations and the Internet works with another, who is less knowledgeable about accessing information from the Internet. Peters (1996) suggests that such interactions extend the less-able partner's zone of proximal development, enabling the child to internalize strategies for successful explorations. Leu and Leu (2000) have argued for a project approach to Internet use, both because of its collaborative nature and because expertise can be shared among students. When students reach the middle grades, projects of all kinds present teachers with highly motivating possibilities (Miller, 2003), and linking projects in various ways to technology seems especially promising.

Other effective collaborations involve a form of electronic pen pals. Garner and Gillingham (1998) explain how students use e-mail to communicate effectively with students in various geographic regions. Beach and Lundell (1998) report that shy students become more interactive and even develop online personalities when they exchange messages through electronic communication systems.

SPECIAL POPULATIONS

Technology can support the literacy learning needs of various types of learners who may be mainstreamed into the classroom. Students at all grade levels who struggle with reading and writing may benefit from particular computer applications. Nonfluent readers, reluctant readers, or children for whom English is a second language may also benefit from features of software. We believe that teachers should approach the use of technology with special populations by following the guidelines we have outlined, namely, through teacher-interactive demonstrations, thematic integration and innovation of software and books, and diverse collaboration.

Supporting Struggling Readers and Writers with Computers

Many children who struggle with learning to read and write in elementary schools may benefit from various types of support available in electronic text formats. Traditional instructional and tutorial approaches for readers experiencing difficulty have been based on a determination of a child's strengths and weaknesses. From this traditional perspective, a teacher or a tutor decides how to support the struggling reader by presenting materials, introducing skills, and managing reading practice at a slower pace than that of the regular classroom (Walmsley & Allington, 1995). Once struggling readers have become familiar with unique features of electronic hypertexts through interactive-teacher or peer demonstrations, they may be allowed to self-select the type of support they believe is the most beneficial, thereby maintaining a pace similar to that of the regular classroom.

How readers use supported text will vary with their developmental level. Emergent readers, for example, will gain more from accessing the full listening version of a text than from more advanced resources. Children like those in Mr. Saunders's class, who are functioning within the decoding stage, can be expected to rely heavily on digitized pronunciations. Those who are approaching fluency will have greater recourse to glossary entries, prose simplifications, digitized video clips, and the like, as they endeavor to acquire content from expository text (Anderson-Inman & Horney, 1998). At this stage, their comprehension will also benefit from accessing linked resources, such as graphic organizers, databases, or electronic encyclopedias. Because the efficacy of these resources is based on aligning software use with a child's stage of reading development, it is important that assessment be aimed at precisely determining that stage, so that a teacher is able to guide the child toward the most appropriate use of such resources (McKenna, Reinking, Labbo, & Kieffer, 1999; Reinking, Labbo, & McKenna, 2000).

For example, a small proportion of struggling middle-grade readers still require extensive decoding support if they are to read successfully. Determining this need and then providing electronic text equipped with support in the form of digitized pronunciations available on demand can dramatically affect their performance. The two applications Mr. Saunders uses in grade one (commercial e-books and teacher-constructed electronic text) have been successfully employed with students in the middle grades who continue to experience difficulties. Hasselbring (1999) provided Don Johnston's *Start-to-Finish* electronic books to this struggling, older population and reported significantly improved comprehension and motivation. McKenna and Shaffield (2002) used *Write Out Loud* to create tailored texts (including scanned textbook passages) for a similar sample of students, and observed increased confidence and success as a result of the support the students received.

A future abundance of supported text will mean both drawbacks and advantages for the struggling reader. Surely, one of the challenges of electronic literacy is the need to develop the ability to navigate strategically through hypertext environments in order to achieve specific purposes. Even when the hypertextual elements are limited to a few helpful resources, the effect of so many choices can appear labyrinthine to a struggling reader. On the positive side, students will be able to read text independently that would have frustrated them without the built-in support of what McKenna (1998) has called "electronic scaffolding" (p. 47). Indeed, the very notion of the instructional reading level will have to be re-examined in electronic environments, because many struggling readers will be able to read at or near their listening levels (McKenna, Reinking, & Labbo, 1997). Mr. Saunders takes full advantage of this potential in his first-grade classroom computer center, where beginning readers success-fully negotiate books written well beyond their decoding ability.

Supporting Nonfluent, Reluctant, or LEP Readers and Writers with Computers

Children who are nonfluent or reluctant readers may benefit from re-peated or echo readings of text that is digitally read aloud. While read-ing to learn new information, a struggling reader may find it useful to compose and record summaries of passages on an electronic clipboard. Burns (1996) notes that multimedia technology can be used to facilitate the English language acquisition of non-native speakers. Multimedia re-sources accommodate the needs of students with limited English profi-ciency (LEP) as they progress in second-language proficiency and gain specific content area knowledge. Some electronic, interactive books have the option of listening to the story in Spanish or another language. More research about the effectiveness of such programs on children's acquisi-tion of a second language, and their understanding of specific reading passage content, is needed.

Finally, speech-synthesizer software offers some promising directions for supporting the spelling development of LEP or nonfluent writers. Shilling (1997) introduced the use of a basic word-processing program and an external speech synthesis unit that gave the children studied a choice of listening to a word they had attempted to spell on the screen, listening to the entire text that they had typed on the screen, or not using speech synthesis at all. Findings suggest that before children consistently benefit from synthesizer software, they need to have acquired some ba-sic concepts about print, phonemic awareness, and a notion of the alpha-betic principle. As the capabilities of speech-synthesizer software improve, continued research in this area is warranted.

IMPLICATIONS FOR FUTURE RESEARCH AND PRACTICE

We hope it is clear in this chapter that digital forms of reading and writ-ing not only can be but also must be integrated into the mainstream of literacy instruction for children in the elementary school. Establishing a program of best practices in literacy instruction today means acknowledg-ing that literacy is no longer a monolithic concept defined by print, pages, and books. Attention to conventional uses of written language centered in a world of print must be balanced by attention to how digital technologies are increasingly moving toward the center of what it means to be literate. Teachers, even those who teach children at the earliest stages of literacy development, must begin to initiate their students into the use of digital forms of expression, with a vigor equal to that they have dedicated to more traditional printed forms.

We would be the first to admit that this is no easy task. To integrate technology into their teaching, teachers must confront many challenges on multiple levels. Not the least of the challenges many teachers face is coming to terms with their own predisposition to favor printed materials, sometimes accompanied by a devaluation of digital reading and writing as inferior. It is hard for some teachers to consider, let alone accept, that emerging forms of electronic reading and writing may be as informative, pedagogically useful, and aesthetically pleasing as more familiar printed forms. To consider that electronic forms of text may in some instances even be superior is undoubtedly more difficult.

A reluctance to embrace technology is often sustained by insecurities over using computer technology. It is not trivial to note that today, for the first time in the modern era, teachers have an obligation to prepare children to become literate in ways in which the teachers themselves might not be fully literate. This situation is created by the juggernaut of change that has occurred in the lifetimes of many teachers today who are witnessing the digital revolution, but who themselves have to some degree been left in its wake. It is hard enough to think about preparing children for the fuzzy future of literacy in a posttypographic world. It is even harder to prepare children for a world in which our print-based literacy skills are less central, let alone for a world that may negate some of our most cherished assumptions about literacy.

Beyond these conceptual issues is a host of practical obstacles that teachers must often overcome. Although the base of computer hardware in schools is generally seen as adequate, many schools do not have the physical or administrative infrastructure needed to use their computers effectively (Morra, 1995). For example, computers are of little use if there is not adequate wiring in places where teachers and students need to use them. Neither are they useful if there is no opportunity for teachers to learn how to use them and to become familiar with software, and how it might be integrated into instruction. Nor are they useful when there are no established instructional niches in the curriculum and school day for computer use, especially in the language arts, at least beyond word processing. Moreover, there are logistical problems involved in bringing students and new technologies together in time and space. This challenge is often faced by teachers who have only one or two computers in their classrooms, or who only have access to a computer lab for an hour or two a week.

So how are teachers to cope in achieving balance between a focus on conventional literacy and electronic literacy? We have found some commonalities among teachers who have successfully achieved this balance, especially among those who do not gravitate naturally to technology. Most teachers have been realistic about both the obstacles they face in using technology and their expectations given these obstacles. Often, they have found a single computer-based activity or application that connects powerfully with their own teaching and their personal conceptions of literacy. They may have found it at a conference, in a university course, or through a colleague, but it is something they find hard to imagine teaching without, once they have discovered it. It may be a simple program addressing in some new way a problematic reading skill, or it may be a more open-ended and sophisticated application involving the Internet. For many teachers, finding such an application stimulates them to confront the challenges of using technology in their teaching. For them, it serves as a gateway to seeking more balance between conventional and digital literacies.

We recommend that teachers who wish to integrate technology into their literacy teaching consider several ideal criteria aimed at transcending perfunctory uses of computers. If technology is used to advance their goals of conventional print-based literacy, software applications should, at a minimum, be consistent with what the teacher knows and believes to be true about reading instruction (Miller & Burnett, 1987). Ideally, use should be made of the unique capabilities of the computer to go beyond conventional materials, addressing some problematic area of literacy that would benefit from a new approach.

Different criteria are relevant if technology is used more to initiate students and teachers into the world of digital literacy. First, like other literacy activities, technology-related activities should ideally involve authentic and personally meaningful communication. Electronic worksheets are in the long run no more meaningful and useful to students' development than are printed ones. Using the computer to enable a kindergarten child to read more texts independently is more worthwhile, as is enabling third-grade children to use e-mail to correspond with other children and adults around the country. Another ideal criterion is that the activity will allow teachers and students to compare and contrast electronic and digital forms of reading and writing. For example, how is an electronic storybook different from a printed one? What are the advantages and limitations of a multimedia encyclopedia over a printed one? How is e-mail similar to or different from sending a letter mailed at the post office? Finally, computer-based activities that increase literacy in the digital domain should allow students to develop functional strategies for reading and writing electronic texts. For example, when might it be appropriate to seek out the pronunciation or definition of a word while reading? How are key words used efficiently to locate information in a computer database?

As Bruce and Hogan (1998) point out, technologies that are truly integrated into daily life are invisible. Fully integrated technologies blend into the environment by virtue of their repeated and natural use. No one views stairs leading from one floor to another as a complicated technology—except someone who is confined to a wheelchair. Integrating computer-based activities into literacy instruction in schools has a long way to go before new technologies are completely unremarkable. Nonetheless, teachers who choose not to wait until digital reading and writing are so widely used as to be scarcely noticed are laying the groundwork for the day when computer technology will be as fundamental to literacy as print technology is today.

DISCUSSION AND ACTIVITIES

Successful integration of computer technology into your own instruction begins with self-assessment. Consider the following lists of hardware and classroom applications. Check the equipment you have available to you and that you feel competent to use (C) or that is available but that you are not comfortable using (A). Then mark the applications that you regularly employ (R) that are not germane to your assignment or grade level (NA), or that you rarely or never employ but that (on the basis of what you have learned from this chapter) may prove useful to you in the future (F).

Hardware

_____ One or more classroom-based microcomputers
_____ High-speed Internet access in your classroom
_____ Scanner
_____ Digital camera
_____ Zip and CD drives
_____ Camcorder

Applications

_____ Integrated Learning System (i.e., a comprehensive, prescriptive software package)
_____ Decoding software that conforms to best practice research
_____ Comprehension software that stresses both higher order and literal thinking
_____ Vocabulary reinforcement software
_____ Electronic books

_____ Text-to-speech software
_____ Software for emerging literates that conforms to theory
_____ Word-processing software
_____ Kid-friendly desktop publishing software with multimedia
 capabilities

Now look again at the hardware you have marked with an "A" and the applications you have marked with an "F." Consider the following questions.

1. Where might you look for useful information that would enhance your expertise?
2. With which of your colleagues might you collaborate to learn more?
3. When would be a convenient time to begin?
4. How might you record your experiences with new applications in order to learn from them and refine your future practice?

Taking stock of what you know and what you might attempt with the tools you have is an important first step, but it is a purely academic exercise unless you act on the results. We encourage you to take the next step and believe it will broaden your practice if you do.

REFERENCES

Anderson-Inman, L., & Horney, M. A. (1998). Transforming text for at-risk readers. In D. Reinking, M. C. McKenna, L. D. Labbo, & R. D. Kieffer (Eds.), *Handbook of literacy and technology: Transformations in a post-typographic world* (pp. 15–43). Mahwah, NJ: Erlbaum.

Beach, R., & Lundell, D. (1998). Early adolescents' use of computer-mediated communication in writing and reading and reading. In D. Reinking, L. D. Labbo, M. C. McKenna, & R. D. Kieffer (Eds.), *Handbook of literacy and technology: Transformations in a post-typographic world* (pp. 93–112). Mahwah, NJ: Erlbaum.

Bruce, B. C., & Hogan, M. P. (1998). The disappearance of technology: Toward an ecological model of literacy. In D. Reinking, L. D. Labbo, M. C. McKenna, & R. D. Kieffer (Eds.), *Handbook of literacy and technology: Transformations in a post-typographic world* (pp. 269–281). Mahwah, NJ: Erlbaum.

Burns, D. (1996, March). Technology in the ESL classroom. *Technology and Learning*, pp. 50–52.

Fatorous, C. (1995). Young children using computers: Planning appropriate learning experiences. *Australian Journal of Early Childhood, 29*(2), 1–6.

Flood, J., Heath, S. B., & Lapp, D. (Eds.). (1997). *Handbook of research on teaching literacy through the communicative and visual arts.* New York: Macmillan.

Fox, B. J., & Mitchell, M. J. (2000). Using technology to support word recognition, spelling, and vocabulary acquisition. In S. B. Wepner, W. J. Valmont, & R. Thurlow (Eds.), *Linking literacy and technology: A guide for K–8 classrooms* (pp. 42–75). Newark, DE: International Reading Association.

Garner, R., & Gillingham, M. G. (1998). The Internet in the classroom: Is it the end of transmission-oriented pedagogy? In D. Reinking, L. D. Labbo, M. C. McKenna, & R. D. Kieffer (Eds.), *Handbook of literacy and technology: Transformations in a post-typographic world* (pp. 221–231). Mahwah, NJ: Erlbaum.

Hasselbring, T. (1999, May). *The computer doesn't embarrass me.* Paper presented at the meeting of the International Reading Association, San Diego, CA.

Haughland, S. W. (1992). The effect of computer software on preschool children's developmental gains. *Journal of Computing in Childhood Education, 3,* 15–29.

Hickman, C. (1994). *KidPix2, Version 2.* Novato, CA: Broderbund Software.

Jones, I. (1994). The effect of a word processor on the written composition of second-grade pupils. *Computers in the Schools, 11*(2), 43–54.

Kamil, M. L., Kim, H., & Intrator, S. (2000). Effects of other technologies on literacy and literacy learning. In M. L. Kamil, P. B. Mosenthal , P. D. Pearson, & R. Barr (Eds.), *Handbook of reading research* (Vol. 3, pp. 773–791). Mahwah, NJ: Erlbaum.

Labbo, L. D. (1996). A semiotic analysis of young children's symbol making in a classroom computer center. *Reading Research Quarterly, 31,* 356–385.

Labbo, L. D. (2000). 12 things young children can do with a talking book in a classroom computer center. *The Reading Teacher, 53,* 542–546.

Labbo, L. D., & Ash, G. E. (1998). Supporting young children's computer-related literacy development in classroom centers. In S. Neuman & K. Roskos (Eds.), *Children achieving: Instructional practices in early literacy* (pp. 180–197). Newark, DE: International Reading Association.

Labbo, L. D., Eakle, A. J., & Montero, M. K. (2002, May). Digital language experience approach: Using digital photographs and software as a language experience approach innovation. *Reading Online, 5*(8). Available at *www.readingonline.org/electronic/elec_index.asp?HREF=labbo2/index.html*

Labbo, L. D., & Kuhn, M. R. (2000). Weaving chains of affect and cognition: A young child's understanding of CD-ROM talking books. *Journal of Literacy Research, 32,* 187–210.

Labbo, L. D., Montero, M. K., & Eakle, A. J. (2001, October). Learning how to read what's displayed on school hallway walls—and what's not. *Reading Online, 5*(3). Available at *www.readingonline.org/newliteracies/lit_index.asp?HREF=labbo/index.html*

Labbo, L. D., Phillips, M., & Murray, B. (1995–1996). "Writing to read": From inheritance to innovation and invitation. *The Reading Teacher, 49*(4), 314–321.

Labbo, L. D., & Sprague, L., with Montero, K., & Font, G. (2000, July). Connecting a computer center to themes, literature, and kindergartners' literacy needs. *Reading Online, 4.* Available at *www.readingonline.org/default.asp*

Leu, D. J. (2000). Literacy and technology: Deictic consequences for literacy education in an information age. In M. L. Kamil, P. B. Mosenthal, P. D. Pearson, & R. Barr (Eds.), *Handbook of reading research* (Vol. 3, pp. 745–772). Mahwah, NJ: Erlbaum.

Leu, D. J., & Leu, D. D. (2000). *Teaching with the Internet: Lessons from the classroom* (3rd ed.). Norwood, MA: Christopher-Gordon.

McKenna, M. C. (1998). Electronic texts and the transformation of beginning reading. In D. Reinking, M. C. McKenna, L. D. Labbo, & R. D. Kieffer (Eds.), *Handbook of literacy and technology: Transformations in a post-typographic world* (pp. 45–59). Mahwah, NJ: Erlbaum.

McKenna, M. C. (2002). Phonics software for a new millennium. *Reading and Writing Quarterly, 18,* 93–96.

McKenna, M. C., Cowart, E., & Watkins, J. W. (1997, December). *Effects of talking books on the reading growth of problem readers in second grade.* Paper presented at the meeting of the National Reading Conference, Scottsdale, AZ.

McKenna, M. C., Reinking, D., & Labbo, L. D. (1997). Using talking books with reading-disabled students. *Reading and Writing Quarterly, 13,* 185–190.

McKenna, M. C., Reinking, D., Labbo, L. D., & Kieffer, R. D. (1999). The electronic transformation of literacy and its implications for the struggling reader. *Reading and Writing Quarterly, 15,* 111–126.

McKenna, M. C., & Shaffield, M. L. (2002, May). *Creating electronic books and documents for poor decoders.* Paper to be presented at the meeting of the International Reading Association, San Francisco, CA.

McKenna, M. C., & Watkins, J. H. (1994, December). *Computer-mediated books for beginning readers.* Paper presented at the meeting of the National Reading Conference, San Diego, CA.

McKenna, M. C., & Watkins, J. H. (1995, November). *Effects of computer-mediated books on the development of beginning readers.* Paper presented at the meeting of the National Reading Conference, New Orleans, LA.

McKenna, M. C., & Watkins, J. H. (1996, December). *The effects of computer-mediated trade books on sight word acquisition and the development of phonics ability.* Paper presented at the meeting of the National Reading Conference, Charleston, SC.

Miller, L., & Burnett, J. D. (1987). Using computers as an integral aspect of elementary language arts instruction: Paradoxes, problems, and promise. In D. Reinking (Ed.), *Reading and computers: Issues for theory and practice* (pp. 178–191). New York: Teachers College Press.

Miller, S. D. (2003). How high- and low-challenge tasks affect motivation and learning: Implications for struggling learners. *Reading and Writing Quarterly, 19,* 39–57.

Morra, L. G. (1995, April). *America's schools not designed or equipped for the 21st century.* Testimony before the Subcommittee on Labor, Health and Human Services, Education and Related Agencies Committee on Appropriations, U.S. Senate. Washington, DC: U.S. General Accounting Office, ERIC Document ED 381 153.

My first incredible amazing dictionary (CD-ROM). (1995). New York: Dorling Kindersley Multimedia.

Neuman, S. B., & Roskos, K. (1992). Literacy objects as cultural tools: Effects on children's literacy behaviors in play. *Reading Research Quarterly, 27,* 202–225.

Papert, S. (1980). *Mindstorms.* New York: Basic Books.

Papert, S. (1993). *The children's machine: Rethinking school in the age of the computer.* New York: Basic Books.

Peters, J. M. (1996). Paired keyboards as a tool of Internet exploration of 3rd grade students. *Journal of Educational Computing Research, 14,* 229–242.

Reading Mansion [Computer software]. (1998). Scotts Valley, CA: Great Wave Software.

Reinking, D. (1994). *Electronic literacy.* (Perspectives in Reading Research No. 4, National Reading Research Center). Athens: University of Georgia Press.

Reinking, D., Labbo, L. D., & McKenna, M.C. (2000). From assimilation to accommodation: A developmental framework for integrating digital technologies into literacy research and instruction. *Journal of Reading Research, 23,* 110–122.

Reinking, D., & Watkins, J. (2000). A formative experiment investigating the use of multimedia book reviews to increase elementary students' independent reading. *Reading Research Quarterly, 35,* 384–419.

Richards, J. C., & McKenna, M.C. (Eds.). (2003). *Teaching for multiple literacies: Cases and commentaries from K–6 classrooms.* Hillsdale, NJ: Erlbaum.

Schwartz, S. (1985). Microcomputers and young children: An exploratory study. In *Issues for educators: A monograph series.* Flushing, NY: School of Education, Queens College, City College of New York.

Shilling, W. (1997). Young children using computers to make discoveries about written language. *Early Childhood Education Journal, 24,* 253–259.

Vygotsky, L. (1978). *Mind in society: The development of higher psychological processes.* Cambridge, MA: Harvard University Press.

Walmsley, S. A., & Allington, R. L. (1995). Redefining and reforming instructional support programs for at-risk students. In R. L. Allington & S. A. Walmsley (Eds.), *No quick fix: Rethinking literacy programs in America's elementary schools* (pp. 19–44). Newark, DE/New York: International Reading Association and Teachers College Press.

Wild, M., & Braid, P. (1996). Children's talk in cooperative groups. *Journal of Computer Assisted Learning, 12,* 216–321.

Children's Literature

Cannon, J. (1993). *Stella Luna.* New York: Harcourt Brace.

Chapter 16

ACHIEVING BEST PRACTICES IN LITERACY INSTRUCTION

James W. Cunningham
Kimberly H. Creamer

This chapter will:

- List and explain the essential conditions for establishing a best practices approach to literacy instruction.
- Describe the conditions that prevent the establishment of a best practices approach.
- Discuss steps for working toward a best practices approach despite the hindrances.

In the first edition of this book, this chapter began with a message of both hope and skepticism: Hope that we, as a field, could and would eventually achieve best practices in literacy instruction; Skepticism about the likelihood of that occurring in the near future. Four years later, we must begin this revised chapter with the same mix of optimism and pessimism. Why do we remain optimistic and hopeful? Because the increasing teacher and principal shortages are making it more difficult for governmental and educational officials to force literacy educators to teach in ways they do not believe are best for children. In many areas of the country, there are none to take their places if they leave to go to other schools or districts, where they will be freer to teach as they believe they should. Why do we remain somewhat pessimistic? Because the conditions necessary for best practices in literacy instruction have not significantly improved in recent years.

The first part of this chapter relates the conditions and hindrances to the establishment of best practices in teaching reading and writing, and considers the likelihood that the present situation may soon improve or deteriorate. In the second and final part of this chapter, we discuss what all of us can do as individuals to work for the day when best practices will characterize the literacy instruction that U.S. public school students receive.

ESSENTIAL CONDITIONS FOR THE ESTABLISHMENT OF BEST PRACTICES IN AMERICAN LITERACY INSTRUCTION

There are at least two essential conditions for the establishment of best practices in literacy instruction in pre-K to grade 12 public schooling: (1) We must stop holding teachers accountable for student literacy learning, and (2) faddism in literacy instruction must give way to a continuing professional consensus.

We Must Stop Holding Teachers Accountable
for Student Literacy Learning

Whether in literacy, mathematics, history, or any other school subject, it is antiprofessional to hold teachers accountable for student learning. Think about it. You cannot successfully sue your doctor just because you did not get well, or your dentist because your teeth still hurt. You cannot successfully sue your lawyer just because you were convicted or lost a civil case, or your clinical psychologist because you are still anxiety ridden. But you can successfully sue your doctor, dentist, lawyer, or clinical psychologist. The basis for any successful suit, however, must be proof that the professional failed to conform to best practices when treating or defending you. The label for such suits, "malpractice," says it all; they are not called "maloutcome" suits! Why can these professionals and others like them be successfully sued but teachers cannot? Because teachers are being held accountable for student learning outcomes. If we held doctors and clinical psychologists accountable for healing people, dentists accountable for ending tooth pain, and lawyers accountable for winning their cases, then none of these professionals could be successfully sued for malpractice either.

Although the ability to be sued successfully is an unfortunate negative indicator of whether one's profession has established best practices, the more-than-compensating positive side is that the members of such professions are free to practice what they know is best, without fear of an outcome they cannot control. Again, think about it. There are lawyers who spend their careers defending the poor or the victims of various kinds of discrimination. Although they seldom get rich, and their percentage of legal victories is often relatively low, they do not live under the constant fear that their state or local government may come in and take over their jobs because they are not "getting results." They are free to practice their profession without fear, where it is needed most.

Similarly, there are physicians who spend their careers treating the victims of diseases for which there is currently no known cure, or for which the cure rate is very low. These physicians do not fear that they will be fired or put on probation because they are unable to cure more of their patients. They, too, are free to practice their profession without fear, where it is needed most.

In contrast to these professions, consider the teaching of literacy. As the push for teacher accountability to reading and writing test scores increases, fewer and fewer teachers want to teach literacy in schools or classrooms with large numbers of struggling readers and writers. And who can blame them? Those who do choose to teach in such places do so at the peril of their careers and reputations. The teachers who are rewarded with merit pay and the praise of their "superiors" are usually those who teach in schools and classrooms with large percentages of middle-class children from highly literate and academically supportive homes.

As long as we hold teachers accountable for student learning, we will not, and cannot, have best practices. To establish best professional practices in literacy instruction, it must be the practices, not the professional, that are held responsible for teaching students to read and write better.

Why We Will Not Soon Stop Holding Teachers Accountable for Student Literacy Learning

There are at least two reasons why it will probably be a long time before we have a best practices model of literacy education in place of holding teachers accountable for students' literacy learning: (1) the nature of our current education elites, and (2) the current politics of public education.

Education Elites

Too many professors of education, employees of state departments of public instruction and central offices in school districts, and public school principals insist on maintaining the current accountability system in some form. Why? Because they do not have to know anything except how to threaten and cajole teachers into "increasing achievement." In a best practices approach, they would actually have to know what those best practices are and how to support and guide teachers' implementation of those best practices in classrooms. It is much easier for them to use, or advocate the use of, carrots and sticks to get teachers to try harder to do what they themselves could not do.

The Politics of Public Education

Democracy is a very good thing, but it has its limits. Why do we not just let people vote on what the best treatments are for, say, lung cancer? Why do we not allow ads in the media for all proposed lung cancer treatments? Would that not be the democratic way? Of course, laetrile, vitamin C, and the laying on of hands might well become the treatments of choice, while chemotherapy, radiation therapy, and surgery might become rarely used!

Politics should play no role whatsoever in determining specific professional practices. Think about it. From professional encounters, you ordinarily cannot tell whether your doctor, dentist, lawyer, or clinical psychologist is a Democrat or a Republican, a conservative or a liberal. Yet, currently, we have representatives and senators in Washington, governors and legislators in many states, and local school board members across the country making curricular and instructional decisions in literacy—prescribing this practice, proscribing that practice, and micromanaging school and classroom instructional activities. Yet the vast majority of those politicians could not teach successfully even one day in a public school classroom.

In 2000, the National Institute of Child Health and Human Development (NICHD) published the report of the National Reading Panel. This panel, commissioned by the NICHD and the U.S. Secretary of Education at the request of the U.S. Congress in 1997, was charged to review and assess the research on teaching reading, with implications for both classroom practice and further research. Asserting "an evidence-based assessment of the scientific research literature" (The National Reading Panel, 2000a, cover; 2000b, cover), this report has already been used to inform policy on literacy education and has begun to serve as a means of enforcement for these policies. In spite of serious flaws (Cunningham, 2001; Pressley, 2002), this report is being used by political conservatives in Washington to mandate their favorite approaches to teaching reading in the public schools of America, especially for poor children.

Why is literacy instruction so political? Because it is so important, because such a large portion of local and state budgets go toward the support of public education, and because everyone has experienced or witnessed some of its failures. Health and medical issues have recently become more political for the same reasons. Why are politicians not legislating medical treatments the way they are legislating literacy instructional materials and methods? Because medicine has a professional consensus, and we do not.

Faddism in Literacy Instruction Must Give Way to a Continuing Professional Consensus

Instead of holding teachers accountable for student literacy learning, our society must hold them accountable for conforming to best practices in their teaching of literacy. Any literacy teacher who conformed to best practice in his or her teaching would then be protected from responsibility for any lack of student literacy learning. To improve student literacy learning in schools or classes where best practices had been used, the definition of what constitutes best practice in that type of setting would have to be changed. In other words, teachers of literacy would be held accountable for employing best practices, and those practices would be held accountable for student literacy learning. The direct link between literacy teachers and student learning outcomes would be severed and replaced by the indirect link all true professions have. Only then will those of us who teach literacy have a profession like dentistry, medicine, clinical psychology, and the law. When we have a true profession with best practices in place, those practices can gradually help achieve the goal of helping all America's children read and write well. Unfortunately, the faddism that has long marked literacy instruction in America prevents the establishment of best practices. Before best practices can be established, faddism must give way to a professional consensus about what constitutes state-of-the-art reading and writing instruction.

The Various Lores of Literacy Instruction Must Be Reconciled

There are many identifiable methods of teaching reading or writing, including methods for teaching particular aspects of the reading or writing process at particular developmental levels. For the most part, each of these methods has a lore—a tradition and a set of beliefs—governing it. Although we would be far worse off without the accumulated wisdom of teachers and other literacy educators, the competition of these lores in the arenas of public and professional opinion prevents us from increasing our overall success very much, if at all—especially for struggling readers and writers.

The problem with lore is that it resists change. Because it depends on tradition and beliefs for its power, it must never allow those traditions and beliefs to change more than would be comfortable for most adherents. Quantum leaps of progress in a lore are just not possible. For example, when medicine was governed by lore, bleeding and the lack of hand washing continued for centuries in spite of few real successes and numerous failures. Because medicine became a profession with established best practices, the rate of change in how different diseases are treated is almost constant.

Best Practices Must Be Defined and Modified by Professional Institutions and Procedures

Best practices are not established in a field because practitioners can generally agree on what the best practices are. Best practices are established because the practitioners can generally agree on how they will decide which practices are best. It is the commitment to a process of evaluating practice, rather than a set of practices, that constitutes the beginning of the establishment of best practices.

In most professions with established best practices, the process to which practitioners are generally committed involves funded research on a broad range of professional practices and representative boards of professionals empowered to modify best practice given new research findings. Literacy education will not have best practices until the majority of us agree on how to settle our disagreements. Almost certainly, the means for achieving a continuing professional consensus in literacy education will include funded research on a broad range of literacy professional practices and representative boards of literacy professionals empowered to apply that research in defining and modifying best literacy instructional practices. Unfortunately, we are worse off than we were 4 years ago, because the National Reading Panel was convened in opposition to professional institutions and procedures. First, the Panel members were selected by the government rather than by professional organizations, at the behest of the government, a huge difference that seeks to impose rather than discover a professional consensus. The members of the Panel were obviously selected because they were expected to go along with what the NICHD had already decided the "scientific" approach to teaching reading should be. Second, the methodology employed by the Panel allowed it to ignore the vast majority of the studies of reading and reading instruction published in refereed research journals.

Why Faddism Will Not Soon Give Way to Professional Consensus

Faddism results from the competition between lores and coalitions of lores. As soon as the lore that is currently in fashion for teaching literacy is widely shown to be less than satisfactory, it is quickly displaced by a competing lore. In several years, the same process will again be repeated.

A Star Trek *Pendulum*?

That education, especially literacy education, is a swinging pendulum is an old metaphor. Any of us who have been around long enough to experience a pendulum swing, such as the most recent one in the mid- to late 1990s from whole language and silent reading to intensive phonics and oral reading, knows that there is certainly truth to the metaphor. By the time one has experienced several such pendulum swings, that person no longer questions the metaphor. There is, however, a serious problem with the pendulum metaphor. Watch a clock that has a pendulum. A real pendulum spends as much time at any one point in the arc as it does in another. That is demonstrably not the case with the literacy education pendulum. Our pendulum spends almost all of its time more or less at rest against one side of the swinging area. When it does swing, it goes through the middle points so swiftly that some question whether it really enters a *Star Trek*-style warp and instantaneously moves to the opposite extreme, without ever going through the middle! Our pendulum swings may each be more like a Kuhnian paradigm shift: a revolution followed by an extended period of "normal" practice defined by that revolution.

If the swinging pendulum, albeit with long periods of rest at each extreme, is a metaphor with much truth to commend it, one must wonder why it works that way. Our answer is simple: The literacy education pendulum is swung or held in place by passion. Consider the eras that American reading instruction has experienced over the past five decades:

- A phonics era (1956–1964)
- A language, literature, and discovery-learning era (1965–1974)
- An individualized specific-skills instruction era (1975–1986)
- A language, literature, and discovery-learning era (1987–1995)
- A phonics and oral reading era (1996–200?)

Of course, different schools and school systems enter or leave an era at various times and implement the new fad to varying degrees, but it is a rare school or system whose reading program remains totally uninfluenced throughout an era.

We believe the case can be made that each of these recent eras in reading education was brought into currency by the zeal of true believers and the tireless efforts of national leaders whom, if this were a history, we could name. As the passion of one set of zealots waned and that of another set waxed, the pendulum was finally wrested from its position and quickly swung over to the other side, where it was again held in position by passion for another 9–12 years. The current advocates for phonics and oral reading are as passionate as any advocates in the history of our field, but they too will eventually have the pendulum wrested from them by advocates of an opposing view, who have grown more passionate than they.

Interestingly, and sadly, our passion hypothesis also explains why our field has never had a "balanced" or "eclectic" era, in spite of the fact that most teachers of reading are and have long been balanced/eclectic in their instructional orientation. The downside of balance/eclecticism is precisely its reasoned moderation, its lack of emotion, its innate wishy-washiness. Yet, at present, only balance/eclecticism allows us a professional means to reconcile competing lores. We do not have the funded research on a broad range of professional practices and truly representative boards of professionals empowered to modify best practice, given new research findings, that are the necessary institutions and procedures to establish best practices.

The Politicization of Educational Research

If research on professional practices is essential for the establishment and maintenance of best practices in literacy education, the recent politicization of educational research in general, and literacy educational research in particular, is a cause for additional concern. Quantitative and qualitative research have recently been taken captive by conservatives and liberals to do their bidding rather than to serve as avenues to new knowledge. For example, today, we hear calls for beginning literacy instruction to be based on (and only on) "scientific, replicable research." Of course, those who use this political slogan are demonstrably disingenuous or, at least, woefully ignorant. If they really believed that, they would be as zealously opposed to retention in grade and grammar instruction as they are in favor of synthetic phonics instruction. Moreover, their zeal for synthetic phonics would be mitigated by the fact that scientific, replicable research has so far found no difference by fourth grade on the comprehension or reading habits of children taught to read by synthetic phonics. They would stop concluding that synthetic phonics is best from studies that compared synthetic phonics with no phonics. They would stop concluding that synthetic phonics is best from studies that only found an advantage for synthetic phonics on a test of nonsense words in isolation. Yet, sadly, the research conducted or cited by those who question the research supporting synthetic phonics is often aimed only at audiences who already agree with the authors; they do not present evidence that could persuade fair-minded moderates. Until literacy educational research becomes depoliticized, faddism in literacy instruction will continue to reign.

The Extremism of the Present Is Always Justified by the Extremism of the Past

The mark of an extremist is that he or she takes the attitude that "those who are not with us are against us." Extremists divide everyone into "them" and "us" (true believers), glossing over differences between moderates and the opposite extreme. The wonderful example today of this kind of extremist thinking is how all those who question intensive, synthetic phonics as the only way to teach beginning reading are labeled by some phonics-firsters as "whole-language advocates," even if they questioned whole language in the past as strongly as they now question intensive, synthetic phonics. Of course, it was not many years ago that some in the whole-language camp labeled everyone else as "behaviorists" in a parallel manner.

If this glossing over of all but extreme differences were restricted to merely labeling moderates as members of the opposite extreme, it would be relatively harmless ("Sticks and stones may break my bones. . . ."). However, this attitude (on the part of whichever group of extremists the most recent pendulum swing has put in position of influence over literacy instruction) causes them to adopt extreme measures to rid classrooms of the vestiges of the now-discredited recent era. Without this attitude, the extremists now in the saddle would have to recognize that, in fact, they share with the moderates a disenchantment with the excesses of the recent era and would work with them to improve matters. Because they would be working together with moderates, the new era would be less extreme, more likely to work, and more likely to last beyond the 9- to 12-year period we can now expect literacy instructional eras to last. The extreme measures of the current group in power or fashion eliminate that which was good about the last era while eliminating the bad and, thereby, alienate the moderates who also had concerns about the last era. If we are ever to move from competing lores to best practices in American literacy instruction, we will have to replace the principle that the extremism of the past always justifies the extremism of the present with the principle that two wrongs do not make a right.

TAKING PROFESSIONAL ACTION IN THE CURRENT ERA

As long as we continue to hold teachers accountable for student literacy learning, and as long as faddism continues to reign in literacy instruction, we believe our field will not, indeed, cannot establish best practices in teaching reading and writing. The question then arises: What should we as literacy educators do in the meantime? To us, the answer to this question is that we should focus our efforts on improving literacy instruction school by school.

As a group, teachers are the strongest link in the educational chain, stronger than principals, school board members, supervisors, or college professors. Yet an individual teacher trying to improve literacy instruction is often powerless against the educational bureaucracy, or even against the consensus of the other teachers in his or her school. Moreover, all children deserve, and many require, a good literacy instructional program every year. One year of good literacy instruction, no matter how effective, is not enough if all our children are to realize their potential in reading and writing. Our efforts to improve American literacy instruction, therefore, cannot focus on just improving teacher education, providing literacy teachers with more money to purchase computers or other instructional materials, or having good system-wide inservices.

On the other hand, much evidence and common professional experience suggest that top-down mandates from Washington, the state capitol, or the central office are unevenly implemented at best. It is particular schools in almost every school district, with their particular principals, teachers, and communities, that excel or fail in teaching literacy. Our efforts to improve American literacy instruction, therefore, cannot focus on adopting the right commercial or other literacy program and mandating it across the board.

It seems that the school is neither too big or too small, but just right as the unit of change in literacy education, at least in the current educational environment. How then can one go about working for improved reading and writing instruction at the building level?

Help the School Achieve a Balance in Literacy Instruction

A balanced literacy program is one that has elements and components from competing lores of the past and present combined into an efficient and practical composite. Although having a balanced program will not ensure best practices in literacy instruction, it is the closest we can ever come to achieving best practices in the current educational environment. Working for balance at the building level means that, in the absence of a national or international professional consensus, individual schools can each construct their own version of how that consensus would likely look.

In our experience, most teachers are balanced/eclectic in disposition, knowing that different emphases from different eras and schools of thought can make a real contribution to some children's literacy learning. The fact that it is so difficult to implement and maintain balanced literacy instruction in schools as a whole indicates how little say teachers have in the way they are expected to teach.

Help the School Achieve a School-Wide Literacy Program

Without the support of the principal and the teachers as a whole, at least at targeted grade levels, there cannot be a true school-wide literacy program. Change can begin in one or a few classrooms as a pilot, but there still has to be leadership and consensus building among teachers if children are going to have consistent, high-quality literacy instruction year after year. Teaching all children to read and write well in a school requires a team approach. All regular education, Reading Recovery, Title 1, and special education teachers have a role to play in helping children move through the grades and toward their maximum literacy ability. The team approach does not mean that there will be no professional discretion or individual differences across teachers, but it does mean that teachers have to be willing to listen, compromise, grow, and work well together with those who disagree with them. In the absence of established best practices, two (three, four, etc.) heads are better than one.

The danger of working toward a school-wide literacy program is that a principal or district administrator will decide that it is "consistency" rather than communication and teamwork across teachers, grades, and specializations that matters for children. Indeed, we have seen a significant increase in the past 4 years of programs being mandated without any attempt to achieve a professional consensus in the school. Such mandated consistency never becomes a true school-wide literacy program. It only results in surface implementation and lip service, without the depth and quality that cannot be achieved overnight by force.

Help Teachers Execute the Fundamentals of Each Component in the School's Balanced Program

It is the nature of top-down mandates in education that those making the mandates believe it is the big things that matter (e.g., what single method of beginning reading you use, what standardized test you administer, what basal reading series you adopt, how many computers each classroom has). Actually, anyone familiar with any professional ability, from cabinet making to golf, can tell you that the little things, the fundamentals, are what really make the difference. In teaching literacy, it is the minute-to-minute, second-to-second execution of discipline and instruction, with all the affective dimensions of both, that determines whether children are learning in that classroom. That, we believe, is the lesson of the classic First-Grade Studies (Bond & Dykstra, 1967/1997) and of more recent research on effective schools (Pressley, Allington, Wharton-McDonald, Block, & Morrow, 2001). Every method can succeed with most children if taught well by a good teacher. That does not mean that some methods are not better or easier to teach well than others, or that one method is better than several done in balance, but it does mean that no method or set of methods will work in the absence of good execution of fundamentals. If we live long enough to see the establishment of best practices in literacy instruction, those best practices will emphasize the execution of fundamentals within whatever broad dimensions of instruction that exist.

Help Teachers and Principals Broaden Their Evaluation of Their School's Literacy Program

As long as we continue to hold teachers accountable for student literacy learning, there will be mandated high-stakes assessments of one type or another. We cannot eliminate or ignore them. The main problem with these assessments for a school is that they tend to reduce what the school is trying to teach to that which the high-stakes test assesses. And the more a school is under the gun because of low scores, the more that school is likely to reduce the breadth and scope of its literacy instruction. Yet because test scores are never as high as someone would like, even schools with good test scores feel some pressure to reduce their instructional goals to match the content or tasks on the high-stakes assessment. In spite of protests to the contrary, we have yet to see a literacy assessment of any type that does not narrow the curriculum when it is given high-stakes status in a state or district.

There is only one solution to this problem: Have school-based assessments of the other important goals of literacy instruction not being directly tested for accountability. Because they are school-based assessments only, they can be informal or observational in nature, inexpensive in terms of time and money costs, and do not have to be shared with anyone outside the school. Their value, however, is considerable. They can help keep teacher morale up when the school is improving its instruction in ways that will not significantly impact the high-stakes test for several years. They can be shared with parents to elicit support for the new instructional program of a school that is still being criticized in the media and at school board meetings for relatively low test scores. Most importantly, they serve as an incentive not to narrow instruction to the high-stakes test to the detriment of children's long-term literacy development.

Schools should take action when their high-stakes test scores are low. The problem is that all worthwhile solutions, all solutions that are good for children in the long run, require gradual improvements in all areas of literacy instruction school-wide. Broadening the evaluation of literacy instruction in the school is the only way to buy time for the school to put good instruction in place, as opposed to instruction designed only to raise student test scores, without actually teaching them to read and write much better.

A FINAL WORD

We can achieve best practices in American literacy instruction, and one day we will. To do so, however, we will have to stop holding teachers accountable for student literacy learning, and faddism in literacy instruction will have to give way to a continuing professional consensus. Of course, we should all work hard for that day to come.

In the meantime, those of us who work in classrooms, schools, central offices, state departments of public instruction, colleges and universities, or other agencies can focus our attention on doing things to help individual schools within our purview develop and execute balanced literacy instruction. We must continue to consult our "professional judgment of what children actually need and when they need it" (Cunningham, 2001). Such efforts may well coalesce over time into best literacy instructional practices that will command national or even international consensus. If not, the improved literacy of the children in the schools we were able to affect will still have been worth all our labors.

DISCUSSION AND ACTIVITIES

1. Consider our discussion on pages 342–345 of the need for professional action during an antiprofessional era. Do you agree with the characterization of teacher professionalism as portrayed by this chapter? Do you feel the actions recommended are possible? Do you feel you are currently being treated as a professional?
2. Think about literacy instruction in your classroom, across your grade level, and in your school. What does it look like? How do you make decisions about literacy instruction? Do you feel best practices determine your instruction?
3. Read the National Reading Panel Report. Consider how this report may affect, or is already affecting, your literacy instruction.

REFERENCES

Bond, G. L., & Dykstra, R. (1997). The cooperative research program in first-grade reading instruction. *Reading Research Quarterly, 32*, 345–428. (Original work published 1967)

Cunningham, J. W. (2001). Essay book review: The National Reading Panel report. *Reading Research Quarterly, 36*, 326–335.

National Reading Panel. (2000a). *Teaching children to read: An evidence-based assessment of the scientific research literature on reading and its implications for reading instruction* (NIH Publication No. 00–4769). Washington, DC: National Institute of Child Health and Human Development.

National Reading Panel. (2000b). *Teaching children to read: An evidence-based assessment of the scientific research literature on reading and its implications for reading instruction: Reports of the subgroups* (NIH Publication No. 00–4754). Washington, DC: National Institute of Child Health and Human Development.

Pressley, M. (2002). Effective beginning reading instruction. *Journal of Literacy Research, 34*, 165–188.

Pressley, M., Allington, R., Wharton-McDonald, R., Block, C., & Morrow, L. (2001). *Learning to read: Lessons from exemplary first-grade classrooms.* New York: Guilford Press.

INDEX

effects of experiences with
literature, 177
Stillwell, Pam, 279–281
Student characteristics
classroom interaction assessment,
217–218
motivation for learning new words,
92–93
prior knowledge as basis for
learning, 15
proficient readers, 10
reading readiness, 45–46
See also Disabilities, students with;
Grouping strategies
Student–teacher conferences, 229–
232
Summarizing, 117
Syntactic awareness, 91
Synthetic phonics, 25, 68, 341

T

Teachable moments, 55–56
Teacher education and training
for assessment, 206
inadequacies in, 203, 205, 206
professional development, 119
Teachers, 203, 205
accountability for student
outcomes, 335–337
desire for learning, 279
exemplary teacher characteristics,
3, 6, 47–48
freedom to make instructional
decisions, 13, 18
Teacher–student relationship
assessment and, 205–206
teacher self-assessment of
classroom interaction, 218,
219–220*f*
Teaching techniques
adolescent literacy, 194–198
best practices, 18
children's literature activities, 168–
171, 182–183
in collaborative learning, 16

comprehension processes
instruction, 114–118
computer applications, 154–155,
310–315, 317–321
content area literacy, 190–192
cross-curricular expository writing,
157–160
degrees of classroom control, 29–
30
demonstrating computer
technique, 316–317, 318, 320
direct instruction in grammar and
composition, 151–154
early reading instruction, 52–54
early writing instruction, 54–55
ecologically balanced, 36
exemplary early literacy
instruction, 47–48, 49–60, 61
extremist stances, 341–342
faddism, 339–340
fluency development, 132–137,
139–140
to foster reading motivation, 16–17
guidebooks for children's texts,
274–275
historical development, 11–12
modeling of comprehension
processes, 119
modeling of word learning, 90–91,
94–95, 98
phonics instruction, 70–71, 72–82
plan book, 52, 56–57
professional consensus on best
practices, 10–13, 14, 14*t*, 18–
19, 337–338
skills contextualization, 31
with special need students, 291–
302
teachable moments, 55–56
use of basal readers, 277, 278–279
vocabulary instruction, 88–99
whole-class instruction, 245
without basal readers, 279–282
writing workshops, 149–151
Text sets, 250
Text-to-speech programs, 314